D1447965

God in the Details

"With this book's smart and insightful authors acting as your guides, you can leave behind the seemingly secular surface of American popular culture, come to understand the religious impulses coursing through music and television, feel their pulse, tap their energy, and in the end reach another country where ordinary things reveal unexpected significance. Be a hero. Take the journey."

> –Joel Martin, co-editor of *Screening the Sacred: Religion, Mythology and Ideology in Popular American Film*

Exploring the blurred boundary between religion and pop culture, *God in the Details* offers a provocative look at the breadth and persistence of religious themes in the American consciousness. This new edition reflects the explosion of online activity since the first edition, including chapters on the spiritual implications of social networking sites, and the hazy line between real and virtual religious life in the online community *Second Life*. Also new to this edition are chapters on the migration of black male expression from churches to athletic stadiums, new configurations of the sacred and the commercial, and post-9/11 spirituality and religious redemption through an analysis of the vampire drama *True Blood*. Popular chapters on media, sports, and other pop culture experiences have been revised and updated, making this an invaluable resource for students and scholars alike.

Eric Michael Mazur is the Gloria & David Furman Chair of Judaic Studies at Virginia Wesleyan College. He is also the author of several works in church–state studies, and the editor of *Art & The Religious Impulse* (2001) and *The Encyclopedia of Religion & Film* (forthcoming 2011).

Kate McCarthy is Professor of Religious Studies at California State University, Chico. She is also the author of *Interfaith Encounters in America* (2007).

God in the Details

American religion in popular culture

Second Edition

Edited by
Eric Michael Mazur and Kate McCarthy

 Routledge
Taylor & Francis Group

LONDON AND NEW YORK

First edition published 2000
This edition published 2011 by Routledge
2 Park Square, Milton Park, Abingdon, Oxon OX14 4RN

Simultaneously published in the USA and Canada
by Routledge
711 Third Avenue, New York, NY 10017, USA

Routledge is an imprint of the Taylor & Francis Group, an informa business

© 2011 Eric Michael Mazur and Kate McCarthy, editorial and selection matter;
individual chapters, the contributors

Typeset in Times New Roman by Taylor and Francis books Ltd,

British Library Cataloguing in Publication Data
A catalogue record for this book is available from the British Library

Library of Congress Cataloging in Publication Data
God in the details : American religion in popular culture / edited by Eric
Michael Mazur and Kate McCarthy. – 2nd ed.
p. cm.
Includes bibliographical references and index.
1. United States – Religion – 1960–62. Popular culture – United States.
I. Mazur, Eric Michael. II. McCarthy, Kate, 1962–
BL2525.G625 2010
306.60973 – dc22
2009041550

ISBN 13: 978-0-415-48536-4 (hbk)
ISBN 13: 978-0-415-48537-1 (pbk)
ISBN 13: 978-0-203-85480-8 (ebk)

To Scott Baradell and William Mandel, who taught me just about everything I know about popular culture, and Jody Mazur, Amy Mazur, and Leslie Needham, who taught me the rest. – E.M.M.

To Duncan, my dearest boy, who made it nearly impossible and understands none of it. – K.M.

Contents

Illustrations

Contributors

Vernon Andrews (Independent Scholar) conducts research on African American culture, sport sociology and urban leisure, health and recreation, and has recently returned from New Zealand, where he lived for 12 years studying rugby, cricket, and elite female athletes. He is currently completing a book on celebratory expression, African American athletes, and the shifting norms of global "sportsmanship." He serves on the board of the *Journal of African American Studies.*

Lisle Dalton (Hartwick College) teaches in the areas of American religious history, religion and popular culture, and religion and science. He currently serves as co-chair of the Religion and Popular Culture Group for the American Academy of Religion.

Julie J. Ingersoll (University of North Florida) teaches courses on the sociology of religion and religion and culture, and is the author of *Baptist and Methodist Faiths in America* (2003) and *Evangelical Christian Women: War Stories in the Gender Battles* (2003), as well as numerous articles on religion, gender, and politics.

Tara K. Koda (Independent Scholar) has taught courses at the University of California, Santa Barbara, and is currently working on a book-length project about early Japanese American cultural practices. Her research interests include Asian and Asian-American religions and cultures, particularly in Japan and in the Japanese American community.

Eric Michael Mazur (Virginia Wesleyan College) is the Gloria & David Furman Chair of Judaic Studies, and teaches courses in Judaism, religion in American culture, and the academic study of religion. He is the author of *The Americanization of Religious Minorities* (1999), co-author of *Religion on Trial* (with Phillip Hammond and David Machacek, 2004), and editor of *Art & the Religious Impulse* (2002). He is currently editing an encyclopedia of religion and film.

Kate McCarthy (California State University, Chico) teaches in the areas of Christianity, religious pluralism, and religion and gender. She is the author of *Interfaith Encounters in America* (2007) and articles on inter-religious dialogue, interfaith families, and feminist theology. She is currently at work on *Jesus Saves!*, a study of popular understandings of the atonement doctrine in contemporary American culture.

Sara Moslener (Augustana College) holds the Conrad J. Bergendoff Fellowship in Religion, and recently completed a book-length research project on the faith-based abstinence movement. Her teaching and research interests include race theory and immigration history, gender and sexuality, and US religious history.

Sarah M. Pike (California State University, Chico) teaches courses on American religions, religion and ethnicity, and new religious movements. She is the author of *Earthly Bodies, Magical Selves: Contemporary Pagans and the Search for Community* (2000) and *New Age and Neopagan Religions in America* (2004). She is currently at work on a project about teenagers, religion, and environmental and animal rights activism.

Leonard Norman Primiano (Cabrini College) teaches courses on vernacular religion, American Catholicism, American religious movements, the history of Christianity, and religious folklife. He is the co-producer and co-founder of "The Father Divine Project," a multimedia documentary and video podcast about The Peace Mission Movement. Recent research and publications include an examination of the St Joseph Day altars and the related devotional practices of Sicilian-Americans in Gloucester, Massachusetts; a consideration of vernacular Catholicism in *The West Wing*; an analysis of the musical culture of Father Divine's Peace Mission Movement; and a study of Roman Catholic ephemeral culture as exemplified by the "holy card."

Wade Clark Roof (University of California, Santa Barbara) is the J.F. Rowny Professor of Religion and Society, and Director of the Walter H. Capps Center for the Study of Ethics, Religion, and Public Life. He is the author of *American Mainline Religion* (with William McKinney, 1987), *A Generation of Seekers* (1993), and *Spiritual Marketplace* (1999), and is currently engaged in a project funded by the Ford Foundation on "Progressive Religious Voices in the United States."

Jennifer Rycenga (San José State University) conducts research on religion and culture, especially in relation to music, sexuality, feminism, and capitalism. She co-edited *Frontline Feminisms: Women, War and Resistance* (with Marguerite Waller, 2000) and *Queering the Popular Pitch* (with Sheila Whiteley, 2006). She is currently writing a cultural biography of white abolitionist educator Prudence Crandall.

James Mark Shields (Bucknell University) conducts research on modern Buddhist thought, Japanese philosophy, comparative ethics, and philosophy of religion. He has published articles and translations in *The Eastern Buddhist, Studies in Religion/Sciences religieuses, Journal of Religion and Society*, and *Philosophy, Culture and Traditions*. He is co-editor (with Victor Sogen Hori and Richard P. Hayes) of *Teaching Buddhism in the West: From the Wheel to the Web* (2003).

Elijah Siegler (College of Charleston) is the author of the introductory textbook *New Religious Movements* (2006), and several articles on subjects ranging from teaching Daoism to religion in the works of Tom Fontana. He is currently working on a book about global Daoism.

Monica Siems (University of Minnesota, Twin Cities) is a service-learning coordinator and an active participant in the movement to preserve and revitalize the Dakota language. She has conducted graduate research on scriptures and hymns translated and composed by Dakota Christians in the nineteenth century, and has taught courses in American religious history and Native American religious traditions at Northern Arizona University, Lewis and Clark College, and Macalester College.

Jon R. Stone (California State University, Long Beach) is the author of *A Guide to the End of the World: Popular Eschatology in America* (1993), *On the Boundaries of American Evangelicalism: The Postwar Evangelical Coalition* (1997), *Prime-Time Religion: An Encyclopedia of Religious Broadcasting* (with J. Gordon Melton and Phillip Charles Lucas, 1997), and editor of *Expecting Armageddon: Essential Readings in Failed Prophecy* (2000) and *Readings in American Religious Diversity* (with Carlos R. Piar, 2007), among others. His most recent essay, "Prophecy and Apocalypse: A Reassessment of Research Testing the Festinger Theory," appeared in the May 2009 issue of *Nova Religio: The Journal of Alternative and Emergent Religions*.

Robin Sylvan (The Sacred Center) is the author of *Traces of the Spirit: The Religious Dimensions of Popular Music* (2002) and *Trance Formation: The Spiritual and Religious Dimensions of Global Rave Culture* (2005). He has taught at the Graduate Theological Union, California Institute of Integral Studies, Naropa University, University of California, Davis, and the College of Wooster, and is currently working on a major study for the Templeton Advanced Research Program on "Music, Religion, Spirituality, and the Human Brain."

Daniel Veidlinger (California State University, Chico) teaches Asian Religions, with a focus on Hinduism and Buddhism. His research uses the lens of media theory to examine the interface of religion and communication technologies. He is the author of *Spreading the Dhamma: Writing, Orality and Textual Transmission in Buddhist Northern Thailand* (2006).

Rachel Wagner (Ithaca College) teaches and writes on religion and culture. She has published a number of articles and chapters, and has been interviewed by public radio and television about her work on religion and film, religion and video games, and religion and popular culture. She is currently working on a full-length book about religion and virtual reality.

Acknowledgments

Our biggest and most heartfelt thanks go to the contributors—some of whom have been involved in the project for what probably seems an eternity—for making this a diverse, thought-provoking, and fun assortment of ideas and insights that we have enjoyed from the very beginning. Though the idea of the collection was ours, the product is theirs, and we are grateful for their participation and support.

Several of the chapters were presented at meetings of various professional organizations, including the American Academy of Religion, the Popular Culture Association, and the Society for the Scientific Study of Religion. We appreciate the members of those organizations who responded thoughtfully to the papers and helped us sharpen the materials presented herein.

Some of the following chapters were tested on students in classes at the California State University, Chico, Hartwick College, Millsaps College, and Bucknell University before publication of the first edition, while others were tested on students at the College of Charleston and Virginia Wesleyan College before publication of the second edition. The comments and reactions from these students (and colleagues), as well as others who have used the first edition in classrooms around the country—and whose pop culture insight was often sharper than our own—have been helpful, and we appreciate their willingness to be guinea pigs for both editions.

Finally, we would like to acknowledge our colleagues in the Religious Studies Department at the California State University, Chico, and the Religious Studies Department at Virginia Wesleyan College, for their assistance, patience, and encouragement for this project. Though conversations sometimes wandered from the sublime to the ridiculous, all of the comments have helped in some way or another. You can stop feigning interest now!

Financial support for the second edition has been provided by the Batten Professor Fund at Virginia Wesleyan College and the College of Arts and Sciences at Bucknell University. We are grateful for their assistance.

Preface

The thing that has been, it is that which shall be; and that which is done is that which shall be done; and there is no new thing under the sun.

Ecclesiastes 1:9

And he that sat upon the throne said, Behold, I make all things new. And he said unto me, Write: for these words are true and faithful.

Revelation 21:5

Since the first edition was published in 2000, there seems to have been an explosion in scholarly interest in religion and popular culture. We are in no way claiming responsibility for this—if anything, we simply benefited from great timing. Rather, there are a variety of events and conditions that likely laid the foundations for the transformation. Depending on how far you want to go back, we could probably identify the Marxian influence on the study of history, starting in the 1970s, which brought into the conversation in a more significant way the influences of markets and class on society; the rise of the field of social history, which took greater interest in the lives of everyday people; and the subsequent rise of the study of material culture for clues to all of this. More than ever before—beyond the field of archaeology—the "stuff" of ordinary people's lives mattered to those who were trying to understand "the people." Shifts in the field of anthropology—which had always had an interest in that "stuff"—meant that a fascination with the "other" as "out there" could be refocused on the "other" as "in here," providing greater analysis of phenomena in our own lives, in our own towns, and not just on islands or in jungles far away; the 1956 Horace Miner article to which we referred in the first edition's Introduction—and to which we continue to refer in this edition—makes this point explicit. The rise of the field of media studies provided tools to investigate the impact of various and expanding media on the lives of the "mediated"—which, despite sounding like a group involved in conflict resolution, represents the mass of humanity affected by the growing web of media contact and the subsequent shrinking of the world. And last, but certainly not least, the coming of age of the "baby boomers," that generation of Americans born after World War II but before 1963, has meant that a generally affluent cohort of people has become sufficiently large to influence markets and marketers, and—for a variety of reasons, suggested in a number of the chapters that follow—has been sufficiently self-interested to make studies of them and their habits worthwhile commercial—in addition to simply scholarly—ventures.

As a result, we have experienced real growth in the field of the study of popular culture—with organizations such as the Popular Culture Association and its various journals and publications—and, more specifically and more recently, the field of religion and popular culture. The American Academy of Religion—the international professional association of more than 10,000 scholars of religion in all of its forms—established a unit devoted to the study of religion and popular culture in the 1990s. A number of journals dedicated to the study of religion and various aspects of popular culture—including *The Journal of Religion and Film* (www.unomaha.edu/~jrf), *The Journal of Religion and Theatre* (www.rtjournal.org), and the *Journal of Religion and Popular Culture* (www.usask.ca/relst/jrpc)—were all founded in the past 10 years, and (tellingly) can be found only on line.

Today, people are almost silly with the exploration of religion in popular culture. Entire published works can be found that address religion and religious meaning in works of fiction (including the real boon to the market, J.K. Rowling's *Harry Potter* series); film (specifically religious films such as Mel Gibson's *The Passion of the Christ*, but also less specifically religious films like the *Matrix* trilogy, and even seemingly non-religious films like George Romero's *Living Dead* films) and filmmakers (such as Francis Ford Coppola and Woody Allen); television programming (such as *Buffy the Vampire Slayer* and its progeny); contemporary secular music (such as that of Johnny Cash); graphic arts (including advertising as well as the fine arts); and even tourism, capitalism, and sports. Unfortunately, one of the casualties of this profusion of publishing has been some confusion over audience, purpose, and method, and the works that are available seem to serve different masters; some are clearly written for fun, some are clearly meant for scholarly reflection—be it in an academic setting or not—and some are clearly meant for religious reflection. Advancements in publishing—and also in book distribution and marketing—seem to have placed all of these works into the same conversation.

It may be the proliferation of works for religious and theological reflection that is the biggest surprise for scholarly readers in this field. There can be no mistake that, in the past 30 years or so (but more rapidly recently), for some (but certainly not all) evangelical Christians, the possibility of finding religion in popular culture has led to a virtual explosion in that sub-genre. But this is not a new development; even in the waning years of the nineteenth century, as the film industry was just being born, conservative Christians were debating amongst themselves just what the medium of film meant to

Christian faith and values. Possibly reflecting some aspect of the "baby boom" media generation—or maybe in response to it—in 1967 John Knox Publishing—a representative of the Presbyterian movement in America—produced *The Gospel According to Peanuts*, a work by Robert L. Short (himself a Presbyterian minister) that used the famous comic strips illustrated by Charles M. Schultz to explore Protestant religious sentiment and biblical teachings in everyday life. By the summer of 2009, as this preface is being written, Westminster John Knox—the original press's institutional descendant—has produced "Gospels" according to "America," the Beatles, Disney, Hollywood, Harry Potter, science fiction, *Star Wars, The Simpsons*, Bruce Springsteen, J.R.R. Tolkien, Oprah Winfrey, and U2. Other publishers representing other parts of the conservative Protestant world—as well as a few representing traditional Catholicism—have explored other aspects of everyday life (film, music, television, the internet, as well as fashions and fads), seeking to understand how these current aspects of the human condition can be reconciled with various elements of their readers' theology.

The mix could not be healthier. It not only brings more voices into the conversation, and adds to the nuance of reflection and analysis of any given topic—or the field generally—but it also reminds all involved that the materials under scrutiny are the warp and woof of our daily lives, and that we are all touched by them, regardless of the fact that we see and understand them differently. Or maybe because of it. The power of any symbol is not in its ability to transmit one meaning, but in its ability to transmit various meanings to various people in various places at various times. It is this that makes the study of religion and popular culture meaningful for so many, and now 10 years later, so meaningful for us again, too.

About the Second Edition

If you read the first edition, thank you! We have heard back from a number of readers, and we have designed this edition to reflect their comments. We felt that we had to remove some wonderful chapters from the first edition that were no longer timely, while at the same time we have updated others. In some cases, we have simply updated some of the language, or supplemented information for ongoing phenomena. In other cases, websites no longer exist, and web addresses (URLs) may no longer work but have been included in good faith with a note identifying them as inoperative. And we have added new chapters on issues that have emerged since the first edition was published. Enjoy!

E.M.M.

K.M.

September, 2009

Introduction

Finding Religion in American Popular Culture

> If our thinking is not to be pseudo-thinking, we must think about life; for such a thinking is a thinking about God. And if we are to think about life, we must penetrate its hidden corners, and steadily refuse to treat anything—however trivial or disgusting it may seem to be—as irrelevant.
>
> Karl Barth 1933, *The Epistle to the Romans*

> What if God was one of us?
>
> Joan Osborne

In a now-clichéd article in *American Anthropologist*, Horace Miner introduces his readers to the strange rituals of a tribe he identifies only as the Nacirema (Miner 1956). He focuses most of his attention on their bodily rituals, particularly their preoccupation with rituals of cleanliness and the body, and describes these people with a sense of wonderment, like the true "outsider" anthropologist, exposing a fascinating system of practices that seems both exotic and yet strangely familiar. Of course, the mystery of the identity of these people lasts only as long as the reader is unable to recognize words written backward and, like many exercises designed to make a point, Miner's piece has proved to be a "one-gag bit"—once you know the Nacirema are in fact Americans, the anthropological point is made, and Miner ends his article quickly and mercifully.

But even after 50 years, Miner's short article continues to have a value to the study of American[1] culture. On one level, it is a reminder that Americans do participate in rituals, like other cultures do, but that we rarely examine ourselves. By maintaining this apparent inability to find ritualized patterns in our own behavior, we all too often assume that rituals are activities only of nonindustrialized, unenlightened "others." And yet, while Miner's lesson was probably a healthy corrective for some early anthropologists, by now the literature examining our own culture is so voluminous as to be overwhelming. Anthropological studies of American culture have taken Miner's jest seriously, and have provided us with ample discussions of our own ritualized behavior.

But there is another point in Miner's small piece that is still of value for analyses of contemporary American culture. If the evidence of ritualization in our own lives is not the lasting point of his article, maybe it is the ability—and even the need—to find meaning in the familiar, even if we exoticize it. We have been shown a method (albeit one that is firmly tongue-in-cheek) of finding meaning where we may not otherwise have looked. In the visit to the dentist, the bathroom, or the hospital, we find meaning—and greater understanding of culture—that would have been missed if we had simply overlooked these areas to concentrate on those events traditionally plowed for "deeper" meaning, such as life-cycle and rite-of-passage events, annual rituals of religious and quasireligious communities, and so on. For both the observer and the observed, religious meaning can be found in activities that are often considered meaningless. That premise is the point of departure for the chapters that follow.

Life In The Borderland

From once dismissing it with disdain, academia currently appears to be in the throes of a full-scale infatuation with popular culture. One can read analyses of Hollywood movies, rap music, and comic books in the most highbrow academic journals, and humanities and social science programs now widely offer courses, if not majors, in the critical study of everything from graffiti to sitcoms. Both the field of popular culture studies and the material it examines, though, seem to be growing at a pace that outstrips the analytical categories and methods available. It is useful, therefore, to clarify what we mean when we use key words in this expanding conversation. What constitutes "culture" (popular or otherwise) and "religion," and where do they meet in everyday experience?

In today's American culture, it seems that religion is everywhere. "What Would Jesus Do?" bracelets can be purchased at huge discount department stores. Pastors of suburban megachurches speak of their "target markets" and "product positioning." There are churches of Elvis, and television dramas about angels. The lines between religion and culture blur in contemporary America in ways that leave scholars dizzy. Though this melding of religion and culture has been going on in the form of popular religion for ages, in the contemporary American world of high technology and late capitalism, the boundaries have blurred more than ever before.

The conventional distinction between popular religion and popular culture is worth noting. Popular religion, whether it be defined by its extrainstitutional status, its nonelite practitioners, its immediacy and informality, or the sheer numbers of people it draws, still refers to behavior and ideas recognized by both participant and observer as *religious*, even if the practices are not condoned by the religious elites. Included here are such phenomena as religious folk art, domestic altars, and practices of interreligious syncretism.

Investigation of this field is enjoying a burst of activity today, enriching and complicating our understanding of American religious identity, past and present.[2] Popular culture, by contrast, includes a much wider range of products and practices that, while they may take on religious connotations, remain ostensibly secular sites of experience that neither the participant nor the casual observer would identify, at least at first glance, as religious. American popular culture studies have examined the deeper significance of everything from soap operas to baseball trading cards, adding new material and methods to countless other fields of inquiry, from history and literature to class and gender studies. Of course, such a contrast between that which is religious and that which is cultural is intelligible only in a society like that of the United States which, for many at least, has made of religion a special category of experience, not the stuff of daily life that it is, and has been, in other places and times.

A major task is to draw attention back to this intersection of religion and culture in the ordinary experience of Americans. It is this strange terrain that these chapters visit: the borderland where traditional religious language, for instance, may not be spoken, but where its accent is clearly heard. Sometimes the authors included in this collection stand closer to the territory of popular religion, as in Jennifer Rycenga's report from the Precious Moments Chapel (Chapter 7), but the gaze from those positions is always outward toward the larger and more confusing world of popular culture. More often, they stand in the territory of popular culture itself, listening for the tastes, accents, and rhythms of the religious world across the border. These are not studies of popular religious ritual, for instance, but—as in the case of Vernon Andrews' study of LeBron James' pre-game behavior and its reception (Chapter 6)—of the *possibility* of ritualizing in the commercial entertainment setting of professional sports. As it turns out, the borderland where religion and culture meet in popular expression is also a borderland of another sort. As the following chapters show, these quasireligious popular culture sites serve as points of intersection—sometimes harmonious, often conflictual— for people of very diverse and disparate identities. The Burning Man festival finds wealthy urban art-lovers sharing tent space with disaffected college students and twenty-something Silicon Valley employees. On the animated television series *The Simpsons*, Hindu, Jew, and evangelical Christian are brought into a kind of dialogue that would leave many ecumenists reeling. Bruce Springsteen concerts bring together working-class conservatives and liberal intellectuals. What is noteworthy is that these are not the casual meetings diverse people experience every day in supermarkets and traffic jams; rather, these chapters show that they are encounters in which questions of ultimate meaning and identity are being struggled over, if not entirely worked out. They are places where members of a society that has tended to privatize religion and demarcate solid denominational lines come (or are thrown) together to explore some very interesting religious questions.

Why should popular culture (rather than the church, the town hall, or the classroom, for instance) be the venue for such encounters? It has long been noted that religion has been edged out of the public square in American culture (Carter 1993; Neuhaus 1984). What this observation has missed, though, is that while institutional religion may indeed have been denied entry into such official public sectors as government and education, the unofficial public square of television, shopping mall, and stadium parking lot have expanded to accommodate the overflow. Media are especially important in this new religious landscape. As Catherine Albanese notes: "The media are mass language brokers and, so, mass culture brokers" (Albanese 1996, 740). In the same way that religion in the West changed dramatically with the introduction of the printing press, so has religion changed drastically with the invention of radio, television and, most recently, the computer. The ubiquitous quality of these popular culture venues (especially by virtue of technologies of mass distribution) make them accessible; that many are entertainment products makes them attractive; and their distance from "official" religious sites makes them flexible and open to many types and levels of interpretation. Church is church, but rock concerts, for instance, seem to be nearly whatever their followers want them to be, often including experiences of intense spiritual transformation. For these and other reasons, popular culture appears well situated as a contemporary religious venue.

Webs of Significance

One way of talking about what people are doing when they are engaged in a religious activity—whether they are singing a hymn, sitting in a Native American sweat lodge, writing theology, lighting a candle, or teaching a child right from wrong—is to say that they are making the world meaningful (or discovering it to be so). When we look at the world around us with this eye toward behavior that carries significant personal and collective meanings, a wide range of apparently nonreligious phenomena become religiously significant. The chapters in this volume represent some of those places where religion, conventionally understood, is not readily—or at least unambiguously—present, but where at least one observer has glimpsed its workings.

To those familiar with various theories of religion, it will not be surprising to find that many of our contributors draw on the work of anthropologist Clifford Geertz. Though other theorists (sociologist Emile Durkheim, history of religions scholar Mircea Eliade, anthropologist Victor Turner, and cultural theorist Michel Foucault, among others) appear throughout the collection, a majority of the authors have relied on the approach articulated by Geertz because of their attention to the "doing" aspect of religion; his functionalist—rather than essentialist—framework permits them to explore what religion does for its adherents rather than what religion is. According to Geertz, religion and culture are not really things in and of themselves; they are the systems of meaning that humans give to things, to the stuff of everyday life. They are the "webs of significance" (Geertz 1973, 5) that connect human thought and behavior, and not so much things that can be calibrated, measured, replicated, or easily diagrammed. They are real enough—or rather, their perception is clothed with "an aura of factuality"— and they are based on things out there (somewhere), but their significance lies in the meanings given to those things by the people who use them in whatever fashion. Using this view here, we are relieved of the burden of finding religious *things*, and can look more widely for the religious meanings attached, explicitly or not, to such activities as eating, dancing.

Important to our collective investigation is Geertz's observation that cultural meanings are necessarily conversational, that is, social and dynamic. In assembling those webs of significance, he argues, we are creating ourselves as social beings. Individual humans don't create culture as a hobby or a byproduct, but need the system of thought created and transmitted collectively in order to survive. Sociologist Peter Berger makes a similar observation when he argues that society is the collective effort to construct meaning that is conferred through processes both external (observed) and internal (intellectual) to the individual. Thus humans are incomplete without the information and meaning encoded in, delivered by, and internalized from the social institutions that they all create without recognizing that participation (Berger 1969). As Geertz concludes, since culture is the process by which collective symbolic meaning is negotiated among individuals, "Culture is public because meaning is" (Geertz 1973, 12).

If culture and meaning are public, it is the task of the observer to learn to read signs and symbols in order to interpret them. In our case, it means scholars need to learn the "language" of particular popular constituencies, language that is communicated often without words, but certainly in a different idiom than that commonly used in the academic world. The observer must get to know not only what the participant knows, but how the participant knows it, and must learn to see what the participant sees but may not question, since it is automatically understood by the participant. In the same way as a non-native must learn the mechanics of grammar as well as the basics of vocabulary in mastering a foreign language, so must the observer, often using terminology and logic unfamiliar to the participant, learn the mechanics as well as the language that the participant has simply "picked up" through the environment.

The Difficulties of Defining Religion

But if culture is the collection of all of the webs of significance, the problem remains of deciding what it is that counts as religious—how one draws the boundaries (if there are any) between religious systems of meaning and other cultural systems. It is hard enough to say exactly what is religious about a sacred text or a worship service; to try to do so for a television cartoon or barbecue is to invite failure. Two principles seemed to serve the contributors to this volume in this effort, though no consensus on such things was sought.

First, obviously, the conception of religion used here is necessarily very broad. If the chapters in this book assume any common definition of religion, it is probably that put forth by Geertz (1973) in his well-known essay "Religion as a Cultural System." Religion, he writes, is "a system of symbols which acts to establish powerful, pervasive, and long-lasting moods and motivations in men by formulating conceptions of a general order of existence and clothing these conceptions with such an aura of factuality that the moods and motivations seem uniquely realistic" (Geertz 1973, 90). But we are content to let it remain fuzzier than that. The identification of such phenomena as Jimmy Buffett concerts, *Second Life*, and Disneyland as "religious" hangs not so much on a definition of religion as on a set of markers that are suggestive of religious meaning. These include the formation of communities of shared meanings and values, the presence of ritualized behaviors, the use of language of ultimacy and transcendence, the marking of special, set-aside "sacred" times and spaces, and the manipulation of traditional religious symbols and narratives. Where one or more of these markers are present, we collectively argue, we have entered terrain worthy of religious analysis. Of course, it is up to each individual author to make the case for the religious significance of the particular phenomenon he or she describes.

Second, aware of how complex, varied, and subjective such phenomena are, the authors of these short studies have strived to stay very close to the experience of those being studied. This is good practice for any well-trained ethnographer; it is vital when you are presuming to attach religious meanings to activities that participants do not recognize as such. Here we think of one of Wilfred Cantwell Smith's criteria for the "humane" study of those of a different religious tradition. While we would not go so far, as he did, as to accept as valid only those statements about our subjects that they themselves would accept (W. C. Smith 1981, 97), we do firmly believe that the participant should at least be able to recognize him- or herself in the scholar's descriptions. We see it as a strength of these chapters, then, that many of the scholars are themselves participants in the communities of meaning they describe.

Objectivity in religious studies, as elsewhere, is a problematic goal. Instead, we more commonly aim for clarity in the relationship between ourselves as observers and the people and things we observe. Anthropologist Ruth Behar speaks of the "vulnerable observer," who "is able to draw deeper connections between one's personal experience and the subject under study," developing "a keen understanding of what aspects of the self are the most important filters through which one perceives the world and, more particularly, the topic being studied" (Behar 1996, 13). In more or less explicit ways, this is the approach taken by the chapters in this book. The contributors are unabashed in their affection for the aspects of popular culture they analyze: Roof is a Southern meat-eater, Dalton and his colleagues are dedicated *Simpsons* viewers, Ingersoll is a self-proclaimed Parrothead. The challenge, then, lies not in overcoming the "otherness" of our subjects of study, but in choreographing the dance that allows us to come into intimate closeness with these subjects and then step back to do critical analysis, then to move in and out again.

A Profile of the Popular

A few comments about our sense of the "popular" in popular culture are also in order. Typically, it is taken to refer to the wide diffusion of the product, usually via mass media;[3] its acceptance by the majority of a given population; or its source in non-elite segments of society. No one of these seems adequate in and of itself; neither can they all be used as criteria for defining the popular, since they are not necessarily compatible descriptors of a given cultural product.

What's more, attempts at defining the "popular" in popular culture have themselves become politically charged acts. The very term "popular culture" implies for some a particular ideological position, a "facile populism that uncritically equates popular cultural forms with the voice of the 'people' and disregards questions of ideology and social control altogether" (Fluck 1987, 3). Aware of the naïveté of venerating popular culture as the source of an authentic, spontaneous expression of the mind and will of the common folk, we nonetheless maintain the connection between the "popular" in popular culture and its Latin root *popularis* ("of the people").[4] Certainly, as many theorists exploring the production of popular culture have noted, much of the mode of communicating popular culture is controlled by the dominant culture—or more specifically, those with the wherewithal to control the expensive technology so important for its dissemination—often making much of popular culture very one-sided. What's more, the purveyors of many popular culture products effectively exploit the power of subcultural symbols and rhetoric in a way that renders the relations between dominant and popular highly opaque. This complex relationship is highlighted in Sara Moslener's analysis of the strategic marketing of the faith-based abstinence movement (Chapter 10), which has cleverly appropriated the language of the sexual revolution for its decidedly culturally conservative crusade.

But the popular culture industry, however exploitative, is successful only to the degree to which it responds to its audience's needs and desires, and therefore its products can tell us something authentic about that audience.[5] In other words, the relationship between the products of popular culture, their producers, and their consumers is complex; each is significantly shaped by the other two. We would expect, then, that the expressions of popular culture can serve accurately as mirrors of that culture, even while they are also reflective of the commercial interests that function as so powerful a part of culture. Thus one descriptor of the "popular" in culture is its authentic connection, however mediated and admittedly manipulated, with broad segments of the population. What's more, modes of communication are democratizing the dissemination of popular culture, and many once subcultural products—notably rap/hip-hop music—have gained wider audiences, making mainstream popular culture somewhat more representative of the diversity of the American population.

A second feature of popular culture that these chapters highlight is its "everyday" quality. If culture is a web of meaning, it is important to note the ordinary source of most of the materials used in that web's construction. What we watch and listen to for entertainment, the clothes we wear, magazines we read, even the foods we eat are the context of our meaning-making. These mundane products are themselves often the basis for much of the construction and maintenance of meaning that is so important in the fabric of culture, playing a larger role, often, than the "official" purveyors of meaning associated with religious and educational institutions.

Another aspect of the popular that bears especially strongly on these discussions of the American situation is what Catherine Albanese, in the introduction to an issue of the *Journal of the American Academy of Religion* devoted to the study of religion and popular culture, calls its "creole" character. Popular culture, she writes, "always pieces and patches together its universe of meaning, appropriating terms, inflections, and structurations from numerous overlapping contexts and using them as so many *ad hoc* tools to order and express, to connect inner with outer, and to return to inner again" (Albanese 1996, 740). There is thus a messy element in the study of popular culture. Just as each piece of popular culture is itself a pastiche of inherited bits and pieces, so each of us works with a wide range of cultural phenomena in making meaning for ourselves. People do not derive their worldview, for instance, solely from their time on *Facebook* or *Second Life*. The challenge is to try to see, as Daniel Veidlinger and Rachel Wagner do in Chapters 11 and 14, how participants in these online activities might be experiencing reality in ways that shape (and are shaped by) their offline experiences and worldviews.

But it is important to emphasize that these popular cultural products do not provide meaning unambiguously. Rather, they often represent those points in the culture where inherited values and actual experience conflict, as several chapters show quite forcefully. A final dimension of our sense of the popular, then, is this ambiguous quality. Popular culture venues are contested sites where multitudes come together and negotiate the conflicts with which individuals, and groups of individuals, must reckon in the course of social participation. In some of the following chapters this tension is the focus of analysis; all of them operate on the assumption that popular culture products are interesting and revelatory precisely because they do not simply mirror or dictate cultural norms, but are ambiguous expressions of conflict and change in social groups.

Toward a Theory of Religion In Turn-of-the-Millennium America

It is entirely possible that those who are studied here will read these chapters and find the religious analyses completely superfluous, if not wrongheaded. As one of our students commented on an early draft of McCarthy's chapter, "Come on. It's just Bruce." Or, one might say of Roof's chapter, "sometimes a spare rib is really just a spare rib." Perhaps. But there is a larger purpose to these chapters that we believe warrants the risk of such responses.

Numerous scholars note that American religion in the second half of the twentieth century was considerably different from what it was in the first half. Sociologists including Phillip Hammond (1992), James Davison Hunter (1991), Robert Wuthnow (1988), and Robert Bellah *et al.* (1986) have all commented independently that in the years following World War II, the structure of religion in the United States changed to reflect the changes in American culture. Some of those changes include a wider mainstream acceptance of non-Christian, or even non-Western, religious traditions, as well as the increasing frequency of a lack of religious affiliation. As historian Robert Handy has noted (Handy, 1984, 1991), religion in the United States, legislatively freed from government control with the ratification of the First Amendment to the Constitution, was by the end of the nineteenth century also ostensibly freed from its Protestant monopoly. By the end of the twentieth century, religious affiliation was loosened significantly from all social institutions generally (Hammond 1992). More and more people have pursued religious commitments based on their personal preferences, and have either abandoned, reinterpreted, or supplemented the religious tradition into which they were born (Roof 1993). The public monopoly once enjoyed by a segment of Protestant Christianity is now a veritable *smörgåsbord* of religious groups, each relatively free to "advertise" to anyone willing to listen.

However, the increased religious freedom has not stopped simply with the expanded ability of non-Protestant religious communities to participate more fully in American society. Individuals can now choose among competitors in the marketplace of meaning construction and meaning maintenance, even among options that traditionally might have seemed nonreligious. As religious institutions have lost their monopoly on the construction and maintenance of meaning, religiosity has found expression in a wide variety of human activities. It is not that religion was slowly disappearing with modernity, as many scholarly observers have predicted throughout this century, but that society was changing the manner in which it expressed itself religiously (Yamane 1997). Notes Hammond:

> In any era, therefore, when religion, at least as commonly understood, is receding, vitality of the sacred may thus come as a surprise. The present era would seem to fit such a description, and we find ourselves unable to comprehend the sacred. The past accretions that transformed the sacred into religion—accretions which in many instances have been corroded by secularization—keep us from the refocusing necessary if we are to study the sacred in a secular age ... unless we can revise our thinking about secularization.
>
> (Hammond 1985, 5)

Eric Mazur and Tara Koda make this their central foundation when they argue (in Chapter 16) that Disney (in all its various and extensive trappings) provides for some a possible replacement for religion. Careful not to suggest that Disney is in fact a religion, Mazur and Koda suggest that, in the creation of a sacred space and sense of sacred time in its parks, and through the inculcation of signs, symbols, and lessons in its various media enterprises, Disney provides for its fans (young and old alike) much that would ordinarily have been provided by religions, traditionally understood.

Does all this mean that every activity in which one can engage is religious? Well, yes and no. It could be that the chapters collected here will provide readers with a better understanding of the limitations of an expansive definition of the religious, just as they might see the limitations of a more restricted definition. The most important check on this possibility is the scholar's ongoing relationship with the popular culture (and its participants) that he or she hopes to illuminate. The academic study of culture and the role of religion in that culture is an endeavor that requires a close examination of the public, and a realization that academic solutions are only as successful as their ability to resonate among those whose activities we are interpreting.

In the end, our sympathies lie with the position taken by David Chidester in an issue of the *Journal of the American Academy of Religion*: "If we only relied upon the standard academic definitions of religion, those definitions that have tried to identify the essence of religion, we would certainly be informed by the wisdom of classic scholarship, but we would also still be lost" (Chidester 1996, 760). Like others before him (J. Z. Smith 1982, for example), Chidester suggests that by providing a definition for religion, the scholar limits what is and is not included in the study. Though working from a definition of religion is perhaps a necessary exercise, it is one that is often not problematized, and scholars fail to ask themselves why some things *shouldn't* be considered religious. "In the end," Chidester continues, "we will need to answer that question. By saying 'we,' however, I refer in this case to all of us who are in one way or another engaged in the professionalized and institutionalized academic study of religion. Participants in American popular culture have advanced their own answers."

Indeed. Part of the motivation behind this collection is to provide comparisons between the seemingly "secular" segments of peoples' lives and the "religious" framework often used only sparingly by scholars of religion. As Geertz (and others) have argued, the search for meaning is at the heart of the question of religion and, though not everything is to be considered religious, everything connected with that search can certainly be compared with those elements usually reserved for institutional religion.

In addition, this collection problematizes the very definition of religion for the readers of these chapters. We want to encourage readers to think about what they mean when they say "religion," particularly in contemporary America, and what others might mean when they deny its presence. We think that the fact that people engaged in the activities portrayed in the collection might deny the "religiosity" of their activities is itself evidence of the significance of the problem of defining religion in our culture. Theorists for decades have noted an increasing suspicion of religious institutions among Americans. Tom Beaudoin, author of *Virtual Faith: The Irreverent Spiritual Quest of Generation X* (Beaudoin 1998), identifies this characteristic as central, for instance, to the spirituality of that generation. For many Americans, it seems, "religion" is identified with institutional religion, and it is precisely their resistance to those institutions that makes such things as music, food, sports, and film attractive alternative sites for meaning-making. It is therefore no surprise that so many would reject any reference to religion as a descriptor for their activities. But we strongly believe this does not mean that the observer ought to be barred from applying religious analyses. This is a difficult issue, and one that many of the contributors address directly in their chapters. It is also one of the most important and interesting issues raised by this project, critical for those who want to explore the meanings of contemporary culture to consider.

Four Organizing Categories

It would be tempting to sort the following chapters according to genre—music, television, radio and film, mass public events, and the like. Such a structure would make it easy for those interested in a particular cultural area to move from one case study to the next, and would likely prompt interesting comparisons and conclusions. But genre, it has become clear, does not necessarily closely correlate with the kinds of religious meaning being found and made in these events. In some cases, authors studying very different kinds of phenomena reached strikingly similar kinds of conclusions about their religious significance. In this case, it seems, the medium is not the message.

In order to bring these religious dimensions to the foreground in the most provocative way, then, we have organized the popular culture expressions examined here into four categories widely used in the study of religion: myth and symbol, ritual, spirituality and morality, and institution ("churches"). These are hardly exhaustive headings for the analysis of religious phenomena; contemporary studies of religion also often employ doctrinal or theological, philosophical, and historical categories, among others. When looking specifically at the quasi-religious aspects of popular culture, though, these four broad categories seem especially useful because of their inherent elasticity. "Myth," for instance, in both its specific references to the sacred narratives of religious traditions, and its broader evocation of powerful, culture-defining symbols and stories, proves to be a fascinating lens for looking at such things as the commercial use of the image of the Buddha and the end-time visions of Hollywood films. Juxtaposing the celebratory displays of professional athletes and the Burning Man festival under the heading of "ritual" likewise raises very interesting questions about the meaning, and indeed the possibility, of shared symbolic activity in a multicultural, multireligious society. Turning to television cop dramas and the social web, for instance, as venues for popular "spirituality and morality," challenges us to take seriously the extent to which such popular forms function for their audiences as spiritual directors and maps of a moral world, complementing if not replacing those offered by traditional religious communities. As alternative "churches," such phenomena as hip-hop culture and the Disney empire are treated in the final section of this book, provoking perhaps the most radical interpretive possibility, that in these popular culture activities we are seeing not only elements once reserved for religious institutions, but fully wrought alternatives to traditional religion.

Overlaying these four religious categories on these (mostly) apparently nonreligious activities does at least two things. It offers a way of demonstrating that what is going on in these activities, because it fits the traditional definitions of myth, ritual, spirituality and morality, and institution, may be comparable with religion as it is traditionally understood. At the same time, it stretches those categories, and therefore our understanding of religion itself, to better accommodate the strange new world of religion in contemporary America. At the beginning of each of the four sections we offer a short introduction highlighting the major themes and possible implications of the chapters that follow—though we hope each reader will be drawn into the interpretive act and will come to see how it is that many Americans are finding God in the details of their lives.

References

Albanese, Catherine L. 1996. "Religion and Popular Culture: An Introductory Essay." *Journal of the American Academy of Religion* 59, 4 (fall): 733–42.
Barth, Karl. [1933] 1968. *The Epistle to the Romans*, 6th edn. Translated by Edwyn C. Hoskyns. New York: Oxford University Press.

Beaudoin, Tom. 1998. *Virtual Faith: The Irreverent Spiritual Quest of Generation X.* San Francisco: Jossey-Bass.

Behar, Ruth. 1996. *The Vulnerable Observer: Anthropology that Breaks Your Heart.* Boston: Beacon Press.

Bellah, Robert N., Richard Madsen, William M. Sullivan, Ann Swidler, and Steven M. Tipton. 1986. *Habits of the Heart: Individualism and Commitment in American Life.* Berkeley: University of California Press.

Berger, Peter L. 1969. *The Sacred Canopy: Elements of a Sociological Theory of Religion.* Garden City, NY: Doubleday.

Carter, Stephen L. 1993. *The Culture of Disbelief: How American Law and Politics Trivialize Religious Devotion.* New York: Basic Books.

Chidester, David. 1996. "The Church of Baseball, the Fetish of Coca-Cola, and the Potlatch of Rock 'n' Roll: Theoretical Models for the Study of Religion in American Popular Culture." *Journal of the American Academy of Religion* 59, 4 (fall): 743–65.

Fluck, Winfried. 1987. "Popular Culture as a Mode of Socialization: A Theory about the Social Functions of Popular Cultural Forms." *Journal of Popular Culture* 21, 3 (winter): 31–46.

Geertz, Clifford. 1973. *The Interpretation of Cultures: Selected Essays by Clifford Geertz.* New York: Basic Books.

Hall, David, ed. 1997. *Lived Religion in America: Toward a History of Practice.* Princeton, NJ: Princeton University Press.

Hammond, Phillip E. ed. 1985. *The Sacred in a Secular Age.* Berkeley: University of California Press.

——1992. *Religion and Personal Autonomy: The Third Disestablishment in America.* Columbia: University of South Carolina Press.

Handy, Robert T. 1984. *A Christian America: Protestant Hopes and Historical Realities,* 2nd edn. New York: Oxford University Press.

——1991. *Undermined Establishment: Church–State Relations in America, 1880–1920.* Princeton, NJ: Princeton University Press.

Hunter, James Davison. 1991. *Culture Wars: The Struggle to Define America.* New York: Basic Books.

Lippy, Charles H. 1996. *Modern American Popular Religion: A Critical Assessment and Annotated Bibliography.* Westport, CT: Greenwood Press.

McDannell, Colleen. 1995. *Material Christianity: Religion and Popular Culture in America.* New Haven: Yale University Press.

Miner, Horace. 1956. "Body Ritual among the Nacirema." *American Anthropologist* 58, 3 (June): 503–7.

Moore, R. Laurence. 1994. *Selling God: American Religion in the Marketplace of Culture.* New York: Oxford University Press.

Neuhaus, Richard John. 1984. *The Naked Public Square: Religion and Democracy in America.* Grand Rapids, MI: William B. Eerdmans.

Orsi, Robert. 1985. *The Madonna of 115th Street: Faith and Community in Italian Harlem, 1880–1950.* New Haven: Yale University Press.

Paglia, Camille. 1992. *Sex, Art, and American Culture.* New York: Vintage Books.

Roof, Wade Clark. 1993. *A Generation of Seekers: The Spiritual Journeys of the Baby Boom Generation.* San Francisco: HarperCollins.

Smith, Jonathan Z. 1982. *Imagining Religion: From Babylon to Jonestown.* Chicago: University of Chicago Press.

Smith, Wilfred Cantwell. 1981. *Towards a World Theology*. Philadelphia: Westminster Press.

Williams, Peter W. 1989. *Popular Religion in America: Symbolic Change and the Modernization Process in Historical Perspective*. Urbana: University of Illinois Press.

Wuthnow, Robert. 1988. *The Restructuring of American Religion: Society and Faith Since World War II*. Princeton, NJ: Princeton University Press.

Yamane, David. 1997. "Secularization on Trial: In Defense of a Neosecularization Paradigm." *Journal for the Scientific Study of Religion* 36, 1 (March): 109–22.

Notes

1 By "American" (here and throughout the text) we mean to refer to citizens and residents of the United States.

2 For a few examples of the excellent work being done in this area, see Hall 1997, McDannell 1995, Moore 1994, Orsi 1985, and Williams 1989. For an annotated bibliography, see Lippy 1996.

3 According to Catherine Albanese, this is the defining feature of popular culture for the contributors to the issue of the *Journal of the American Academy of Religion* for which she wrote the introduction (Albanese 1996, 737).

4 *The American Heritage Dictionary of the English Language* (2nd college edition, Houghton Mifflin, Boston, 1991) defines "popular" as: "Widely liked or appreciated ... Of, representing, or carried on by the common people or the people at large ... Fit for or reflecting the taste and intelligence of the people at large ... Accepted by or prevalent among the people in general ... Suited to or within the means of ordinary people ... Originating among the people." (The second definition, referring specifically to a person as the object of popularity, has been omitted.)

5 In this vein, Camille Paglia has written: "Academic commentary on popular culture is either ghettoized as lackluster 'communications' tamed up with semiotics, or loaded down with grim, quasi-Marxist, Frankfurt School censoriousness: the pitifully witless masses are always being brainwashed by money-grabbing capitalist pigs. But mass media is completely, even servilely commercial. It is a mirror of the popular mind. All the P.R. in the world cannot make a hit movie or sitcom. The people vote with ratings and dollars. Academic Marxists, with their elitist sense of superiority to popular taste, are the biggest snobs in America" (Paglia 1992, ix).

Part I

Popular myth and symbol

At a conference on using popular culture in the university classroom, an English professor makes the case that the popular 1990s sitcom *Friends* was a clever repackaging of Shakespeare's *Much Ado about Nothing,* that *Star Wars* retells Book One of *The Faerie Queene,* and that *The Simpsons* is really a contemporary take on Goldsmith's *She Stoops to Conquer.* A given culture, such parallels would suggest, has a finite number of good stories to tell. But good stories are capable of infinite retelling.

Some of the best stories with some of the richest symbols are to be found in the religious traditions that have had profound effects in shaping cultures. Virgin births, hero journeys, stories of death and resurrection, battles between good and evil, revelatory encounters with supernatural beings—these are what enliven the sacred scriptures of the world's religions. In a monocultural society, common knowledge and public retelling of such myths reinforce the religious and social identities of community members. In a culturally diverse and officially secular society such as the United States, there is no central fire around which a singular set of stories gets told by an authoritative narrator. Instead, as the following chapters explore, the myths and symbols of various religious traditions resurface—by themselves, in fragments, and in strange combinations—in what look like wholly secular spaces, in a process that both keeps the stories alive and radically reframes their meaning.

Many of the narratives that inform traditional religious institutions are alive and well in American popular culture, though those "reading" them—in song lyrics, movies, even in Victoria's Secret swimwear—may be completely unaware of their sacred roots. In some cases, the stories are preserved with their basic narrative structure and cultural function largely intact. Kate McCarthy (Chapter 1) traces the language and imagery of the biblical *Exodus* account through three decades of Bruce Springsteen's music, where it serves, as it has for countless Jewish and Christian generations, as a powerful symbol of personal and collective promise, as well as "an indictment of America's failure to make real its transcendent promise." McCarthy sees this myth and all its troubling ambiguities being retold not only in Springsteen's song lyrics, but also in concert parking lots, internet chatrooms, and in the persona of Springsteen himself. While listeners may or may not catch the biblical references, she argues, Springsteen's use of the story of deliverance from bondage into a promised land of opportunity and grace makes the ideological stakes higher here than they are in most rock music.

A mythic genre from the other end of the Bible, apocalypses akin to the *Revelation* of John, also survives in secular popular culture, according to Jon Stone's analysis of popular film (Chapter 3). Stone defines the genre carefully, reminding us that not all accounts of a cataclysmic end of the world are apocalyptic. Rather, apocalypses involve a consistent set of markers, including otherworldly revelation and warning and heroic intervention. Stone goes on to examine three types of apocalyptic film that reveal how compelling and flexible the genre has been in allowing several generations of Americans to reckon with the fear of perceived threats to our world—whether they be nuclear, environmental, or technological—just as it helped first-century Christians cope with Roman persecution. The difference is that those who absorbed these and other mythic stories through Scripture as interpreted by traditional religious communities understood the texts as divinely revealed, while contemporary fans of Springsteen and the *Terminator* movies are conscious of the wholly human origin—in the mind of the filmmaker and musician—of these cultural products. An interesting question raised by these discussions is what difference this difference makes: is confidence in an otherworldly source requisite for cultural narratives to have life-shaping impact, or has the human imagination now taken over that role?

The stories of exodus and apocalypse, though they are radically resituated, largely maintain their original shape in the popular manifestations considered by McCarthy and Stone. Other religious narratives arrive in popular culture in fragments, their powerful component symbols resurfacing alone or in interesting combination with other secular and religious elements. James Shields' contribution on the controversy surrounding a Victoria's Secret swimsuit emblazed with iconographically accurate images of the Buddha (Chapter 4) raises questions about the implications of extracting such a symbol from its religious context and inserting it into one that is non-religious and, in fact, highly sexual. Questions about the *intent* of symbolic representation are important to consider here, and help explain why the stakes are so high when those doing the representing are seen as outsiders to the religious tradition. According to Shields' analysis, the outcry of protest against the "Buddha bikini" is in one sense surprising, given the long tradition of Buddhist representation of both the Buddha and sexualized female figures. The setting of this particular symbolic representation, though, angered many Buddhists from around the world for its trivialization and exploitation of a non-Western sacred symbol for Western commercial purposes. The encounters represented by this episode—East–West, commercial–religious, sexual–sacred, reverence–iconoclasm—prompt reflection by scholars and lay people alike about the *religiousness* of religious symbols when they are also highly sexualized products for sale in an ostensibly non-religious market. In this case, do long-running intra-Buddhist conversations about iconography and iconoclasm even apply? How do the terms of such a conversation change when the cultural setting is global, multireligious, and profit-driven?

Leonard Primiano observes another process of symbolic dislocation in his analysis of the religious imagery and themes of the HBO vampire drama *True Blood* (Chapter 2). Focusing especially on the series' weekly introductory credits, Primiano finds a "fantasia on American religion" that exposes new patterns in lived or "vernacular" religion and the traditional symbol sets in which it is enmeshed. *True Blood*'s vampires, Primiano argues, inherit the dark sexuality of their classic ancestors, but also reflect the recent literary trend of valorizing vampires as "undead anti-heroes" characterized by emotional and moral complexity. Situated in the context of rural Louisiana religiosity, these characters are part of a new iconography of American religion, in which traditional symbols and theological narratives are fragmented, inverted, and reimagined. The pronounced individuality and eclecticism often observed in contemporary American spirituality is evident in Primiano's treatment of *True Blood*, in the downplayed, if not damning, images of organized religion, and the show's continuous evocation of the "power derived from an appreciation and acceptance of one's own unique talents and abilities, and the subsequent openness to others and their differences."

But Primiano's mediation on the spirituality of *True Blood* goes a step further. In addition to a kind of splintered iconography in which pecan pie becomes sacramental and the American flag trumps the cross, Primiano finds a new and quite radical American iconoclasm in the show's – and especially the opening title sequence's – implicit theology. That montage, and the characters' experiences across the first two seasons, express a dark ambivalence about a God who is real but distant, absent from the usual venues, and usually disappointing if not openly hostile. To the emerging picture of contemporary American religion, Primiano adds the suggestion that this ambivalence is a significant element since 9/11, and especially for many gay people, who have felt abandoned by organized religion, if not by God, for much longer.

One of the most exciting things going on in the popular retelling of sacred stories and reworking of sacred symbols is the emergence of countless new voices in the storytelling process itself. Who tells the story, and who has the authority to interpret it, are critical factors in determining the meaning or meanings of a given myth or symbol. The vampires of *True Blood* can easily be seen as a metaphor for gays and lesbians and others struggling for assimilation, according to the show's openly gay creator and producer. Bringing them and their complex human counterparts to the center of the narrative shifts interpretive authority from institutional and cultural sources to individual religious experience which, however bleak, involves authentic moments of transcendence and redemption.

But all these reinterpretive sites, though populist and potentially empowering, are also, these authors remind us, commodified and conflict-ridden. Because popular culture sites are very often commercial sites, their role in religious meaning-making is always ambiguous. Certainly, the "products" of traditional religious organizations have always been commodified in various ways, but the central (and legitimated) place of commercial interests in the television, fashion, and film industries that are the vehicles of these popular myths and symbols add an additional layer to the retelling of these classic stories. While such sites can be venues for the self-expression and redefinition of marginalized groups, they can also, and simultaneously, represent back that marginal status when to do otherwise threatens the profitability of their stories as products. Sensitivity to this possibility certainly lies behind some of the vociferous objections to the Buddha bikini by Buddhists in America and around the world who (erroneously, Shields notes) often assumed that Western religious symbols would never be subject to comparable treatment.

Because they are so multivocal, popular use of myths and symbols makes visible a truth that is not always evident within traditional religion: the abundance of their interpretive possibilities. A story whose meaning is fixed and universally agreed upon is not, by definition, a myth; the potency and longevity of myths lie in their ability to mean different things to different people in different historical settings. Paradoxically, while myths unite groups of people in common appreciation of the story, they also serve as venues for intragroup conflict. As historian of religion Wendy Doniger puts it, "[a] myth is like a gun for hire, like a mercenary soldier: it can be made to fight for anyone" (*Myth and Method*, University Press of Virginia, 1996, 119). This conflictual element is prominent in McCarthy's treatment of Springsteen, where she highlights the odd ways his music brings together those with very different ideological identities, from liberal intellectuals to disenfranchised Vietnam veterans to working-class conservatives. Shields notes that one of the most interesting aspects of the Buddha bikini controversy was the degree to which it drew out a single, nonsectarian Buddhist consciousness; angry responses coalesced from culturally and denominationally diverse communities of Buddhists around the globe.

The power of symbols and myths, these chapters show, is this power to connect, amiably or confrontationally, those with otherwise very disparate lives and views. In a multi- or nonreligious society, the power of myth is somewhat obscured but no less real. The stories become divorced from their institutional and doctrinal contexts, get fragmented and remixed, and reappear in sometimes startling ways in popular culture. From campfire, pulpit, and family dinner table, the telling of the myths shifts to, among other places, concert hall, television, chat group and, oddly, sexy swimwear. We learn from the popular materializations of these stories some things that might not otherwise be clear. Television vampire shows reveal that Americans are still deeply interested in the supernatural; Victoria's Secret swimwear catalogues tell us that anxiety about sensuality and spirituality is a global phenomenon complicated and intensified by globalization; the popularity of Bruce Springsteen indicates that Americans are still profoundly idealistic (and therefore in conflict) about what it means to be an American; apocalyptic films expose our deep and persistent fear of the military, industrial, and technological powers we so celebrate. While they lose the specificity of their transcendent referents, sacred stories and symbols as employed in popular culture continue to help us reckon with questions of meaning and identity and to promote real cultural encounters in a society for which that is increasingly difficult.

Chapter 1

Deliver Me from Nowhere

Bruce Springsteen and the Myth of the
American Promised Land

Kate McCarthy

We got one last chance to make it real
To trade in these wings on some wheels
Climb in back, heaven's waiting on down the tracks
Oh come take my hand
We're riding out tonight to case the promised land
Bruce Springsteen, "Thunder Road"

The importance of bar bands all across America is that they nourish and inspire
that community. So there are the very real communities of people and characters, whether it's in Asbury Park or a million different towns across the land.
And then there is the community that it was enabling you to imagine, but that
you haven't seen yet. You don't even know it exists, but you feel that, because of
what you heard or experienced, it could exist.
Bruce Springsteen, interview, *Double Take*, spring 1998, 36–43

In the first months of 2009, Bruce Springsteen performed at arguably the two
most iconic events in American culture: the Presidential inauguration and
the Superbowl. The ritual quality of the inaugural performance was
strengthened by its setting in front of the Lincoln Memorial and by the red-
robed choir that backed him, while the Superbowl show framed him as both
preacher and ultimate referee. Clearly, these events seemed to suggest, this
music by this performer *means something*. While not all reviews of his half-
time performance were raves—some wincing at his near collision with a
cameraman following a cross-stage slide perhaps better left to a younger
rocker—these appearances suggest that Springsteen's stature as an American
institution is firmly resolved. And while such gigs may be seen as trophies
awarded to has-beens, Springsteen's commercial success has never been
greater. According to *Billboard*, Springsteen had the second-highest-grossing
tour of 2008, bringing in more than $204 million (*Billboard* 2008).

The story of Bruce Springsteen as American culture hero is one I am
steeped in. I grew up in an assortment of East Coast suburban towns, where
devotion to Springsteen was like a local dialect. I remember lying on the

living room floor with my sisters, studying album covers and fantasizing ourselves as Mary, the archetypal girlfriend in "Thunder Road," dancing out the screen door to meet Bruce, who would drive us away to meet our destinies. Years later, I would return to those same songs with feminist rage. Still, I was moved and challenged by the later Springsteen's tender portraits of struggling workers, illegal immigrants, and 9/11 widows, for whom the American Dream had slipped out of sight, even while I bristled at the fact that those songs were written in the comfort of a multimillion-dollar southern California mansion. And I would still point to Springsteen concerts as some of the most transcendent experiences of holy community I have ever had. Apparently, I am not alone in my highly charged response to this musician. Like only a few other popular musicians, Springsteen is the subject not only of glossy fan panegyrics, but of major academic analyses pursuing such themes as his relation to the American literary tradition of Whitman and Twain and the dynamics of gender in his lyrics.[1] Relatively few fans read studies like these, but they contribute to a consensus formed among critics, cultural analysts, and politicians who have invoked his music that there is something going on in this music that is more significant than the stuff of most Top 40 hits.

Such assessments are conceivable and often compelling because Springsteen is linked with a myth much larger than himself, a myth that reaches back not only to the formation of American identity, but to the Bible. Specifically, Springsteen's work and person invite analysis in terms of the biblical themes of exodus and promised land, themes widely invoked in his lyrics, but also applicable to the phenomenon of Springsteen's performances, social commentaries, and status as cultural icon. By virtue of that mythic connection, Springsteen's music and persona become contested sites for ongoing negotiation over what is good and true—and ugly and shameful—about America.

Certainly, the mythic lens I employ here is only one among several possible interpretive tools for this music; much of it is better read as standard-issue rock-and-roll celebrations of freedom, sex, and rebellion. And I do not impute intentionality to musician or fan in the religious meanings I read in their words and behavior (though often these meanings are explicit). But I am convinced by the pervasiveness of this imagery that analysis of the symbols of exodus and promised land provide one useful route into one place in the culture where real conversation about the spiritual meanings of being an American is occurring.

Promised Land As Myth

One of the most potent narratives of the Jewish and Christian traditions is the story of the Hebrew people's escape from slavery in Egypt and journey to a land promised them by God, as told in the books of *Exodus, Numbers,*

Leviticus, and *Deuteronomy.* The power of this story is attested by its place in an ostensibly secularized America. Though many Americans know the story more from Cecil B. DeMille than from the Bible, this religious text has become a foundational narrative in American (usually Christian) self-under-standing. It is cited by politicians and social activists, exploited by advertising agencies, and emerges frequently in the long history of American popular music, from African-American spirituals to Chuck Berry.

It is important to note that this is a cultural (as opposed to a cosmological) myth; its focus is on a particular group, and the impact of the story depends on appropriating that group's perspective. If we were to read it from the perspective of the Egyptians, or the Canaanites already inhabiting the "promised land," for instance, its meaning would be radically altered. If we assume the Hebrews' perspective, though, the story presents the following elements for ongoing cultural appropriation.

First, it offers an account of human suffering. The book of *Exodus* opens with a description of the oppression of the Hebrew slaves wrought by their Egyptian taskmasters who "made their lives bitter with hard service in mortar and brick and in every kind of field labor" (*Exodus* 1:14). Identification with the Hebrews' misery provides one important entry into this story. Generations to follow have found in these words resonance of their own suffering under conditions of (perceived) injustice, and thereby made sacred meaning of that suffering.

Second, the story tells us that God is on the side of these victims of oppression, and shares empathically in their grief. "I have observed the misery of my people who are in Egypt," God says; "I have heard their cry on account of their taskmasters, indeed, I know their sufferings" (*Exodus* 3:7). This is a God who will intervene on behalf of the Hebrews, who promises to deliver them from their suffering and lead them to "a good and broad land, a land flowing with milk and honey" (*Exodus* 3:8). The biblical theme of chosenness, whereby God elects one particular person or group for a sacred destiny, is a strong element in this narrative.

A third theme of this text that is relevant to its resurfacing in popular American culture is that of the sacred journey. God does not liberate the Hebrews immediately; rather, they are forged into a holy nation through a 40-year period of God-led but often conflictual migration. This motif of a transformative journey, through which a person or group gains freedom, new identity, and transcendent wisdom, is common in myth; this particular version resurfaces in a wide range of American expression, from the Joads' drive across the dusty plains in Steinbeck's *Grapes of Wrath* to *The Wizard of Oz*.

Finally, the concept of the promised land itself is packed with interpretive possibility. It is significant that the Hebrews do not inherit the land for which they have been working for generations, but are led by God to a new place, one already occupied by others but whose conquest God mandates. It is no wonder, then, that this myth should figure so prominently in American rhetoric. The conviction of divine right to a particular piece of geography is a powerful current in American political and cultural history.

To claim that Bruce Springsteen's music is mythic, then, is on one level simply to point to the frequency of allusion to these elements in his lyrics. But more important, it is to see in this music the ongoing function of myth to crystallize complex cultural issues. When Springsteen invokes this myth, he is engaging in a dialogue not only with the Bible and the Jewish and Christian religious traditions, but also with long traditions of American history and self-understanding.

City On A Hill: The American Promised Land Tradition

American history is deeply infused with the conviction that this particular land has a unique place in God's plan. That conviction emerges in evocations of the exodus narrative for a variety of purposes, from national self-congratulation to radical cultural criticism. The Puritans of the Massachusetts Bay Colony were convinced that their communal experiment was one of divine significance comparable with that of the ancient Israelites. John Winthrop's sermon "A Model of Christian Charity" (1630), in which the New England plantation is identified as the "City upon a Hill" on which all eyes were focused (cited in Cherry 1971, 43), established a permanent theme in American religious reflection. It is heard in Jonathan Edwards' revivalist confidence that "the latter-day glory is probably to begin in America" (Cherry 1971, 55), served the Mormon self-definition as a persecuted people led by God to a western Zion, and was put to extraordinary use in a speech by Senator Albert Beveridge in 1900 defending US imperialism in the Pacific. Such expansion, he argued, was America's "high and holy destiny" (Cherry 1971, 153).

Images of exodus and promised land have also worked as vehicles of radical self-criticism in America. Henry Ward Beecher used these images to sustain the abolitionist cause in the face of "the Red Sea of war" (Cherry 1971, 165), seeing in the biblical parallel more of a terrible challenge than a mandate. Martin Luther King Jr claimed the exodus narrative for African Americans who had borne the brunt of society's claims to a holy destiny. His last speech made clear that the promised land is conceivable, but does not exist, cannot exist in racist America. A generation later, Mario Cuomo chided Ronald Reagan's 1984 invocation of the Puritan city on the hill motif, reminding us that America is a shining city "only for those relative few who are lucky enough to live in its good neighborhoods" ("Two Cities," cited in Bellah et al. 1987, 413). Evocation of the promised land has been a powerful way to express competing constructions of American destiny and multiple deconstructions of the hypocrisy underlying such conceptions and their mockery of the real experience of millions of Americans.

A comparable range of meanings can be discerned in popular music's treatment of these images. Evocations of exodus and promised land have figured centrally in the music of African Americans. The connection between their situation and the Hebrews' is explicit in the spirituals; but even in the blues, these biblical themes are evident. In their uncompromising reckoning with the painful realities of black existence in racist America and their expression of confidence in the possibility of *another* reality, access to which is symbolized by journeys—by foot, on buses, and on trains—blues artists continued to express a communal will to be, an exertion of "somebodiness" in a world bent on denying it,[2] and continued to invoke biblical imagery in the process.

Inheritor of these traditions, rock music has kept alive this theological tradition with deep American roots; we hear refrains from *Exodus* in a wide range of rock songs, from Chuck Berry's "Bye Bye Johnny" to Creedence Clearwater Revival's "Up Around the Bend" to Sheryl Crow's "Leaving Las Vegas." The post-World War II generations of white Americans who have been the main producers and consumers of rock have tended to repudiate both the institutions of American Christianity and its historic confidence in this society's holy destiny. But there remains in their musical expressions a profound sense of the transcendent possibilities of this place; while the music rejects the dominant culture and its institutions, it does so in a way that re-establishes the legitimacy of language of ultimacy—mythic language—to describe America. This is nowhere clearer than in the songs of Bruce Springsteen, who emerged from and aims to speak for the white, lower-middle- and working-class Americans who are the inheritors of this myth and its increasingly problematic meanings.

Casing The Promised Land: The Songs

The complex interplay between myth and music(ian) is most simply approached through lyric analysis. In Springsteen's case, such an analysis reveals a consistent use of biblical imagery to evoke the transcendent dimensions of experience, whether of family conflict ("Adam Raised a Cain"), sexuality ("Fire"), or a factory worker's despair ("Youngstown"). Springsteen's frequent use of the promised land theme is highly ambiguous and often ironic, serving the same cultural–critical function it has had for centuries of American artists and rhetoricians. His songs celebrate the American road and its joyous possibilities (in industrial New Jersey of all places), but beneath these celebrations is an indictment of America's failure to make real its transcendent promise. Springsteen's critique of the "runaway American dream" is a rock 'n' roll take on the working-class laments of John Steinbeck and Woody Guthrie, laying bare the exploitation and alienation that have built the city on the hill. From the image of his father "walking through them factory gates in the rain" in *Darkness on the Edge of Town*

(1978) through his depictions on *The Ghost of Tom Joad* (1995) of the plight of Mexican immigrants, ex-cons, and unemployed workers, Springsteen's music has turned a light on the limits of America's promise. For all their grimness, Springsteen's songs also project hope in a real American promised land. These songs are full of defiant movements out of conditions of limitation and toward, if not into, worlds of possibility.

Early Road Songs: Exodus as (Sexual) Escape

In his earlier songs these limits are usually personal—dead-end jobs and relationships, oppressive small towns, and restrictive familial obligations. Exodus accounts on these early records—*Greetings from Asbury Park N. J.* (1973), *The Wild, the Innocent & the E Street Shuffle* (1973), and *Born to Run* (1975)—are simple escapes, usually temporary, often sexual, almost always in cars. His 1975 anthem "Born to Run" stands as an archetype of this 1970s version of exodus as escape, where "tramps like us" can "ride through mansions of glory on suicide machines."

The overwhelming impact of this song, with its huge guitar sound, is one of surging masculine power. While the protagonist identifies with the chrome-wheeled, fuel-injected machine sprung free on Highway 9, Wendy is invited only to hold on, to "wrap your legs round these velvet rims and strap your hands 'cross my engines." It is this kind of exodus via sex and machine on American highways, where men have agency and women have flowing hair, that one also hears in Steppenwolf's "Born to Be Wild" and any number of '70s and '80s heavy metal songs.

Another similar expression comes through in "Thunder Road" (1975), which gets at the fuller spiritual import of automotive exodus. It opens with Mary, the mythic girl who figures in so much of Springsteen's music, dancing across her porch to Roy Orbison's "Only the Lonely." "Thunder Road" becomes a plea for Mary to get in the singer's car and come away with him, and in the process creates a vivid description of both the bondage of their lives and the alternative world waiting out on the highway.

The religious references are explicit. Mary has been "praying in vain for a savior to rise from these streets," one who would release her from the suffocation of getting older and going nowhere in a "town full of losers." He makes clear that he is not that kind of savior, but he does tell Mary that "heaven's waiting on down the tracks," which they can reach if they are willing to "trade in these wings on some wheels." Reflecting the Christianized reading of the promised land myth that dominates American culture, Springsteen explicitly identifies it with heaven: "we're riding out tonight to case the promised land." The conflation of these two symbols—this-worldly promised land and otherworldly heaven—points to a major and long-standing tension in American spirituality: is our religious destiny to be fulfilled here in the real world, or is that world only prelude to our true destiny of personal spiritual fulfillment after death? In this song Springsteen offers one rough attempt at an answer, one that apparently resonated with a sizable portion of baby boomers in the early 1970s.

The car becomes a metaphor for the rejection of otherworldly religious promises and the affirmation of the possibility of an alternative, this-worldly redemption. He and Mary can stay where they are, in a kind of death-in-life suggested by images of burned-out Chevrolets and ghosts haunting dusty beach roads, or they can *move*, pull out and leave it all behind for a more real life, in which ordinary—especially sexual—experience itself is the source of meaning and connection. Heaven/the promised land can be reached by car, "Thunder Road" suggests, but only by those who are willing to give up prayer but show faith in the night, give up crosses but also sacrifice dreams.

There are, of course, problems with the automotive exodus experience for those of us who view it through Mary's eyes. Throughout rock music, the traps from which male artists depict liberating flight are typically those of the family or meaningless labor. Symbolic flights of this kind are often identified as the hallmark of youth and subcultural expression. But, as Angela McRobbie argues, there are often overlooked gender implications to this pattern. She reminds us that "it is monstrously more difficult for women to escape (even temporarily)" and that "these symbolic flights have often been at the expense of women (especially mothers) and girls." Recalling Springsteen's invitation to Wendy in "Born to Run," she notes, "in the literary sensibility of urban romanticism that resonates across most youth cultural discourses, girls are allowed little more than the back seat on a drafty motorbike" (McRobbie 1980, 69).[3]

In these early songs, Springsteen's women are silent accessories to male fantasy. Later they will become somewhat more complex, and honored for their greater ability to manage life's complexity, as in 1987's "Spare Parts," in which the young man is too afraid to deal with the responsibilities of unexpected parenthood, while the young woman pulls herself together and gets on with it. Such changes are part of the larger evolution of Springsteen's songwriting toward a vision of a promised land that is real, complicated, and inclusive of the domestic world from which these early heroes seek escape. Still, women in Springsteen's songs still remain secondary figures, defined, not unexpectedly, by the male protagonists who maintain the subject position.

More Road Songs: Exodus as Personal Redemption

Another layer of meaning is added by songs from *Darkness on the Edge of Town* (1978), *The River* (1980), and *Nebraska* (1982). *Darkness*'s "The Promised Land" summarizes the album's recurring themes: alienating work, intergeneration conflict, relationships that become traps—all made more painful by the awareness, however vague, that another kind of life is possible.

Despite "feel[ing] so weak I just want to explode," the protagonist still ends each refrain with the insistence that "Mister, I ain't a boy, no I'm a man/And I believe in a promised land." Here the promised land has no more specific content than its contrast with conventional life. Importantly, it is evoked through violent imagery: explosions, knife fights, twisters. It is as if these acts of destruction are the only way the speaker can convince himself of his own existence. Consciously or not, Springsteen here taps into an old blues tradition, the assertion of manhood, of "somebodiness," through acts of violence against a world whose more subtle violence the protagonist can no longer bear.

This sense of exodus as escape out of anonymity into an authentic sense of self is still connected with the automotive experience, as indicated by "Open All Night" (*Nebraska*), a tight, tense song about a worker finishing a long shift, on "an all-night run to get back to where my baby lives." A drive through north Jersey becomes its own exodus, through the power of the car and its radio. The sound is at once lonesome and exhilarated, moving at a deliberate, urgent pace that threatens to—but never quite does—burst its restraints. The opening lines, "I had the carburetor cleaned and checked/With her line blown out she's hummin' like a turbojet," are reminiscent of the macho world of "Born to Run," but there's something else going on here. The singer is uneasy, and brings us in on that uneasiness: "This turnpike sure is spooky at night when you're all alone." He's low on gas, late for arrival, and can't find a gas station or a pay phone. The mood is heightened by the mounting pressure of the lyric structure; there is not a repeated line in the song.

Finally, it is the music on the radio that offers release. Fighting through frequencies "jammed up with gospel stations," he prays, "Hey Mr. Deejay, won'tcha hear my last prayer/Hey ho, rock and roll, deliver me from nowhere." In this prayer, Springsteen offers a précis of this stream of his rock 'n' roll theology: it rejects the Christian faith the culture offers, identifying it with an irrelevant, and often oppressive, otherworldly spirituality, but at the same time reaches for its own "long-distance salvation" through rock 'n' roll radio. This music claims the power to reorient experience so dramatically that only the language of religion is adequate to expressing it. It "saves" and "delivers" its listeners by connecting them not only with this music, but also, through the shared radio experience, with each other. Here Springsteen takes part in a long-standing tradition of rock 'n' roll radio as both source and medium of holy community, in which the radio transports the listener into a virtual, temporary promised land.

This communitarian element is central to Springsteen's vision of an ideal America. Even in those lyrics that depict cars and highways as a celebratory escape from the cares of the long workweek, there is an element of collective salvation. Jim Cullen (1997) points to the importance of the shift to the first-person plural in the last verse of *Darkness*'s "Racing in the Street." The song is evocative of Martha and the Vandellas' "Dancin' in the Streets" (1964), a pop dance hit whose widely known subtext was an ebullient announcement of the urban riots of the '60s. Springsteen's much quieter song seems to lack any of the larger social meaning, until the last verse. The refrain lines about blowing away all comers in drag races on the strip have been heard twice by this point. Then, just before the final refrain, comes this verse:

> For all the shut-down strangers and hot-rod angels
> Rumbling through this promised land
> Tonight my baby and me we're gonna ride to the sea
> And wash these sins off our hands

The collective redemptive power of the singer's own purificatory drive is then reflected in the song's last lines:

> Tonight, tonight, the highway's bright
> Out of our way mister you best keep
> 'Cause summer's here and the time is right
> For racin' in the street ...

The plural pronoun suggests that Springsteen's use of promised land imagery is developing a more complex theological meaning; escape from the world of those who "start dying little by little, piece by piece" can't be had alone. The compassion of the last verse indicates a sense of the collective quality of human suffering and the necessarily collective nature of liberation, even when it takes the form of a drag race. "Play becomes communitarian, something one does not only to save oneself, but also something one does for (or at least in honor of) others" (Cullen 1997, 121). This shift marks the beginning of Springsteen's development of a fully wrought vision of an American promised land built on the premise of mutual responsibility.

The Folk Songs: Exodus as Populist Plea

Beginning with *Nebraska* (1982), and more explicitly in *The Ghost of Tom Joad* (1995), Springsteen's use of promised land and exodus imagery is put to increasingly political use. In these stripped-down acoustic albums the limits to authentic life in America are increasingly seen as collective; his lyrics tell us that America cannot be the promised land until it is made hospitable to the likes of Vietnam vets, downsized steelworkers, farmers, single mothers, and illegal immigrants. Springsteen expresses a personal sense of culpability for this national failure, a sense that he urges upon us all. As he said at a Vietnam veterans' benefit concert in Los Angeles, preparing to sing Woody Guthrie's "This Land Is Your Land": "There's a lot in [United States history] ... that you're proud of and then there's a lot of things in it that you're ashamed of. And that burden, that burden of shame, falls down. Falls down on everybody" (quoted by Gilmore 1990, 295). For Springsteen, the space between rock 'n' roll performance and political activism has become thin; he hopes that the images that drive his songs will also drive concert-goers and CD-buyers into their communities as spokespeople for the voiceless.

The grimness of the *Joad* album led some critics to argue that Springsteen had abandoned hope in America's transcendent possibility.[4] But the songs on *The Ghost of Tom Joad* can be read differently. The title song sets a scene very close to despair, with a "shelter line stretchin' 'round the corner/ Welcome to the new world order." In this America, the road is a metaphor of failure, not promise. "The highway is alive tonight," Springsteen sings, echoing dozens of earlier lyrics, "but nobody's kiddin' nobody about where it goes." This is a road that ends in homeless shelters, jail, or death. In one of the bleakest of his allusions to the promised land, he resurrects Steinbeck's Preacher, who is

> Waitin' for when the last shall be first and the first shall be last
> In a cardboard box 'neath the underpass
> Got a one-way ticket to the promised land
> You got a hole in your belly and a gun in your hand

Here the promised land images seem to serve nothing but irony; the wait for that day and the ticket to the promised land seem equally hopeless. A similar effect is achieved in the songs about Mexican immigrants. "Across the Border" evokes the outsider's hopes for America as promised land, but set beside "Sinaloa Cowboys," "The Line," and "Balboa Park," these images become something like a cruel joke. In these songs, the immigrants who make it across the border are reduced to hustling, drug dealing, smuggling, and a variety of ignominious deaths, as other people's cars "rush by so fast."

But the last verse of "The Ghost of Tom Joad" offers the barest hint that redemption is still possible in this hard land. The luckless narrator who sits with "no home, no job, no peace, no rest" invokes Steinbeck's Everyman and recounts his parting words to his mother:

> Now Tom said, "Mom, wherever there's a cop beatin' a guy
> Wherever a hungry newborn baby cries
> Where there's a fight 'gainst the blood and hatred in the air
> Look for me, Mom, I'll be there"

By raising Tom Joad's ghost this way, Springsteen situates his dark vision of America within a rich populist tradition. The stories of the album's tragic characters are enlarged and dignified by this association, and their portrayals become a plea for the more humane and inclusive America that we have at least collectively imagined. *We Shall Overcome: The Seeger Sessions* (2006),

Springsteen's only album of music he didn't write, reaches more deeply still into the American folk tradition to help revive this memory. These songs, from "John Henry," to "Erie Canal," to the title anthem, confirm that for Springsteen, America is still worth singing about, still a source of mythic tales, and in this sense still a holy landscape.

Rock Songs Redux: Exodus As Personal And Political Hope Post-9/11

Springsteen's three rock-oriented studio albums of the new millennium, *The Rising* (2002), *Magic* (2007), and *Working on a Dream* (2009), form a trilogy that reckons with the new realities of American identity after 9/11. Interspersed with the folk *Devils and Dust* (2005) and *Seeger Sessions*, these albums give coherent new shape to his career-long concern with national possibility and responsibility. After a seven-year studio gap, *The Rising* was a huge popular and critical success, and won the Grammy for best rock album of 2002. Many of *The Rising*'s songs were written as explicit responses to the attacks—the fear, the losses, and the heroism of the rescue workers—an apparent effort to contribute to the national mourning process.

In the struggle to make sense of these events, several rhetorical frameworks competed for national consensus in the first months following 9/11. Was this an act of war akin to Pearl Harbor, to which the language of national unity and defense was appropriate? Was it a criminal act requiring cool-headed investigation and legal prosecution? Was it the consequence of years of foreign policy errors calling for national reflection and reassessment? Or was it the opening salvo in a religious war, to which only the language of crusades and divine purpose could speak? With its juxtaposition of excruciating depictions of loss in a song like "You're Missing" ("Coffee cups on the counter, jackets on the chair/Papers on the doorstep, you're not there") with the Sufi music and references to the possibility of love across lines of difference "'neath Allah's blessed rains" in "World's Apart," *The Rising* offers another rhetoric, one in which love and rock and roll offer the possibility of meaning-making amidst the horror. "His concern is not with a national uprising but with a rising above: the transcending of ever-mounting losses and ancient hatreds" (Loder 2002). This album still shows faith in the redemptive power of the exodus-style journey, though, as in "Further On (Up the Road)," the road is still "out in the desert," and "if there's a light up ahead well brother I don't know," but it is a road on which those who believe in good times can still meet. The album ends on a prayer, in "My City of Ruins," for faith, love, the lost, the world.

Five years later, deep in the Bush quagmire, *Magic* seems to step back from the possibility of redemption; the magic of the title is a kind of nasty, lethal sleight-of-hand performed by the powerful on the weak, who never seem to catch on. The road imagery in this album is bleak. The "Long Walk

Home" reverses the sacred trip, as the narrator returns to his hometown where everything's closed, the courthouse flag that his father said stood for something no longer signifies "Who we are, what we'll do and what we won't," and the sign on the diner just says "gone." Gone is John Winthrop's high rhetoric of American purpose, or even Woodie Guthrie's commitment to its possibility. In "Livin' in the Future," set on the morning after election day, when the protagonist admits "my faith's been torn asunder," the ship of liberty has "sailed away on a bloody red horizon." This album's other road song, "Magic," is similarly grim. The sun is sinking, and there are bodies hanging from the trees. The sleight-of-hand man threatens, with a shiny blade, looking for a volunteer. On this road, freedom drifts like a ghost through the trees, and you are advised to "carry only what you fear."

If *The Rising* represented a moment when a possible promised land came into view from a peak moment in American history, and *Magic* the blood-soaked downward slide from that possibility, *Working on a Dream* (2009) might be seen as the slow climb up the other side, toward something like home. The third of his full-throttle rock albums made with the reconstituted E Street Band, *Working on a Dream* recovers the joyous spirit of early Springsteen records, hard won by the work in between. The persona of this album is vintage Springsteen, the "honest striver redeemed by love and hard work" (Chanin 2008), but the view is more cosmic. The album's lyrics are full of images of suns, stars, skies, planets, moons, gravity, the big bang, telescopes, stardust. At the same time, many of the songs are intensely intimate, reflections on the survival of love amid political and interpersonal disenchantment. Exodus themes no longer dominate, perhaps because, these songs suggest, we've traveled those roads to their ends. Instead of looking back or ahead to a place where troubles disappear, *Working on a Dream* invites us to look up, at a cosmos that relativizes all claims to special destiny, and down, at the things in our lap that redeem an imperfect world. In one of the album's most beautiful lines, the lover in "This Life" brings the two together: "I finger the hem of your dress, my universe at rest."

What I have presented thus far is an unambiguous reading of the meaning of these ancient symbols in one site of American popular culture. Were we to stop here, we could enjoy a neat picture of Springsteen as a contemporary Moses, putting transcendent truths in understandable words, pointing to a better reality, a holier destiny, chiding us when we fail to live up to the promises we have made ourselves and each other. But the reality is far more ambiguous, because the lyrics discussed above do not exist simply on the page, but (1) as performed, in both recorded and live contexts; (2) as interpreted through the experiences of those who encounter those performances; and (3) as refracted by the public personae of Springsteen not only as musician but also as hometown hero, adulterer, businessman, family man, activist, and multimillionaire. These concentric interpretive contexts add complexity to the music's reports of the American promised land and point to the truly mythic—because multivalent—meaning of popular culture.

"Do You Have Enough Beers In Your Car?": Parking Lot Promised Land

Springsteen's fans are a devoted lot. The adoring "Bruuuuuce" that greets him when he appears on stage is something akin to what the Pope receives on visits to Latin America. In parts of New Jersey a negative comment about him is cause for violence. It is not unusual to hear his significance put in religious terms, as the editor of a long-running fanzine does, recalling his first show: "Springsteen ended up playing a guitar solo standing atop my table, and as he dripped sweat on me that hot summer night, I imagine I was baptized in some alien way" (Cross 1989).

For many, the impetus for such adulation goes far beyond musical appreciation. Fans adore Springsteen because he offers a vision of themselves and their society as inhabitants of a promised land that is truer, more authentic than their daily experiences. The word "real" shows up with striking frequency in discussions of Springsteen's music, in concert and album reviews, and in fans' reports of what the music means to them. But just what does "real" mean in this context? Intersecting, overlapping, and conflicting understandings of the promise held out by Springsteen's music show the complexity of apparently shared cultural symbols like the promised land.

On the one hand, what is real about Springsteen is the people his songs depict. These are unglamorous, working-class folks who drive real cars on real New Jersey highways, are too tired to play with their children, and see themselves facing the same destinies for which they cursed their parents. But Springsteen grants a dignity and a hopefulness to these characters that make their plight seem meaningful. The "real" world of screen doors, backstreets, factory gates, and neighborhood bars is presented in the lyrics as a world of sublime possibility, where transcendent moments—windows rolled down, hair blown back, radio up loud—shine a transformative light on everything else.[5]

For fans, Springsteen concerts often become such moments. At a Springsteen concert at the New Jersey Meadowlands in 1984, I was stuck in one of two very slow-moving lines of cars making their way into the huge parking lot. The summer evening was still hot, the air damp and sticky in our un-air-conditioned car. Windows were open all down the lines, and conversations struck up over bootlegged tapes. Noticing our California plates, a young woman in the crowded car next to us leaned out and called, "You came all the way from California? Do you have enough beers in your car?" One assumes this is not an offer she would have made stopped at a traffic light just outside the stadium. I have had similar encounters in suburban Los Angeles and outside Boston Garden, where I saw panic move down a line of college-age ticket-buyers when it was learned that the box office would not accept checks. I watched as those who had extra cash took checks from those who didn't, the only apparent concern being to maximize the number of us who would get to see Bruce. These are moments of what Victor Turner would call spontaneous *communitas*,[6] here made possible by common connection to a particular vision of America, one in which time moves slowly, neighbors are trusted, and the good life can be had over a shared beer. The performance context thus suggests that in addition to *depicting* a kind of promised land, the music also conjures it, makes it temporarily real for those participating.

Like all ritual, Springsteen performances and their peripheral events are able to sustain the intense *communitas* experience by virtue of their removal from "real" space and time. In this case, people share beer, money, and affection with others who, outside the performance context, they would be unlikely to share a conversation with. Lines of class, politics, and geography (though not, notably, race) seem to dissolve within the "sacred" space and time of the concert experience. And while rock concerts of many varieties can be, and have been, identified as sources of this kind of experience, in this case the sense of intimate, uncomplicated, unstructured connectedness is powerfully aided by the mythic quality of the images in the music. Were Springsteen to explicitly lay out a sociopolitical analysis of American ideals and failures, such a vision would appeal to only a small portion of the audience. As it is, his reports of "badlands," out of which one can drive on "streets of fire" past "the mansion on the hill" to "the river" to "wash these sins off our hands," invite liberal intellectuals and conservative blue-collar workers alike to read themselves into the narrative. In these songs, the story of enslavement ("the working, the working, just the working life") and the promise of deliverance ("I believe in a promised land") are made relevant to contemporary American experience, but at the same time are sufficiently removed from the actuality of that experience to remain available for appropriation by diverse if not competing constituencies.

This was illustrated in a bizarre way in the controversy that erupted in 1984 over the Reagan campaign's effort to appropriate Springsteen's "Born in the USA" as a conservative anthem. Columnist George Will offered a review of a Springsteen show that cast Springsteen as Republican cheerleader: "He is no whiner, and the recitation of closed factories and other problems always seems punctuated by a grand, cheerful, affirmation: 'Born in the U.S.A.!'" (quoted by Cullen 1997, 3). Reagan himself invoked Springsteen a few days later at a campaign stop in New Jersey, where he aligned himself with Springsteen's "message of hope" (Gilmore 1990, 298). Springsteen distanced himself from the president's embrace in comments at subsequent shows, and later said: "I think people got a need to feel good about the country they live in. But what's happening, I think, is that that need—which is a good thing—is getting manipulated and exploited. And you see

the Reagan re-election ads on TV—you know 'It's morning in America.'
And you say, well, it's not morning in Pittsburgh. It's not morning above
125th Street in New York. It's midnight, and, like, there's a bad moon risin'.
And that's why when Reagan mentioned my name in New Jersey, I felt it
was another manipulation, and I had to disassociate myself from the president's kind words" (Loder 1984/1996, 154). Springsteen seemed to recognize, at this point in his career, that his own effective use of mythic symbols
for the purposes of American cultural critique depends on their not being
tied too closely to any particular American agenda.

Moses In The Hollywood Hills: Springsteen As Ambiguous Culture Hero

The "realness" celebrated by Springsteen fans also refers to the musician
himself. Coming to national celebrity in an era of synthetic disco sounds,
and performers defined as much by costume and makeup as music, an era in
which rock had become unabashedly big business, Springsteen was celebrated as the real thing, a return to rock's purer, simpler roots, when the
music was what mattered. Jon Landau's famous designation of Springsteen
as the future of rock 'n' roll was part of a larger statement in which he
expresses this widespread image of Springsteen:

> In my own moments of greatest need, I never gave up the search for
> sounds that can answer every impulse, consume all emotion, cleanse and
> purify—all things that we have no right to expect from even the greatest
> works of art but which we can occasionally derive from them. Tonight,
> there is someone I can write of the way I used to write, without reser-
> vation of any kind. Last Thursday, at the Harvard Square theatre, I saw
> my rock 'n' roll past flash before my eyes. And I saw something else: I
> saw rock 'n' roll's future and its name is Bruce Springsteen.
>
> (quoted by Goodman 1997, 226–27)

The hyperbole of Landau's assessment of Springsteen points to the religious
quality of this popular image of Springsteen and his music as somehow more
authentic than the rest. Landau here invests rock and roll with a salvific
function and identifies Springsteen's music as the genuine article, the sound
that can, at last, fulfill that holy promise. There is a baptismal quality to
what Landau celebrates in these lines; the Harvard Square show has left him
cleansed, purified, feeling reborn.

But to hear others tell it, behind all this reality and authenticity is in fact a
carefully orchestrated presentation by record producers, promoters, critics and,
at least since the release of *The River*, Springsteen himself, that masks
the wide cracks that have developed between New Jersey working-class
guitar hero and savvy businessman. The most obvious of these gaps, of

course, is money. The son of Freehold, New Jersey, now owns several multi-million-dollar homes and faces none of the hard realities against which his songs' characters struggle so nobly. "Money changes everything," Cyndi Lauper realized. So did Springsteen, according to Fred Goodman, who argues that as his popularity increased, the naïve young rocker gradually came to accept and even embrace the music industry's profit-driven logic. That Goodman should devote the better part of a 400-page book to documenting this transformation in Springsteen is itself evidence that with this artist the stakes are very high. It is significant that Springsteen should have sold out to this version of the American dream precisely because of his iconic representation of a holier America, one defined by the dignity of labor, the loyalty of family, the integrity of community, the transcendent power of sexual love. As the local boy who made good, Springsteen has been represented as one who did not just write and sing about, but also embodied this American promised land, re-presenting its values back to those from whom the vision might have begun to recede.

Exposing the tycoon beneath the leather jacket as Goodman seeks to do, then, is book-worthy because it problematizes important aspects of American self-understanding. Mainstream American culture, if such a thing can still be talked about, is perhaps unique in seeing itself as simultaneously elect and common; one reason the exodus narrative remains so relevant to this culture is because of its fusion of divine chosenness with social and political powerlessness. The breakdown of Springsteen's identification with the disempowered masses he represents throws into question the possibility of our own arrival in the promised land, or at least of arriving with souls intact and of finding there something other than a theme-park version of what was promised.

This breakdown is even more evident in the increasing ideological gap between Springsteen and many of his listeners. Springsteen's audiences, almost exclusively white, have always been an interesting mix of working-class locals and liberal intellectuals in from the suburbs. The small size of the latter class, however, has always made the former the core Springsteen constituency. As his music, and especially his performances, have become more explicitly identified with liberal political causes, and eventually with the Obama presidential campaign for which Springsteen performed, the ideological distance between Springsteen and this fan base has grown. "Hobokencoach," a contributor to the "Springsteen Forum" on NJ.com, resents Springsteen's frequent defense of illegal immigrants: "The 8 million illegal number being thrown around in the election by the Dems? Try 20 million. The drain on our resources and economy is staggering, Sinaloa Cowboy. This is why BS' politics and pontificating at events makes me sick. He's a great songwriter and understands the human condition in a poetic sense but dammit if he isn't simplistic and dumb about so many things he spouts off about" ("Springsteen Forum", NJ.com; comment posted April 15 2009).

More recently, fans have blamed Springsteen for holding back the best concert seats for insiders, when regular ticket-buyers end up in the cheap seats. "This so-called working man's hero is nothing but an elitist, liberal, 'do as I say, not as I do' scumbag. I used to think that I had an equal shot at getting front row seats as everyone else. Seems THAT priviledge [*sic*] is reserved for his well-connected friends. Thanks, A$$HOLE!" ("Springsteen Forum", NJ.com; comment posted June 15 2009). Springsteen's insider status with the Obama administration further alienates many longtime fans, as indicated by this response to the reported presence of Obama staff members at a May 2009 concert reported in the *Washington Post*: "One of many reasons I opted not to go to the concert (despite the fact that the first concert I ever saw was the Boss in '85) was to avoid the self-congratulatory Democratic [expletive deleted]" (Akers 2009; comment posted May 19 2009).

Springsteen himself appears to be well aware of these gaps, and of the inherent ambiguity of enormous wealth and celebrity built on a "regular guy" image. The very personal songs on 1992's *Lucky Town* and *Human Touch* acknowledge how good he has it, but insist that a satisfying life is as elusive for those of privilege as it is for the poor. His wealth and fame have made a myth of Springsteen himself, he has said, one from which he has had to struggle to free himself:

> It's like you're a figment of a lot of other people's imaginations. And that always takes some sorting out. But it's even worse when you see yourself as a figment of your own imagination ... [Y]ou can get enslaved by your own myth or your own image, for lack of a better word. And it's bad enough having other people see you that way, but seeing yourself that way is really bad. It's pathetic.
>
> (Henke 1992/1996, 322)

To get past this myth, Springsteen seems to have turned to the work of interpersonal intimacy, as reflected in the more stationary images that fill *Tunnel of Love* (1987), *Human Touch*, and *Lucky Town*, the dark, scary intimacy of the tunnel replacing wide-open highways.

Springsteen's music continues to depict and decry the huge American wealth gap, but does so now from knowledge of life on the other side of that chasm. While it will not be persuasive to all, his ruminations about how hard it is to get comfortable in the mansion on the hill at least indicate an awareness of the complexity of the relationship between wealth and happiness. One of the most dangerous versions of the American promised land myth is the one that identifies the promise with the trappings, he tells us.

> I understood that it's the music that keeps me alive, and my relationships with my friends, and my attachment to the people and the places I've known. That's my lifeblood. And to give that up for, like, the TV, the

cars, the houses—that's not the American dream ... Those are the booby prizes. And if you fall for them—if, when you achieve them, you believe that this is the end in and of itself—then you've been suckered in ... So you gotta be vigilant. You gotta carry the idea you began with further. And you gotta hope that you're headed for higher ground.

(Loder 1984/1996, 164–65)

His own reckoning with the gap between myth and reality seems to add another layer to the meaning of an American promised land for Springsteen, suggesting that it must be an interior as well as exterior landscape.

Springsteen's "authenticity" is thus a common flashpoint in debates about his music. As his work has become increasingly explicit in its identification with liberal political causes, his credibility with critics seems to improve, while it disgruntles his working-class fan base. His music, by invoking the biblical language of a promised land to cast American ideals and realities in mythic terms, has thus become a contested site, prompting a series of hard questions for its listeners: What makes America a promised land? To whom was the promise made? How far, and at whose expense, can its offer be extended? Whose responsibility is its massive failure to deliver on the promise? How much does our individual and collective arrival in that land depend on internal, spiritual dispositions, and how much on outward social and political struggle?

The Myth Of The Promised Land And American Popular Culture

The biblical myth of exodus and promised land has been good to Bruce Springsteen, allowing him to evoke powerful responses in a wide range of American listeners. Viewed collectively, these evocations offer insight into the evolving spirituality of an ostensibly secularized segment of the American population, by sketching changing understandings of what it is that constitutes human bondage, what redemption from that captivity might feel like, and what vehicles might take one there.

From the adolescent sexual frustration of "Rosalita" (1973), to the alienation of meaningless anonymous labor in "Factory" (1978), to the abandonment by their country of Vietnam vets in "Born in the USA" (1984), to the dead-end route of illegal Mexican immigrants in "Sinaloa Cowboys" (1995), to the injured soldier in "Devil's Arcade" (2007), Springsteen's songs depict experiences of bondage that are given weight by religious language and allusion. Similarly, journeys—on motorcycles, cars, and amusement park rides, and across towns, rivers, and state and national borders— become, by means of these references, symbols of personal and collective salvation. In their superimposing of biblical with American landscapes, these songs evoke (positively or negatively) profoundly idealistic visions of

American possibility. But the weight of biblical references also points to the burden of claiming a chosen status, the challenges of establishing and defending the borders of a promised land and the invisible, interior struggles the journey there requires.

As his own and the national life have shifted, so has Springsteen's use of these images, but they consistently explore the tension that Robert Bellah and his colleagues have identified as a defining feature of the contemporary American character: the drive for individual freedom of all kinds, but especially from institutional determination, and the simultaneous quest for a meaningful sense of community (Bellah *et al.* 1985, 144). *Born to Run* uses the exodus theme to express the raw power of the former; *Tom Joad* uses it to press the moral imperative of the latter. This tension is inherent in *Exodus* itself. The biblical story of the escape from Egypt and the journey to the promised land of Canaan is a complex study in social inclusion and exclusion; the Hebrews are the excluded outsiders trapped inside Egypt but become, in their journey, the included of God, led to a place where they claim the divine right to exclude the native inhabitants. And, of course, within their own community are degrees of inclusiveness; the promise made to Moses apparently did not extend equally, for instance, to the Hebrew women (Plaskow 1990, 25–28). The push to freedom, the story implies, is always accompanied by the challenge of new opportunities to include and exclude.

The applicability to the American experience is obvious. In Springsteen's music, the tension between these two perspectives, those of the trapped insider wanting out and the excluded outsider wanting in, is a defining theme. In this sense, Springsteen's work is conservative in an important way. His characters do not want to tear down but to find a meaningful place *within* the system: "My characters aren't really antiheroes. Maybe that makes them old-fashioned in some way. They're interested in being included, and they're trying to figure out what's in their way" (Percy 1998, 38).

What's in their way has changed from album to album, involving increasingly complex issues of class, race, global politics, and interpersonal and ultimately personal soul-searching. The intersection of these issues reminds Springsteen's listeners that getting to the promised land is not a matter of simple escape from one place to another. It must be imagined, negotiated, pieced together out of the scarce resources at hand in the places we already live. At its best, Springsteen knows, his music fosters that kind of imagination.

But, as indicated above, audience experiences of Springsteen and his music are not univocal. It is the complexity of these responses that points to the truly mythic quality of this work. In religious settings, myths are the central stories in light of which individual and collective lives are made meaningful in some ultimate sense. They do not require that all members of the myth-sharing group derive the same meanings, only that all remain in some way tied to the story. In fact, the contested text is the real locus of encounter; without it, the differing constituencies have neither the impetus nor the resources for real conversation.

References

Akers, Mary Ann. 2009. "Bruce Sprinsteen Sends a Sign to Obama." Washington-post.com (May 19). http://voices.washingtonpost.com/sleuth/2009/05/obamaites_-turn_out_for_real_bo.html

Bellah, Robert N., Richard, Madsen, William M. Sullivan, Ann Swidler, and Steven M. Tipton. 1985. *Habits of the Heart: Individualism and Commitment in American Life.* (Berkeley: University of California Press).

——, eds. 1987. *Individualism and Commitment in American Life: Readings on the Themes of Habits of the Heart.* (New York: Harper & Row).

Billboard. 2008. "Top 25 Tours—Billboard Year in Music 2008." www.billbaord.com/yearend/2008/charts/top25-tours.shtml

Chanin, Nate. 2008. "Playlist: Lucky Days and Marvelous Times." *New York Times,* December 12. www.nytimes.com/2008/12/14/arts/music/14play.html?_r=2

Cherry, Conrad, ed. 1971. *God's New Israel: Religious Interpretations of American Destiny.* Englewood Cliffs, (NJ: Prentice Hall).

Cone, James. 1972. *The Spirituals and the Blues.* (Maryknoll, NY: Orbis Books).

Cross, Charles R., and the editors of *Backstreets* magazine. 1989. *Backstreets: Bruce Springsteen: The Man and His Music.* (New York: Harmony Books).

Cullen, Jim. 1997. *Born in the USA: Bruce Springsteen and the American Tradition.* (New York: HarperCollins).

Gerics, Joseph. 1996. "A Melancholy Boss: Springsteen's New Sound." *Commonweal,* February 9, 20–21.

Gilmore, Mikal. 1990. "Bruce Springsteen: What Does it Mean, Springsteen Asked, to Be an American?" Reprinted in *Bruce Springsteen: The Rolling Stone Files,* ed. editors of *Rolling Stone* (New York: Hyperion, 1996), 291–302.

Goodman, Fred. 1997. *The Mansion on the Hill: Dylan, Young, Geffen, Springsteen and the Head-On Collision of Rock and Commerce.* (New York: Random House).

Greeley, Andrew. 1988. *God in Popular Culture.* (Chicago: Thomas More Press).

Henke, James. 1992/1996. "The *Rolling Stone* Interview: Bruce Springsteen." Reprinted in *Bruce Springsteen: The Rolling Stone Files,* ed. Editors of *Rolling Stone,* (New York: Hyperion), 318–33.

Loder, Kurt. 1984/1996. "The *Rolling Stone* Interview: Bruce Springsteen." Reprinted in *Bruce Springsteen: The Rolling Stone Files,* ed. Editors of *Rolling Stone,* (New York: Hyperion), 151–65.

——2002. "Album Review: Bruce Springsteen, *The Rising.*" *Rolling Stone* 903 (August 22): 80–81.

McRobbie, Angela. 1980. "Settling Accounts with Subcultures: A Feminist Critique." Reprinted in *On Record: Rock, Pop, & the Written Word,* ed. Simon Frith and Andrew Goodwin. (New York: Pantheon Books, 1990).

Palmer, Gareth. 1997. "Bruce Springsteen and Masculinity." In *Sexing the Groove: Popular Music and Gender,* ed. Sheila Whiteley. (New York: Routledge).

Percy, Will. 1998. "Rock and Read: Will Percy Interviews Bruce Springsteen." *DoubleTake* 12 (Spring): 36–43.

Plaskow, Judith. 1990. *Standing Again at Sinai: Judaism from a Feminist Perspective.* (New York: HarperCollins).

Spencer, Jon Michael. 1992. "Rhapsody in Black: Utopian Aspirations." *Theology Today* 48 (January): 444–51.

Symynkywicz, Jeffrey B. 2008. *The Gospel According to Bruce Springsteen: Rock and Redemption from Asbury Park to Magic.* (Louisville: Westminster John Knox).

Turner, Victor. 1974. *Dramas, Fields and Metaphors: Symbolic Action in Human Society.* Ithaca, (NY: Cornell University Press).

Notes

1 See for instance Cullen 1997, Goodman 1997, and Symynkywicz 2008.

2 This idea is developed fully in James Cone's *The Spirituals and the Blues* (Cone 1972). Jon Michael Spencer argues for a similar function of contemporary rap music: "Rap, as a resentment listening music, collectively comprises the power of emancipated knowledges, the determination to change established society, and the anticipation of liberation" (Spencer 1992, 448).

3 For an analysis of the construction of masculinity in Springsteen's music, see Palmer (1997).

4 See, for instance, Gerics (1996, 20).

5 It is for this revelation of the transcendence of the ordinary that Catholic sociologist Andrew Greeley praises Springsteen and other popular culture artists who display a "Catholic imagination." See Greeley (1988).

6 According to Turner (1974, 274), *communitas* refers to the antistructural component of ritual life, characteristic of the relationships of those jointly undergoing ritual transformation. *Communitas* relationships are "undifferentiated, equalitarian, direct, extant, non-rational, I–Thou (in Feuerbach's and Buber's sense) … Communitas is spontaneous, immediate, concrete—it is not shaped by norms, it is not institutionalized, it is not abstract."

Chapter 2

"I Wanna Do Bad Things With You"

Fantasia on Themes of American Religion from the Title Sequence of HBO's *True Blood*[1]

Leonard Norman Primiano

"What Are You?"

It is a warm Louisiana night. The air is thick with humidity. The time is the very near future. A comely young waitress from a local bar and grill walks through an old cemetery located between residential properties. The woman is not alone. She is speaking to an attractive, even handsome, figure of a male. She seems strangely drawn to him, even though—while open to new experiences, and especially those individuals she perceives as marginalized members of society—she does feel some trepidation. She is distinctly aware that this person, who communicates in a courtly manner and is obviously physically present, standing and talking with her, is, in fact, not mortal. He is a member of a unique category of legendary creature: the living dead, better known as a vampire. Instead of desiring to drink this female's blood, the vampire is himself actually drawn to and quite fascinated with this woman as an individual, and they engage in spirited conversation. In the course of their time together over the past three days, he has sensed something unique about her humanity—supernatural gifts—which is an intrinsic aspect of her being, an important part of her everyday life. He has directly inquired several times during their initial meetings, sincerely and with great curiosity: "What are you?" What will eventually prove to be not only a personal but an intimate relationship has begun.

The evocative interrogatories described above concerning one's personal sense of spiritual self, as well as unexpected role reversals—a vampire being moved to ask questions about the surprising nature of a human, for example—can be found in the opening episodes of the HBO network's vampire romance and drama *True Blood*. While it is impossible to know over the course of a multi-year television series the direction that creators will take during an entire production—even one emanating from popular novels—it is my contention that the state of personal spirituality, as well as organized religion in America, is central to the serial's first two seasons (2008–09). In the audio commentary accompanying the release on DVD of the first year of the series, creator and executive producer Alan Ball recalls a rather cryptic summary of the series that he once hastily offered a studio executive at HBO: "It is about the terrors of intimacy" (Ball 2009). The intimacy to which Ball refers could be understood exclusively as interpersonal, but a more generous consideration opens up this sense of intimacy to include relationships that individuals feel with their deity, with their organized religious tradition, or with their personal spiritual selves, what I have described elsewhere as their "religious idioculture" (Primiano 1995, 48–51).

Stanley Cavell distinguishes masterpieces of film and television with the assessment that "what is memorable, treasureable, criticizable is primarily [not] the individual work [of television], but the program, the format, not this or that day of *I Love Lucy*, but the program as such" (Cavell 1984, 239). This analysis extends beyond Cavell's point to engage both episodic examples and the entire program, *True Blood*. I propose that *True Blood*, as evidenced from the past two years of its broadcasts, presents a rich, disturbing, ironical, critical, depressing fantasia on American religion in general—both in its institutional expressions and also in its lived, hybrid, vernacular expressions. More specifically, the program can be seen as serving an array of interlocking functions. As a reflection of multidimensional religious life in contemporary America, the evocative program communicates a multitude of conflicted and conflicting perspectives. It acknowledges religion's power socially and individually; it recognizes the viability of vernacular religion ("religion as it is lived, as human beings encounter, understand, interpret, and practice it", Primiano 1995, 44) as a consistently negotiated reality; it opens up a consideration of religion not as emanating from cultural sources, but as an experience-centered phenomenon; and finally it perceives and portrays faithful believers as bound for disappointment by an apparently detached God, unmoved by human pleas for assistance, transcendence, or immanence.

This article explores the link between *True Blood*'s re-telling of the legend of the vampire and the state of normative religious traditions and vernacular spirituality in contemporary America. This constellation of concerns invites closer scrutiny. As provocative as the actual dialogue and action of the drama is, my essay centers its focus on the clues provided by the show's weekly introductory credits, arguing that their visual style speaks not only to a "new iconography" (Hoover 2001), but quite possibly to something much larger: what I see as a "new iconoclasm" of American religion being mediated by this television fantasia in the post-9/11 era.[2]

"I Don't Think Jesus Would Mind, If Somebody Was A Vampire."

In June 2008, the cable network Home Box Office first offered its series *True Blood*, a chronicle of vampire/human societal interaction set in contemporary northern Louisiana. A second season of first-run episodes continued in June and concluded in September 2009. For readers unfamiliar with the creative context and content of the drama, the brief abstract of the show offered on the official website of the series is a suitable introduction to the program:

> Thanks to a Japanese scientist's invention of synthetic blood, vampires have progressed from legendary monsters to fellow citizens overnight. And while humans have been safely removed from the menu, many remain apprehensive about these creatures "coming out of the coffin." Religious leaders and government officials around the world have chosen their sides, but in the small Louisiana town of Bon Temps, the jury is still out.
>
> Local waitress Sookie Stackhouse (Anna Paquin), however, knows how it feels to be an outcast. "Cursed" with the ability to listen in on people's thoughts, she's also open-minded about the integration of vampires—particularly when it comes to Bill Compton (Stephen Moyer), a handsome 173-year-old living up the road. But at the service of Bill's less virtuous vampire associates, Sookie is drawn into a series of catastrophes that will put their love to the test.
>
> The latest hit series from *Six Feet Under* creator Alan Ball, *True Blood* delves into the meticulously-crafted world of novelist Charlaine Harris. Described by the Emmy-winning Ball as "popcorn for smart people," the first season of *True Blood* caused an overnight sensation—and the new installments only build on his colorful cast of supernatural misfits.
>
> (HBO 2010a)[3]

This television adaptation of literary vampires certainly continues the well-known metaphorical association of vampires with sexuality, observed most notably in Bram Stoker's novel *Dracula*, and the popular films made from this book featuring such actors as Bela Lugosi, John Carradine, Christopher Lee, and Frank Langella as the elegantly mannered and formally-coiffed Eastern European Count.[4]

True Blood also builds on another contemporary trend: that of viewing vampires as "moral," "noble," "sympathetic," even "self-controlled," undead anti-heroes, supernatural creatures who do commit immoral actions against humans, but who also possess a conscience about the existential context and implications of their eternal existences and needs for survival. In some literary and cinematic incarnations, therefore, male vampires possess much angst about their existence, supernatural orientation, and relationships to female acquaintances. Such vampires are less survival-oriented, animalistic, supernatural phantasms, and more sentient creatures possessing consciousness, guilt, emotional pain, and reflexivity.

A 2008 article about vampire metaphors in the popular periodical *Newsweek* expands on the theme of evocative metaphorical fluidity; it notes that "the idea of vampire as artistic metaphor is as deathless as the creatures themselves ... Depending on whom you ask, vampire stories can be read as symbols of venereal disease, capitalism, immigration, industrialization, colonialism, AIDS, homosexuality, mental illness, anti-Semitism, technology or class warfare" (Yabroff 2008, 74). William Patrick Day is one of many scholars (see also Gelder 1994; Auerbach 1997; Gordon 1997; Hallab 2009) who indicate that the strength and resiliency of vampire mythology rests in its applicability as a metaphor and avenue for addressing societal, cultural, and personal problems. In the introduction to his book, Day both agrees with the analysis of literary scholar Nina Auerbach, for example, but also adds his own interpretation of the matter:

> I agree with Auerbach that, at least in the last forty years, the vampire has changed shape and meaning and that power, sexuality, and gender form a significant part of the vampire story. But the other side is ethics, and I think that the vampire story has responded even more sensitively and complexly to the search for an ethical understanding of human identity, which emphasizes not our place in the grip of power beyond our control but our desire for significant choices about who and what we are.
>
> (Day 2002, 8)

Such a search for "an ethical understanding of human identity" is observed in the thought and actions of major *True Blood* character, the telepathic Sookie Stackhouse, who reflects the power of choice when she begins an intimate relationship with a vampire. She offers to her loving grandmother her response as a Christian to the contemporary moral problem of life with the undead in America: "I don't think Jesus would mind, if somebody was a vampire" ("The First Taste").[5] From her vernacular religious perspective, God would naturally expect humanity to appreciate the multifaceted variety of all of creation. Sookie's Jesus is very much the loving, open-minded Christ, who himself knows something about existence after death. Sookie's grandmother, Adele, in another conversation, complements Sookie's perspective by adding her own vernacular religious world view on God, the created world, and special gifts: "I just think there is a purpose for everything that God creates whether it's a unique ability or a cup of overpriced coffee with too much milk or a vampire. God will reveal that purpose when the time is right" ("Mine").

The power derived from an appreciation and acceptance of one's own unique talents and abilities, and the subsequent openness to others and their differences, is a continuous theme of *True Blood*, whether the characters are gay or telepathic, African American or shape-shifters, women or vampires. In a *New York Times* interview prior to the series premiere, the show's openly gay creator and producer Alan Ball observed that it undoubtedly engages in such larger cultural and personal issues:

I love the fact that these creatures are struggling for assimilation. I can relate to that in certain ways ... Certainly it's very easy to look at the vampires as metaphors for gays and lesbians ... But it's very easy to see them as metaphors for all kinds of things. If this story had been done 50 years ago, it would have be a metaphor for racial equality ... But I can also look at the vampires and see them as a kind of terrifying shadow organization that is going to do what they want to do, whether they have to break the law or not. And if you get in the way, they'll just get rid of you. So, it's a very fluid metaphor.

(Rhodes 2008)[6]

The fluidity of that metaphor and the "shadow" or dark nature of its character is especially observed in the status of one organized structure in the show: religious institutions. Organized religion plays a negative role in the first two seasons of the series as represented by an evangelical-like Christian mega-Church called the "Fellowship of the Sun." This new religion seeks to praise Jesus by not allowing vampires to enter into society with the rights of mortals. It is portrayed as deceptive, hypocritical, violent, even militaristic. In Bon Temps, Louisiana, religious life certainly exists—people talk about God quite frequently—but there appears to be an absence of rational, organized, active religious life represented by mainline institutions. Images of organized religion are negative or scarce. The only instance of the interior of a Christian church being used, for example, is not for a service, but for an address by vampire Bill to a Civil War remembrance society. When Sookie's grandmother dies, there appears to be no service in a church building, but a graveside one in the fluid social environment of the town cemetery that is nestled in-between the properties and homes of the residents.

The series' lack of observable forms of organized religion is especially intriguing in the face of the fact that images of organized, congregational religion are visible from the very start of the program. They can be found in the visuals encountered in the drama's opening credits which, when structured as they are here as a separate sequence of their own, are known as a "title sequence." This montage of images appears in the episode's first few minutes as cast members and creators' names unfold. In the case of *True Blood*, this sequence follows the dramatic opening scene, known as a "cold open," introducing or recapping the story of each episode.

"When You Came In The Air Went Out ... "

Jostein Gripsrud, in his 1995 book *The Dynasty Years: Hollywood, Television, and Critical Media Studies*, observes:

The title sequence of a show is its self-presentation and self promotion. It is made with particular attention to its audible qualities, so that its particular music, etc. can signal throughout its viewers' homes that a particular show is about to start ... Since they are designed to identify a particular show, they will capture and express a particular affective mode which the producers wish to associate with it.

(Gripsrud 1995, 183–84)

I have been not only conscious of, but entertained by, film and television title sequences for many years. The very first credits of any television or film that I ever took notice of and appreciated as a youth were the wild montages of bright colors, guns, and undressed women in Maurice Bender's opening credits of James Bond films of the 1960s and 1970s. They were cinematic entities unto themselves, and I anticipated what Mr Bender would present in the next entry in the series, and how it would complement or be completed by John Barry's lush 007 theme scores. Within the history of American television, particularly striking credits have been associated with some supernaturally-themed shows of the 1960s such as *The Twilight Zone* (CBS, 1959–64) and *The Outer Limits* (ABC, 1963–65) with their airs of mystery and suspense and distinctive sound and musical effects (for a discussion of title sequences in films, see, for example, Allison 2001, 2008; Stanitzek 2009).

The *True Blood* credits, which will be used on the show for its entire run despite any changes or events that may occur within the story, were nominated for an Emmy award in the category of "Main Title Design" in 2008.[7] The work of a team of artists from the "hands-on" Seattle-based creative digital "engagement marketing" agency and production company Digital Kitchen,[8] the title sequence is described by the firm on its website with the following quote:

A truly hand-made sequence for one of the most watched dramatic series in HBO's history. The final edit contains over 65 shots comprised of original documentary, studio, tabletop photography and found footage. 6 separate shoots took place in Louisiana, Seattle, Chicago on 7 different still, film, and video cameras. 3 new babies were born at DK between award and delivery. No divorces. 1 Bolex [a motion picture camera or lens] passed peacefully in the night.

(Digital Kitchen 2010)

What one observes in this opening montage, accompanied by the song "Bad Things" sung by Jace Everett (which begins with the lyric: "When you came in, the air went out ... "), are many murky images from the world. These are scenes from the grimier and carnivorous side of animal and plant nature (an odd-looking fish submerged in a swamp, a waiting alligator, a dead possum, an irritated rattler, and some sort of Venus fly trap in the process of feeding on a frog) intermeshed with the expressive culture of humans (dirty dancing and other sexual positions of men and women, displays of their undergarments and bare skin). There is also historical footage of racially-motivated political expression including a KKK-clad child; as well as the countenances and body language of average folk—from an adult relaxing on a rocking chair on what could be his back porch to berry-crazed children. Pointedly dispersed throughout, or juxtaposed with, these images are seemingly ethnographic scenes from rural Louisiana religious life: a Pentecostal church service, a cemetery, a cross, an African American church choir, the laying-on of hands, the experience of being slain in the spirit, and finally full bodily immersion and symbolic resurrection from a baptismal rite in a body of water.

These credits present a *tableaux* of paradoxical images: the decay within nature and the lewdness of humanity is juxtaposed with the fervor of Christian religious experience, the pure expression of contact with the Holy Spirit, and the drama of baptismal rites of passage. Lead creative producer of the credits Rama Allan and editor Shawn Fedorchuk explain, in an article in the trade journal *American Cinematographer*, the guiding conceptualization: "We wanted to juxtapose concepts like the 'sacred versus the profane' and present nature as a predator … " Fedorchuk edited the material to resemble "the POV [point of view] of a predatory, beast-like entity that views humans with ambivalence—there's repulsion, but also a blood-lust, and there's a perversity to that. They're also attracted to the human beings and their way of life" (Stasukevich 2008, 10, 14). Digital Kitchen's executive producer Mark Bashore comments that his team's approach was to avoid using footage from the actual production and instead "create images from the ground up" (*ibid.*, 10). With a goal of presenting "roughed up" and especially found footage, some material was heavily altered in post-production and editing, but the overall perspective was to suggest "a transformative animal state."

The scenes within a Pentecostal church service actually originated in the urban context of Chicago, and have the appearance of footage from an ethnographic documentary. According to the explanatory short film, also on the Digital Kitchen web site, this spiritual setting was not naturally induced and then filmed, but artificially induced at the request of the filmmakers from Digital Kitchen (" … at the last minute, working with a line producer in Chicago … we had, we essentially casted [sic] a church … ").[9] The religious experiences filmed while induced do not appear to have been "staged" or "performed" by actors or even the church members themselves. The short company website film does offer one perspective on the decisions made about the construction of the visuals in this arresting montage:

And the whole piece is a crescendo. I mean it definitely, it definitely builds and builds and builds until—the idea was basically, to make it feel like you couldn't possibly take anymore, and then there's this almost cathartic release at the very end where you have this night baptism, and it's a redemption of all the previous evils that you've seen leading up to this in the sequence ...[10]

These words refer to a redemption from evils, and I take that to mean that the creators of these credits are reflecting on a positive function of religious ritual. In light of the above statement, the website provided by Digital Kitchen also includes a seeming contradiction that is not addressed. The positive assessment of religiosity represented in the credits offered by their producers is tempered by a fascinating detail. As a visual prelude to Digital Kitchen's website material on the preparation of the *True Blood* credits ("Case Study"), there is posted an unattributed motto/quotation in a hand-written script:

Whore and choir girl are often one and the same despite sanctimonious claims to the contrary

(Digital Kitchen 2010)

Is such a statement meant as an aspersion on the sincerity of the women in the pictured church choir? Do these creators actually see little difference in the moral character of those who engage in occasions of sexuality and occasions of religiosity? Is the usefulness of such questions that they assist in the attempt to understand the visual messages these credits are communicating to the viewer? Should their visual message be understood as a duality: raw versus cooked; nature versus culture; good versus evil; sacred versus profane? Or should they be understood as expressing a single meaning or implication?

Though the church scenes were filmed in a city, the frame of the montage sets them in the wild, where the redemptive work of the religious with their ecstatic writhing bodies emerges out of the same rural instincts as the sexualized dancers. Might the totality of all of these images just as well be read as a collection of predatory images *only*? Are the young berry-stained children more like little beasts wickedly engorging themselves on berries patiently picked by others; can the sacred be as perverse as the profane; is American religion filled with dangerous paradox and hypocrisy; does religious affiliation and practice lead to much trouble for those who choose an association with it; does the true nature of religion linger in its shadowy margins, and cause considerable decay and death? Finally, is God, not vampires, the predatory beast attracted to humans' adoration, but still treating them with ambivalence?

The *True Blood* titles combine the ethnographic religiosity of the church sequences with the staged and found images of everyday encounters with nature, sexuality, prejudice, etc. One wonders: did the Christians in these church scenes really understand the purpose and end of their filmed images? This *mélange* of "the terrors of intimacy," recalling Ball's phrase, makes for an affecting juxtaposition of sacred and profane planes of existence, but certainly not one that observant Christians might find appropriate. According to Alan Ball, the premise of Charlaine Harris's book, on which *True Blood* is based, is that "humans are at times more threatening than the vampires." If vampires have enough self-control to resist the lure of human blood, should humans possess sufficient self-control to resist organized religion? Are the religious humans pictured in these title images perceived of as threatening to certain viewers of the program? Are they threatening to the creators of the titles or the television producers themselves?

In his DVD audio commentary, series creator Alan Ball offers his own cryptic perspective on these opening credits:

> I love this title sequence. I didn't want to see any vampires or anything supernatural, but I did want it to, just sort of like, set the tone—set the world—you know, create that strange mix of religious fervor and gettin' [*sic*] drunk at the bar on the weekend and, you know ... how they both sort of are two sides of the same coin. The need, the human need to sort of have some sort of transcendent experience.
>
> (Ball 2009)

Ball's reading of the credits, of course, is very much in harmony with the overall nature of the series itself. The human need and search for transcendence takes many forms. It can be attempted through experiences of sexuality, alcohol, drugs, as well as religion. Human characters, for example, use vampire blood (called "V" in the show) as a sort of magical Viagra to enhance their experiences of sex. They believe in the efficacy of exorcism to rid them of personal demons causing *trouble* in their lives, even if the exorcist herself turns out to be a charlatan. While transcendence out of the human condition exists for humans in recognizable and unrecognized forms, it nonetheless still emanates from an unidentifiable and what could also be described as an uninvolved source. The characters do occasionally indicate that "God" is one such spring of transcendence, but never that organized religion is the proper path to that source. An incredible ambivalence about God and religion resonates in the words and actions of characters throughout the first two seasons of Mr Ball's production of *True Blood*. They act as a link to the visual ambivalence toward religion and the relationships that Americans have with their gods, as seemingly reflected in the title sequence.

"Was There No God?"

In this series, an encounter with organized and especially traditionally conservative religion calls for as much care and caution for an individual as does a private meeting with a vampire, which the character Tara Thornton describes as: " ... trouble lookin' [*sic*] for a place to happen." Indeed, organized religion, spirituality, God are all characters in *True Blood*, but in intriguing, disparate proportions: organized religion, or rather organized Christianity, as already noted, is suspiciously portrayed in the second season in the form of a fundamentalist Christian group led by an unsavory, hypocritical televangelistic couple determined to remove the rights of and destroy all vampires. Vernacular spirituality—religion as it is lived, interpreted, and created by individuals—is consistently expressed, but never as succinctly or paradoxically as by openly gay character Lafayette, a seller of sex, drugs, and vampire blood, who remarks when he recites a prayer he learned in childhood at a moment of difficulty and intercessory need: "Jesus and I agreed to see other people. Now, that don't mean we still don't talk from time to time" ("New World in My View"). When a *maenad* terrorizes the community of Bon Temps, where anti-hero vampire Bill has decided to make his home and, moreover, to live openly as a vampire, Bill consults Sophie-Ann, the Vampire Queen of Louisiana, who tells him that these creatures—like mortals—spend too much time pursuing a god who will not respond to them.[11]

SOPHIE-ANN: Maenads are sad, silly things. The world changed centuries ago and they're still waiting for the god who comes.

BILL: Does he ever come?

SOPHIE-ANN: Of course not. Gods never actually show up. They only exist in humans' minds, like money and morality.

BILL: If I can't kill her, how do I get her to leave Bon Temps?

SOPHIE-ANN: She has to believe that she has successfully summoned forth Dionysus in hopes that he will ravish her and quite literally devour her until she is lost to oblivion.

BILL: So she seeks death, the true death. The one thing she has evolved beyond.

SOPHIE-ANN: Ironic, isn't it? You know, they're really not that smart, these maenads.

BILL: So, how does she summon this nonexistent god of hers?

SOPHIE-ANN: I never said he was nonexistent, just he never comes ...

("Frenzy")

These lines of dialogue highlight this drama's view that contemporary religious belief is rooted in a theistic conundrum, and that such attitudes bear an association with the history of American religion. These words undeniably question the willingness of the sacred other to act in any specific way in the everyday lives of humans, evoking an American deistic perspective of a God who creates, tinkers, leaves qualities of the divine, but then does not directly interfere (Albanese 1992, 439–41). A God who inexplicably loves, forgives, even possesses humans, but all from a great distance. A God whose creation and gifts humans have yet to comprehend and appreciate fully. The maenad is a powerful creature, who murders humans without any feelings of guilt; yet obviously, and in her own way, she is firmly "religious," an absolute believer in her deity. She is killed in the climactic final episode of Season Two by the shape-shifting bar-owner Sam Merlotte, who assumes the form of her Earth-centered God of nature—a bull—and gores her, also pulling out her blackened heart. And what is her response at this moment of her demise: "Was there no god?" Like the humans around her, this supernatural creature is faced with the same existential longing for a God that just is not there, is not dependable, does not seem to care. The drama is populated with characters who believe that God is a source of all that they encounter in their existences, freely acknowledging the religious idioculture of individuals—be they vampire or human—to create their own religion, while leaving open the possibility that such belief is mere delusion.

"We Vampires ... Can Stand Before A Cross, Or A Bible, Or In A Church ... "

The visual dilemma that television faces in terms of the representation of religion in the late twentieth-/early twenty-first-century era of loose institutional "religious" or denominational affiliation, but strong personal "spiritual" association, has been identified by religion and media scholar Stewart Hoover. Both Hoover (2001) and Lynn Schofield Clark (2003) have indicated what "a new iconography" of religion might look like in this time: from the now seemingly out-of-place clerical garb of a minister in an episode of *Northern Exposure* (CBS, 1990–95) to the magical realism of a new breed of teen angels and punk demons on *Buffy the Vampire Slayer* (WB, 1997–2003). "To rising generations that are increasingly ignorant of traditional religion and its sacred and popular iconographies, these images will become more and more determinative of their understanding of faith and spirituality" (Hoover 2001, 156).

In the case of a drama such as *True Blood*, centered on the traditional mythic creatures known as vampires, strongly associated as they are in Western consciousness with Catholic sacramental images such as the crucifix, the host, and holy water, it seems almost impossible that the production could not involve a notable presence of religious imagery, especially in the form of material culture (see Primiano [forthcoming]). Indeed, *True Blood* is not insensitive to sacred materiality or sacramentalism, but its treatment of religious iconography seems to mirror the splintered state of contemporary American religiosity represented by (1) traditional, (2) new iconographic, and (3) even new iconoclastic categories of the visual culture of American religion. It might be helpful to cite an example from each category: a major object offered frequently in the action of the drama taken from the tradition of material/visual vampire lore is the deterrent of pure silver, for example in a chain or a ring, highlighted from the series' first episode, though the particular reason for its power has yet to be explained. Suggesting new iconographic turns is one of the most moving scenes from the first season, the act of personal mourning over the loss of a beloved family member, in this case Sookie's murdered grandmother Adele. This mourning is centered not on her person, her coffin, her grave, her personal Bible, but brilliantly on one-half of a pecan pie, the last "thing" that the woman crafted for her family with her own hands. After the funeral, Sookie sits alone in her kitchen weeping. She connects with the physical reality of the love and gifts of her grandmother once more by eating that pie, forkful by forkful, with the reverence and dignity of the reception of the Eucharist at a funeral Mass. The visual gesture of eating and the visual object of the pie exemplify that new sense of religious iconography referenced above by Hoover, in this case a fresh visual form of mourning and connection with a spirit of the dead.

Another example of such a fresh iconographic vision of religion is the emotionally compelling exchange about the forgiveness of God ("I Will Rise Up") between Sookie and Godric, one of the oldest vampires in North America. Godric decides to end his existence by greeting the sunlight on a vampire hotel roof in Dallas, and Sookie waits with him for his end. She speaks of her certainty of God's forgiveness when he speculates about it. As she cries for him, Godric remarks that here, at the end of a long existence, he sees God in the tears and countenance of this human who mourns for him. This quintessential reflection on the possibility of finding God anywhere or in any person exemplifies the meaning of the Christian theological concept of "sacramentality," "the understanding of all reality as potentially or actually bearing and expressing the sacred presence of God; the created world not only embodies the sacred, but it can itself serve as a sacred, divine, or ultimate source" (Primiano 2007, 121). Such episodes add to the paradoxical nature of the show that, in true vernacular religious fashion, crafts a complex expression of religion as it is lived with its doubts, its fears, its creativity, its recognition of beauty.

A final example of the visual culture of American religion, but in this case an iconoclastic one, is based in the treatment of material Christian forms, also from the program's first season ("Sparks Fly Out"). This instance of change in the perception of Christian imagery needs some unpacking to illustrate its power exemplifying what I see as a new iconoclastic perspective, and I use this term to mean not a literal "breaking of sacred images," but a visual and material diminution of religious iconography on par with the equation of religious practice with sexuality, prejudice, and the underworld of nature evident in the program's title sequence.[12] Visual religion scholar David Morgan, in a discussion of the term "image" as a keyword in religion, media, and culture, notes:

> Implicit in the fear of images are notions of their power, of their relation to the structure of thought and feeling, and of the subtle but compelling linkage of human bodies to one another and to social bodies of various

kinds. One task for the study of images in religion and media is to make visible the network of submerged assumptions that do so much to make seeing what it is and, very commonly, what it is not.

(Morgan 2008, 110)

A sea of submerged assumptions pour into this compelling episode where vampire Bill Compton is asked to speak, as an actual veteran of the nineteenth-century American Civil War, to a twenty-first-century gathering of relatives and friends of descendents of that national conflict who maintain a remembrance association. Because of great community interest in Bon Temps, the organization's administrative board decides to accommodate the crowds in a town church of some unreferenced Protestant denomination. As the vampire waits in the church's back kitchen to be introduced, town busybody Mrs Maxine Fortenberry notices one unattended detail: no-one remembered that there stands in the center of the sanctuary's back altar the church's central brass cross. For fear, not of the vampire defiling the cross, but of its deleterious effect on this supernatural creature, Mrs Fortenberry, and then her son Hoyt, work to pull—and then, when it stubbornly refuses to budge, literally attempt to yank—the Christian symbol of Christ's mastery over death out of the stone altar. No minister appears to stop any of this potentially damaging altar and cross transformation. When the cross refuses to be removed, the Fortenberrys decide to hide it from view by covering the cross with, of all objects, the flag of the United States of America. The national symbol itself is draped over the cruciform image as if to suggest that, in the contemporary struggle of allegiance to nation or church, "Old Glory" wins, even if a bit disheveled. After his introduction, but before speaking from the pulpit, Bill acknowledges the concern over the cross by pulling away the flag from the sacramental object, to the startled response of the audience. He explains: "We vampires are not minions of the devil. We can stand before a cross or a Bible or in a church just as readily as any other creature of God." He then takes the American flag and replaces it on its pole, noting how he respects it and the country it represents.

It is useful to consider the meaning of this scene in the context of the manifestation of contemporary American religion as a personal spirituality, as well in light of scholarly reflections on the social and cultural meaning of horror tales featuring vampires. Lynn Schofield Clark, in her study of the link between teen culture, the media, and ideas about the supernatural and the roots of "Christian beliefs and the genre of horror" (Clark 2003, 64), calls her readers' attention to the ideas of cultural studies scholar Edward J. Ingebretsen (1996). It is the opinion of this critic that literary horror "finds its initial impulse and articulation within the central stories of Christianity" where they "can be seen as inversions of the Incarnation: they examine the 'horrific possibilities' of mixing supernatural and natural worlds" (Clark 2003, 64). I would like to complement this reading regarding the action of the vampire to reject and fear the cross, the Bible, or the church sanctuary, as a continuation of a series of responses related to the central inversion of a core principle of Christian theology. I see reflected in the vampire's legendary fear of the cross, holy water, and the consecrated host a consistent reminder of the social and spiritual power of the institutional Catholic Church. Under the principle of sacramentality (Primiano 1999, 2007), the Church stands as the arbiter of the sacred: identifying these human-made objects; mediating their availability and use; and controlling which objects are designated potent reservoirs of potential holiness (see Brown 1981, 106–27). Subsequently, in *True Blood*, the discovery that these religious objects are no longer effective against the undead is surprising for the humans gathered, but is it equally unsettling to viewers? The message communicated by this contemporary change in the vampire legend is that, like organized religion in America, these once vital religious images need to be reinterpreted as—at least as far vampires are concerned—more inclusive, but also significantly they are less powerful, even impotent, manifestations of the presence of God. Here is another example that God is actually not present in the lives of humans.

It would take an extensive interview with series creator Alan Ball to gain a full sense of how he sees religion in his own life, and how he has expressed that feeling in this media creation. Having studied the response to organized religion by gay men in America (Primiano 1993, 2004), it is understandable that Ball would feel an acute sense of abandonment by organized religion, most certainly Christianity, as well as by fellow religionists who readily condemn the gay person (and practice of sexual expression) as not a creature of God. The building of voluntary organizations for gay Christians, for example, has been equally criticized by the gay community and by conservative Christians as misguided and futile. Is it any wonder that such feelings of futility about American religions, their gods, and even the creative religious negotiations of fellow citizens come to the surface in Ball's media creation? Additionally, it is quite easy to speculate that individuals indeed feel that God has abandoned them in the decade following the 9/11 terrorist attacks on America in 2001, filled as it has been with challenges to personal, international, and economic safety (Primiano 2009).

These reflections take us back to those credits that introduce *True Blood* to viewers. These visuals do more than use the landscape of land and humans found in the American South to establish a peculiar, haunting mood to complement the evening's hour-long supernatural narrative. The credits are also not just an abstract homage to American variations on the legend of the vampire. What they express is a message about the state of religion in America post-9/11, in this first decade of the twenty-first century—where religion as institution is questioned, but where American religiosity is also ever needed and firmly associated with the American national character. Though Americans' association with and knowledge of specific religious institutions wanes, and their general religious literacy about world or even local religious traditions abates (Prothero 2007), what scholars and now the general public might refer to as the "spirituality" of Americans remains abundant in the country (Roof 1993, 1999; Ammerman 1997; Wuthnow 1998; Primiano 2001). To tell the story of American religion today is to tell the story of that spirituality, a type of religiosity quite ephemeral and difficult to capture because of the very way it splinters into bits of knowledge, subjective truth, and experience (Clark 2003; Freitas 2008). European friends tell me that what they particularly love about America is the abundance, resoluteness, and uniqueness of the way European religion grew on American soil and how America developed its own hybrid religiosity. The credits of *True Blood* can be seen to showcase, exploit, adore, and simultaneously stand suspicious of that American religious hybrid. Framing the plot lines of the show, these credits highlight Americans' fascination with occult or secret knowledge, their attraction to the supernatural, and their devotion to personal, experiential religion, even while often denying affiliation with institutional religions.

The *True Blood* credits, though seemingly tangential, actually tell a story of the American religious experience as a sort of cultural roadkill: a subject of endless fascination to us. Once we or someone else hits it, or it hits us for that matter, we cannot stop slowing down, staring at it, reliving the experience, and appreciating what it says about the limitations and yet boundless possibilities of human reality. Still, while fascinating, it can remain an object recognizable, if misshapen, but also feared and without life. Reflections on God are quite benign in *True Blood*; in fact, religion as an organized expression of belief and practice, like the frequent sex between humans and between humans and vampires in the show, acts more like a fetish than an intrinsic human need. God is certainly not dead in *True Blood*, recalling the theological ideas of Gabriel Vahanian, Paul van Buren, William Hamilton and Thomas J. J. Altizer; but God, even as this divine transcendent force is spoken of as forgiving, still seems—evoking the drama's theme song—most certainly waiting and wanting to do bad things to us.

References

Albanese, Catherine L. 1992. *America: Religion and Religions*, 2nd edn. Belmont, CA: Wadsworth.

Alexander, Bobby. 1994. *Televangelism Reconsidered: Ritual in the Search for Human Community*. Atlanta, GA: Scholars Press.

Allison, Deborah. 2001. *Promises in the Dark: Opening Title Sequences in American Feature Films of the Sound Period*. PhD Dissertation, University of East Anglia.

——. 2008. "Title Sequences in the Western Genre: The Iconography of Action." *Quarterly Review of Film and Video* 25, 2: 107–15.

Ammerman, Nancy T. 1997. "Organized Religion in a Voluntaristic Society." *Sociology of Religion* 58: 203–15.

Auerbach, Nina. 1997. *Our Vampires, Ourselves*. Chicago: University of Chicago Press.

Ball, Alan. 2009. "'Strange Love': Audio Commentary." *True Blood: The Complete First Season*. Home Box Office. DVD.

Bellafante, Ginia. 2009. "The Week Ahead: June 14–20." *New York Times*, June 14. http://query.nytimes.com/gst/fullpage.html?res=9402E2DE1339F937A25755-C0A96F9C8B63

Brown, Peter. 1981. *The Cult of the Saints: Its Rise and Function in Latin Christianity*. Chicago: University of Chicago Press.

Cavell, Stanley. 1984. *Themes Out of School: Effects and Causes*. Chicago: University of Chicago Press.

Clark, Lynn Schofield. 2003. *From Angels to Aliens: Teenagers, the Media, and the Supernatural*. New York: Oxford University Press.

Cotton, Trystan T. and Kimberly Springer. 2010. *Stories of Oprah: The Oprahfication of American Culture*. Jackson, MS: University Press of Mississippi.

Day, William Patrick. 2002. *Vampire Legends in Contemporary American Culture: What Becomes A Legend Most*. Lexington: University Press of Kentucky.

Decker, Jeffrey Louis. 2006. "Saint Oprah." *Modern Fiction Studies* 52, 1 (Spring): 169–178.

Digital Kitchen. 2010. "HBO: True Blood Main Title." www.d-kitchen.com/projects/true-blood-main-title

Forbes, Bruce David. 2000. "Introduction." In *Religion and Popular Culture in America*, eds Bruce David Forbes and Jeffrey H. Mahan, 1–20. Berkeley, University of California Press.

Freitas, Donna. 2008. *Sex and the Soul: Juggling Sexuality, Spirituality, Romance, and Religion on America's College Campuses*. New York: Oxford University Press.

Gelder, Ken. 1994. *Reading the Vampire*. New York: Routledge.

Gibbs, Christopher H. 2009. "Te Deum." *PLAYBILL: The Philadelphia Orchestra* (September 24–29): 40–43. New York: PLAYBILL Inc.

Gordon, Joan, ed. 1997. *Blood Red: The Vampire as Metaphor in Contemporary Culture*. Philadelphia: University of Pennsylvania Press.

Gripsrud, Jostein. 1995. *The Dynasty Years: Hollywood, Television, and Critical Media Studies*. New York: Routledge.

Hallab, Mary Y. 2009. *Vampire God: The Allure of the Undead in Western Culture*. Albany, NY: State University of New York Press.

HBO. 2010a. "*True Blood*: About the Show." Home Box Office. www.hbo.com/true-blood#/true-blood/about

——. 2010b. "*True Blood*: Seasons and Episodes." Home Box Office. www.hbo.com/true-blood#/true-blood/episodes/index.html

Hoover, Stewart. 2001. "Visual Religion in Media Culture." In *The Visual Culture of American Religions*, eds David Morgan and Sally M. Promey, 146–59. Berkeley: University of California Press.

Howard, Robert Glenn. 2005. "A Theory of Vernacular Rhetoric: The Case of the 'Sinner's Prayer' Online." *Folklore* 116, 3: 175–91.

——. 2006. "Sustainability and Narrative Plasticity in Online Apocalyptic Discourse After September 11, 2001." *Journal of Media and Religion* 5, 1: 25–47.

——. 2009. "The Vernacular Ideology of Christian Fundamentalism on the World Wide Web." In *Fundamentalisms and the Media*, eds Stewart M. Hoover and Nadia Kaneva, 126–41. New York: Continuum.

Illouz, Eva. 2003. *Oprah Winfrey and the Glamour of Misery: An Essay on Popular Culture.* New York: Columbia University Press.

Ingebretsen, Edward J. 1996. *Maps of Heaven, Maps of Hell.* Armonk, NY: M. E. Sharpe.

Lofton, Kathryn. 2006. "Practicing Oprah; or the Prescriptive Compulsion of Spiritual Capitalism." *Journal of Popular Culture* 39, 4: 599–621.

Mazur, Eric Michael and Kate McCarthy, eds. 2001. *God in the Details: American Religion in Popular Culture.* New York: Routledge.

Mitchell, Jolyon. 2007. "Questioning Media and Religion." In *Between Sacred and Profane: Researching Religion and Popular Culture*, ed. Gordon Lynch, 34–46. New York: I. B. Tauris.

Morgan, David. 2005. *The Sacred Gaze: Religious Visual Culture in Theory and Practice.* Berkeley: University of California Press.

——. 2008. "Image" In *Key Words in Religion, Media and Culture*, ed. David Morgan, 96–110. New York: Routledge.

Porter, Jennifer and Darcee McLaren, eds. 2000. *Star Trek and Sacred Ground: Explorations of Star Trek, Religion, and American Culture.* Albany, NY: State University of New York Press.

Primiano, Leonard Norman. 1993. *Intrinsically Catholic: Vernacular Religion and Philadelphia's "Dignity."* PhD Dissertation, University of Pennsylvania.

——. 1995. "Vernacular Religion and the Search For Method in Religious Folklife." *Western Folklore* 54: 37–56.

——. 1999. "Post-Modern Sites of Catholic Sacred Materiality." In *Perspectives on American Religion and Culture: A Reader,* ed. Peter W. Williams, 187–202. Malden, MA: Basil Blackwell.

——. 2001. "Oprah, Phil, Geraldo, Barbara, and Things That Go Bump in the Night: Negotiating the Supernatural on American Television." In *God in the Details: American Religion in Popular Culture*, eds Eric Michael Mazur and Kate McCarthy, 47–63. New York: Routledge.

——. 2004. "The Gay God of the City: The Emergence of the Gay and Lesbian Ethnic Parish." In *Gay Religion: Innovation and Continuity in Spiritual Practice*, eds Scott Thumma and Edward R. Gray, 7–30. Lanham, MD: AltaMira Press.

——. 2007. "The Vow As Visual Feast: Honoring St. Joseph in Sicilian American Homes." *Traditiones* 36, 1: 113–25.

——. 2009. "'For What I Have Done and What I Have Failed to Do': Vernacular Catholicism and *The West Wing*." In *Small Screen, Big Picture: Television and Lived Religion*, ed. Diane Winston, 99–123. Waco, TX: Baylor University Press.

——. Forthcoming. "Material Culture." In *Encyclopedia of Global Religion*, eds Wade Clark Roof and Mark Juergensmeyer, Newbury Park, CA: Sage.

Prothero, Stephen. 2007. *Religious Literacy: What Every American Needs to Know— And Doesn't.* San Francisco: Harper San Francisco.

Rhodes, Joe. 2008. "After All the Funerals, A Prime-Time Auteur Digs Up the Undead." *New York Times*, August 3. www.nytimes.com/2008/08/03/arts/television/03rhod.html

Roof, Wade Clark. 1993. *A Generation of Seekers: The Spiritual Journeys of the Baby Boom Generation.* San Francisco: Harper San Francisco.

——. 1999. *Spiritual Marketplace: Baby Boomers & the Remaking of American Religion*. Princeton, NJ: Princeton University Press.

Schmidt, Leigh Eric. 2005. *Restless Souls: The Making of American Spirituality from Emerson to Oprah*. New York: HarperCollins.

Stanitzek, Georg. 2009. "Reading the Title Sequence." *Cinema Journal* 48, 4: 44–58.

Stasukevich, Iain. 2008. "*True Blood* Titles Set Southern-Gothic Tone." *American Cinematographer* 89, 12: 10–14.

Wilcox, Rhonda V. 2005. *Why Buffy Matters: The Art of Buffy the Vampire Slayer*. London: I. B. Tauris.

Winston, Diane. 2009. "Introduction." In *Small Screen, Big Picture: Television and Lived Religion*, ed. Diane Winston, 1–14. Waco, TX: Baylor University Press.

Wuthnow, Robert. 1998. *After Heaven: Spirituality in America since the 1950s*. Berkeley: University of California Press.

Yabroff, Jennie. 2008. "A Bit Long in the Tooth: Hollywood Found New Blood with 'Twilight,' but the Vampire Metaphor is Positively Deathless." *Newsweek*, December 15. www.newsweek.com/id/172558

Notes

1 This chapter was first presented at the 2009 meeting of the American Folklore Society in Boise, Idaho. I wish to thank Deborah Ann Bailey, Father Michael Bielecki, O.S.A., Kevin Eppler, Roger Klaus, Margaret Kruesi, Kate Luce, Will Luers, Kathy McCrea, Jodi McDavid, Lisa A. Ratmansky, Katie Reing, Joseph Sciorra, as well as Anne Schwelm, Michael LaMagna, and Corey Salazar of Cabrini College's Holy Spirit Library for their assistance. Mark Bashore and Julie Pereyra of Digital Kitchen graciously provided me with information about the production of the credits sequence. I am especially grateful to Eric Mazur for his unfailing support, and to Nicholas Rademacher and, especially, Nancy Watterson, who read final drafts of the article.

2 A note on the scholarly lineage of this article is in order. As religion became somewhat less powerful in nineteenth-century European society, many of its attributes and consolations were transferred to the arts—or so Christopher H. Gibbs explains in his program notes for a Philadelphia Orchestra performance of Hector Berlioz' *Te Deum* (Gibbs 2009, 40). The concert hall, for example, emerged as a kind of sanctified space and concert attendance increasingly took on the sort of aura formerly associated with going to church. In the past 50 years in the United States, various scholars of religion and media have searched for the affective quality of another forum of the popular arts—namely, television—for communicating religion, religious presence, or a critique of religion in a powerful, persuasive manner (see, for example, Alexander 1994; Porter and McLaren 2000; Hoover 2001; Mazur and McCarthy 2001; Clark 2003; Wilcox 2005; Winston 2009).

In opening comments to the first edition of this volume, editors Eric Michael Mazur and Kate McCarthy proclaim with an almost missionary zeal that "religious meaning can be found in activities that are often considered meaningless" (Mazur and McCarthy 2001, 3). They further explain that any reflection on contemporary religion that fails to consider the human-made creations known as "popular" culture—whether mass produced or massively consumed, whether in historical or contemporary perspective, whether interpreted as meaningless or not—is sadly missing a significant and vibrant generator of ideas influencing twenty-first-century belief and practice. In making these statements, Mazur and

McCarthy (2001, 1–15) are responding to those who criticize the overall content of popular culture, with particular reference to television across genres ranging from situation comedies to serialized dramas, reality television, talk shows, etc.—much/most of which has been evaluated negatively as devoid of merit. The act of watching television itself has likewise been described as meaningless and a harmful, uncritical act of valueless, capitalistic cultural consumption (see Mitchell 2007, 34–38 for a discussion of critical iconoclastic assessments of the dangers posed to religion by various forms of media).

Almost a decade later, Diane Winston, in her collection of essays directly considering "television and lived religion," reiterates past scholarly and societal concerns about the weakness of the television medium as a serious bearer of any form of meaning, and especially religious meaning, when she notes that: "Calling television a religious text may strike readers as oxymoronic" (Winston 2009, 2). Winston argues (*ibid.*, 1–14, 427–31), as do the essays in her collection, that watching television both opens one up to a tradition of sacred stories and the performance of such stories, as well as functioning "as a discursive place for constituting both individual and communal religious identity." This act of viewing television content and then personally responding to it through virtual communities on the World Wide Web (see Howard 2005, 2006, 2009 for a discussion of contemporary online vernacular religious expression) is significant for a growing number of the religiously unaffiliated population who live their religion "unmediated by institutional authorities" (Winston 2009, 14). In light of the national trauma faced in the decade following the 9/11 terrorist attacks on targets in the United States in 2001, "the experience of watching, and responding to, TV characters' moral dilemmas, crises of faith, bouts of depression, and fits of exhilaration gives expression—as well as insight and resolution—to viewers' own spiritual odysseys and ethical predicaments" (*ibid.*, 6).

As a contributor to both of these volumes, my own scholarship resonates these points that popular culture, and most certainly television, can be an extraordinarily rich reservoir of, and testimony to, what I call the "vernacular religion" of the American population, reflections of their own acts of religious creativity, artfulness, negotiation, and interpretation within everyday life (Primiano 1995). My earlier study of television in the first edition of *God in the Details* (Mazur and McCarthy 2001, 47–63) considered the role of the 1980s and 1990s television talk show. As a product of this mass medium, these programs crystallized religious/spiritual beliefs and ideas under the rubric of the "supernatural," what has surely been identified by media scholars as instances of "religion *in* popular culture," but also "popular culture in religion" (see Forbes 2000, 1–20 for an elaboration of these terms). In the past 10 years, television talk shows have morphed into completely new forms with, for example, Oprah Winfrey's wildly successful talk program changing as many times in the past 10 years as its host's weight, hair, clothes, and bank account. I, however, have not been particularly interested in taking the "popular culture as religion" perspective, where I might have examined figures like Phil Donahue and Oprah Winfrey as occupying quasi-sacerdotal roles, in which they use the divine power of individual celebrity to provide their audiences with moral stability and guidance; that is, use the electronic mass medium of television to cultivate a sense of a cohesive folk community of believers (for discussions of the spirituality associated with Oprah Winfrey and her television talk show, see Illouz 2003; Schmidt 2005; Decker 2006; Lofton 2006; Cotton and Springer 2010).

In Diane Winston's book, I again considered the performing art of television, this time concentrating on television serial dramas, the theme of that particular volume. Using Aaron Sorkin's *The West Wing* as my foundation, I examined its dramatic embodiment of "vernacular Catholicism" in unusually rich character-izations, particularly "the gift of improvisation in reinterpreting and reusing Church teaching, as well as the transformation of religion that individuals make in their lives" (Winston 2009, 116). Though such acts of reinterpretation seem to challenge normative institutional beliefs and practices, a drama such as *The West Wing*, and talk-show episodes dealing with supernatural subjects, still positively connect Americans to institutionalized religion such as the Roman Catholic Church, and to religion in America in general.

HBO's vampire saga *True Blood*, as a television serial drama centered on the supernatural, has allowed me to combine the genres and themes of the pro-grams from these past articles. *True Blood*, however, in relation to Oprah Winfrey's chat show or *The West Wing*, is much more ambiguous—one might even say, jaundiced—about religious institutions, functionaries, and beliefs in general as they exist in America. So what exactly are the submerged assumptions present in the *True Blood* opening montage, a vernacular fantasia of American life featuring religious Americans in its representation of the everyday? These images, as well as some potent visuals from the show itself, deserve a closer consideration.

3   The value judgment of the show's characters as "supernatural misfits" by the producers of the *True Blood* website is surprisingly out of touch with the actual message of appreciation for individuality—especially for those with talents, abilities, perspectives, even natures different from the norm—as portrayed on the show.

4   I would be remiss, of course, if I did not also mention that obvious recent tease of vampire-human sexuality, Stephenie Meyer's *Twilight* series of novels and films, which I feel actually speaks much more to Meyer's Mormon sexual sensibilities of abstinence before marriage and the value of repressed sexual urges than it does to fantasies of actual intercourse with non-humans, but that is another article altogether.

5   Episode titles have been taken from the episode guide provided online by Home Box Office (HBO 2010b).

6   In fact, the program has been described by another *Times* reporter as a "gay civil rights allegory about vampires assimilating into small-town Louisiana life despite the rampant prejudices" (Bellafante 2009).

7   Lasting one minute and 31 seconds, the *True Blood* opening credits can be viewed online via YouTube.com (www.youtube.com/watch?v=vxINMuOgAu8).

8   The creators of these titles discuss their production and meaning in two valuable sources: an article in *American Cinematographer* (Stasukevich 2008), and on the website of the company Digital Kitchen (2010), which offers a short documentary on the making of the montage ("Making of"), as well as notes accompanying its creation ("Case Study").

9   Taken from the voiceover of "Making of" (Digital Kitchen 2010). Mark Bashore of Digital Kitchen (personal communication, May 17, 2010) clarified to me that the choirs singing in the Chicago church scenes were, indeed, an assembly of church choirs, as well as an African American theatre group. The choir perfor-mers broke into performance unprompted, "and we rolled cameras on it. So the performance was staged, yet largely improvisational and even 'documentary' in the sense that a very realistic chorus broke out in front of cameras." All partici-pants knew the purpose of the filming. The baptism scene was also staged and featured three non-professional actors, two of whom actually work for Digital Kitchen. The two blackberry-eating boys in the credits montage were

Mr Bashore's own children. "They are in fact very clean eaters and we had to get messy for the desired effect."

10 *Ibid.*

11 A *maenad* is a Greek mythological creature (in the physical form of show character Maryann Forrester) who served the God Dionysus.

12 Morgan (2005, 71–73, 129–46) discusses a more traditional sense of iconoclasm as the destruction of images.

Chapter 3

A Fire in the Sky

"Apocalyptic" Themes on the Silver Screen

Jon R. Stone

The wildly evocative image at the conclusion of Stanley Kubrick's 1964 movie *Dr. Strangelove*, of Slim Pickens riding the "Bomb" downward through the sky, as if he were trying to tame a raging bull, points out, in perhaps the most perverse way, the irony of a society living in fear of the very weapon it sees as its salvation from fear. As we know from the film, an insanely paranoid US Air Force General (Sterling Hayden) has sent a flight of bombers on a pre-emptive nuclear airstrike against the Soviet Union. By the final scene of the movie, with the threat of Soviet retaliation looming over them, the US authorities have succeeded in their frantic attempts to recall the bombers or have them shot down. All of the planes and their crews have been neutralized except one: *Leper Colony*, the renegade B-52 Strato-fortress piloted by Pickens' character, Major T. J. "King" Kong. Over the drop site *Leper Colony*'s bomb-bay doors jam, and when they do open, a new complication arises. The bomb will not deploy. Without a second thought, Pickens throws himself atop its steely back, and with a bump and a yelp, he releases the "bull" from its pen. Both rider and beast plummet earthward: mission accomplished.

The message of *Dr. Strangelove*'s comically dark conclusion seems clear enough: a society can no more safely hold the destructive power contained in a nuclear warhead than it can control the unbridled spirit of a wild and willful beast. In fact, this beast has a way of controlling those who think themselves its master. Tragically, modern society's predicament becomes an inescapable dilemma: our future is as much in our hands as it is out of our hands. Once it is been unleashed by human science, the destructive power of nuclear weapons is no longer ours to control. The bomb becomes as much a demon as it is a god. In the end, the only logical response to this Damocle-sian dilemma, as *Dr. Strangelove*'s subtitle wryly puts it, is to learn "to stop worrying and love the bomb."

The twisted humor of the closing scene—the Soviets' swift and devastating nuclear retaliation that destroys the world, with the final burlesque of A-bomb explosions mushrooming high into the Earth's atmosphere—is not meant to frighten the moviegoer as much as it is to accustom the viewer to the sight, the sound, and the grand drama and pageantry of the end of humankind. There is, as it were, an exaggerated Vaudevillean quality that takes away the sting even as it stings: actors and audience laugh at the absurdity of each other and at the senseless circumstance into which they have together fallen. That is, actors and audience see themselves and their situation in the reflection of the other. Both are doomed. The unfortunate fact about the bomb that stays with the audience even after the house lights have gone up is the realization that the images on the screen and the precarious circumstances of modern life are really no laughing matter.

Postwar American Angst

Living in the shadow of the mushroom cloud was an inescapable fact of life for Americans who came of age soon after World War II ended. Ironically, though a remarkably resourceful and resilient generation of Americans had defeated one fascist regime after another, it could not evade the truth that, in doing so, it had resorted to military technologies possessing a destructive force that could not be imagined or described except in biblical—that is, "apocalyptic"—terms. Now, for the first time in human history, human beings had the power to annihilate whole civilizations, the power to inciner-ate their own planet, the power, indeed, to destroy themselves and even the memory of themselves. The atomic exclamation point that ended World War II became a looming question mark over the future of world civilization. For the immediate postwar generation, then, who saw the newsreel footage of the war's thunderous conclusion, the destructive power that it had unleashed to save the free world from the nightmare of fascist totalitarianism became an even greater power to fear.

Notwithstanding its menacing presence, the atomic bomb represented but one of a number of inescapable existential facts with which Americans living during the postwar period and into the present have had to grapple. Threats to the natural environment, as predicted by Rachel Carson in her 1962 exposé, *Silent Spring*, about the consequences of the unchecked use of pes-ticides, were likewise couched in "apocalyptic," end-of-the-world, language. As a result of the unprecedented growth of industrial civilization in the nine-teenth and twentieth centuries, human society had created the conditions under which, by the latter half of the twentieth century, ecological meltdown became not only possible but almost inevitable. While humankind had made significant advances in science and technology—advances that lengthened and improved the lives of people throughout the world—those same humans were contaminating their environment through the unregulated dumping of toxic waste and other pollutants into the sky, the land, and the sea. Even as humanity was attempting to escape the nightmare of a nuclear holocaust through diplomacy and détente, it was poisoning itself through careless management of the environment. An environmental holocaust was in the making, one in which humankind would slowly choke itself by its own polluted hands.

The blame, many believed, lay entirely at the feet of the twin gods of science and technology. Science and technology, heralded as the champions of modern civilization, had proven instead to be its betrayers. The promise that human science and technology held out of a greater tomorrow did not come without serious problems. Their supposed benefits had unpredictable, and sometimes deadly, consequences for human society. In fact, as some would claim, the very advances that science and technology offered as solutions to one urgent problem oftentimes gave rise to a series of new problems which, in turn, demanded even more urgent solutions. For instance, while the automation of factory assembly lines sped production and provided less expensive products for middle-class homes, it inadvertently led to factory layoffs of large populations of unskilled laborers as well as the downsizing of many skilled workforces. At the same time, technology, especially in the computer field, advanced beyond the capacity of a workforce it was intended to aid, making many "virtual" slaves of the machines that had been created to serve them. The Y2K computer scare, in which some experts predicted widespread economic disaster, illustrates yet another instance of human subservience to technology.

So, as with the atomic bomb and with industrial pollution, by the latter half of the twentieth century, technology itself, the idea of human progress through the application of scientific discovery, had likewise threatened to destroy humanity even as it sought to save it. It is not surprising, then, that such fears found expression in the film and print media of the postwar period, especially in science fiction films, a genre well-suited to "apocalyptic" themes. It is upon this genre of film that this essay focuses.

"Apocalypse" and "Apocalyptic"

It has become commonplace to speak of any cataclysmic event as an "apocalypse" or as "apocalyptic." Such colloquial misuse of these potent terms, though widespread, stems from a conceptual and definitional misunderstanding. By definition, apocalypses are revelatory texts whose sources of knowledge are otherworldly or divine. As such, an apocalypse reveals a reality not previously known to the apocalypt, the recipient of the revelation, or to its intended audience. As a literary genre, an apocalypse has two common elements: its revelatory narrative framework and its eschatological orientation, an orientation that anticipates final judgment and punishment of the wicked. Apocalypses sometimes include other elements, such as belief in the supernatural control or divine predetermination of human history, in the inevitable triumph of good over evil, in divine judgment of all persons living and dead, and in the renewal of the cosmos or in the eventual restoration of a golden age. To be sure, while what is usually revealed to the apocalypt is sometimes pandemic in its scope and often cataclysmic in its effect, one should not confuse the *source* of the apocalypse with its eschatological (end-of-the-world) *content*, especially if one seeks to draw analytical distinctions among genres of literature or, in this case, film.[1] To do so would empty literary terms of their analytical usefulness. Put differently, while a common motif of an apocalypse is the destruction of the wicked, an end-of-time conflagration, with its resultant triumph of good over evil, does not an apocalypse make. The prediction of imminent and utter destruction may very well be part of an apocalypse, but such content does not define this genre as a whole. An apocalypse has a deeper and more intentioned meaning that goes far beyond fire and brimstone.[2]

Interestingly, as a world view or as a way of making sense of human events, the elements that typify apocalyptic literature are found in other cultural media, media that likewise make claims of otherworldly sources. Indeed, one can discern the apocalyptic or revelatory worldview in a variety of cultural artifacts of modern American society, from popular fiction to popular films. This revelatory element is especially evident within films broadly classed as science fiction.

"Apocalyptic Fiction"

Movies function both as a reflection and as a critique of society. Most, however, while pointing to perilous flaws in modern life, do not point to otherworldly sources as the basis for their critique of culture. But, over the past several decades, a more specialized genre of science fiction film has developed that presents a vision of what the future may hold for those living in the modern scientific age. We might call this revelatory genre of film *apocalyptic fiction*, not because its subject is cataclysmic *per se* but because its generic form is similar to that of an apocalypse, and its underlying function is that of a warning of imminent danger and of a way to avert impending doom.[3]

Indeed, the medium through which apocalyptic fiction conveys its revelatory material—the motion picture—is well suited as a channel of divine or otherworldly warning in that, like ancient apocalypses, its dramatic message is also broadcast through the immediacy of words and a parade of vivid images. The pictures cast upon the movie screen not only project images that are intended to shock and awaken the audience, but these images also reflect back to society something of its own fears and concerns. As a mediator between the revealed message and its intended audience, the "silver screen" fulfils two purposes: it is at once a *medium* that displays images of interest and concern to the audience, and at the same time a *mirror* that reflects back upon its viewers. In the latter instance, much like a mirror that reveals what stands before it as it really appears, the movie screen becomes a device that shows us ourselves—warts and all.[4] As before, it is this revelatory aspect of the movie screen that interests us in this essay, for it is in this genre, "apoc-alyptic fiction," that the latent uneasiness of postwar American society dra-matically reveals itself.[5]

If an apocalypse is a revelation of esoteric or previously inaccessible knowledge, then it is fair to ask what specific kind of knowledge apocalyptic fiction reveals. In essence, the revelation is of a reality not previously known to the apocalypt, such as the revelation of a heavenly realm, of coming destruction, or of cosmic regeneration. For instance, while in the case of the film *Blade Runner* (1982), the revelation may be of a bleaker tomorrow, the revelation may also be of a brighter tomorrow; such is the case with the one-time popular futuristic movie *Logan's Run* (1976).[6] In addition to the revelation of either a pessimistic or optimistic future for humankind, we might add that apocalyptic fiction also contains a number of elements that may or may not be present in other types of popular science fiction films. These include: (1) the tyranny of science and technology; (2) human helplessness in the face of an evil system or corrupt world order; (3) height-ened Cold War antagonisms, usually resulting in a nuclear holocaust; (4) a messianic component in which an anointed person will rescue humanity; (5) the inescapable fact that the protagonist must embrace his or her destiny or calling; (6) the expectation of the eventual destruction of the world through some humanly engineered disaster; and (7) the need for outside or otherworldly intervention to remedy hopeless circumstances.

Additionally, there seem to be two key differences between literary apoc-alypses and what here I am calling American *apocalyptic fiction* films, one having to do with the *message* and the other with the *messenger*. The first difference is that in every case it is assumed that the predicted cataclysmic event can be averted by human action. The second difference is that, in most, though certainly not all, cases, the messenger of the apocalypse or the one to whom the message is given becomes the agent of salvation, that is, the savior of humanity. In American apocalyptic fiction films—and perhaps in American films more generally—there appears to be an underlying optimism that defies the bleak outlook these films initially portray.[7] There is, in short, an underlying belief that circumstances need not be as they are, and that acquiescence in the face of doom is not the proper heroic response. Indeed, despite the dictates of destiny, when faced with trouble or looming disaster, Americans are wont to take matters into their own hands.

At the same time, the narrative *pattern* we find in most apocalyptic fiction films differs somewhat from the standard science fiction tales that typically feature a male hero who ventures forth to seek his fortune, or to rescue a captive maiden, or to discover his true identity and fulfill his cosmic destiny.[8] By contrast, the most pervasive thematic structure in apocalyptic fiction films, which frames the plot, is that of revelation and rescue: society will be saved, and this despite its disbelief in or disregard for the message of warning that the hero or heroine brings. In this instance, the hero or heroine plays a dual role, serving as both messenger and savior. This apocalyptic pattern, then, is threefold: first, the hero or heroine receives a special message or revelation, usually from outside the present circumstances; second, the civil authorities (or so-called experts of society) reject the warning or refuse to act to avert catastrophe (instead, their energies are absorbed harassing the hero); third, the hero or heroine, along with a ragtag collection of compatriots, rescues society from near disaster, destroys the menacing force, and makes the world safe once more.[9]

In the sections to follow, this essay will examine apocalyptic fiction in terms of the three conditions of postwar American society that seemed to point toward inevitable doom. What is revealed to postwar society through the steady production of apocalyptic fiction films is a culture on the brink of nuclear, environmental, and technological destruction. In addition, the films within this genre tend to follow the same narrative pattern discussed above, that of revelation of coming disaster, of resistance from society and its authorities, and of eventual rescue by the heroic efforts of the recipient of the revelation. I will return briefly to the discussion of this recurring pattern in the conclusion of this essay. But first, let us consider these three main types of apocalyptic fiction.

Nuclear Apocalyptic Fiction

Since the very first atomic bombs were detonated over Japan at the end of World War II, the potential of another nuclear conflagration and its frightening aftermath of sickness and suffering has remained fearfully fresh in the mind of postwar American society. With the heightening of Cold War tensions during the late 1940s and early 1950s, punctuated by news that the Soviet Union and then Red China had the bomb, it is not surprising to find the silhouette of mushroom clouds rising above the fictional cityscapes in numerous science fiction films of the period. The escalation of hostilities between East and West that led to the Korean crisis and armed conflict between China and the United States gave rise to fears that a nuclear exchange between the superpowers was inevitable.

During this period, some science fiction films also took a turn toward the apocalyptic, not in their portrayal of the coming nuclear nightmare, but in their collective message that such a war could not be won and therefore must not be contemplated, let alone fought. One such film, still considered a cult classic among science fiction devotees, is the 1951 full-length feature *The Day the Earth Stood Still*, directed by Robert Wise. Released during the "hot" period of the Korean War, this mysteriously gripping film used aliens from a near-distant planet as its messengers. These aliens, led by Klaatu (Michael Rennie), had traveled to Earth with a special mission of warning: human aggression and nuclear terror must not expand into the Solar System. "Man," they explained, was not only a threat to his own kind, but he and his growing nuclear arsenals were a threat to all intelligent life. Resistance to the alien mission by the US military only confirmed their message: humans were hell-bent on destroying themselves and thus were in need of extraterrestrial mediation.[10]

More recent examples of nuclear apocalyptic elements in popular films include the Mad Max *Road Warrior* series, particularly *Beyond Thunderdome* (1985), and the youth-oriented nuclear suspense thriller *WarGames* (1983). While both movies concern the use of nuclear warheads, the first, starring Mel Gibson as Mad Max, reveals a post-nuclear holocaust world that thrives, and for the most part survives, on the production of methane gas from pig excrement. Though what remains of human civilization has sunk to a crude subsistence level in a place called "Bartertown," run by a bosomy no-nonsense matriarch, Aunty Entity (Tina Turner), the story actually concerns a troupe of children who were in-flight during the bombings and thus escaped annihilation. In hiding among the desert caves beyond the reach of Bartertown, the children anxiously wait for the coming of a prophesied savior, who they come to believe is the unassuming but handsome hero, Gibson. In the movie's climactic battle scene, Gibson unwittingly fulfills his destiny, first by destroying the evildoers, and then by freeing the society from its *lex taliones* structure, a structure in which every offense is punished either by a duel to the death or by banishment to the outer desert.

The latter film, *WarGames*, starring Matthew Broderick as a computer whiz-kid who accidentally hacks his way into the US nuclear defense system, focuses instead on contemporary American society whose serenity is about to be disrupted through a chain of events that, it seems, will inevitably lead toward thermonuclear world war. As a result of Broderick's hacking, "Joshua" (Hebrew for Jesus, meaning "savior"), the gigantic mainframe computer that controls the US nuclear arsenal, has decided to launch a preemptive strike on the Soviet Union. All safeguard measures fail; a computer-initiated nuclear war is inescapable. Interestingly, while in the *Mad Max* saga the main character is hailed by the children he rescues as the messiah—a mantle Gibson's character reluctantly accepts—Broderick's fresh-faced character employs his computer expertise to save the planet. Seconds before the destructive launch, Broderick's character breaks the security code and convinces the renegade mainframe computer, who thinks Broderick is its long-lost creator, not to initiate its planned nuclear attack.

While *Beyond Thunderdome* seems aimed at quelling Reagan-era arms race bravado through its grim portrayal of a post-nuclear holocaust world, the message *WarGames* communicates is the futility of waging nuclear war in the first place. Since all parties involved would be utterly destroyed, there can be no real winner in such a contest. Or, as the computer Joshua announces at the end of the movie, the only real way to win the nuclear war game is not to play it.

What is common to these two examples of nuclear apocalyptic fiction is that they reveal a humanity pitted against itself through mistrust and fear, tragically unable to accept its cultural and political differences. What is likewise revealed in these films is that civilized life is really no more than a thin veneer masking human savagery and incivility. The response to the threat of nuclear destruction arises not from humanity's collective unconscious fear of death, but from its unspoken fear of returning to its cave-dwelling, barbarous past. As we are reminded, whether it results in the deaths of millions or in the death of civilized life, nuclear terror is an inescapable fact of modern life, a radioactive cloud that will continue to cast a large shadow of uncertainty over the future of humanity. Apocalyptic fiction is meant to convey the message that it does not have to be this way. Human civilization need not live in fear of such weapons of mass destruction, but should work instead to avert this deadly man-made threat.

Environmental Apocalyptic Fiction

During the postwar period, active concern in environmental issues by interest groups and government agencies heightened. As many scientists and activists began to warn of imminent environmental disaster, the civil authorities responded with legislation aimed at reversing the effects of decades of environmental negligence. In 1956, for instance, the Water Pollution Control Act, which mandated waste water treatment, was passed. Soon after, other environmentally sensitive measures were put into place, ones that sought (1) to ban above-ground testing of nuclear weapons (the 1963 Nuclear Test Ban Treaty), (2) to address the problems of acid rain and airborne pollutants (the 1970 Clean Air Act), and (3) to phase out the use of harmful pesticides such as DDT (passed in 1972). In 1970, the year the United States held the world's first Earth Day observance, President Nixon established the Environmental Protection Agency. The country seemed to be right on track toward putting its environmental house back into order.

But all this public awareness and all these governmental initiatives did not prevent environmental disasters from happening. Oil spills off the California coast in the early 1970s left once-pristine beaches and shorelines forever marred. But this only spelled the beginning of a series of environmental mishaps that marked the years to follow. In 1978, Love Canal, New York was evacuated after it was discovered that it had been the site of a major chemical dump, creating concerns over the health of its residents and their children. The very next year, in March 1979, a near reactor-core meltdown occurred on Three Mile Island, Pennsylvania, when its nuclear power plants malfunctioned. And in 1986, a reactor meltdown and explosion at the nuclear power plant in Chernobyl, Ukraine killed workers and some residents and caused widespread contamination of the air and soil throughout the old Soviet Union and much of northern Europe. As if that were not enough, about that same time, a release of highly lethal chemical gases in Bhopal, India killed thousands of people and raised questions about the effectiveness of existing industrial safeguards in preventing such deadly disasters. With each environmental mishap, the peoples of the Earth were repeatedly reminded of the fragility of the natural world and of their own negligent stewardship.

Environmental concerns such as these did not escape the notice of filmmakers, who began producing a host of movies depicting the destructive consequences of human mismanagement of the natural world.[11] Among a number of environmentally oriented sci-fi films produced during this period, two stand out as examples of this genre. The first, *Logan's Run* (1976), reveals a hopeful future for humankind and its relation to the natural world, while the second, *Soylent Green* (1973), presents a very bleak picture of human life to come.[12]

The resilience of nature, despite the poisoning of its rivers and oceans, the contamination of its soil, and the decimation of its bird and fish populations by human nuclear and industrial waste, is at the heart of *Logan's Run*'s futuristic (and hedonistic) Edenic setting. Human society lives underground, presumably having been forced centuries earlier to seek safety from mounting environmental disasters. Generations have passed and the memory of life above ground has faded into legend. Since this new Eden can be sustained only through rigorous control of the human population, all persons are compelled to die at age 30. The passing of time is marked by a luminous flower-shaped disk implanted in the palm of each person's left hand. When one's time has expired, the disk begins flashing. Death takes place daily through an elaborate communal renewal ritual called "Carousel," in which masked participants wearing flame-emblazoned white robes revolve in the carousel chamber. As the crowds of people chant "renew," the participants are drawn up into the sky by a magnetic force and then electrocuted by a flash of artificial lightning. All die. No one is ever renewed. Indeed, those who try to escape the ritual—called "runners"—are hunted down by a special security force—called the "sandmen"—and summarily eliminated.

The revelatory element of *Logan's Run* comes when the state decides to investigate and root out rumors of a "sanctuary," where runners are said to be hiding. The main character, Logan, a "hunter" played by Michael York, though sent to infiltrate this sanctuary, discovers instead that the world above has "renewed" itself and can once more sustain human life. The human channel of this revelation is the Old Man, played by Peter Ustinov. The Old Man becomes the link between the old and new worlds, and serves as a human repository for society's treasured knowledge, presumed to be lost when the previous world died. After his encounter with the Old Man, Logan returns to the world below as an apocalypt. Through his heroic efforts, Logan breaks the hold of the central authority—appropriately, a computer—

and leads the people out of their underground prison and into a true Edenic paradise.

In the movie *Soylent Green*, the audience is presented with the bleak image of a future world irreparably polluted by chemical and industrial waste, a world with scarce resources, little fresh food, and far too many people for its polluted surface and meager resources to sustain. Human society has become a police state, in which panic and near chaos are the order of the day, and the misery of human life is exacerbated by totalitarian controls on population growth and life-sustaining resources. The human diet has been reduced to the eating of protein-enriched soy and lentil crackers of differing colors called "soylent." Even this bland diet is not enough to promote or sustain healthy life, as evidenced by the piles of dead and dying bodies that line the streets—presumably overcome by the combined effects of malnutrition, and air and water pollution—only to be scooped up and hauled away like garbage by the city's sanitation trucks.

The main character in *Soylent Green*, Officer Thorn (Charlton Heston), is a twenty-first-century metropolitan New York cop investigating a high-profile murder. His attention is diverted after a death-by-euthanasia-bed conversation with Sol Roth, an elderly friend and retired police researcher played by Edward G. Robinson (in his last screen role), who tells Thorn what human life was like before the world was overrun by people and pollution. Roth, like Ustinov's character, serves as a mediator between old and new worlds, and opens Thorn's eyes to a reality that he had not previously known, or even considered: the sea is dying, and all earthly life with it. Though the plot sometimes verges on camp—the movie is clearly a child of the '70s—the depressing backdrop of the film sets the stage for the hero's great discovery, which, in horrifying disbelief, he proclaims to the aimless hordes of human cattle at the movie's dramatic final scene: "Soylent green ... is people!" Having destroyed its environment, humanity, he learns, is reduced to feeding off its dead.

Technological Apocalyptic Fiction

Dehumanization and the loss of personal autonomy and self-worth that has resulted from society's over-reliance on technology have become inescapable facts of modern life. Machines not only rule people's lives, but also make much of human labor virtually unnecessary. What is more, human thought and ingenuity are slowly being replaced by artificial intelligence. In fact, some critics of modern technology fear that machines designed to think for humans will slowly become machines that act independently of them, eventually coming to control their lives.

The revelatory element of "techno" apocalyptic fiction is one in which humans are seen as inadequate before machines and are therefore insignificant to the workings of the modern world. Three themes characterize these films. First, we find the recurring message that technology can be cruel and dehumanizing. People who live in technologically-controlled societies live cold and emotionally detached lives, devoid of existential meaning or purpose. Second, while technology is meant to provide greater freedom for humanity, in truth it has enslaved humankind—individually as well as collectively—and controls our future. Because of their over-reliance on technology and a naïve willingness to surrender control over all aspects of their lives, humans have become subservient to their own machines. Third, in "techno" apocalyptic fiction, science and technology are clearly the villains, with humanity pitted against machines in a life-or-death struggle. In many cases, the techno-villain is himself a personification of technology: cold, calculating, brutal, the very face of mechanized evil.

With perhaps the exception of the bad-to-the-bone Darth Vader in the *Star Wars* trilogy (which, incidentally, is *not* an apocalypse in form or content),[13] there are probably no better examples of this personification of technological evil than in the film *The Terminator* (1984) and its highly popular sequel, *Terminator 2: Judgment Day* (1991), both directed by James Cameron of *Titanic* (1997) fame.

In the first *Terminator*, we learn from Kyle Reese (Michael Biehn), a visitor from the future, that by the year 2029 the world will be under the ruthless domination of machines, which have turned on their human creators and subdued them by computer-initiated warfare. No match for the technological and military superiority of the machines, humans have become a hunted breed. There exists, however, a small but strong underground resistance movement led by John Connor, a resourceful and charismatic leader. In order to root out the resistance, the machines concoct a plan to kill Connor's mother, Sarah (Linda Hamilton), before he is born. To carry out this deed, the machines send back in time—to the year 1984—a Terminator cyborg unit (Arnold Schwarzenegger), a relentless and virtually unstoppable killing machine. Having learned of the plan, Connor sends Reese, his most loyal lieutenant, back in time to warn and protect his not-yet-pregnant mother. (In a strange, mind-bending twist, we learn that Reese, who does not survive the movie, is in fact Connor's father, in essence both siring a son—during a brief lull in the action, Reese and Sarah Connor have a steamy carnal romp—and then dying nearly two decades before he himself is born.)

Programmed to kill, the Terminator does not deviate from its pursuit of Sarah Connor. As it moves through the streets of suburban Los Angeles, it literally kills or maims everyone in its way. In the end, human ingenuity—and a lot of luck—triumphs over this symbol of runaway scientific technology. Though the now-pregnant Hamilton is safe—at least for the time being—the future of humankind remains in doubt. Before the credits roll, Hamilton drives south into the Mexican desert to hide out until her son is born, matures, and takes his place in the fight against technology.

In the sequel, *Terminator 2: Judgment Day* (or simply *T2*), the pre-teen John Connor (Edward Furlong) is living in a foster home, his mother having been committed to a mental institution because of her obsession over the future rebellion of the machines. In *T2*, Sarah Connor is more wild-eyed doomsday prophetess and anti-technology militant than the helpless and harried mother-to-be in *T1*. Interestingly, while she is haunted by the grim vision of a future high-tech world, her son, who is of the generation not frightened by rapid technological advances, becomes a mediator—a messiah of sorts—between present and future worlds.

The premise of *T2* is simple: the machines that rule the future world send a more advanced T-1000 Terminator unit (Robert Patrick) back to the present, this time to assassinate the young Connor. Learning of this mission, the Connor of the future world sends a rival but weaker T-800 Terminator, played once more by Arnold Schwarzenegger, to protect his present-day self. To his mother's initial discomfort, her old nemesis is now one of the good guys. While the boy and his Terminator are running from the marvelously protean T-1000, the mother is bent on finding and killing Miles Dyson (Joe Morton), the scientist responsible for designing the computer chip that sets the entire end-time scenario into motion. (Part-way through the film, in a chilling dreamlike playground scene, Sarah envisions the fiery nuclear destruction of civilization. Rather than continue to brood over the fate of humanity, she decides to join the others in their efforts to change the course of the future.) At the climax of the movie, both Terminators and the special chip are destroyed in a vat of molten steel, and the Connors—mother and son—save human civilization. (Dyson dies earlier in an explosive hail of fire and bullets.)

Aside from the conceptual difficulties and implausible premises of the *Terminator* films, of which two more have since been made,[14] we discover a number of things about the ambivalence of modern society in the face of technological advance. (Ironically, the films themselves are technological marvels.) While in one breath we praise the boundless genius of the human mind to create, at the same time we are struck dumb by the realization that humans are often unable to see beyond what appear to be the immediate benefits of their creative ideas. Humans, we learn, rarely consider the unforeseen and unintended consequences of their ideas or their actions. But, additionally, we learn that the fruits of human ingenuity need not be destructive. The warning that the American apocalypt issues has an underlying message of hopefulness: Men and machines can work together for the benefit and advance of humankind.

Concluding Comments

The main point of the foregoing discussion of apocalyptic fiction is that, in an analysis of contemporary films, it is not enough to say that movies that depict the end of the world or scenes of cataclysmic destruction of human civilization are *apocalyptic*. As a genre of film, apocalyptic fiction possesses several common elements that distinguish it as *apocalyptic*, the most telling of which is its revelatory framework. This is not to say that apocalypses differ from other film genres because they *reveal* something. All films have a reflective quality. That is, all films naturally reflect their times and reveal something about the cultures in which they are produced. But in the case of what I am calling apocalyptic fiction, the revelatory characteristic refers to a message whose *source* comes from elsewhere—that is, outside the present conditions or circumstances—and is mediated through an agent who stands between these worlds. Whether the agent or the receptor of the message becomes the hero is irrelevant to classifying a film as apocalyptic fiction. The revelatory framework, the otherworldly source of the message, its mediated character, and its inherent call to change destiny are what differentiate apocalyptic fiction from other genres of film.

At the same time, what we have discovered in the above discussion is that the source of the revelation need not come from another world *per se*. While in one of the examples of nuclear apocalyptic fiction—*The Day the Earth Stood Still*—the apocalypt did come from outer space, in other examples the apocalypt came from the world of the future or was connected to the world of the past. In other words, the apocalypt is someone (or something) not altogether belonging to the society in danger, that is, someone (or something) from the outside.

What is more, not only is the source of the revelation otherworldly, but the message that the apocalypt brings contains a warning, usually of impending doom or of cataclysmic destruction of the world *in toto*. It is this unforeseen threat that inspires the apocalypt, and this same threat that frames the content of his or her message.[15]

But the apocalypt is not, in all cases, simply an appointed messenger. In some cases, he or she becomes the savior as well. In these instances, not only does the apocalypt deliver a message of warning, but he or she also delivers society from the imminent danger, either by providing the necessary information to save society or, in many cases, the necessary fire-power. Indeed, this apocalypt-*cum*-redeemer plot device in apocalyptic fiction films tends to follow a similar pattern, in which the messenger or the person to whom the message is directed must likewise act on the revelation him- or herself. The pattern, again, is threefold: (1) after receiving the revelation, (2) the hero(ine) warns society of its precarious circumstances. After being rejected by the civil authorities, (3) the hero(ine) determines to save society through his or her own actions. As before, while most action and suspense movies tend to follow a similar plotline, what makes this *apocalyptic* is the revelatory framework of the film, that is, the *otherworldly* source of its revelation.

We see an example of this apocalypt-*cum*-redeemer in *Logan's Run*. After he discovers that the renewed world above is a greater paradise than the world below, to save his fellow humans from death at age 30, Logan must fight against and defeat the system. We see another example of this in *Terminator 2*, in that the T-800 Terminator is the messenger and, for the most part, a heavily-armed savior. This apocalypt-*cum*-redeemer device is also evident, but to a lesser extent, in some of the other films highlighted in this essay, such as *Mad Max: Beyond Thunderdome* and *WarGames*. One can also see evidence of this plot device in films not touched on above, such as *The Sacrifice* (1986), *Waterworld* (1995) and, perhaps, *Contact* (1997).

A final observation that one can make from the foregoing discussion is that while apocalyptic fiction films tend to demonize technology as destructive and dehumanizing, it is interesting to note that these same films also hold out the hope that technology, if properly applied, can likewise be salutary. The defining difference is in the ways technology is used, and in the intentions of those who use it. In other words, whether technology is used as a tool or a weapon rests squarely in the hands of those who possess it. Accordingly, in the epic struggle against the deleterious effects of modernity that apocalyptic fiction films seek to portray, the tale these films likewise tell is one of caution: take care, lest the knowledge and wisdom of modern science be rooted out as well.

But, as these films also reveal, the faith that people have in science, technology, medicine, and the like may very well be a misplaced faith that, like faith in politics or religion, leaves them vulnerable to visionary promises of utopia. In a touch of irony, apocalyptic fiction films point out that our faith in these technologies, and the beguiling promise they hold out of heaven on Earth, may very well damn us to a hell of our own making. In the end, they may condemn humanity to living in a cold and inhospitable future world, one defined—in truly biblical proportions—by warfare, disease, starvation, totalitarian governments, savage barbarism, and death.

References

Barkun, Michael. 1986. *Disaster and the Millennium*. Syracuse, NY: Syracuse University Press.

Boyer, Paul. 1992. *When Time Shall Be No More*. Cambridge: Belknap/Harvard.

Bull, Malcolm, ed. 1995. *Apocalypse Time and the Ends of the World*. Oxford, UK: Blackwell.

Cohn, Norman. 1970. *The Pursuit of the Millennium*. New York: Oxford University Press.

Collins, John J. 1984. *The Apocalyptic Imagination*. New York: Crossroad.

——. 1997. *Apocalypticism in the Dead Sea Scrolls*. London and New York: Routledge.

Dixon, Wheeler Winston. 2003. *Visions of the Apocalypse: Spectacles of Destruction in American Cinema*. New York: Wallflower Press.

Gordon, Andrew. 1995. "*Star Wars*: A Myth for Our Time." In *Screening the Sacred*, eds Joel W. Martin and Conrad E. Ostwalt, Jr, 73–82. Boulder, CO: Westview Press.

Harvey, David. 1990. *The Condition of Postmodernity.* Oxford: Basil Blackwell.

Hellholm, David, ed. 1983. *Apocalypticism in the Mediterranean World and the Near East.* Tübingen: J.C.B. Mohr.

Jewett, Robert and John Shelton Lawrence. 1977. *The American Monomyth.* New York: Doubleday.

Miles, Margaret R. 1996. *Seeing and Believing: Religion and Values in the Movies.* Boston: Beacon Press.

Newman, Kim. 2000. *Apocalypse Movies: End of the World Cinema.* New York: St Martin's Press.

Ostwalt, Conrad E., Jr. 1995. "Hollywood and Armageddon: Apocalyptic Themes in Recent Cinematic Presentation." In *Screening the Sacred,* eds Joel W. Martin and Conrad E. Ostwalt, Jr, 55–63. Boulder, CO: Westview Press.

Robbins, Thomas and Susan J. Palmer, eds. 1997. *Millennium, Messiahs, and Mayhem: Contemporary Apocalyptic Movements.* London and New York: Routledge.

Shapiro, Jerome. 2001. *Atomic Bomb Cinema: The Apocalyptic Imagination on Film.* New York: Routledge.

Stone, Jon R. 1993. *A Guide to the End of the World: Popular Eschatology in America.* New York: Garland.

——, ed. 2000. *Expecting Armageddon: Essential Readings in Failed Prophecy.* London and New York: Routledge.

Strug, Cordell. 1995. "Apocalypse Now What?: Apocalyptic Themes in Modern Movies." *Word and World* 15, 2 (Spring): 159–65.

Thompson, Kirsten Moana. 2007. *Apocalyptic Dread: American Film at the Turn of the Millennium.* Albany, NY: State University of New York Press.

Walliss, John. 2004. *Apocalyptic Trajectories: Millenarianism and Violence in the Contemporary World.* Oxford: Peter Lang.

Walls, Jerry L., ed. 2008. *The Oxford Handbook of Eschatology.* New York: Oxford University Press.

Weber, Timothy P. 1987. *Living in the Shadow of the Second Coming: American Pre-millennialism, 1875–1982.* Chicago: University of Chicago Press.

Wessinger, Catherine, ed. Forthcoming. *The Oxford Handbook of Millennialism.* New York: Oxford University Press.

Notes

1 An apocalypse (or "revelation") is a genre of visionary literature that emerged during the Hellenistic period of Western antiquity (*c.* 200 BCE–200 CE) and is characterized by the revelation of heavenly knowledge through means of a heavenly journey or through the visitation of a heavenly messenger. The use of "apocalypse" and "apocalyptic" as metaphorical synonyms for "cataclysmic end of the world" is derived from the *Apocalypse of John*, the Greek title of *The Revelation to St John the Divine*, the final book of the Christian Bible. The Revelation (always singular) recounts the heavenly vision that the Apostle John received concerning God's destructive judgment upon a sinful, unbelieving world. While the book, traditionally dated about 96 CE, is more than likely a veiled critique of the Roman Empire's anti-Christian policies, its revelatory content has inspired countless predictions of "imminent destruction" and "kingdom come" by

overly zealous biblical interpreters—both learned and unlearned—throughout the past nineteen centuries (for specific examples see Cohn 1970; Barkun 1986; Weber 1987; Boyer 1992; Stone 1993, 2000; Bull 1995; Robbins and Palmer 1997; Walliss 2004; Walls 2008; Wessinger forthcoming 2011). It should be stated that while the Book of Revelation is the model apocalypse for Christian theologians, it is not *the* model for this essay on revelatory elements in postwar American films. References to apocalypse and apocalyptic in this essay should be taken as references to a genre of which the Book of Revelation is simply one example.

2 There are five identifying features common to all apocalypses. First, apocalypses typically feature a supernatural source from which a secret knowledge comes. These sources of special knowledge often come through visions, dreams, angelic visitations, heavenly journeys, and the opening of a heavenly book or sealed scroll. A second identifying feature of apocalypses is their interest in otherworldly forces, usually angelic and demonic. The angels and the demons have material or quasi-material form—usually human—as well as cosmic names or titles. These titles include such descriptive words as Lightbearer, Destroyer, Morning Star, Accuser, and the like. A third characteristic feature of apocalypses is the firm belief in divine intervention in human history, usually culminating in the end of an evil person or power, or sometimes the end of time itself. Also characteristic of apocalyptic literature is the restoration of paradise on Earth. The scenario of this fourth feature includes the termination of the old world and its transformation into a new world order. A final feature of an apocalypse is the dispensing of rewards and punishments to men and women in the afterlife. The reward or punishment is determined by the degree of faithfulness to God that a person showed in this life, especially in the face of trial and persecution (see Collins 1997, 1–8, 1984, 1–32; see selected essays in Hellholm 1983).

Apocalyptic literature differs from eschatological literature in that the knowledge provided by means of the heavenly journey or by the heavenly messenger does not always speak of the future in end-of-the-world imagery. An apocalypse may or may not be grounded in millennial expectation and may or may not speak of the dawning of the millennium, the golden age of peace. Also, though the message of the apocalypt may anticipate the coming of a messianic figure who emerges to rescue those in distress, messianic intervention is likewise not a defining feature of an apocalypse. With the foregoing discussion in mind, it is therefore not surprising that the *metaphorical* use of "apocalypse" and "apocalyptic" has led to flawed and confusing analyses, even by scholars who claim a measure of expertise regarding things apocalyptic. (For examples of the metaphorical use of "apocalypse" and "apocalyptic" in the analysis and interpretation of American films, see Ostwalt 1995; Miles 1996; Newman 2000; Shapiro 2001; Dixon 2003; Thompson 2007.)

3 While films such as *Dr. Strangelove* certainly communicate to their audiences the sense of impending doom that awaits human society if it does not act to avert disaster, these films are not apocalyptic in form. There is no otherworldly source, *per se*, that reveals impending doom or that recommends a course of action that will avert disaster. By definition, then, what we are calling "apocalyptic fiction" does not include films about nuclear buildup, Cold War tensions, or the aftermath of nuclear holocaust, such as *Fail-Safe* (1964), *On the Beach* (1959), or the then-shocking TV movie *The Day After* (1983). It also does not include pseudo-religious films about the coming of an anti-Christ or a prophesied end of the world, such as *The Omen* theater trilogy (1976–81), *The Seventh Sign* (1988), *The Rapture* (1991), or *End of Days* (1999). This essay, then, is not merely a survey of movie titles lumped haphazardly under a catch-all metaphorical category called

"apocalypse," but an attempt to approach the subject of religion and film more critically by applying religious typologies and literary genres with greater analytical precision.

4 With Nietzsche, who wrote in *Beyond Good and Evil* that "when you gaze long into an abyss the abyss also gazes into you," we might likewise say that if we as a society gaze long at the silver screen, it soon begins to look into us. The screen shows us ourselves in objectified form and, in so doing, reveals to us something of the terror of living in the (post)modern technological age. It also shows us the urgent need for salvation from our predicament, either coming from within ourselves or from someone or some force standing outside our precarious circumstances. Of course, Nietzsche, through the mouth of his prophet Zarathustra, strenuously argued for the former.

5 A criticism of this scheme might come in the fact that all movies "reveal" something to the viewer, that is, they all have a point their writers and directors are trying to make. This critical aspect is understood. However, in keeping with the proper meaning of the word "apocalyptic" as "revelatory," the distinction this essay seeks to make is between movies that are apocalyptic in form, not simply revelatory in content or in intention. Otherwise, it would make little sense to speak of apocalypse as a distinct genre of literature or film.

6 David Harvey (1990) provides an interesting postmodernist "reading" of the film *Blade Runner* in his well-known study, *The Condition of Postmodernity.*

7 As Cordell Strug has noted, "[t]he very fact that dramas are being conceived as post-apocalyptic implies that we think we—or someone—will survive" (Strug 1995, 161). It is quite possible that, deep down, humankind knows that civilized society is merely one global disaster away from a return to the Hobbesian state of nature. And yet, humanity seems ever hopeful that a disaster of such magnitude can be averted.

8 See, for instance, Gordon (1995), whose analysis centers on the movie *Star Wars* (1977).

9 This comment is not meant to suggest that an apocalypse involves revelation and rescue, only that many, if not most, American apocalyptic fiction films combine the apocalypt and the savior in one character.

10 In December 2008, a remake of *The Day the Earth Stood Still* was released. In this version, starring Keanu Reeves as Klaatu, the threat that triggers extra-terrestrial intervention is no longer nuclear proliferation but global warming, an issue made popular by former Vice President Al Gore in his prize-winning ecomentary, *An Inconvenient Truth* (2006). In the remake, Klaatu believes that the only way to save Earth's environment is to exterminate all of its human inhabitants.

11 Disaster movies of all kinds were in popular demand during the 1970s. Such notable films produced during this period include *Airport* (1970), *The Poseidon Adventure* (1972), *The Towering Inferno* (1974), *Earthquake* (1974), *Tidal Wave* (1975), *The Swarm* (1978), and *Meteor* (1979). Though depicting catastrophic events, none of these films is *apocalyptic* in the true sense of the word.

12 It should be noted that, while many of the films in the postwar period call attention to the destructive consequences of environmental negligence by human society—to the extent that in some cases nature begins to fight back, as in M. Night Shyamalan's *The Happening* (2008)—not all environmentally-interested sci-fi films, including *Silent Running* (1971), can be typed as apocalypses. Likewise, films that depict the terrifying consequences of plagues and pandemics, such as *The Last Man on Earth* (1964) and its remake *The Omega Man* (1971), *The Andromeda Strain* (1971), *Outbreak* (1995), *Ever Since the Earth Ended*

(2001), *28 Days Later* (2002), *28 Weeks Later* (2007), *Resident Evil* (2007), and *Doomsday* (2008), do not appropriately fall within the genre of film I am identifying as *apocalypse/apocalyptic*. The few exceptions worth noting are *Twelve Monkeys* (1995), *The Reaping* (2007), and *I Am Legend* (2007).

13 As an aside, though it may appear to have apocalyptic (revelatory) features, the *Star Wars* trilogy (1977–83) and its "prequelogy", *The Phantom Menace* (1999), *Attack of the Clones* (2002), and *Revenge of the Sith* (2005), do not properly fit the apocalypt-*cum*-redeemer pattern. This series of films more closely resembles the so-called American monomyth (Jewett and Lawrence 1977; Gordon 1995).

14 *Terminator 3: Rise of the Machines* (2003), directed by Jonathan Mostow, was a 109-minute afterthought meant to revive box office interest in the *Terminator* franchise. It starred Nick Stahl as a late-adolescent John Connor, and once more featured Arnold Schwarzenegger as a Terminator unit, in his last starring role before becoming Governor of California. The twist in *T3* is that "Judgment Day," set for year 2004, is not averted. Instead, John Connor and a suitable young female heroine are unwittingly led to a civil defense command bunker deep with a Montana mountain, there not to stop "Judgment Day" but to survive it. It is from this shelter that a new Adam and Eve will emerge.

In the final installment of the *Terminator* tetralogy, *Terminator Salvation* or *T4* (2009), set in the year 2018, John Connor (played by Christian Bale) develops the command skills necessary to lead the human resistance against Skynet (the machines) and its menacing army of cyborgs.

15 Incidentally, the recently-released film *Knowing* (2009), starring Nicholas Cage, provides a near-perfect example of an *apocalypse* in the true sense of the word. In this film, MIT astrophysics professor John Koestler (Cage) uncovers a code that serves as the key to determining when doomsday will occur. But in this case, nothing can be done to avert the end of all life on Earth. Shortly before the Earth is seared by a colossal solar flare, quasi-angelic aliens arrive in spaceships to transport the chosen children of Earth to an extraterrestrial home—a new heaven and a new earth—reminiscent of the Garden of Eden.

Chapter 4

Sexuality, Blasphemy, and Iconoclasm in the Media Age

The Strange Case of the Buddha Bikini[1]

James Mark Shields

> Sudhana saw the lay disciple Prabhūta upon a seat made of the precious gems and metals. She was a very young woman: beautiful, gentle, and fair to behold with the first touch of youth … Her limbs were without ornament. Her petticoats and sari were white. Aside from the Buddhas and Bodhisattvas, no one comes to see her whom she does not overwhelm with her physical and mental superiority, the luster of her spiritual fire, her exquisite complexion, and her beauty.
>
> *The Harmony of the Young Sapling Sutra*

> There is virtually no other item of clothing linked with so many ideas, images and preconceived impressions. For the bikini belongs to the mythology of today that shapes our concept of reality. In much the same way as the speed of a motorcar bestows on its driver an intoxicating sense of power, and indeed just as a gold credit card has the power to avail its possessor of infinite possibilities, the bikini represents a blank screen open to a person's imagination … So when a woman wears a bikini, she … is wearing a magical thing, something that will transform her and turn her into someone else.
>
> Patrik Alac 2002, *The Bikini: A Cultural History*

According to an oft-cited study of sex and advertising, "Every media consumer is alert to 'sex in advertising.' Its pervasive use and misuse are constantly before us, and typically elicit strong criticism" (Richmond and Hartman 1982, 53). Numerous studies over the past few decades (e.g. Cebrzynski 2000) have largely confirmed the truism that, at least within certain limits, "sex sells"—or, more correctly "sexiness sells"—and it is not hard to see why. Indeed, setting aside for the time being related ethical and gender issues, this fact itself requires little by way of further analysis. More interesting, though much less studied, is a question more germane to the present investigation: does *religion* sell?

A recent study investigating the question of whether "spirituality sells" found that, compared with sexuality, religious content in advertising is surprisingly infrequent: only one per cent of television and magazine advertisements (Moore 2005, 5). This may be due to the fact that, even more than with sexuality, there are limits that must be negotiated—advertisers employing religious themes and images tread dangerous water. Perhaps sensitivity to what might be considered "blasphemous" is stronger today than sensitivity to what might be considered "obscene." Having said that, in terms of the commercial use of sex, any limit is also a potential boundary that can be pushed and, short of a full-fledged consumer boycott, the surrounding controversy in itself frequently serves to increase attention to (and potentially sales of) the offending product. In a different and more provocative vein, extrapolating the work of James Twitchell, it may be that contemporary consumer culture has no need to adopt religious themes and images in selling products, because the culture of advertising already, in and of itself, performs the same functions as traditional religions (see Twitchell 1996). As Charles Taylor has argued, in order to succeed, religions require at least a partial commitment to the goal of "human flourishing"—even while they pursue goals that transcend worldly understandings of such (Taylor 2007). It follows that any attempt to proselytize must rely at least in part on themes and images that evoke, display, or promise worldly benefits, which is precisely the *modus operandi* of advertising.

Whatever the reasons for this relative lack, it is important to note the discrepancy in the treatment of Western and Asian religions in contemporary advertising. Moore notes that whereas Western religions are more frequently used to sell "cultural products" (books, magazines, films), Asian religions tend to be used to sell goods and services; whereas Western religious images tend to be historical, Asian ones are contemporary; and whereas, on the whole, ads containing images from Asian religions tend to be "respectful," this is much less the case with ads containing images from Western religions, which are more likely to use humor to undercut or question the validity of Western religious beliefs or practices. On the whole, research has found that Asian religions, when represented in contemporary advertising, tend to be portrayed in a positive (if naïve or romanticized) light. And while Rick Moore misidentifies one of the Asian images, the yin/yang symbol, as being "Buddhist"—it is in fact Daoist or, at any rate, a pan-Chinese symbol that long pre-dates the arrival of Buddhism in East Asia—he nonetheless concludes that "Buddhism and Taoism are cool... Judaism and Christianity are not" (Moore 2005, 6–9, 11).

The Perfect Storm: Sexuality, Religion, and Commercial Advertising

In early 2004, popular American lingerie company Victoria's Secret launched a new brand of bikini, in form little different from standard (revealing) Victoria's Secret fare, but in content quite unique in that the swimsuit was adorned with traditional Buddhist iconography, including a prominently displayed Buddha image on the left breast. As Gregory Levine notes, the swimsuit—called by Victoria's Secret (2004) the "Asian Floral Tankini"—conflates the tropical lushness of South Asia with its presumably colorful spirituality (Levine 2005).[2] In other words, the exoticization of Buddhism appears as one feature of a more general exoticization of the tropical, sensuous Other—extending an orientalist motif that can be traced back in visual art to Paul Gauguin (1848–1903). The bright florid style is indeed fairly typical of Indian and south Asian religious art, though the iconography suggests a more specific Himalayan aesthetic, of the Nepalese or Tibetan sort.

The main image on the tankini top is a seated Buddha giving a combination of the "explanation" and "meditation" *mudras* (ritual hand gestures). The combination of these two gestures indicates that the Buddha is Shakyamuni—the "historical Buddha," otherwise known as Siddhartha Gautama (*c.* 563–483 BCE). Further down on the torso is an image of Bhaisajyaguru—the "medicine Buddha"—who is always depicted holding a medicine jar in his left hand, his right hand upraised in the "gift-giving" *mudra*. The blue color of his robes indicates the lapis lazuli paradise over which he reigns. Finally, cut off at the model's midriff, we glimpse an image of Tsongkhapa (also known as Je Rinpoche, 1357–1419), the founder of the Geluk or "Yellow Hat" school of Tibetan Buddhism (out of which emerged the lineage of the Dalai Lamas). His teachings emphasized the union of *sutra* (canonical writings, usually attributed to Gautama Buddha) and *tantra* (esoteric writings associated with the Vajrayana or tantric schools of Buddhism, the dominant form of Buddhism in Tibet), as well as the *vinaya* (monastic) code. Beyond being revered as a great teacher, his wisdom and compassion were such that he is sometimes called a "second Buddha," or as an emanation of Manjushri, the bodhisattva of wisdom. Whether or not it is to Victoria's Secret's credit, these designs are accurate in their representation of traditional iconography. That is to say, despite the objections of some critics who decried the bikinis as lacking in aesthetic taste and proper representation, they are not in themselves misrepresentations, stereotypes, or caricatures, as one sometimes sees in Western commercialization of Buddhism. On the other hand, the verisimilitude of these images may be part of the problem, since any sacred status they accrue by virtue of being "correct" images makes them theoretically more prone to being "defiled" by the way in which they are reproduced and employed. Bernard Faure cites several cases in which "Asian icons, because of their verisimilitude, their mimetic quality, are able to arouse people" (Faure 1998b, 780).

Though there was little immediate response to the "Buddha bikini," presumably because most regular consumers of Victoria's Secret swimwear were not particularly concerned with the matter, within weeks protest began to emerge, initially coming from Asian-American and Asian Buddhists and Buddhist leaders. The response triggered a second wave of protest from non-Asian Buddhists in the USA and a few other Western countries, many of whom chimed in with their fellow Buddhists about the "tactlessness" and "orientalism" of the suits and the offending company. Employing the internet as a source for protest, Buddhists worldwide launched a campaign against Victoria's Secret.[3] Against the growing barrage of criticism, the company discontinued the line, though they did not offer a recall of the sold products, and were initially hesitant to offer an apology to those who were upset by the Buddha bikinis. Indeed, in a public statement the company denied knowledge that the image on the suit was indeed "the Buddha," and proceeded to pass the blame to the manufacturer, a Columbian company called OndadeMar. OndadeMar, in turn, discontinued its own version of the Buddha bikini, which it called the "Baby Buddha Bikini" (Figure 4.1), and promptly removed all offending images from its website (www.ondademar.com).

Figure 4.1 OndadeMar's "Baby Buddha Bikini." Image used with permission.

Figure 4.2 Detail of Abercrombie & Fitch's "Buddha Bash" t-shirt. Image used with permission.

The Buddha bikini was not, in fact, the first case in which commercialized images of the Buddha were the cause of controversy in the USA. In early 2002, trendy retailer Abercrombie & Fitch got into hot water for its new line of Asian-themed T-shirts, one of which was festooned with a stereotypical image of a pudgy Buddha wearing what (inexplicably) appears to be a Hawaiian *lei*, along with the words "Buddha Bash: Get Your Buddha on the Floor" (Figure 4.2).[4]

Presumably the humor lies in the similarities of the words Buddha and the slang term "booty," but members of the Asian-American Students' Association at Stanford University were not laughing: they demanded an apology and called for a boycott of Abercrombie & Fitch goods. The main criticism in this case, as voiced by spokesperson Michael Chang, was that the company was trading in outdated and offensive stereotypes of Asians, as well as, at least in the case of the "Buddha Bash" shirt, trivializing "an entire religion and philosophy" (Strasburg 2002). Though the company did eventually apologize and pull the shirts from its shelves, it insisted that people should not be upset, because Abercrombie & Fitch "makes fun of everyone," and was in fact marketing the shirts to young Asian-Americans as a kind of inside joke.

Unlike the case of the Victoria's Secret swimsuit, the main complaint against Abercrombie & Fitch was that it was peddling products with "racist" images (though it must be said that, of the various shirts under attack, the

Buddha Bash T-shirt was probably the *least* offensive in that respect). However, as with the Buddha bikini, the incorporation of religion into the mix certainly contributed to the perceived slight, because of the widespread perception that using religious images to sell products is a trivialization of something sacred and powerful. What this controversy lacked, however, was the element of sexuality—the final touch to an already explosive brew. In fact, Abercrombie & Fitch—a company that is "notorious for using men as sexual objects in their advertising" (Blair *et al.* 2006, 4)—seems to have purposely exaggerated the Buddha's unattractiveness, in flat contradiction to the early Indian and southeast Asian tradition, which is at pains to emphasize the Buddha's physical beauty and even, at times, his virility. Ultimately, unlike the relatively localized response to the Abercrombie & Fitch T-shirts, the Buddha bikini débâcle took on global proportions.

Let us examine the actual complaint in more detail. What, exactly, was it about the Buddha bikini that was so offensive to so many, especially Asian and Asian-American, Buddhists? The answer can be broken down into a number of broad categories. The first is simply a display of ignorance or lack of respect for Buddhism as a "foreign religion." Along these lines, Kieu Dam Trang, one of the organizers of the campaign, criticized both companies for lacking "common sense" and "respect for religious differences," and for being "inconsiderate" (cited by Aoyagi 2004, 1). This is the weakest level of complaint, since it does not malign the intentions of the swimsuit-makers, simply their lack of foresight, but it was perhaps the most common theme among reactions by Western Buddhists on the now-defunct Buddhist News Network. Moreover, the criticism of lacking respect for "religious differences" is interesting, since it seems to imply that, *unlike* Christians, Muslims, or Jews, Buddhists themselves would never allow such an irreverent display of their holy founders and/or deities. Perhaps a more accurate statement of this critique would be to say that Victoria's Secret and OndadaMar showed a lack of respect for "religious similarities"—a recognition that Buddhists, too, might be sensitive to thoughtless use of images sacred to their traditions.

Once we get beyond the level of mere "disrespect"—once we delve into more substantive complaints about the Buddha bikini—the debate becomes fraught with contradictory, misleading, and frankly erroneous claims and assumptions about Buddhism, images, and sexuality. In short, from a cultural studies perspective, this is where things get interesting. For instance, Kodo Umezu, a "priest" of the Buddhist Churches of America (a name that in itself indicates the Westernization of Buddhism), locates the main problem with the Buddha bikini in the commercial aspect, noting that Buddha images "represent something very meaningful for many Buddhists," and that "we [Buddhists] do not like these images to be used in a design" (Aoyagi 2004, 1). Underlying this complaint is the assumption that Victoria's Secret is attempting to capitalize crassly on the recent cachet of Buddhism (and Asian design more generally) in the West. Though the company may not have meant intentionally to malign Buddhism, it knew full well that it was appropriating "sacred" images and using them to sell products in order to make a profit.

But there may be something more at stake here. Reverend Kodo implies that it is not just the commercialization of the suits that is problematic, but the very idea of *duplication* of Buddhist images in any form of design. This puts it onto shaky ground as far as Buddhism goes, since the reproduction of Buddhist images—and the sale of such—has been part and parcel of Asian Buddhist traditions for centuries (Faure 1998b, 802). Indeed, in many Buddhist countries the reproduction of Buddhist images is one of the best ways to gain merit (*punya*), which will lead one to a better rebirth. Today in Japan, any visit to a Buddhist temple provides one with the opportunity to purchase a whole range of goods, including images of the various buddhas and assorted heavenly beings. While it is true, of course, that the buddha and bodhisattva images on sale in various Asian Buddhist countries are not generally plastered on provocative swimwear, we may be witnessing here an adoption by Buddhist critics such as Reverend Kodo of what might be termed a "Protestant" critique against image-worship and idolatry, rather than anything remotely "Buddhist."

Within Buddhist ethics, intention plays a significant role. Indeed, though a number of scholars have noted that Buddhist ethics is difficult to classify in terms of classic Western ethical paradigms (e.g. Keown 1992; Harvey 2000), a focus on intention is one element that Buddhist ethics cannot do without. In Buddhism, as opposed to various other Indian religious systems such as Jainism, *karma* itself is intricately connected to intention—indeed, these terms can sometimes seem to collapse into one (Harvey 2000, 17). It is only fitting, then, that intention plays a part in the controversy surrounding the Buddha bikini. As noted above, many critics raised the point that Victoria's Secret was clearly hoping to profit from trendy images, even ones that happen to be sacred to millions of Asians. If this were not enough, they managed to trump the effrontery of other merchandisers such as Abercrombie & Fitch by putting the image on a *bikini*—which, it may be assumed, is an item of clothing designed to flaunt sexuality (or cultivate insecurity) in women and inspire lust in males.[5] According to this argument, then, all those involved in the making and distribution of the Buddha bikini are guilty of using "sacred" Buddhist images to encourage thoughts and behaviors antithetical to traditional Buddhist teachings. This sounds like a reasonable argument, and it is one that dovetails to some degree with feminist critics of the more general use of the sexualized female body to sell products—whether the target is men or women (Blair *et al.* 2006, 4). Yet it brings up a number of related concerns.

Clearly, the problem with the Buddha bikini runs more deeply than feelings of disrespect, or sensitivity to the commercial reproduction and sale of

Buddha images. The deeper issue lies in the fact that these images are on *bikinis*, and bikinis are, in our present global culture, understood as highly sexualized items of clothing—especially when displayed within the pages of a Victoria's Secret publication, the only mail-order catalogue that can make the claim of being as popular among men as women. Of course, depending on one's cultural background and politics—and perhaps, to a lesser degree, one's religion—bikinis can signify sexual liberation, sexual oppression, or sexual laxity. In the case of the Buddha bikini, not only are the Buddha images situated on a bikini, the bikini itself is displayed on the body of a swimsuit model—posed in a highly suggestive way. That is to say, there are actually two levels at which the problem of images arises: the printed cloth that makes up the bikini itself, and the printed page that displays the product on the body of the model.

The History of Buddhist Iconography, Iconoclasm, and Images of the Female Body

As with virtually all world religions, Buddhism at times has struggled with images—is it appropriate to depict sacred beings, and if so, what forms should these images be allowed to take, and to what uses may they be put? There have been periods in which anthropomorphic images of the Buddha are few—or even, in Chan/Zen streams, deliberately destroyed—and periods (much more common) in which the use and production of such images abound. In particular, the few centuries following the death of Siddhartha Gautama show a noticeable lack of figurative imagery—the Buddha himself is generally represented by symbols such as a footprint or a parasol. Scholars still debate the specific reasons behind such wariness (see Foucher 1917; Coomaraswamy 1927; Mus 1935; Gombrich 1966; Dehejia 1990; Hunting-don 1990). On one side is the idea that the very "humanity" of the Buddha, combined with his teaching of impermanence and widespread belief in his own "final nirvana" upon decease, meant that any visual depiction of him was conceived as a delusory and harmful grasping after something that had gone "poof" (e.g. Gombrich 1971, 112; Snellgrove 1978, 23–24). At the opposite end of the spectrum is the more familiar notion that the very awe-someness of the Buddha as a spiritually enlightened being renders any attempt at his physical representation hopeless at best, presumptuous at worst. Though the former seems to fit better with the early Buddhist teach-ings, the latter is, we might say, the more typically human response. And indeed, given what we know about the relatively rapid development of Bud-dhist devotion and worship, especially in the Mahayana, it may be the more plausible explanation.

At any rate, this an-iconic period appears to have ended by the first cen-tury BCE, and from that point on we see a flourishing of Buddhist images in architectural relief, sculpture, and cave paintings, first in India and Central

Asia, and eventually spreading via the Silk Road to China and East Asia and to southeast Asia via Sri Lanka (see Faure 1991, 148–78; 1996, 237–63). Most Buddhists—monks and laypeople alike—came to accept images as part and parcel of their religious practice. Besides being invaluable tools for visualization/meditation, religious icons were also the most effective way to spread the teachings, particularly to those—and they were the vast majority—who could not read the often impenetrable Buddhist texts (Faure 1998b, 799). Perhaps the most common early subjects of artistic representation were the stories of the past lives of the Buddha—the so-called "Jataka Tales." These pre-Buddhist moral fables, rooted in Indian folk traditions, served as teaching tools to convey simple Buddhist values such as compassion and charity. Some of the most striking examples of Jataka-themed art can be found in the Ajanta caves in northern India, which were painted between the first and fifth centuries CE (Figures 4.3, 4.4 and 4.5).

It is hard not to be struck by the sensual nature of these images, not only the attention to color and the flowing lines, but the way the figures—both male and female—are portrayed. An early scholarly consensus was that the sensuality of especially the later Ajanta paintings is a clear indication of the growing "degeneracy" of Indian Buddhism into "crude" tantric practices. Though *tantra* may have played some role in the Ajanta aesthetic, it is more likely that the artists were continuing an already existent Indian sculptural tradition that emphasized the body—especially, but by no means exclusively, the female body—as an auspicious emblem of fertility and good fortune (see Young 2004, 30–31; also Faure 1998b, 789 n. 58).

In addition, the depiction of bodhisattvas, lesser deities, and holy figures in a sensual fashion has strong precedent within later Buddhist traditions, beyond India. Faure notes that, while standard depictions of the major buddhas (Jp. *honzon*) tend toward "valorized stillness," icons of "distinct worthies" (Jp. *besson*) are frequently shown in a more dynamic fashion: "when they seem to be on the move, their movement often goes hand in hand with a certain sexualization." Moreover, as opposed to the *honzon*, the *besson* are "more dynamic and clearly gendered (sometimes even quite explicitly, like images of the goddess Benzaiten, whose unclothed body is distinctly feminine)" (Faure 1998b, 770). It seems clear that whoever created these famous images had little problem with depicting the human form in all its sensual glory.

Buddhism, Sex, and the Female Body

Students and practitioners of Buddhism in Western countries have long been informed that the Buddhist view of sex is that it is simply "no big deal" (e.g. Kornman 1999). Indeed, this is without a doubt one of the factors that drew so many young people to Buddhism (and Hinduism) in the '60s and '70s: the appeal of a religion that—so unlike Christianity—does not frown on sex, the body, or women.[6] Yet, in the case of the Buddha bikini, it so happens that a

Figure 4.3 Detail of wall painting from the Ajanta caves, Ajanta, India, *ca.* 6th century CE. Image used with permission.

Figure 4.4 Detail of yakshi on East Torana of Great Stupa, Sanchi, India, *ca.* 1st century BCE–1st century CE. Image used with permission.

Figure 4.5 Sculpture of yakshi at Srirangam Temple. Image used with permission.

number of complaints focused less on the general issue of the duplication or commercialization of sacred images discussed above than on the *sexualized context* of the images, in a double sense: as an advertisement in a highly "sexualized" swimsuit catalog; and as sacred icons that, in the advertisement itself (and, presumably, on the consumer who buys the item), are in direct contact with a naked female body—and more specifically, with the most "sexualized" parts of that body—breasts and crotch (Faure 1998b, 778).[7] Continuing a long and unfortunate, but nonetheless inescapable, history of misogyny in Asian Buddhist cultures, these body parts are continually referred to by critics of the bikini as "dirty," "impure," and "defiled." One well-meaning (but perhaps naïve) Western Buddhist critic of the Buddha bikini suggested that Victoria's Secret simply "apologize" by putting out another Buddha-theme swimsuit—albeit a more conservative one-piece with a single Buddha image over the heart.

Any serious study of Buddhism—whether Theravada, Zen, Pure Land, or even tantric—quickly complicates naïve, romanticized or simplistic assumptions about Buddhism, gender and sexuality (Paul 1985; Gross 1993; Faure 1998a; Young 2004). Despite the Ajanta Caves, early Buddhist writings tend to take a fairly dismissive view of sex and the body, which are more often than not viewed in terms of the attachment, suffering, and affliction that they can cause.[8] Early Buddhist attitudes towards the female body, in particular, are laced with ambiguities and ambivalence—with the textual tradition tending towards conservative attitudes ranging from mildly sexist or patriarchal to outright misogynist (Paul 1985).[9] While some of the ambivalence stems simply from the combination of a male-dominated *Sangha* (monastic assembly) that viewed sexuality itself—and female sexuality in particular—as a threat to spiritual progress, and a lack of specific prohibitions against women's capacity for awakening, it is also important to note the lingering effect of pre-Buddhist (or extra-Buddhist) notions of women as symbols of fertility and cosmic creativity. Though early Buddhists relegated this aspect to the material realm—for example, the striking images adorning the caves, as well as the sculptural *yakshi* adorning the early *stupa* (burial mound, or structure containing relics) gates—this powerful positive aspect of the Buddhist "feminine" reappears with a flourish in Tibetan tradition, with the Great Mother Tara, and also in the transformation of the Indian male bodhisattva Avalokiteshvara into the East Asian Guan Yin/Kannon.[10]

In general, there appears to be much more acceptance of the female body in Buddhist images than in texts. Besides the figures in Ajanta, a good number of Buddhist images in India and East Asia depict positive female spirits such as *apsaras*, *yakshis*, *tennin*, *naginis*, and *dakinis* (Young 2004, 12). *Dakinis*, in particular, are often depicted naked to represent the truth, and are described as "highly insightful females who often act as messengers, reminders, and revealers to the student of Vajrayana" (Gross 1993, 108–9).[11] Moreover, far from being passive objects of the male gaze, *dakinis*, like *yakshis*, have shape-shifting powers that they employ as a kind of iconographic *upaya* or "skillful means." As Young puts it: "They are in charge of their images, through which they assert their roles as the source of men's [and sometimes women's] enlightenment" (Young 2004, 129).

These are not atypical. South Asian Buddhist (and Hindu) sculpture abounds with voluptuous and scantily clad female forms, visions that understandably shocked the pants off Victorian missionaries to these heathen lands. While it may be countered that these are more often than not spatially—and thus symbolically—peripheral to early Buddhist sacred sites, another typical sculptural representation within early Buddhism is a tableau depicting the birth of the Buddha in which the Buddha's own mother, Queen Maya, is depicted as a *yakshi*—that is, a fertility spirit, nude, voluptuous, and life-giving.[12] This and other images of the Buddha's birth are particularly noteworthy for the tension that exists between the emphasis on women's bodies/fertility and a reluctance (reflected in the texts) to allow the pure Buddha baby to be born out of Maya's "defiled" womb—thus, in most images, the infant Siddhartha emerges out of her side or, in some East Asian cases (where nudity is less acceptable), the sleeve of her garment. In some early images, the artist has chosen not to bother with depicting the infant at all, so that the viewer's attention is fully focused on the body of Maya, flanked by her attendants (Young 2004, 24–41).[13]

Of course, modern feminists will have trouble swallowing the notion that the use of naked female bodies as fertility symbols is much of an advance in terms of religious egalitarianism, since such depictions may have the effect of relegating women to one particular aspect of life—however powerful or cosmically significant. Moreover, in Buddhist terms, it is hard to see such as anything less than a lingering essentialism regarding gender, however positively encoded.[14] And indeed, there is little evidence that such iconography had a role in supporting the spiritual advancement of actual Buddhist women. Yet the argument could be made that it is this symbolic power, located largely if not exclusively in early Buddhist iconography, that allowed for the emergence of strong female figures in Mahayana and Vajrayana devotion—Tara and Guan Yin—even while female bodies and sexuality remained as a "threat" within the most prominent early Buddhist texts.[15] In the Mahayana, images of women extend well beyond the "eternal feminine" triad of fertility, motherhood, and mercy to include bliss, instruction, friendship and, with the goddess Prajnaparamita, whose name implies the very "perfection of wisdom" itself, a goddess whose goal is to reveal this world for what it truly is. Not only is she lionized in the sutras as "the genetrix, the mother of all Buddhas" (*Perfection of Wisdom in 8000 Lines*, cited by Macy 1977), Prajnaparamita is also, according to Gross, the "desired lover" of the Mahayana practitioner (Gross 1993, 76–77).[16] Ironically, these more developed aspects of the Mahayana feminine ideal may have emerged precisely because both motherhood and fertility were largely confined in

Buddhism to the secular sphere. Indeed, as Paul notes, the great female characters of Mahayana literature are largely women who break with conventional social roles—nuns, of course, but also "married laywomen without children, prostitutes, or young unmarried women" (Paul 1985, 61).[17]

Once we move to the esoteric or tantric sects of Buddhism—found today mainly in the Himalayan countries of Tibet and Nepal, but also in Japanese Shingon—representations of the female body are taken well beyond the powerful but conceptually limited aspect of fertility. Tantric iconography is often explicitly sexual—most famously the *yabyum* embrace, which represents the union of male (compassion) and female (wisdom) principles.

Of course, such images are not *simply* erotic, but to imply, as most texts do, that they are *not erotic at all*, is to impose a conceptual dualism that is unwarranted.[18] What exactly is this category of the "erotic" that is presumably too shallow or frivolous to be associated with "serious" religious art? Esoteric Buddhism is quite clear in teaching that the passions can and should be cultivated and channeled towards enlightenment, and we should bear in mind that the images that adorn the Victoria's Secret Buddha bikini are clearly based on esoteric/tantric iconography. Although intentionality seemed to play a significant role in the criticism of the Buddha bikini, from a Buddhist perspective it is also important to note the way in which such images are understood and employed by the viewer. As Diana Paul rightly argues, "[i]n Buddhism both men and women were to regard evil as ignorance, a mental attitude. Evil was not an external object or force as it is in this text ['The Tale of King Udayana of Vatsa']. The concept of evil expressed in these verses consequently is not Buddhistic" (Paul 1985, 58 n. 68). Ultimately, as with so much else in Buddhism, their meaning is what we make of them.

A common theme among those who complained about the Buddha bikini was that there was no way that a company would even attempt to market a Jesus or Virgin Mary swimsuit. Yet, as we might expect from Moore's results on comparative religion in advertising, this is not the case. The following are just a sampling of items that can be purchased via the internet (Figure 4.6).

The thong gives us a fairly standard WASPy/kitsch image of Jesus (together with the motto "Jesus was a liberal Jew"). Also noteworthy in this regard was a 2001 controversy surrounding an art exhibition in Santa Fe, New Mexico, which displayed a small collage of the Virgin of Guadalupe in a bikini—a floral patterned one, no less—which, according to Roman Catholic Archbishop Michael Sheehan, made the Mother of God look "as if she were a tart" (Associated Press 2001).

Granted, this is a somewhat different issue, since it involves questions of the limits of art and free expression and has little to do with commercialization—yet it does bring together issues of sexuality, media, and religion, as well as help put to rest the argument that Westerners—some Westerners—would never treat Christian holy figures in a way that might be insensitive to Christians. Indeed, blasphemy is a staple subgenre of modern Western art,

Figure 4.6 Kalacakra in yabyum embrace with Visvamata, 17th century. Image used
with permission.

and recent studies of the use of religious motifs in US advertising indicate
that, if anything, Western religions are more likely to be mocked or derided
than their Eastern counterparts (Moore 2005).

More to the point, all this tit for tat betrays a highly questionable
assumption or set of assumptions: that the treatment of religious imagery
and icons is, or should be, equivalent across religions and cultures—and/or
that outsiders should treat the images of other faiths in ways equivalent to

how they treat their own, regardless of the status or use of these images in their respective traditions. Buddhism is a complex and multiform set of traditions, and there is certainly no single correct answer to the way a specific image should be treated—yet we are left with the problem of respect. How far do the media or companies need to go to refrain from hurting the feelings of others?

Gregory Levine has argued that one lesson of the Buddha bikini controversy is that we should be wary of accepting the "anything goes monoculture" that is being foisted upon us by the media and big business, lest we find ourselves sliding down a "slippery slope" of commercial exploitation (Levine 2005). While Levine has a point, I believe the nature of the responses to the Buddha bikini tells us as much about contemporary Buddhism—or should I say *Buddhisms*—as it does about contemporary consumer culture. For one, the legacy of misogyny—the fear, mistrust, and loathing of women's bodies and female sexuality—remains a deep if frequently unacknowledged element of Asian Buddhism. Second, like members of other world religions, modern Buddhists continue to struggle with issues of sacred representation in an age of consumerism and mechanical reproduction. And yet one unforeseen product of globalization may be a convergence of religious attitudes towards appropriate religious imagery, or perhaps a division that runs less along religious lines than between "liberals" and "conservatives" of all traditions. Third, for better or worse, Buddhists seem to have developed a global nonsectarian consciousness of being Buddhists—a sort of interlinked Buddhist *umma* (a Muslim term used to identify the entire Muslim community, in the broadest sense). How else can we account for the fact that the complaints about the Buddha bikini rolled in from virtually all Asian countries— even, or especially, those such as Vietnam and Thailand, whose Buddhist beliefs and iconographic traditions differ significantly from the tantrically inspired swimsuit?

Obviously, compared with more recent protests surrounding European cartoons of the Prophet Muhammad, the case of the Buddha bikini is relatively tame in that, as far as I am aware, no-one was physically injured, and Victoria's Secret's reputation was only slightly sullied, even if one Vietnamese– Canadian Buddhist made a veiled threat that the honchos at Victoria's Secret would ultimately suffer the same karmic fate as the Bamiyan Buddhadestroying Taliban. Yet the threats by Buddhist protesters were passionate and strongly-voiced, and the suffering caused by Victoria's Secret to many Buddhists was evident. In the end, the highly "postmodern" image of a sensually posed Western swimsuit model adorned with tantric Buddhist icons poses a challenge for scholars and lay Buddhists alike to rethink not only the limits of the public and commercialized use of religious symbols, but also conventional attitudes within Buddhist traditions towards sex and the female body. Along these lines, a comment by Bernard Faure serves as an apt conclusion to this essay:

Our use (or abuse) of these [non-Western] icons may be not only the unavoidable outcome of modern commodity fetishism but also part of a Western pragmatic which consists in installing cultural fragments in another context (Malraux's *musée imaginaire*), reinscribing them in another structure, and thus establishing another circulation of power.

(Faure 1998b, 811)

References

Alac, Patrik. 2002. *The Bikini: A Cultural History.* New York: Parkstone Press.

Aoyagi, Caroline. 2004. "Buddhists Decry Use of Bodhisattva Images on Swimwear." *IMDiversity.com*, May. www.imdiversity.com/Villages/Asian/arts_culture_media/archives/pc_buddha_swimwear_0504.asp

Associated Press. 2001. "N.M. Governor: Bikini-clad Virgin Mary Should Stay on Display." 9 April. [Posted online by the Freedom Forum First Amendment Center: www.freedomforum.org/templates/document.asp?documentID=13636]

Associated Press. 2004. "Thailand Blasts Victoria's Secret for New Buddha Swimsuit," ReligionNewsBlog.com, April 21. www.religionnewsblog.com/6886/thailand-blasts-victorias-secret-for-new-buddha-swimsuit

Bays, Gwendolyn (trans.). 1983. *The Voice of the Buddha: The Beauty of Compassion (*Lalitavistara*).* Oakland, CA: Dharma Press.

Blair, Jessica Dawn, Jason Duane, Stephenson, Kathy L. Hill, and John S. Green. 2006. "Ethics in Advertising: Sex Sells, but Should it?" *Journal of Legal, Ethical and Regulatory Issues* 9: 1–2.

Cebrzynski, Gregg. 2000. "Sex or Sexy? The Difference is that One Sells, and the Other Doesn't." *Nation's Restaurant News* 34, 11: 14.

Coomaraswamy, Ananda K. 1927. "The Origin of the Buddha Image." *Art Bulletin* 9, 4: 287–328.

Dehejia, Vidya. 1990. "Aniconism and the Multivalence of Emblems." *Ars Orientalis* 21: 45–66.

Falk, Nancy. 1974. "An Image of Women in Old Buddhist Literature—the Daughters of Mara." In *Women and Religion*, eds Judith Plaskow and Joan Arnold Ramura, 105–12. Missoula, MT: Scholar's Press.

Faure, Bernard. 1991. *The Rhetoric of Immediacy: A Cultural Critique of Chan/Zen Buddhism.* Princeton, NJ: Princeton University Press.

——. 1996. *Visions of Power: Imagining Medieval Japanese Buddhism.* Princeton, NJ: Princeton University Press.

——. 1998a. *The Red Thread: Buddhist Approaches to Sexuality.* Princeton, NJ: Princeton University Press.

——. 1998b. "The Buddhist Icon and the Modern Gaze." *Critical Inquiry* 24, 3 (Spring): 768–813.

Foucher, Alred. 1917. *The Beginnings of Buddhist Art and Other Essays in Indian and Central-Asian Archaeology.* Paris: Paul Geuthner.

Gombrich, Richard. 1966. "The Consecration of a Buddhist Image." *Journal of Asian Studies* 26: 23–36.

——. 1971. *Precept and Practice: Traditional Buddhism in the Rural Highlands of Ceylon.* Oxford: Clarendon Press.

Gross, Rita M. 1993. *Buddhism After Patriarchy: A Feminist History, Analysis, and Reconstruction of Buddhism*. Albany, NY: State University of New York Press.

Harvey, Peter. 2000. *An Introduction to Buddhist Ethics: Foundations, Values and Issues*. Cambridge: Cambridge University Press.

Huntingdon, Susan L. 1990. "Early Buddhist Art and the Theory of Aniconism." *Art Journal* 49 (Winter): 401–8.

Keown, Damien. 1992. *The Nature of Buddhist Ethics*. London: Macmillan.

Kornman, Robin. 1999. "Sex & Buddhism: No Big Deal." *Shambala Sun* (July): 40–41, 75.

Le, Lotus. n.d. "Victoria Secret's Lack of Respect for Religion." *PetitionOnline.com*. www.petitiononline.com/VSlotus/petition.html

Leach, Edmund R. 1983. "The Gatekeepers of Heaven: Anthropological Aspects of Grandiose Architecture." *Journal of Anthropological Research* 39 (Fall): 244.

Levine, Gregory. 2005. Remarks on a panel entitled "Buddhism Sells: Buddhist Concepts and Images in American Advertising," given at the Center for Buddhist Studies/Institute of East Asian Studies Conference entitled "Speaking for the Buddha? Buddhism and the Media," University of California, Berkeley, February 8–9.

Macy, Joanna Rogers. 1977. "Perfection of Wisdom: Mother of all Buddhas." In *Beyond Androcentrism: New Essays on Women and Religion*, ed. Rita M. Gross, 243–60. Missoula, MT: Scholars Press.

Moore, Rick Clifton. 2005. "Spirituality that Sells: Religious Imagery in Magazine Advertising." *Advertising & Society Review* 6, 1.

Mus, Paul. 1935. *Barabudur: Esquisse d'une histoire du bouddhisme fondée sur la critique archéologique des textes*. Paris: l'École Français d'Extrême Orient.

Paul, Diana. 1985. *Women in Buddhism: Images of the Feminine in the Mahayana Tradition*. Foreword by I. B. Horner. Berkeley, CA: Asian Humanities Press.

Richmond, D. and T. Hartman. 1982. "Sex Appeal in Advertising." *Journal of Advertising* 19, 1: 14–22.

Snellgrove, David L., ed. 1978. *The Image of the Buddha*. Paris: UNESCO.

Strasburg, Jenny. 2002. "Abercrombie & Glitch: Asian Americans Rip Retailer for Stereotypes on T-shirts." *San Francisco Chronicle* 18 April: A1. http://articles. sfgate.com/2002-04-18/news/17540580_1_abercrombie-fitch-t-shirt-wong-brothers-laundry-service/2

Taylor, Charles. 2007. *The Secular Age*. Cambridge, MA: Belknap Press.

Twitchell, James B. 1996. *Adcult: The Triumph of Advertising in American Culture*. New York: Columbia University Press.

Young, Serinity. 2004. *Courtesans and Tantric Consorts: Sexualities in Buddhist Narrative, Iconography, and Ritual*. New York & London: Routledge.

Notes

1 This is a revised version of a paper delivered at "World's Religions after September 11: A Global Congress," Montréal, Québec, September 15, 2006.

2 Despite the title of this article, the item in question is not actually a bikini but rather a tankini—a combination of a traditional bikini bottom and a tank top. Having noticed the Indian-sounding lilt of the word tankini, I broke the word down into its Sanskrit roots to discover that *tan* implies "to stretch," while *kini*,

meaning "dancer," forms the base of the word *dakini*, defined as "a supernatural female with volatile temperament who serves as a muse for spiritual practice." Though purely coincidental, this fortuitous etymological link provides an auspicious entry into some of the historical and iconographic issues at stake here. Citing corporate policy, Limited Brands—the parent company of Victoria's Secret—refused to grant permission to reproduce an image of the tankini in this article. However, a simple online image search ("Buddha bikini") will produce images used across the Web, presumably without permission. See, for example, Associated Press (2004), reprinted on ReligionNewsBlog.com on April 21, 2004.

3 This and other similar comments were taken from the "Buddhist News Network," an online discussion located at www.buddhist news.tv/current/bikini-reaction-230404.php. This link no longer works; it seems the Buddhist News Network is now "The Buddhist Channel" and located at http://buddhistchannel.tv. Unfortunately, the comments related to this story have been eliminated from the site. A petition posted on PetitionOnline.com (Lotus Le, n.d.) titled "Victoria's Secret Lack of Respect for Religion" reads [original text remains unedited]:

To: Victoria Secret, President & CEO

We are shocked and disturb at Victoria Secret's recent line of graphic swim wear. We are absolutely stunned to find the Buddha and Bodhisattvas images, two of the most revered Buddhas, were printed on swimming suits in the Victoria Secrets Catalog, name : "The Hot Issue swim 2004 Mexico", item name: "Asian Floral Tankini" and item number: IR 173–444. Displaying the images of the Buddha and Bodhisattvas on the swim suite currently markets through Victoria Secret Catalog is an appalling and serious insult to all Buddhism believers, not just in America, but also to over 500 hundred million Buddhists around the world. The lacking of respect for religion, as Victoria Secret has shown, also could be leading to a very regretful outcome while America, as a nation, is more than ever needing a united and determined effort for a religious tolerance and harmony. We understand fashion is made creatively; however it should never be permitted to make contempt of any religion. Let's think of an ending if Victoria Secrets Catalog has used the spiritual founders other than Buddhas on the same swim suite. A simple ignorance, in many cases, would cause a mankind disaster. Considering the blatant lack of respect, we must then question the sensitivity and intelligence of every employee at every level responsible for designing and marketing the swim wear. We are forming this petition to let Victoria Secret and all other companies know how much business you can lose through religion insensitivity, not only from Asian American consumers but from all Americans with a social conscience. To help restore a mutual understanding and respect for religion, we truthfully ask Victoria Secret to immediately stop distributing the catalog, remove the product from the market, and recall all sold items. Victoria Secret's promotion of Buddha images on their products, not only shows lack of respect for religion, but shows ignorant of history and is highly offensive.

Sincerely,

The Undersigned

As of January 10, 2008, there were a total of 10,587 signatories to this petition.

4 In the ad, Chinese characters to the left (somewhat obscured by the words "Buddha Bash") can be loosely translated as "dangerous or indecent young woman"—or, perhaps more fittingly, given the alternative meaning of the first glyph as "festival"—"party girl."

5 Patrik Alac gives the following "definition" of a bikini: "The bikini is a bathing costume that is narrow and in two parts, of a maximum area of 7 square inches (45 square centimetres), and not specifically intended for bathing. It can be sold in a matchbox, or folded easily into a handbag compact. It represents clothing for a woman such that she does not feel completely naked, yet leaves her sufficiently undressed to be irresistibly attractive to men" (Alac 2002, 16).

6 As is often the case with such interreligious comparisons—especially, though not exclusively, at the popular level—analysis of sexuality and gender issues in Buddhism is distorted by blindness to the forces of history and societal context. Whereas Western religions tend to be (negatively) judged in terms of actual history and "facts on the ground," Buddhism is (positively) appraised by virtue of its ideals and certain decontextualized texts.

7 Faure cites Edmund Leach, for whom "works of art are not just things in themselves, they are objects carrying moral implications. What the moral implication is depends upon where they are" (Leach 1983, 244). As such, Faure argues, "what we call the loss of aura results in this case from the displacement of the icon from its religious context and not merely, as Walter Benjamin argued, from mechanical reproduction" (Faure 1998b, 778). The images on the Buddha bikini are, in a quite literal sense "profaned" (Latin *profanum*, to be placed outside the temple).

8 "The body, born from the field of karma, issuing from the water of desire, is characterized by decay. Disfigured by tears and sweat, by saliva, urine, and blood, filled with filth from the belly, with marrow, blood, and liquids from the brain, always letting impurities flow—bodies are the abode of impure teachings and ugly stenches ... Having seen this, what wise man would not look upon his own body as an enemy?" *Lalitavistara* (Bays 1983, 314–15).

9 Paul repeats the common criticism (e.g. in Falk 1974) that early Indian Buddhism in particular holds a misogynist view of women as temptresses of monks, a view that Rita Gross (1993, 44–48) sees as "quite one-sided and incomplete," in that the fear of sexual temptation on the part of all Buddhist monastics—whether monks or nuns—goes beyond a simple association with women and women's bodies. According to Gross: "When the various stories of attempted seduction and temptation are analyzed, many variants and motifs, rather than a single theme of misogyny, emerge." Gross concludes that while traditional Buddhism is undoubtedly androcentric, "it is not especially misogynist" (*ibid.*, 119).

10 Interestingly, in her discussion of Falk's assertion of the "negative feminine principle" of early Indian Buddhism, Gross neglects the sculptural tradition in which positive and presumably archetypal female forms abound (see Young, 2004, xxi). In suggesting, *contra* Falk, that "the kind of archetypal, mythic and symbolic thinking that is so much a part of the feminine principle is entirely foreign to the thinking of early Indian Buddhism," Gross seems to be privileging the textual tradition over that of early Buddhist material culture—or perhaps making an implicit assumption that material culture or ritual is not related to "thinking" (Gross 1993, 48).

11 Gross notes that *dakinis* are not simply a focus for male spiritual advancement, but can be—and are—frequently encountered by women as well. Also see Young 2004, 142, 224–25. Steven Hodge notes "The gloss (lit. Sky Dancer) is given for Dakini. This is inaccurate though very loosely based on the Tibetan translation of the term, *mkha'-gro-ma*, she who travels the sky. However, this rendering is based on a false Sanskrit etymology for an Indic word which is probably of Munda

origin. It is likely that dakinis were originally tribal shamanesses who chanted, drummed and invoked spirits as suggested by cognate words" ["Talk: Dakini (Buddhism)." *Wikipedia*, 01:19, April 25, 2005. http://en.wikipedia.org/wiki/Talk: Dakini(Buddhism).]

12 "Casting Queen Maya in this pose directly connects her with these powers [of fertility], and it incorporates these chthonic powers into Buddhism. Statues and carvings of Maya, *yakshis*, and similar female images were included to empower early Buddhist sites with their auspiciousness. Consequently, these images are all about womanliness: they have large, full breasts and broad curving hips that stress fertility and stimulate male desire. They are a celebration of female biology, but they also carry powerful religious meanings as bestowers of fertility and wealth in all its forms" (Young 2004, 30).

13 In distinction from Gross, Young's analysis of the early Indian sculptural tradition allows her to posit a strong link between early Indian Buddhist traditions and later tantric affirmations of female sexuality (Young 2004, 113–14).

14 At another level, as Faure (1998b, 787) suggests, such images may be as much the product of individual male fantasies as of a more generalized (and academically rendered) social imaginary.

15 "Fools lust for women / like dogs in heat. / They do not know abstinence. / They are also like flies / who see vomited food. / Like a herd of hogs, / They greedily seek manure. / Women can ruin / The precepts of purity. / They can also ignore / Honor and virtue. / Causing one to go to hell / They prevent rebirth in heaven. / Why should the wise / Delight in them?" ("The Tale of King Udayana of Vatsu" ["*Udayanavatsarajaparivartah*"], *The Collection of Jewels* [*Maharatnakuta*], assembly 29. T. v. 11. N. 310, pp. 543–47).

16 This process of liberation may be said to culminate in the *Vimalikirti Sutra*, in which Shariputra is reproved by the goddess for his blindness regarding gender essences: "I have been here for twelve years and have looked for the innate characteristics of the female sex and haven't been able to find them" (Goddess chapter, *Vimalakirti-nirdesa-sutra*, quoted by Paul 1985, 230).

17 Most famous of the Mahayana prostitutes is of course Vasumitra of the Flower Garland and Harmony of the Young Sapling sutras, who uses her physical charms as an *upaya* (skillful means, as in doing whatever it takes to bring about awakening) for the awakening and merit of the various beings who approach her. She is "beautiful, serene, and fair to behold … Her hair was very black and her complexion golden. Her form in every limb and all limbs together were well proportioned. The glorious beauty of her features, form, complexion, and color exceeded that of celestial and human beauty in all the realms of desire" (Paul 1985, 159; also see Faure 1998a, 121).

18 As Faure notes, even if we grant that tantric images should be seen as "merely a symbolic expression of the philosophical 'conjunction of opposites' … it is obviously clear that such dialectical images lend themselves to a multitude of interpretations." Furthermore, along with other motifs such as that of Guan Yin as a prostitute, such "sexualized" images "must have had a power of arousal that we no longer suspect" (Faure 1998b, 787).

Part II

Popular ritual

When does eating become a ritual? Certainly when it occurs in a religious context, like a Passover *seder*, and also, most would probably agree, when it is part of secular family and cultural celebrations, like Thanksgiving. We might even see ritual in the intensely personal and carefully choreographed food manipulation of the anorexic. In Chapter 5, Wade Clark Roof suggests that we might also find ritual, with all its powerful religious undertones, in the preparation, consumption, and celebration of pork barbecue in the "pig-loving" American South. If this is so—if the most (apparently) mundane visit to the neighborhood barbecue joint can be said to bear transcendent meaning—it would seem that nothing is safe from the ritual theorist's gaze.

And this is perhaps as it should be. For while many Americans have loosened their ties to organized religious institutions, they do not seem have lost their need for ritualized meaning-making activity; rather, they've relocated it to places like athletic fields and art festivals. While the contributors to this section might not agree on what exactly constitutes ritual behavior, religious or otherwise, they uncover several themes in their explorations of the ritual dimension of popular culture that collectively point to both the permanent power of ritual and its unique place in contemporary America.

The first of these themes is the power of ritual to define a space and/or time set apart from daily experience, a kind of sacred setting where issues of ultimate concern come into focus. Churches and temples are such places, as are Native American sweat lodges, the holy sites of Mecca, and the River Ganges. So, too, one could argue, are Graceland and the Vietnam Memorial. This notion of ritual as the encounter with sacred space and time is powerfully evoked in Sarah Pike's Chapter 8, on the Burning Man festival held annually in the Nevada desert. In this three-day extravaganza of ironic art and alternative community, Pike sees a group of people making a pilgrimage to a place so removed from ordinary life that radical experimentation with self and community becomes possible. Through symbolic city-making, body-marking, various forms of ritualistic art, and chronologizing that defines events in relation to the festival (pre-Burning Man and post-Burning Man), festival participants act out what historian of religion Mircea

Eliade identified a generation ago as a fundamental need of the religious person—to periodically reimmerse him/herself into a time and place perceived as eternal and indestructible (*The Sacred and the Profane*, 1959). It turns out that may be a need shared by many ostensibly nonreligious Americans as well.

In a setting so different that it makes the mind reel, Jennifer Rycenga (Chapter 7) finds at the Precious Moments Chapel in Carthage, Missouri, at Christmastime, a ritualized space that fosters "total absorption in the 'holiday spirit,' centered around buying and selling." The demarcation of sacred space and time may be less evident in considerations of southern barbecue and professional sports, but in these, too, we can see the marks of ritualized time and space. The almost taboo aura of the barbecue pit, the power of the barbecue joint to break down powerful regional social boundaries, as Roof describes it, and the evocation of centuries-old African American religious expression in black athletes' pre-game rituals, slam dunks, and end-zone dances—all of these indicate that in these settings, too, participants have stepped out of ordinary time and space into another world, where different rules inhere and new possibilities emerge.

In a multiethnic and religiously diverse society like the United States (which of course includes a huge portion of purportedly nonreligious people), the sacredness of certain times and spaces is not a given, as it is, say, for the Catholic in Rome during Holy Week or the Jew in Jerusalem during Yom Kippur. It is an interesting feature of the American religious landscape that while in traditional religious experience, the space and time themselves create the sense of the sacred for the participant, in the secular spaces and times considered here, participants imbue the sites with meaning through their own ritualized actions. By reference to powerful experiences or deeply held values—whether national, regional, subcultural, or even purely personal—places like sports arenas, an anonymous and barren piece of the Nevada desert, and even a local restaurant can become sites of intense ritual meaning.

A second theme that surfaces repeatedly in these analyses of popular ritual is that of transformation. Set off as they are from everyday existence, these rituals, like their traditional religious counterparts, apparently create a space in which personal and sometimes collective change can occur. In his influential work on ritual, anthropologist Victor Turner focused on the transformative nature of ritual, especially rites of passage and their power to move an individual from one social status to another. While none of the events described by our authors would typically be called a rite of passage, they do share this transformative power.

According to Turner, subjects involved in ritual transformation pass through a liminal phase in which the structures of the society are temporarily suspended, even upended and mocked, and where intense experiences of *communitas*, or a sense of communion of equal individuals, occur among participants. This kind of liminality is clearly evident in Pike's description of the Burning Man festival (Chapter 8), where every imaginable aspect of contemporary American culture (and especially its institutional religions) is lampooned. But Pike's analysis of post-Burning Man reports on internet bulletin boards suggests that this play is actually part of a serious ritual restructuring of identity. Many festival-goers describe finding their true selves and their true "homes" in this stripped-down but wildly imaginative desert setting. Burning Man is also, Pike indicates, a place of potential social transformation, where utopian visions of a society—defined by all of that which (in the participants' view) strait-laced, consumerist, Christian America is *not*—can be imagined and briefly experienced.

But it's not always this dramatic. To identify ritual as a site of transformation is simply to note that we are somehow *different* after partaking in the ritual from how we were when it began. Southerners might find that ties of family, church, and geography feel a little stronger following a shared barbecue supper. An African American aesthetic might find itself a little more fully integrated into mass media culture after the ritualized gestures of LeBron James are taken up by Nike ads.

In traditional religious ritual, the safe release of antistructural (playful, nonhierarchical, anti-authoritarian, subversive) energy is contained within the ritual action, and the rules and status systems governing the way things are normally done re-emerge intact at the other end of the ritual process. Mardi Gras, the traditional reveler knew, would inevitably be followed by Ash Wednesday. In this way, the release ultimately serves to strengthen that which it ritually challenges. Whether or not the secular rituals of popular culture similarly reinforce the structures of the wider society or whether they might, at least in some cases, more radically alter the inherited cultural system is an interesting question raised by the studies in this section. Does Burning Man's revolutionary art yield any lasting social or personal change? Does the blood ritual of barbecue have any real "jollifying" impact on the sober Protestantism of the South? It is tempting to argue that ritual divorced from the doctrines and institutions of organized religion has more potential for lasting subversive impact, as illustrated, for instance, in Vernon Andrews' analysis of the transgressive rituals of black sportsmanship and their effects on the dominant culture (Chapter 6). But it is evident that many secular rituals can also have profoundly conservative effects. Pilgrimage to the Precious Moments chapel at Christmastime is nothing, Rycenga tells us, if not a festal reauthorization of "patriotism, patriarchy, respect for authority, and Christian exclusivism."

It is also important to note that these secular rituals are bound up with a different kind of structure, that of commercial enterprise. It may be that the commodification that attends these rituals (even, increasingly, Burning Man) works as its own kind of damper on the antistructural force of the ritual. In places like the Precious Moments Chapel (ironically the only site considered here with explicit religious content), the intersection of ritual and commerce is shamelessly displayed, and antistructural forces stand no chance at all. On the other hand, as noted above, it is the mass media's embrace of such ritualizing gestures as LeBron James' pre-game powder toss that has, according to Andrews, advanced the normalization of black expressivity in American society.

A third theme these chapters raise is the way in which ritual of all kinds both exposes and helps resolve conflicts of various sorts. There are tensions involved in even the most carefully scripted religious rituals, as theorists have pointed out for nearly a century. The moment when an adolescent undergoes the rite of passage into adulthood, for instance, is fraught with tensions surrounding changes in sexual and social status. The threat those tensions pose, in fact, can be seen as a primary explanation for the closely controlled action of ritual. It is as if the repeated words, the predictable action, and the familiarity of the ritual acts offer a safe and comfortable route through crisis situations. One way of thinking about ritual, then, is as an organized set of behaviors that both heighten and ultimately help to resolve, or at least diffuse, the conflicts that threaten personal and collective life.

In each chapter in this section, the authors see powerful conflicts crystallized in ritualized actions. In Andrews' discussion, the tension arises from conflicting cultural codes expressed in professional sports. Andrews argues that what many white observers (and rule-makers) deride as crass self-aggrandizing displays on the part of some black athletes are actually ritual affirmations of communal identity with deep roots in the black church. Roof's treatment of southern barbecue sees it as a culinary resolution of the intracultural conflict between the "two cultures" of the American South—one folk, kin-based, and sensuous; the other official, ecclesial, and ascetic. The Burning Man festival, according to Pike, exposes and struggles with the conflicts between radically individual self-expression and the quest for a community of common ideals. Making a Christmas journey to the gift shop-encased Precious Moments Chapel, Rycenga argues, helps devotees to maneuver among some powerful conflicts—Christian piety and consumerism; the efficiency of mass production and the desire for the singular; American individualism and an interdependent economic system. By "acting out" their habitual norms in these formalized ways, partakers in these secular rituals are working out (sometimes consciously, sometimes not) significant conflicts that are engendered by, but unresolvable within, the structures of regular existence. Conflict is inherent in all religious ritual, but it offers an especially useful interpretive key to ritual in American culture, where so many conflicting worldviews and identities intersect.

A final theme suggested by these case studies of secular ritual is not only the diversity of contemporary American ritual, but also the diversity of meanings attached to ritual activity when it operates independently of religious structures. Divorced from the specific mythic narratives that accompany much of traditional religious ritual, activities like these take on as many meanings as they have participants, for while the scholars here have all hazarded interpretations of what these activities "mean," they all also suggest how fluid and multivocal those meanings are. This may suggest that when it comes to ritual, the doing is more important than the interpreting; that is, it is possible to come together in organized, deeply meaningful activity with those for whom that meaning is significantly different. It may be that the need for communion in so large, diverse, and fragmented a society as the United States feeds the ritual impulse and draws us together into shared acts of eating, dancing, spectating, and buying, so that even if we can't agree on what we believe, we can at least feel that, for a few moments anyway, we all hold on to a slim thread of communal life.

Chapter 5

Blood in the Barbecue?

Food and Faith in the American South

Wade Clark Roof

Anyone growing up in the American South, or even a visitor just traveling through the region, knows that barbecue and Dixie go together like honey and flies. No other food is so distinctively southern, as obvious in the signs seemingly everywhere for barbecue, or simply BBQ, posted on billboards, the sides of buildings, and menus of restaurants, cafés, and honkytonks scattered from Mississippi to Virginia. By barbecue, I mean mainly pork (but it can include beef and chicken) cooked slowly and basted often with carefully prepared sauces; hence the word as southerners use it refers both to the food and its style of preparation. Anything less is not barbecue; indeed, southerners bristle when outsiders casually talk of barbecuing but really mean just grilling burgers or throwing some chicken legs on a burner. To defame the word *barbecue* in this way is not just a sign of ignorance, but a violation of a sacred regional norm.

In this chapter, I look at barbecue as a deeply embedded symbol in southern culture. Food symbols are important in any culture; more than just an object of curiosity or taste, they are bound up with a people's way of life, their deepest values and identities. That being the case, food symbols inevitably are implicated in religious and political matters. In fact, I shall argue that barbecue—and especially barbecue pork—is of crucial symbolic significance for the South, for both its unity of experience and cultural distinctiveness as a region.

Barbecue as Symbol

Why single out pork barbecue? It could be argued that barbecue is a national food today, particularly at truck stops across the country. Yet it is also true that regional preferences remain deeply embedded when it comes to the choice of meat: pork is preferred east of the Mississippi; beef in the cattle country and in the West (Fabricant 1996). And nowhere is there as much variety in eating pork as found in the South. Southerners like pork fixed in endless ways, be it chicken-fried pork chops, cracklins or pork rinds, pickled pigs' feet and snouts, sausage, ham, or bacon, but mainly it's pork barbecued—whether chopped or pulled or sliced or made into hash—that they like the most. Indeed, hash in many southern towns has lost its generic meaning as a type of food; the term refers simply to a pork dish served on rice, alongside a bountiful supply of slaw and pickles. And then there are ribs. Mouth-watering ribs basted with a home-made sauce and dry rubbed to seal in the juices, cooked with dry, cool smoke—for this there is no substitute this side of heaven.

Like any food that becomes so much a part of the culture, pork in the South is more than just the meat of choice. It's a fundamental symbol whose meanings penetrate deep into the region's way of life. Evidence for this is apparent even in the sheer number and types of signs for pigs, in one form or another, found all over the South. Well-known observer of southern culture, sociologist John Shelton Reed of the University of North Carolina at Chapel Hill, writes:

> For years I've kept a mental log of barbecue joint signs. I've seen pigs reclining, running, and dancing; pigs with bibs, with knives and forks, with crowns and scepters. I've seen pigs as beauty contest winners, pigs in Confederate uniforms, and pigs in cowboy hats (one with a banjo). I've seen Mr. and Mrs. Pig dressed for a night on the town, and Mr. and Mrs. Pig as American Gothic. But I've never seen pigs like I saw in Memphis. Pigs in chess hats and volunteer firemen's helmets. A pig in a Superman suit rising from the flames. A pig reclining in a skillet; another on a grill, drinking beer. Two pigs basting a little gnomish person on a spit, and (on the T shirts of a team called the Rowdy Southern Swine) a whole trainload of partying pigs. It's a hard call, but my favorite was probably some pigs with wings and haloes, from a team called Hog Heaven.
>
> (Reed 1995, 148)

Pigs are extraordinarily versatile: they can be dressed in popular garb to fit any audience—working-class, middle-class, or upper-class—no matter how formal or informal the occasion. The animal takes on almost totemic proportions, as anyone knows who has ever heard University of Arkansas Razorback football fans chant, calling the hogs—WooooOOOOOOOOOOOO! Pig! Suuuuuuuuuueeeeeeeeeeee! And like any symbol as pervasive as this one, it serves to bring southerners together around celebrations and common activities. Few other places in the South enjoy as much joviality, sociality, and sharing as do those places where pig symbols are displayed. Like in any liminal moment or setting, old boundaries tend to lose force and a new basis of social solidarity emerges. To quote John Shelton Reed (1995, 47) again: "A good barbecue joint may be the one place you'll find Southerners of all descriptions—yuppies, hippies, and cowboys, Christians and sinners, black and white together."

Of course, Reed is speaking about barbecue in the New South, where increasing numbers of southerners (both old-timers and newcomers) find a pig sign more acceptable than a Dixie flag. Southerners of late have been hunting for a new regional emblem, and the pig ranks high on that list. The fact that pigs and barbecue have all gone mainstream in recent times helps— Memphis has its World Championship Barbecue Cooking Contest; Hillsboro, North Carolina, its annual Hillsboro Hog Day; Climax, Georgia, its Climax Swine Time; and not to be overlooked, there's the Chitlin Strut in Salley, South Carolina. These aren't just commercial ventures to attract tourists, efforts at trading on southern tradition for hungry outsiders (though southerners aren't averse to making a little money on it); they are symbolic markers of sorts, reminding a changing, expanding world of the continuing importance of barbecue. The fact that southern barbecue is now exported to other regions of the country reinforces the need for dramatizing its symbolic presence and significance within the homeland. If nothing more, it reminds people who live in the South and those who grew up there of a reality that borders on the timeless. Upscale magazines like *Southern Living* do their part, as well, to package barbecuing as a southern fine art. These magazines regularly carry recipes for suave, middle-class southerners interested in advancing the skills of making good sauces and concocting new culinary delights like "cheesy barbecue popcorn." Hence barbecue—replacing grits—emerges as the symbol of a new, more prosperous and respectable South.

But these celebrations and upscale recipes notwithstanding, the real meaning of barbecue in the South lies in its more traditional setting—in the joints and shacks where most of it is still served, close to the pits where it is cooked. Largely a male enterprise, barbecuing in this context has long signaled an ordered world of social patterns and activities. Anthropologist Mary Douglas (1972, 61) writes: "If food is treated as a code, the message it encodes will be found in the pattern of social relations being expressed. The message is about different degrees of hierarchy, inclusion and exclusion, boundaries and transactions across boundaries. Food categories therefore encode social events." One could not find a better example in the South of what Douglas has in mind than with the preparation and serving of that most favorite of foods—pit-barbecued pork and the "fixins."

In a basic sort of way, eating barbecue defines a southerner. This is true not just in the sense of "you are what you eat," which of course is to some extent true, but also in the sense that groups are known by their food habits. Especially in a region with so distinct a consciousness of itself as being over against others—in-group versus out-group—foodways function as a symbol of group identity. The practices surrounding even the homeliest and most mundane of food easily emerge as significant. Barbecue pork is just such a homely and mundane food, long serving as a visible boundary distinguishing southerners from other Americans. That boundary has not disappeared; if anything, it may have become even more visible as southern-style barbecue has spread across the country, creating a space for southern culture in the most alien places—like Yankee territory. The boundary is increasingly tied less to physical space, and more to the presence of southerners wherever they live. Both within the region and outside of it, southerners continue to relish being different, even to the extreme of boasting about it, as we know from bumper stickers proclaiming that "Southerners do it slower" or, as in Hank Williams's classic lyric, "If heaven ain't a lot like Dixie, I don't want anything to do with it." Moreover, the fact that such bumper stickers show up in great numbers on cars, pickups, and vans outside barbecue joints where Hank Williams's music still plays on jukeboxes underscores something of Mary Douglass's point about food categories encoding social realities.

Certainly for the major social institutions of southern life, barbecue is very much at the center of action. For example, it continues to be the favorite food at political rallies. Democrats and Republicans, and nowadays mostly Republicans, routinely hold political events featuring barbecue—often chopped pork with hash, rice, slaw, and hush puppies. That tradition reaches far back into the past. Even as far back as the election of 1832, the *Louisville Journal* reported that "swallowing a pig" was an effective technique in winning the voter's favor (Remini 1971). Then, as now, eating dramatizes and enacts fundamental cultural values—it combines taste with rhetoric and conveys not just what is good to eat, but what people feel about how things are going on the farm, in the town, for themselves, and for the larger world. Even more important, for southerners a political rally with barbecue bonds the group and symbolizes a world governed by law and order. It communicates something of the sacred and the profane, the two at some point juxtaposed against one another. The most profane of things, as Emile Durkheim reminds us, has the capacity to evoke the presence of the sacred; and conversely, that which is regarded as sacred mingles freely in and around the profane. In many rural areas and small towns, radios still carry, often at noontime, daily reports on local stock prices interspersed with Gospel music—"hogs and hymns," as we called it in South Carolina when I was growing up. The latest prices on hogs and cattle come together with inspirational and country music, and often a political commentary, in what amounts to a mediated ritual of southern identity and celebration.

God approves of barbecue, or so it would seem considering the thousands of church cookbooks published across the region. Just about every First Presbyterian church has a cookbook and, for sure, the biggest Southern Baptist and United Methodist churches in every city have one, and all have recipes for barbecue sauces. Often the recipes are personalized, such as "Miss Maggie Clark's BBQ Sauce" with instructions about how to prepare it. It is common for such information—the "esoteric knowledge" of barbecuing—to come from someone who is widely known and respected within a church, and often it has been handed down from a master cook from a previous generation. The church supper is of course the occasion *par excellence* for eating barbecue, symbolizing a shared religious and social world and communal belonging. Both the frequency of church suppers and the attention given to food in religious gatherings for southerners point to the symbolic significance of food. The meal mediates between the individual and the community and serves as a ritual affirmation of the gathered community itself. Because both the political and religious institutions are closely identified with the same food—with barbecue pork and fried chicken, the latter being the second best-known food of the region—the two institutions themselves are closely linked symbolically. It might even be said that, for many southern churchgoers, food is a key ingredient in ordering and sustaining a phenomenological world bringing the religious and political together.

Barbecue and Sacrifice

Links between food and religion run deep in any culture—provoking powerful religious emotions associated with food. Pigs especially seem to evoke strong religious emotions. So strong, anthropologist Marvin Harris suggests, that the world can be divided into two types of people, pig lovers and pig haters. Pig hating among Jews and Muslims is well known, but pig loving is common as well, particularly in Celtic cultures. Pig hating and pig loving differ in how they symbolize relations between people and food. Pig hate leads to carefully prescribed dietary regulations and food prohibitions. Here the pig symbolizes those boundaries with a taboo-like quality: don't eat, don't touch. Pig love arouses a more mystical, unifying experience, a bringing together of the people world and the animal world. Its power to solidify is astounding, shown by Harris to work its magic in many cultures. "Pig love," he writes (Harris 1974, 46) "is a state of total community between man and pig. While the presence of pigs threatens the human status of Muslims and Jews, in the ambience of pig love one cannot truly be human except in the company of pigs." Hence, not surprisingly, in those places around the world where you find pig love, you also observe close contact of people and pigs: people often have pigs in pens adjacent to where they live, sometimes even in barns attached to human dwellings. It is not uncommon for people to talk to their pigs, to call them by names; people will feed them from the family table—"slopping," as people below the Mason and Dixon are fond of saying, meaning that they care so much for their choice swine they share with them their own leftover human food. Obviously, southerners are pig lovers.

Given this close association with pigs, we can speak, not inappropriately, of the "cult of the pig" in the South. And unlike in India in the case of cows, the veneration of the pig results in obligatory sacrifices and celebratory occasions for eating pigs. To quote Marvin Harris again:

Because of ritual slaughter and sacred feasting, pig love provides a broader prospect for communion between man and beast than is true of the Hindu farmer and his cow. The climax of pig love is the incorporation of the pig as flesh into the flesh of the human host and of the pig as spirit into the spirit of the ancestors.

(ibid., 46)

Communion with pigs! Obviously there's something deeply mystical about such communion binding pig lovers and their pigs. And it doesn't take a great deal of imagination to leap from this depiction of incorporating the pig as flesh to the high and holy act of eating the body and blood of Christ as practiced by Christians. In a region where there is both so much pig love *and* Christ love, and frequent eating of the flesh of both kinds, might there be an affinity between these two sacred feasts? Might there be blood in the barbecue, so to speak?

The South's "Two Cultures"

The question is not as far-fetched as it might first seem. Among white Southerners, blood has long assumed a special status. It is *the* life force: a potent symbol of family and kin bonding, of unity among people, especially in the face of an external threat. Some might go so far as to say—indeed, people have said—that blood is an obsession among white Anglo-Saxon Protestant southerners. Certainly concern about racial purity is a defining feature of southern history. Racial purity came to be a concern particularly in the years after the Civil War, when southerners, suffering from defeat, sought to defend and romanticize their way of life by means of Jim Crow segregation laws and a system of rituals and etiquette respecting their pride and identity. Defensiveness and pride resulted in a powerful psychology that unified much of the southern white world around folk symbols—including the mystique surrounding blood and ancestry. This regional psychology would perhaps reach its apex in the veneration of the southern "soldier saint" who fought valiantly and spilled his blood on behalf of a way of life. It is a psychology, too, that would produce cultural distortions in its unyielding and obsessive devotion to a cause. To quote John Shelton Reed (1982, 131), who paraphrases Irving Babbitt's comment about the Spanish: "There seems to be something southern about southerners that causes them to behave in a southern manner."

Religion is a crucial element in southern identity and culture, but it is a complex reality since, as Samuel S. Hill (1972) points out, there are "two cultures" juxtaposed in southern experience. What emerged after the Civil War and Reconstruction in the latter decades of the nineteenth century, Hill argues, were two overlapping ritual systems: one celebrating regional and folk values; the other affirming historic Christian beliefs and practices. Much of southern tradition ever since is a playing out of the tensions between these two ritual systems. The fact that the love ethic of Christianity was muffled in popular religious life, forced to accommodate a prideful and racially sensitive regional culture, is a big part of what makes southern religion so distinctive; in effect, social justice took back seat to a more personal, Christ-centered piety. Added is a peculiar guilt-oriented theology paralleling regional experiences of slavery and war, which brought to prominence themes of sacrifice and atonement through the blood of Christ. This theological construction would dominate much of popular religious life after the fall of the Confederacy and the era of Reconstruction—which is to say, the great majority of believers, upward of 80 per cent or more in some counties of Baptists, Methodists, and other low-church, sectarian Protestants. Regional values created an operative southern theology of the "problem–solution" sort, with an emphasis upon the all-important work of salvation by Christ, whose death on the cross satisfied God's violated holiness and thereby made redemption possible for any individual if only he or she would accept what had been done for him or her. As Flannery O'Connor so rightly claimed, the South became "Christ-haunted," and to understand what that means, one must grasp how themes of sacrifice and atonement play out not just in church but throughout the culture.

A "Christ-haunted" culture finds expression in the region's sacred and quasi-sacred music. Nothing quite occupies the place within southern life as those old hymns like "The Old Rugged Cross," "Nothing but the Blood," and "Blessed Assurance," all pitched to deep mystical meanings surrounding the cross, blood, and salvation. Journalist Marshall Frady (1980, XVff) sums up this underlying message lying at the heart of southern piety in the following way:

> Religion in the South was principally a romance about the cross—a dire melodrama of thorns and betrayal and midnight anguish, with nothing in the life of Jesus mattering quite so much as his suffering and his death. The Southern Jesus was an almost pre-Raphaelite figure of pale languishing melancholy, with a tender, grave, bearded face much like those thin faces of young Confederate officers that stare, doomed, out of ghostly tintypes. And nowhere was this Southern Christ so passionately defined as in those old heavy-hauling hymns that most Southerners had sung, at least once in their youth, at some summer night's revival in a bug-swarmed tent on the ragged outskirts of town: *What can wash away my sins? Nothing but the blood of Jesus ... Oh! precious is the flow that makes me white as snow ... in agony and blood, He fixed his languid eyes on me ... O Jesus, Lord! how can it be that Thou shouldst give Thy life for me, to bear the cross and agony in that dread hour on Calvary ... Oh, how I love Jesus! Oh, how I love Jeees-SUSSS!*

But how do we get from revivals and such heavy hymns back to barbecue? The answer, it would seem, has to do, in one way or another, with blood, sacrifice, and mystical communion. The "two cultures" of the South, though distinct, are drawn together through symbols and rituals—those of both the official religious system and the folk culture. The greater the cultural integration, in fact, the greater the chances that what happens in one ritual system will bear upon the other. And because southern culture continues to be rather tightly bound, combining distinctive regional and religious themes, it follows that folk rituals will reinforce the dominant religious and cultural themes and, to some extent, develop analogues of myth, practice, and boundary-defining mechanisms in lived experience similar to those of the official religious establishment. It is in this latter sense that food as symbolism and barbecuing as a specific practice take on deep ritual meaning and significance for southerners, even if only vaguely perceived.

Food, Place, Kin, and Church

To start with, we might look for what Durkheim would call the "elementary forms of ritual sacrifice" in the popular culture. And barbecuing as a cultural practice certainly offers opportunity to do so. Much mystery surrounds barbecuing as a "food event": pork is traditionally barbecued in pits requiring careful attention to the fire, the cooking, and the sauces. The pit itself is not unimportant. The pit qualifies as sacred space of sorts, and hence is usually covered when not in use. When in use, it is a place of awe and mystery, the primordial depths from which good things come. Amid the smoldering logs and smoke streaming from the bottoms of the pit, magical forces turn the raw meat into something mouth-watering and delectable. A vigil-like atmosphere prevails as the meat cooks slowly, and especially when it is cooked overnight, as is frequently the case. It is a time of watching and stoking the fires, of telling and sharing stories. Even today, when backyard grills have taken over much of the barbecuing and turned it into a private and family-based activity, good old boys still come together to watch the pits overnight as they prepare meals for the Lions Club, a church, or a political rally.

The fact that those watching the fires and telling the stories—the high priests—are almost always men is itself important symbolically. Cooking in the region is commonly women's work, but not so with pit barbecuing. It is viewed as a special act, set apart from regular cooking, requiring special knowledge, and hence a man's job. This ritual reversal of cooking responsibilities signals an enduring male authority, and locates the artistry and craft of turning pork into barbecue clearly within a quasi-sacred province of which only men may take charge. Barbecuing is part work, part sport, and part performance, and much lore surrounds those cooks who possess what amount to esoteric skills, knowledge of recipes, and techniques of food preparation (often handed down from older males). It is not uncommon to hear stories praising the best barbecue cooks in a community and conferring upon them great respect and status, defining them as functional equivalents to a high priest officiating a sacred feast.

But there's more involved than preparing barbecue—eating it takes on particular significance as well. No blasphemy is intended when I say that loving Jesus and loving pigs have much in common: both types of love are expressed in feasts, and even more importantly, in both the act of eating is symbolically related to the crucial flow of vital life forces. The first—shared feasts—is obvious enough, but what about this latter? Is pig love an occasion for the flow of vital life forces?

To grasp how this might possibly be, it is important to remember that in the South historically there have been strong, overlapping attachments to place, kin, and church. Southern religion is closely bound up with locality and kinship. Jean Heriot's ethnography of a Southern Baptist congregation in South Carolina nicely underscores the fusion of these three types of identity: "Being Baptist (is) more than a statement of doctrinal belief," she writes, "it (is) also a statement about family, kinship ties, place, and history" (Heriot 1994, 57). Polls and surveys show that attachments to local communities remain stronger in this region than anywhere else in the United States which, in turn, reinforces kinship and religious ties. Local attachments undergird a local world view with its own sacred canopy and drama of sin and salvation, played out in a context bounded, to a considerable degree, by community and kinship ties. Close links between church and family abound. In Appalachia, for example, the proliferation of churches is known to result often from kin groups breaking off and organizing their own churches (Bryant 1981). And nowhere on Earth are there more family reunions, cemetery associations, and church-organized homecomings—social gatherings where family and religious identities easily fuse. Moreover, such gatherings almost invariably include dinner on the grounds, frequently at a church, and often with the same people who are at church on Sunday morning, meeting to eat with extended family and kin later in the afternoon. Put differently, in the context of the South's two cultures, ties of kinship and place are organizing social principles bound up with religious identity, ties so strong they often overshadow the deeper historic, universal themes of the official religious community.

Place, family, and church are all bound by ancestry, but practically speaking, it is the food practices more than anything else that keep memory alive and visibly symbolize this underlying historical unity. Eating, and certainly eating barbecue, is the one thing—sometimes it seems like the only thing—that kin groups do when they come together. By sharing a meal together, they reaffirm the ties that bind—of one to another and of all to place. But why is barbecue so important in this respect? Part of the answer lies in the fact that traditionally, stoking the barbecue pit has been a man's job. Despite clear norms about cooking as a female activity, public and outdoors cooking with a male head is important because it reaffirms the traditional social order, the unity of all things past and present. It seems reasonable to expect, in fact, that the stronger the overlapping identities of place, family, and church, the more likely outdoor food practices will take on great symbolic significance. Even in the New South of interstate highways, shopping malls, and family Web pages in cyberspace, the "food event" remains of great importance to families. Gwen Neville (1987) argues that reunions, homecomings, and other such occasions involving big spreads of food provide for southerners who have left their home communities a chance to return and to renew their ties with their primal community. Such occasions are really like pilgrimages to places of origin, opportunities to re-create meaningful ties to a sacred community encompassing kin and fellow believers. Gathered around the table, often not far removed from the barbecue pit, generations of people bound by family, kin, and religious ties all come together, if only briefly, in what amounts to a ritual celebration of *communitas*, of the ties that really bind and give expression to the vital life forces.

Gathering around the table and pit takes on semi-sacred significance, even replacing the church for some as the dominant arena for the celebration of *communitas* for still another reason. And this has to do with the particular style of popular southern religion. While southerners are known for their high levels of religiosity, Holy Communion, or the celebration of the Eucharist, is not a particularly prominent part of the region's tradition. Low-church, evangelical Protestantism set the style historically, with its emphasis upon emotions and individuals accepting Christ in their hearts, rather than upon liturgical worship and celebration, or the sacramental observance of a gathered community. In practical effect, religious food was robbed of some of its mystical power. Thus communion services in southern churches historically were infrequent, often "quarterly" (meaning every three months) among Baptists, Methodists, and other low-church denominations. Even when Holy Communion is served, grape juice replaces wine in the popular faith traditions. It was a Methodist dentist, Dr Thomas Welch, who saw to it many years ago that unfermented grape juice was substituted in the Lord's Supper, a practice that caught on among low-church groups in the South, where drinking, or activities related to drinking, was viewed as a serious moral problem. Once again, the "two cultures" thesis sheds light upon the situation. Southerners forged a popularly based unity in an official ascetic-religious call for total abstinence from alcohol—including wine—in the interest of personal piety, but in so doing created a pale imitation of the historic Christian mass that was originally modeled after the account in First Corinthians where Jesus took a cup of wine and pronounced, "This is the new covenant in my blood. Do this in remembrance of me." Grassroots southern religion—that is, the dominant religion—is left with strong moral power over individuals, but weak in its sacramental rituals and mystical celebrations.

As a consequence, much of southern religion suffers from a moral asceticism and blandness, or an inability to "enjoy Jesus" in ways that Christian traditions in other cultural settings often do. Southerners tend to celebrate Jesus emotionally within the more narrow confines of their individual lives, but far less so in a lively and shared partaking of Jesus's body and blood. Yet as one commentator, Donald Horton (1943), has pointed out, a vital aspect of lived religion is its "social jollification," or the actual enjoyment people experience with food and drink as they celebrate the mystical bonds of faith. Food has a sensuous and rejuvenating quality in a religious context, if given ritual expression. But if this doesn't happen in the communion services within popular church life, then where else might it happen?

Casual observation suggests that communion with the pig is an occasion for social jollification. In this proto-ritual moment, vital life forces flow, helped in no small part because barbecue is often eaten with beer, and on occasion even bourbon—and not infrequently under a Dixie flag or guns, or some other symbol of regional significance. Nor is it a coincidence that the usual place for eating barbecue is called a "joint," for it is in shacks and honkytonks that eating and drinking come together in what amounts to a hearty display of enjoyment. Even the more upscale places that try to disassociate barbecue from the seamier aspects of southern life like to bill themselves as places where you can enjoy yourself casually as you eat and drink. No matter where the place, or the socioeconomic status of the clientele, eating barbecue seems to make people happy and gregarious: they seem to get excited just making simple menu selections; even coming together around this special food seems rejuvenating in a Durkheimian sense. In a very simple, yet profound sort of way, regional bonds are affirmed and the simple act of eating becomes "time out of time," a moment of celebration and mystical unity. Food and memory are always bound together, but especially so in a context where emotions are less restrained and the natural unities of people easily surface. In effect, the barbecue joint and the social occasions on which barbecue is served accomplish what the church often fails to do: create an opportunity for affirming the mundane world of family, kin, and friends in an open, jovial atmosphere.

Just because the symbolic blood in the barbecue overshadows the pale substitute of the church-based communion does not mean that what happens at church is unimportant. My point is not to downplay the role of religious institutions; indeed, the many church suppers, overt friendliness, and stress upon fellowship—often a code word for getting together to eat—help to sustain the importance of food symbolism and its meaning in southern life. Rather, the two—barbecue and church—can be, and often are, mutually enforcing and are not easily separated in the ritual performance of southern identity in a context in which place, kin, and religion are all symbolically linked. What we learn in all of this is a basic Durkheimian principle: that even in the most profane, everyday activities such as eating, the underlying vital forces of social life and of primordial human bonding find sacred expression. So the next time you hear the familiar southern chant— WooooooOOOOOOOOOOOOOO! Pig! Suuuuuuuueeeeeeeeeeee!—remember, it is about more than just pigs.

References

Bryant, F. Carlene. 1981. *We're All Kin: A Cultural Study of a Mountain Neighborhood.* Knoxville: University of Tennessee Press.

Douglas, Mary. 1972. "Deciphering a Meal." *Daedulus* 101, 1 (Winter): 61–81.

Fabricant, Florence. 1996. "The Geography of Taste." *New York Times Magazine,* March 10.

Frady, Marshall. 1980. *Southerners: A Journalist's Odyssey.* New York: Meridian.

Harris, Marvin. 1974. *Cows, Pigs, Women, and Witches: The Riddles of Culture.* New York: Vintage.

Heriot, M. Jean. 1994. *Blessed Assurance: Beliefs, Actions, and the Experience of Salvation in a Carolina Baptist Church.* Knoxville: University of Tennessee Press.

Hill, Samuel S., Jr. 1972. "The South's Two Cultures." In *Religion and the Solid South,* eds Samuel S. Hill, Jr, Edgar T. Thompson, Anne Firor Scott, Charles Hudson, and Edwin S. Gaustad. Nashville: Abingdon Press.

Horton, Donald. 1943. "The Functions of Alcohol: A Cross-Cultural Study." *Quarterly Journal for the Study o f Alcohol* 4: 199–320.

Neville, Gwen. 1987. *Kinfolks and Pilgrims: Rituals of Reunion in American Protestant Culture.* New York: Oxford University Press.

Reed, John Shelton. 1982. *One South: An Ethnic Approach to Regional Culture.* Baton Rouge: Louisiana State University Press.

——. 1995. *Kicking Back: Further Dispatches from the South.* Columbia: University of Missouri Press.

Remini, Robert V. 1971. "Election of 1832." In *History of American Presidential Elections 1789–1968,* ed. Arthur M. Schlesinger, Jr. New York: Chelsea House Publishers.

Chapter 6

Rituals of the African American Domus

Church, Community, Sport, and LeBron James

Vernon L. Andrews

> It is a story of the public presentation of the black body, a search for the cultural imperatives that have influenced the ways in which African Americans have clothed themselves, styled their hair, and communicated meaning through gesture, dance and other forms of bodily display... within the confines of an oppressive social system, African Americans have been able to develop and give visual expression to cultural preferences that were at variance with those of the dominant group.
>
> (White and White 1998, 2)

African American religious, social, and sports rituals are all interconnected. The Black Church has served as the institutional conduit and transfer point of cultural ways of singing, shouting, preaching, and testifying, and the phrase "make a joyful noise unto the Lord" has been taken quite literally by many black congregations over the centuries. Given the importance of the Black Church to the black community from slavery through the Civil Rights Movement, it should be no surprise to find that African Americans rework religious ritual into cultural ways of ritualizing in everyday society. Desegregated sport, especially since the Civil Rights Movement, has allowed African Americans like current National Basketball Association (NBA) star LeBron James to succeed at the game while they have embodied the African-American dream of the freedom of cultural expression.

My primary focus in this chapter is on African American behavior patterns and social rituals with deep roots in the Black Church. As such, the bulk of my argument will be to show how ministers, congregants, and choirs forged unique modes of expression in the Black Church that spread into surrounding communities. I elaborate on how "ordinary rituals in everyday behavior" forged in and around urban and rural black churches serve as the framework that informs contemporary athletes, such as James, who ritualize in sport. The new churches of African American expressivity are stadiums and arenas all over America. I will focus on three rituals that flow from everyday life and black religious life into both professional basketball and football—the ring/circle ritual, the call-and-response ritual, and the individual creative expressivity ritual—in the context of research highlighting nascent ritualizing and creative ritualizing.

Though both men and women create and continually rework black expressive rituals in churches and neighborhoods across America, the bodies most prevalent in popular sport are African American males, and as such they are the focus of this chapter.[1] For the sake of space, I will limit my analysis to four examples of these types of expressive ritual that have made their way into popular culture via sport: pre-game circular rituals designed to both harmonize and "fire-up" teams before play begins; LeBron James's ritual powder-toss; slam-dunking as ritual in basketball; and end-zone dancing as professional football call-and-response ritual.[2]

The Ring and Circle in Black Sport

If there was any doubt about the convergence of sport and religion, behold the naming of NBA player LeBron James as "King James" and "The Chosen One" to whom we all bear "Witness."[3] James emerged into the professional ranks straight out of high school in 2003, and until recently played for the Cleveland Cavaliers. Nike uses the two honorific religious titles (after all, the most foundational translation of the Bible in the Western [Protestant] world was commissioned by King James of England)—in conjunction with "witness"—to promote James (with Kobe Bryant and Tiger Woods, their premier athlete endorsers) in billboard ads, television commercials, and with "branding" on basketball shoes. ESPN, ABC, and TNT—television networks that all broadcast NBA games—highlight James in slow-motion commercials. This combination of media and advertising worship and the phenomenon of Cleveland Cavalier fans who bear "witness" on T-shirts illuminate how James is viewed as much more than a star athlete: in a sporting sense, he is seen as the second coming of Michael Jordan—"chosen" at birth to attain to new levels of greatness.

Ronald Grimes notes in his definition of ritualizing that "ritualizing transpires as animated persons enact formative gestures in the face of receptivity during crucial times in founded places" (Grimes 1982, 60). If naming "King" James "the chosen one" is any indication, then fans, advertisers, and the media are certainly receptive to the various formative gestures enacted by LeBron James in arenas ("founded places") around the USA.

LeBron James, Michael Jordan, Kobe Bryant, and many other contemporary black athletes who have achieved success since the rise of boxer Muhammad Ali, have all developed their own individual styles of play. On occasion, some of these performed acts have become ritual, including the ring or circle ritual in which teams engage as they prepare for the game. In a typical such ritual, LeBron James stands in the center of a circle made up of his teammates, and dances, chants, and sings as they all indicate their support of him in the outer ring. He smiles, snaps his fingers, chants, and gestures. Other teams in professional basketball (the Los Angeles Lakers, for one) and football (the Baltimore Ravens, among others) also engage in this now-common ritual. Gena Caponi notes the African roots of this black cultural practice:

> In the majority of cultures across Africa, group rituals were performed in a circle, dancers danced in a circle, and individuals performed solos in the center before returning to the surrounding circle of community. The circle helped to keep everybody involved, active, and interdependent. In addition to the circle, African rituals used…individual improvisation and stylization…dialogic interaction or call-and-response. Taken together they form the basis of most African cultural expressions—the basis of African aesthetics.
>
> (Caponi 1999, 9)[4]

Ritualizing in the ring and circle is widely practiced in African American culture. At many black wedding receptions, guests initiate a "ring dance" by forming a circle while dancing and singing in unison, and then one-by-one joining the circle, performing an improvised dance move or their own signature move—often to laughter and chants—and then returning to the outer ring. Individuality is supported, and the more exaggerated the dance move or gesture, the more laughter there is, and the more it is supported by the group. According to Roger Abrahams:

> Each player is encouraged to show off in some way, either through some kind of individualized dance step … or through strutting, teasing, flirting, and wiggling, with everyone else clapping, commenting, and joking in support. This is the point. For while the player is at the center he or she is never alone, rather there is constant commentary and support by the ring.
>
> (Abrahams 1992, 104)

Black athletes have transferred common ritualizing in the ring to professional basketball and football games via the circle of community. Athletes are never separate from the team or the crowd; they perform *for* the crowd and team. This is part of the larger ritual of call-and-response in black culture and, specifically, in the Black Church.

Some Distinctions in the Study of Ritual, Ritualizing and Black Culture

Legend has it that former President William Howard Taft—at 300 pounds, the heaviest president in history—inspired a baseball ritual quite by accident:

In 1910, as a game between the Washington Senators and the [Philadelphia] Athletics wore on, the rotund, six-foot-two president reportedly grew more and more uncomfortable in his small wooden chair. By the middle of the seventh inning he could bear it no longer and stood up to stretch his aching legs—whereupon everyone else in the stadium, thinking the president was about to leave, rose to show their respect. A few minutes later Taft returned to his seat, the crowd followed suit, and the "seventh-inning stretch" was born.

(Emery 2009, 1)

The same thing was done at the following game, until the "stretch" became a ritual across America.

In his early work on ritual theory, Ronald Grimes notes that narrow definitions of ritual tend to concentrate on mature instances—such as Passover or Mass—and tend to overlook emergent behaviors that are *nascent* ritual, or what Grimes describes as "ritualizing." Traditional theories of ritual have argued that rites "originated but cannot originate," which is, Grimes argues, a conservative fallacy. Rather, "we want to call attention to their originative moments" (Grimes 1982, 61), such as in the case of the seventh-inning stretch. Ritual is not an unchanging given; Grimes suggests that we can engage in "ritual creativity," which may lead to ritual.

Though African Americans differ regarding the appropriateness of displaying black cultural ways in various milieux (Kochman 1981), the practice by African Americans of ritualizing in predominantly white public spaces requires that we understand these acts as more than merely acts of asocial behavior (see Jones 1986). What sometimes appear as resistant social acts by black athletes might be ritualizing instances that, if sustained rather than swiftly aborted by traditional rules and norms, could become part of the social fabric—what Grimes loosely describes as "rites of passage, seasonal rites, meditative practices, carnival celebrations, and so on"—rather than snuffed-out as simply "meaningless gestures and cultural symbols" (Grimes 1982, 62).

There is an ongoing visual conversation of gestures and practices of African American life that informs views of the world and speaks into that world with verbal and nonverbal cultural stylings. As John Edgar Wideman notes on African American expressivity, "our stories, songs, dreams, dances, social forms, style of walk, talk, dressing, cooking, sport, our heroes and heroines provide a record ... so distinctive and abiding that its origins in culture have been misconstrued as rooted in biology" (Wideman 1990, 43), hinting that African American rituals get passed on intergenerationally through "stories, songs [and] dreams."

The African American aesthetic—which informs ritualizing—is a way of being in the world that is passed down generation after generation through "cultural expressions such as dance, religion, music, and play, [where] societies articulate and transmit the ideas, values, and beliefs that bind people together" (Caponi 1999, 7). And though religion is the major temple from which these aesthetic values emanate via bodily and verbal expression, one need not attend church on a regular basis in order to be acculturated.[5]

Ritual and the Birth of the Black Church

The Black Church has long been identified as the one American institution free of white entanglement. As Albert Raboteau (1995) notes, the influence of this black-controlled space was crucial for community development:

> As a center for social organization, economic cooperation, educational endeavor, leadership training, political articulation, and religious life, the ... church exercised unrivaled influence in many black communities. It was ... the one institution that African-Americans controlled.
>
> (*ibid.*, 79–80)

Today, the Black Church continues to serve a broad purpose for African Americans (see Battle 2006). It often serves as a community center and social gathering place, festival and anniversary site, and a place where baptisms, weddings, and funerals are held. People meet their spouses, raise their kids, sing in the choir, and seek fellowship there. It is the *how* of doing church that separates this original black institution from its white counterpart, though this difference was not envisioned by the whites who originally gave Christianity to the slaves. Initially considered a way by which slavemasters could maintain peace on the plantation, Christianity has, as Reverend Calvin Marshall argues, empowered African Americans with its resistant nature:

> Long before there was a college degree in the race, there were great black preachers, there were great black saints, and there were great black churches. The [white] man systematically killed your language, killed your culture, tried to kill your soul, tried to blot you out—but somewhere along the way he gave us Christianity, and gave it to us to enslave us. But it freed us—because we understood things about it, and we made it work in ways for us that it never worked for him.
>
> (quoted by Holt 1972, 331)

There was no notion among whites of how African Americans would transform church rituals to fit their ends. Later, blacks took the "white man's religion and from within the Black Church developed routines and variations of form, substance, and ritual to satisfy black psychological needs" (*ibid.*, 332). Raboteau (1995) goes further in his analysis of the black incorporation of Christianity, noting that black Christians rejected the notion that

Christianity was a white man's religion, and instead notes that "Christianity and slavery were antithetical. Christianity was not false; the American version of it was" (*ibid.*, 61). And thus a vehicle for black expressivity and ritual was born.

The Black Minister, Black Style, and Black Ritual

The identity of the black minister was intimately tied to his (rarely, before the Civil Rights Movement, *her*) ability to use his creative expressiveness— within the context of the church ritual of preaching—to bring about an emotional release from audience members. Raboteau (1995) discusses the distinctive style of black preaching as "the chanted sermon" (*ibid.*, 41), and notes that though this style is not inclusive of all black ministers—and indeed, some white ministers follow this style—it is "as much a staple of African-American culture as spirituals, gospel, blues, and tales" (*ibid.*, 142). Further, the chanted sermon style is discernable among black ministers who can perform it with " ... skill, fluency, spontaneity and intensity" (*ibid.*, 142). Grace Holt elaborates:

> The ritual begins with the preacher "stylin' out," which the audience eagerly awaits ... "Stylin' out" means he's going to perform certain acts, say certain things with flourish and finesse ... The preacher walks, body swaying from side to side, slightly bent, from one side of the pulpit to the other ... He waits until he gets to one side, stands straight up, and makes a statement about sin ... with a strong sense of melody and rhythm.
>
> (Holt 1972, 334)

If ever there was an original ritual in African American culture, it is the expressive performance of the black preacher in synchronicity with the black congregation. This was not a monologue, but a dialogue between pastor and flock, setting up the cultural aesthetic of the call-and-response:

> The verbal exchange between preacher and audience throughout the service is accompanied by a variety of counterpoint. When the preacher makes his charges of sin he may shout or whisper, point a finger, lean on the pulpit, pause, or look long and hard at the audience, letting the words sink in for effect ... The white handkerchief, wiping the face, pausing to get a drink of water, and changing to a shaking voice all signal to the audience that the preacher is really going to get down and preach; the spirits of the audience lift ...
>
> (*ibid.*, 336–37)

The pastor's personal expression is grounded in tradition, and his or her own "signature" style involves "moves, gestures, dances, [and] speaking with body as well as voice" (Raboteau 1995, 144). The gestures and movements by the pastor are part of the build-up. The audience is aware of each movement as part of the nonverbal communication, part of the pastor saying "I'm tired, but this is so worth saying that I will fight my fatigue in the name of the Lord."

Given the exalted status of ministers and the church in the black community, it is little wonder then that these call-and-response ways of interaction have flowed from the pastor to the choir, throughout the church, and right down the steps into the black community. There has always been a strong receptivity not only to the message of the healing of earthly wounds, but also to the enactment—the form of delivery that has become sacred ritual in African American culture. As Grimes puts it:

> Ritualizing is enactment in the face of imagined, socially experienced, or mythologically construed receptivity. For ritualization to occur, the surroundings must expose a vulnerable (*vulner* = wound) side…in order for ritualizing to gestate. The more deeply an enactment is received, the more an audience becomes a congregation and the more a performance becomes ritualized. "Sacred" is the name we give to the deepest forms of receptivity in our experience.
>
> (Grimes 1982, 62)

Thus black ministerial ritualizing is a performative enactment to a deeply receptive congregation steeped in historical wounds. These styles of interaction are sacred on Sundays, to be sure, but they are also sacred rituals in the black community generally. And as there is diversity in American society, so there is diversity in both black and white churchgoing and ritual. Though one might assume that from a common past might flow a singular style of expression in African American culture, there is a range of ways individuals choose to (or are able to) express themselves in any given social situation.

J. L. Hanna comments on what she has observed in relation to dance and the Black Church, implying that there is neither an essentially Black Church nor a black way of being:

> … dancing is not innate among blacks; middle-class Afro-Americans [*sic*] often move like whites. So do Africans who are educated in British or American settings as I discovered in my African fieldwork. Some do not know how to dance. Furthermore, as there are black churchgoers who "feel the spirit," as their manifest body movement bears witness, there are also middle-class black churchgoers who are as physically restrained as their white counterparts.
>
> (Hanna 1997, 382)

First and foremost, the Black Church provides its congregants with an opportunity to cleanse themselves of worldly pain and suffering, seek forgiveness for sins, and commune with others. But in ways uncommon in white congregations (white Pentecostals and middle-class blackness not-withstanding), the Black Church has served as a safe haven for creative expressivity. All of this lived expressivity and the transference into black everyday life is summarized well by rhythm-and-blues guitarist Johnny Otis (1993), who noted:

> I never had to instruct my horn players how to phrase a passage ... The music grew out of the African American way of life ... the emphasis in spiritual values, the way reverend Jones preached, the way Sister Williams sang in the choir, the way the old brother down the street played the slide guitar and crooned the blues, the very special way the people danced, walked, laughed, cried, joked, got happy, shouted in church.
>
> (*ibid.*, 117)

The day-to-day practices have forged distinctive ways of living, and are ritualized and reinvented with each new generation, adding character to the African American way of life. While reinvention happens in homes, on street-corners, and on playgrounds, ritualization certainly happens weekly in black churches.

Black Social Ritual and the Black Domus

There are two key social rituals that are learned in the Black Church and transferred into everyday life: the call-and-response nature of interaction between all parties in the church, and the free-flowing acceptance of bodily expressivity by members in the church. The choir is especially important to this process of call-and-response and emotional catharsis. As Mellonee Burnim (1985) notes: "When the expectations of the black congregation or audience are met, performer and audience merge: they become one. The personal interpretation of a given gospel selection generates a sense of ethnic collectivity and spiritual unity" (*ibid.*, 157). The verbal and nonverbal individual expressivity by choir members—especially the lead vocalist—provides the personal interpretation. What is the ideal outcome for the congregation?

Olly Wilson (1992) argues that the audience is seeking solidarity, release; "the expected goal is a point in the performance when the expressive power of the performer is so overwhelming that it demands a spontaneous response from the audience" (*ibid.*, 169). The church "performer" who dis-tances him- or herself from the audience does not gain broad acceptance in the African American religious community; this is also true, to a lesser degree, in sports.

The Sunday emotional release and expressive communion with the body by peers in the sacred space of the church has resonated with the black community since Christianity was introduced to the slaves. The Black Church—with its choirs, usher boards, deacons, ministers-in-training, and musicians—has always served as a community center as well as a place of worship; this was the original *black* Facebook. This is where its members shared what happened the past week, what they were feeling and where we were going, and where they asked for help in how to get there. Through this portal, this physical space, local networks met once a week, exchanged stories, testified, supported each other, and listened to some preaching and singing.

The notion of the domus—developed by Robert Orsi in his analysis of the family-centered culture of Italians in Harlem between 1880 and 1950—provides a useful tool to understand the transfer of African American ideals from church to community. In his work, Orsi sought to understand how this structure influenced all other aspects of local Italian society. In essence, the domus was the extended family, but the family—or domus—extended its reach throughout the community. As Orsi illustrates, there was a natural interweaving of the domus and the community:

> Life in Italian Harlem was very public. Although there was ... a strictly maintained core of privacy in the domus itself, the life of the domus spilled out into closely watched streets and hallways. Women leaning out of buildings, men sitting on stoops, children playing in courtyards—all served as a kind of urban chorus surrounding the intimacies of the domus ... The lines between neighborhood and domus were not sharply defined. People had to be careful how they behaved in the streets because these too were a theater of the domus.
>
> (Orsi 1985, 92)

In the African American community, the Black Church is the domus, and the larger community is the "closely watched streets" and the "urban chorus" surrounding the domus.[6] Indeed, church culture shapes a variety of community and voluntary association patterns in black society (see Pattillo-McCoy 1999), and all manner of issues are discussed therein, including community issues, politics, family matters, unemployment, crime, and drug usage, making it the extension—or "theater"—of the domus. Catherine Bell (1997b) notes that involvement in a "highly ritualized community is often based on an interest in ethnicity as a framework of community, identity, and a sense of tradition and belonging" (*ibid.*, 270). And whereas Orsi's Italian family-centered domus saw priests as outsiders—since they do not have families and thus are not central—the black domus sees the pastor as exactly the opposite: the center of life, culture, history, and hope. The Black Church's expressivity and its influence on black culture in the greater community are intimately connected.

The Transition from Church to Secular Bodily Expression

Regular church attendance has diminished among African Americans (Hunt and Hunt 2001), especially among poor (Clemmitt 2007) and black youth (Ramirez and Brachear 2006). Given more social choice since desegregation, African American society might be experiencing a higher degree of secularization and individualization. Bell (1997a) notes this would not be the first time secularization gave way to different affiliations, arguing that "In a secular society, people have many more choices about what to believe, how to act, and where to affiliate and devote their energies." This has the effect of putting "greater emphasis on the individual as the basic unit of the society and less on the family or clan or group as a whole" (*ibid.*, 199). So, while some have analyzed the effect on religion of the increasingly intermittent nature of modern black church attendance (Hunt and Hunt 2001), others— following Bell's argument that "secularization does not entail the progressive demise of religion in general but a transformation of its form" (Bell 1997a, 202)—have examined how African Americans have found many other public spaces in which to enact ritual behaviors, including corporate functions, picnics, bowling leagues,[7] and, as we shall see, professional sports.

What is the connection, then, between the black body performing in church and the black body performing in stadiums and arenas? The expressive minister and congregation can certainly influence the domus of the church and greater community, but there still has to be a motivation to perform black ritual in white spaces. Perhaps the Civil Rights Act—an official statement of desegregation made by the ruling elites—was the official social blessing African Americans needed to begin socially expressing years of denied freedom in public spaces. African Americans began an association with the body as alive and expressive, and as divine temple:

> In a society chronically split between body and spirit, African American ritual exemplifies embodied spirit and inspired body in gesture, dance, song, and performed word. In worship the human becomes an icon of God … the person is of ultimate value as image of the divine.
> (Raboteau 1995, 190)

Raboteau implies that inspired black creativity and individuality with the body somehow speaks to being in touch with something deeper and spiritual and—if someone is very good at expressing—something divine.[8] In church, our verve and inspired singing or testifying translates into being in touch with not only ritual, but a spiritual force. That same spark of embodied spirit that flows into creative ritualizing with the body in the black domus is carried into collegiate and professional sports by black athletes.

Black bodily expressivity in integrated settings can carry costs as well as individual and group rewards. Many African Americans learn that homogenized bodies in tune with white social ritualizing in institutional settings controlled by whites might be more apt to be promoted (Gordon 1964).[9] But in a heavily commodified and commercialized marketplace, sometimes the opposite is true for black bodies. It is the complexities of African American ritualizing in the context of professional sports to which we now turn.

LeBron James' Ritualizing: The Powder-Toss and the Slam Dunk

There are two ritualized acts in which LeBron James engages that embody the call and response of the Black Church and community: the powder-toss to the crowd before the game, and the slam dunk. Although Kevin Garnett, currently with the Boston Celtics, was the first to throw powder, James has taken the powder-toss to an entirely different level; to ritual form. Before play begins, he takes a handfull of chalk (used to keep hands dry during the game) and walks in front of the scorer's table, faces the crowd, and then tosses the powder high into the air. With feet and legs together, arms spread wide at right angles to his body, with palms upward and head tilted back, he appears every bit as Jesus might have on the cross. Is he blessing the sacred space? Is he sprinkling holy water? Or is he offering himself up as "chosen" to entertain? In keeping with his anointed status, he might also be calling out: "This I do for you."

To be sure, it *is* baby powder; but it is the symbolism of the act that is important. The powder-toss is highly suggestive of a religious ritual, and is so loved by Cleveland fans that they have also, at times, been given confetti to join in the act: as James releases the powder high into the air, fans toss up their handfuls of colorful bits of paper. This acknowledgement of the crowd as part of the game is call-and-response behavior that breaks down the "fourth wall" between audience and performer (see Goffman 1959), akin to what black ministers do when they interweave congregants' life-dramas and look to the audience for cues.

LeBron James also loves the slam dunk. His style is to clutch the ball in an arm outstretched far behind his head, before crashing the ball home into the basket—an emphatic slam dunk over the opposition. James, like others in the NBA, watches the crowd go wild and then stops for a brief moment to scream at the top of his lungs *in response* to the crowd. Thus his call (the slam), the audience's thunderous response (cheers), and James's reaction (the scream); the slam dunk itself has become a ritual in American sports.

Basketball's slam dunk is the single most individualistic and expressive act of "performance while scoring" in any American sport, while football's end-zone dance (to be examined shortly) is the most individualistic and expressive act "performed after scoring" *in* America; African American athletes have taken slam dunks and end-zone dances to ritualistic heights. But, notes Gena Caponi, "the 'in-your-face' style" of these moves is "so intimidating that rules were changed to eliminate it." As she describes it:

> The NCAA banned the slam dunk in 1967 because of Kareem Abdul Jabbar's (then Lew Alcindor) performances for UCLA, and the move didn't return until Julius Erving ("Dr. J") and others helped popularize it in the American Basketball Association (ABA) of the 1970s. Likewise, professional football has banned "excessive celebration" after touchdowns, a rule scholar Joel Dinerstein ironically terms "illegal use of black culture."
>
> (Caponi 1999, 4)[10]

The slam dunk is an important ritual in ways that still elude explanation. When a slam dunk is performed with individuality and creativity, it is the ultimate in expressive brilliance in the black community, akin to a great sermon ending on a high note, or a jazz band reaching its conclusion with a swirling crescendo. It is a moment of truth—the one play that can send the crowd over the top in ways that no other sporting moment can. In these moments of elevation, time can stand still. Lasting only a split-second or so, there is a stoppage of time in that one moment of brilliance that many have witnessed elsewhere with choirs, musical performers, and ministers.

The brilliance and resonance of these acts are what transfer expressive ritualizing to the next generation. The epitome of this expressive moment is embodied in the Nike logo for "Air Jordan"—the silhouette of the outstretched arms and legs of Michael Jordan leaping to the basket for a slam dunk in mid-flight that adorns Jordan's clothing line and many of Nike's basketball shoes.[11] Since 1984, there has been a slam dunk competition before the NBA All-Star game.

John Wideman (1990) describes a player's brilliant slam dunk as executing a "move so spectacular that glory reflected instantly on all of us because he was one of us out there in the game and he'd suddenly lifted the game to a higher plane ... he needed us now to amen and goddamn and high-five and time-out" (*ibid.*, 395). What is key in Wideman's quote is the "amen," as it implies the spirituality in the moment the act is conceived and performed. Likewise, Caponi reflects what composer Olly Wilson calls the "soul focal moment" in black music performance, where the player performs the unexpected to such a level that he or she "elevates the community through his or her individual effort, and the community bursts into spontaneous applause, responding as one body" (Caponi 1999, 5). This is classic Black Church call-and-response. Caponi notes that athletes and individuals can create "moments of transcendence and fusion for all involved; transcendence of the ordinary, and of the boundaries between community and individual" (*ibid.*).

Grimes advises practitioners of ritual studies to look to gestures as significant to ritual enactment, noting that "social values can penetrate ritual gestures" (Grimes 1982, 66). He notes that "formative gestures" need to be attended to, such that we look at the "style and rhythm of the dance's gestures ... " (*ibid.*), making a distinction between form (which assumes models and archetypes) and "formative" (the flow-like, verb-like qualities) inherent in ritualizing. Things flow and change and take new shape, and have no obvious "intent." The formative gestures have no deep or hidden religious meaning to athletes who perform them; rather, the ever-changing use of gestures is symbolic of a dialogue and interaction with black expressive practice that flow from neighborhoods, homes, playgrounds, and the Black Church. The nonverbal culture and symbolic significance in African American gestures require that scholars reconceptualize them as "possible symbols rather than toss them away as 'meaningless'" (Grimes 1982, 66; see also Andrews and Majors 2004).

The End-Zone Dance and Traditional Rules and Rituals in Sports

African American bodily ritualizing in traditionally white collegiate and professional sports has not been without contestation. There were always subtle codes of conduct—referred to as "sportsmanship"—that were in play before blacks ever entered the top levels of sports in America; white middle-class ritualistic codes of conduct formed in England and repackaged in various ways in United States sporting codes (Abe 1988). These "sportsmanship" codes conflict with many African American expressive codes and interaction norms (Kochman 1981; Ashe 1988; George 1992; Dyson 1993; Andrews 1996, 1997; Andrews and Majors 2004).

There has always been an undercurrent among many blacks that public displays of expressivity might confirm whites' thinking of African Americans as "primitive" and only capable of communion with the body, rather than as complex and conscious individuals (DuBois 1903), particularly given historical criticisms of black behavior and prevailing images of the "Sambo," "Coon," and "Happy Darkie" by whites (Riggs 1987; Weisenfeld 2007). Many white objections center on the usefulness of the action ("Is that necessary?") and the lack of humility ("Why don't you act like you've been there before?"). The policy of the National Football League (NFL) toward expressivity by (primarily) black players echoes the above sentiment and notes the ring component of end-zone celebrations and individual expressivity:

> The Committee is unanimously opposed to any prolonged, excessive or premeditated celebration by individual players or groups of players. Antics such as unrestrained dances, wild flailing of arms and legs, simulated dice games, "high-five" circles in the end zone, imitations of

gun-fighters, and similar behavior are deemed to be contrived exhibi-
tionism that has no place in the sport and should be penalized five yards
for unsportsmanlike conduct.

(in Pierson 1991, 8)

Further, there are codes of conduct in collegiate sport that have been in place
for a number of years and that look at individual creative expression
(whether by white or black athletes) as a gesture of poor sportsmanship. The
National Collegiate Athletics Association (NCAA) ruled in 1995:

Players will express excitement over a great play but must never address
remarks or gestures to opponents or spectators, nor may they spike the
ball or throw it into the air. Choreographed or delayed spectacles have
no validity in football and detract from its honored traditions.

(NCAA 1995, 10)

While at some point in time everyone involved might have agreed on behavioral norms—such as in the '30s and '40s, when teams were all white, and
black athletes were banned—collegiate ranks and the NFL are now heavily
populated with African Americans, many of whom are not steeped in similar
traditions, norms, rituals, and ritualizing. Bell (1997a) argues that groups
with oral traditions (such as African Americans) are much more flexible than
text-based "literate" societies, and that this can cause conflict. Despite the
rise in access to education and firmly established written traditions after the
Civil War, African American culture continues to refer to—and reflect—an
oral tradition more than a written tradition; change in language and slang is
constant, playful, and in a dialogue with those oral traditions of the past.
It could be said that not only does African American society dance to a
different beat than white society, but that African Americans dance with the
English language in ways far more flexible than traditional white normative
ways, given the resonance of rural and street-level oral traditions. As Bell
notes, in an oral society ...

the embodiment of tradition can flexibly change to keep pace with the
community and win people's assent as remaining true to tradition and
appropriate to the current climate. Ritual can change without necessarily
being very concerned with change as such. In literate societies with
written models, however, change itself easily becomes a problem that is
viewed as a threaten [sic] to tradition and authority ... In other words, in
literate societies change can be very untidy.

(ibid., 204)

Black athletes may well be "untidy" while working within a community
aesthetic that diverges from traditional white normative values; many

African Americans (and many whites, also) might well contextualize end-zone celebrations as normal emotive behavior, as reasonable, and as acts that draw attention to themselves as part of a larger ritual of community-in-the-round that need not provoke opponents. Religion scholar Jonathan Smith (1987) notes that, "ritual is a means of performing the way things ought to be in conscious tension to the way things are" (*ibid.*, 37). When we oppose one set of norms in favor of another set of values based primarily in "tradition" and without any critical analysis, we reaffirm (in this case) white privilege: *the way things are.*

Thus, rather than view black creative bodily expression in the end zone as embarrassing, arrogant, or stereotypical, the expressive freedom athletes initiate and ritualize might show us how limitless the body's capability for joy and spirituality in the moment can be. Maybe expressive calls to the audience are not intended to alienate teammates or embarrass and humiliate the opposition, but rather an outcome of different historical ways of knowing the body and different cultural rituals. The global transmission and acceptance of African American music (Raboteau 1994) in addition to dance styles, youth slang, and clothing style speaks to the resonance of black culture. Caponi (1999) notes with dignity a broader vision of the crowd's actions and reactions to black performers:

> From another perspective, while the slam-dunking and one-on-one competitions may temporarily distract attention from a team organization, they nevertheless take place within a larger organic community that is following every nuance, a community that in each action, each comeback is being resurrected, strengthened, and dignified.
>
> (*ibid.*, 6)

The notion of a black organic community is pivotal, as it points to ritualizing as a process of becoming something altogether different from the neatly trimmed formality of institutional America, especially as found in American sport and perpetuated by rules and traditions. In truth, ritualizing by African Americans in black churches and communities was no problem for American society until the ritualizing began to creep into professional sports and white public spaces after desegregation.

Gaining Our Rituals, Losing Our Religion

It is possible that the dispersal of African Americans away from each other and their churches in urban neighborhoods threatens the continuity of stories passed down, the traditions and the ritual of black life (Hunt and Hunt 2001); that indeed those rituals and rites and ways of behaving and talking and walking—all those good and bad qualities that come from being raised within an enclave similar to Orsi's Italian domus—might be slipping away.

This is an unforeseen consequence since 1965 of obtaining equality of movement in American society. African Americans—like previous ethnic groups that slowly saw their American enclaves dissolve—want to preserve culture while at the same time take full advantage of new avenues toward social mobility (Steinberg 1989; Hraba 1994). Until recently, scholars have argued that part of what gave rise to black creativity was the community's underdog status and "lot" in life. What happens when the future for African American culture looks brighter? What happens when middle-class status and movement away from the black domus shifts the color and ethnicity of our neighborhood friends, our co-workers, our spouses, and even our pastors? What happens to the underdog status when the occupants of the White House are black? This growing diversity of black culture and ways of seeing ourselves in the world might mean a shift in how black culture is expressed verbally and physically in the future. Rituals will surely live as they are needed or die as they lose resonance.

For now—and into the near future—a variety of cultures will continue to resonate with black athletes' calls to the audience in many sports. Before black expressive rituals become obsolete, we can continue to enjoy athletes communing in the ring-circle with one another before games as they build camaraderie; we can enjoy slam dunks and end-zone dances; and we can reflect that, though times have been tough and the road difficult for African Americans in obtaining expressive freedom, long-suffering humility has its rewards. If we are lucky, we can catch a glimpse of the giddy embodiment of black joy in a local church, a local black barbershop, or on a sacred playing field in any city in America.

References

Abe, Ikuo. 1988. "A Study of the Chronology of the Modern Usage of 'Sportsmanship' in English, American and Japanese Dictionaries." *International Journal of the History of Sport* 5, 1: 3–28.

Abrahams, Roger D. 1992. *Singing the Master: The Emergence of African American Culture in the Plantation South*. New York: Pantheon.

Andrews, Vernon L. 1996. "Black Bodies—White Control: Race, Celebratory Expression and the Contested Terrain of Sportsmanlike Conduct." *Journal of African American Men* 3, 2: 33–59.

——. 1997. "African American Player Codes on Celebration, Taunting and Sportsmanlike Conduct in College Football." *Journal of African American Men* 4, 1: 57–92.

Andrews, Vernon L. and Richard G. Majors. 2004. "African American Nonverbal Culture." In *Black Psychology*, ed. Reginald Jones, 313–51. Hampton, VA: Cobb and Henry.

Ashe, Arthur R. 1988. *A Hard Road to Glory: A History of the African-American Athlete*. New York: Warner Books.

Battle, Michael. 2006. *The Black Church in America: African American Christian Spirituality*. Hoboken, NJ: Wiley.

Bell, Catherine. 1997a. *Ritual: Perspectives and Dimensions.* New York: Oxford University Press.

——. 1997b. "Ritual Reification." In *Ritual and Religious Belief: A Reader*, ed. Graham Harvey, 265–85. New York: Routledge.

Braxton, Edward K. 1998. "The View from the Barbershop: The Church and African-American Culture." *America* (February 14): 18–22.

Burnim, Mellonee V. 1985. "The Black Gospel Music Tradition: A Complex of Ideology, Aesthetic, and Behavior." In *More than Dancing*, ed. Irene V. Jackson, 147–68. Westport, CT: Greenwood Press.

Capone, Stefania. 2007. "Transatlantic Dialogue: Roger Bastide and the African American Religions." *Journal of Religion in Africa* 37: 336–70.

Caponi, Gena Dagel. 1999. "The Case for an African American Aesthetic." In *Signifyin(g), Sanctifyin' and Slam Dunking: A Reader in African American Expressive Culture*, ed. Gena Caponi, 1–41. Amherst: University of Massachusetts Press.

Clemmitt, Marcia. 2007. "Black Churches Cater to Suburban Middle Class: Poor, Inner-city Blacks are being Left Behind." *CQ Researcher* 17, 43: 122–23.

DuBois, W.E.B. 1903. *The Souls of Black Folk: Essays and Sketches.* Chicago: A. C. McClurg.

Dyson, Michael Eric. 1993. *Reflecting Black: African-American Cultural Criticism.* Minneapolis: University of Minnesota Press.

Emery, David. 2009. "The Seventh-Inning Stretch: Origin (or not) of a Baseball Tradition." *About.com.* http://urbanlegends.about.com/cs/historical/a/seventh_inning.htm

Floyd, Samuel A., Jr. 1995. *The Power of Black Music: Interpreting its History from Africa to the United States.* New York: Oxford University Press.

Fordham, Signithia. 1993. "Those Loud Black Girls: (Black) Women, Silence, and Gender 'Passing' in the Academy." *Anthropology and Education Quarterly* 24, 1: 3–32.

George, Nelson. 1992. *Elevating the Game: Black Men and Basketball.* New York: HarperCollins.

Gilroy, Paul. 1993. *The Black Atlantic: Modernity and Double-Consciousness.* New York: Verso.

Glazier, Stephen D., ed. 2001. *Encyclopedia of African and African-American Religions.* New York: Routledge.

Goffman, Erving. 1959. *The Presentation of Self in Everyday Life.* New York: Doubleday Anchor Books.

Gordon, Milton. 1964. *Assimilation in American Life.* New York: Oxford University Press.

Grimes, Ronald L. 1982. *Beginnings in Ritual Studies.* Washington, DC: University Press of America.

ter Haar, Gerrie. 1995. "Ritual as Communication: A Study of African Christian Communities in the Bijlmer District of Amsterdam," in *Pluralism and Identity: Studies in Ritual Behavior*, eds Jan Platvoet and Karel van der Toorn, 115–44. New York: Brill Academic Publishers.

Hanna, J. L. 1997. "Black/White Nonverbal Differences, Dance and Dissonance: Implications for Desegregation." In *Nonverbal Behavior: Perspectives, Applications, Intercultural Insight*, ed. A. Wolfgang. Seattle, WA: Hogrefe & Huber.

Herskovits, Melville J. 1941/1958. *The Myth of the Negro Past*. New York: Harper and Brothers. [Reprint, Boston: Beacon].

Holloway, Joseph E. and Winifred K. Vass. 1993. *The African Heritage of American English*. Bloomington: Indiana University Press.

Holt, Grace Sims. 1972. "Stylin' Outta the Black Pulpit." In *Signifyin(g), Sanctifyin' and Slam Dunking: A Reader in African American Expressive Culture*, ed. Gena Caponi, 331–47. Amherst, MA: University of Massachusetts Press.

Hraba, Joseph. 1994. *American Ethnicity*. Itasca, IL: F. E. Peacock.

Hunt, Larry L. and Matthew O. Hunt. 2001. "Race, Region and Religious Involvement: A Comparative Study of Whites and African Americans." *Social Forces* 80, 2: 605–31.

Jones, James M. 1986. "Racism: A Cultural Analysis of the Problem." In *Prejudice, Discrimination and Racism*, eds John F. Dovidio and Samuel L. Gaertner, 279–314. San Diego: Academic Press.

Kochman, Thomas. 1981. *Black and White Styles in Conflict*. Chicago: University of Chicago Press.

NCAA. 1995. *NCAA Rules*. Section 2, Non-contact Fouls: Unsportsmanlike Acts. Indianapolis: National Collegiate Athletics Association.

Olson, Ernest. 2001. "Signs of Conversion, Spirit of Commitment: The Pentecostal Church in the Kingdom of Tonga." *Journal of Ritual Studies* 15, 2: 13–37.

Orsi, Robert A. 1985. *The Madonna of 115th Street: Faith and Community in Italian Harlem, 1880–1950*. New Haven, CT: Yale University Press.

Otis, Johnny. 1993. *Upside Your Head! Rhythm and Blues on Central Avenue*. Hanover, NH: Wesleyan University Press.

Pattillo-McCoy, Mary. 1999. "Church Culture as a Strategy of Action in the Black Community." *American Sociological Review* 63: 767–84.

Pierson, Don. 1991. "Icky Rule is Proving to be Sticky for NFL." *Chicago Tribune* (March 24): 8.

Raboteau, Albert J. 1994. "Fire in the Bones: African-American Christianity and Autobiographical Reflection." *America* (May 21): 4–9.

——. 1995. *A Fire in the Bones: Reflections on African-American Religious History*. Boston: Beacon Press.

Ramirez, Margaret and Manya A. Brachear. 2006. "Struggling to Fill Needs, Pews." *Chicago Tribune* (February 12): B1.

Rickford, J. F. and A. E. Rickford. 1976. "Cut-eye and Suck-teeth: African Words and Gestures in New World Guise." *Journal of American Folklore* 89: 294–309.

Riggs, Marlon, dir. 1987. *Ethnic Notions*. San Francisco: California Newsreel.

Sered, Susan S. 1992. "Ritual Expertise in the Modern World." In *Women as Ritual Experts: The Religious Lives of Elderly Jewish Women in Jerusalem*, 121–37. New York: Oxford University Press.

Smith, Jonathan Z. 1987. "To Take Place." In *Ritual and Religious Belief: A Reader*, ed. Graham Harvey, 26–50. New York: Routledge.

Stallybrass, Peter and Allon White. 1986. "Introduction." In *Ritual and Religious Belief: A Reader*, ed. Graham Harvey, 139–62. New York: Routledge.

Steinberg, Stephen. 1989. *The Ethnic Myth: Race, Ethnicity and Class in America*. Boston: Beacon Press.

Stephenson, Barry. 2003. "Ritual criticism of a contemporary rite of passage." *Journal of Ritual Studies* 17, 1: 32–41.

Takahashi, Melanie and Tom Olaveson. 2003. "Music, Dance and Raving Bodies: Raving as Spirituality in the Central Canadian Rave Scene." *Journal of Ritual Studies* 17, 2: 72–96.

Thompson, Robert Ferris. 1966. "An Aesthetic of the Cool: West African Dance." In *Signifyin(g), Sanctifyin' and Slam Dunking: A Reader in African American Expressive Culture*, ed. Gena Caponi, 72–86. Amherst, MA: University of Massachusetts Press.

——. 1983. *Flash of the Spirit: African and Afro-American Art and Philosophy.* New York: Random House.

Weisenfeld, Judith. 2007. *Hollywood Be Thy Name: African American Religion in American Film, 1929–1949.* Berkeley: University of California Press.

White, Shane and Graham White. 1998. *Stylin': African-American Expressive Culture from its Beginnings to the Zoot Suit.* Ithaca, NY: Cornell University Press.

Wideman, John Edgar. 1990. "Michael Jordan Leaps the Great Divide." In *Signifyin(g), Sanctifyin' and Slam Dunking: A Reader in African American Expressive Culture*, ed. Gena Caponi, 388–406. Amherst, MA: University of Massachusetts Press.

Wilson, Olly. 1992. "The Heterogeneous Sound Ideal in African-American Music." In *Signifyin(g), Sanctifyin' and Slam Dunking: A Reader in African American Expressive Culture*, ed. Gena Caponi, 156–71. Amherst, MA: University of Massachusetts Press.

Notes

1 For examinations of African American women and expressivity, see Fordham (1993); Andrews and Majors (2004). On not defining the male sphere of ritualizing as normative for women, see Sered (1992).

2 A broader study might include greeting and congratulatory rituals, such as the fist-bump made famous by (then-Senator) Barack Obama and his wife, Michelle, as he accepted the Democratic nomination for President. For a discussion of other gestures, see Andrews and Majors (2004).

3 The very titles—LeBron "The King" James and "The Chosen One"—are reminiscent of Ray Allen's portrayal of Jesus Shuttlesworth in Spike Lee's movie *He Got Game* (1998), a critique of basketball—and collegiate and professional sport in general—and its exploitation of African American athletes.

4 Anthropologists, black nationalists, sociologists, historians, and geneticists have debated the presence of Africanisms in African American culture at least since the turn of the twentieth century. (See Herskovits 1941/1958; Thompson 1966, 1983; Rickford and Rickford 1976; Gilroy 1993; Holloway and Vass 1993; Floyd 1995; Caponi 1999; Glazier 2001; Capone 2007.) For African ritual in Amsterdam, see ter Haar (1995).

5 By way of analogy, a child of Catholic parents need not be Catholic him or herself—nor have ever been to a Catholic church—in order to have had Catholic *ways of being* infused into his or her life processes.

6 For a discussion of religion and culture in the context of a black barbershop—another center of the black domus—see Braxton (1998).

7 The growing secularization of society has led scholars to investigate what may have replaced church-going rituals and rites. For a discussion of how boys and girls fashion their own rites of passage, see Stephenson (2003). For a discussion of the ritualizing of dance and music and the influence of DJs on youth, see Takahashi and Olaveson (2003).

8 Ernest Olson notes: "The Pentecostal church has an exuberance of music, preaching, and prayer that clearly demarcates the denomination's presence in the Tongan Islands" (Olson 2001, 14).
9 Milton Gordon defined cultural assimilation as a "change of cultural patterns to those of the core society" (Gordon 1964: 71).
10 For an extensive discussion of "transgressions and the attempt to control them," see Stallybrass and White (1986, 160).
11 During the 2009 NBA Playoffs, media commentators even suggested on-air that the "Air Jordan" slam-dunk leap be made the association's new "logo," replacing the iconic 1960s image of Los Angeles Laker Jerry West.

Chapter 7

Dropping in for the Holidays

Christmas as Commercial Ritual at the Precious Moments Chapel

Jennifer Rycenga

"Christmas is the season to visit the chapel. Even if you've been here before, you must come and see the lights." This enthusiasm poured from a receptionist at the Precious Moments Chapel in Carthage, Missouri, describing the glories of the yuletide displays. When I actually arrived in mid-December, however, the lights were not what caught my eye.

Entering the chapel grounds requires one to navigate through a phalanx of gift shops. The first such emporium I encountered, to my left, was a special seasonal store. Thematically decorated Christmas trees, rows of porcelain ornaments, and other tinny, tiny geegaws proliferated in the small space, swallowing the consumer/collector in their elaborately and abundantly precious universe. The other "regular" gift stores were similarly sagging under the pressure of the commercial truism that the Christmas season is the financial "make-or-break" point for the entire year. Indeed, for all employed at the chapel, Christmas is the season when they pray you will visit.

The Precious Moments universe is the creation of nondenominational evangelical artist Sam Butcher. Coming from a background in the Child Evangelism Fellowship, Butcher designed a series of note cards in 1975 featuring children with large heads, compressed bodies, and the iconic attribute of teardrop-shaped eyes. Picked up by the Enesco Corporation in 1978, the Precious Moments children were transferred to the medium of porcelain figurines, where they met with unqualified (and still growing) success. Now the top grossing line of porcelain figurines (finally outstripping their illustrious European predecessor the Hummels in the mid-1990s), they are sold internationally, and a vigorous secondary market flourishes for fans and collectors. The participants in Precious Moments culture consider the chapel to be a primary pilgrimage site, both because of Butcher's ongoing creative work there, and because of the gift stores, which offer the widest selection, as well as pieces unique to the chapel grounds (Martin 1994, 20; Wells 1995, 160–61).[1]

Butcher deftly crafts his figurines to combine common cultural themes of childhood innocence, domesticity, and a simple Christian faith. His art is dependent on two salient features of Christianity: its narrative richness, and its theological claim that people can be saved despite being sinful. Both of these features give Butcher leeway to depict his characters sentimentally. For example, a figurine shows the baby Jesus in a crèche, with two little children looking in on him. The girl is whispering to the boy "His Name is Jesus" (the title of the figurine; Martin 1994, 242). Theologically, this portrays the frailty and ignorance of the human condition, but not in a condemnatory manner. We are invited to project our limited selves into the salvific situation, and imagine that we could have played a role—perhaps as cute comic relief—in the cosmic drama. Since this cosmology assumes that we are all children in the eyes of God, each of us has the potential to be similarly winsome and lovable. God's transcendence is maintained, especially given the evangelical overtones of the figurine's title, but that transcendence is ultimately no more unbridgeable than that between parent and child.

Hand-wringing over the commercialization of Christmas is as old as the holiday's prominence in America (Nissenbaum 1996, 140, 318). Christians of many denominations have decried the appropriation of Jesus' birth in the service of fattening corporate profits (Schmidt 1995, 5–6). Genuine though these concerns may be, they tend to overlook larger cosmological contexts—specifically, the overarching universalism of contemporary capitalism and the ambiguous design of placing God amid these business details. The Precious Moments Chapel happily provides a site for baptized capitalism, where a religious sheen enhances the magic and greases the wheels of commerce. The chapel's ritual of Christmas shopping represents the annual rebirth of a gentle apotheosis of capitalist calculation.

Ritual commonly uses sacred objects: props such as incense, flowers, vestments, animals, food, and coins. Similarly, any commodity, in its use-value, "is, first of all, an external object, a thing which through its qualities satisfies human needs" (Marx 1867/1977, 125). Despite the fact that both capitalism and ritual employ material objects, they disengage from that very materiality, deliberately projecting a cosmological overlay or abstract meaning onto objects. Instead of linking us to our physicality, our bodies, and our materiality, the processes of elevation in formal rites and of leveling quantification in capitalism tend to alienate participants from the material qualities of objects and from the ways in which they are made and exchanged (Marx 1867/1977, 126–28; Grimes 1990, 14).

Of course, such alienation has not gone unnoticed, and various attempts have been made to overcome it. The more radical wings of the Protestant Reformation, for example, repudiated the inherited ritualism of the medieval church. But such total rejection brought in its wake a strengthening of body/mind dualism, and therefore did nothing to ease the alienation from matter. A seemingly more promising route emerged when the domestication of white urban America throughout the nineteenth century entailed moving both ritual and the exchange of commodities into the charmed, intimate circle of home. No moment better encapsulates this strategy than the Christmas season, and few places rival the Precious Moments Chapel as an illustration of the collapsed logics of religious sentiment and capitalism. Christmas shopping becomes an adjunct ritual, a public enactment of one's commitment to the ritual affirmation of personal domestic bliss. Sentimentality must be highlighted at every turn, either in the hopes of providing authenticity, or in the calculation and manipulation of human desires. As a ritual about buying commodities, Christmas shopping reinforces ritual and religious logic. The seasonal decoration of the grounds of the Precious Moments Chapel supports an atmosphere of total absorption in the "holiday spirit," centered on buying and selling. Contradictions emerge when one inquires how, and how much, the entire operation is commercialized, and when one views the extent to which the attempts to disguise commercialization are both (and sometimes simultaneously) sincere and disingenuous.

Christmas is, indeed, the season to see just how cute theology can get. Upon entering the Christmas store at the chapel complex, the ornaments currently in production are arrayed for purchase.[2] They include a ballerina entitled "Lord, Keep Me on My Toes"; the starchily uniformed but smiling visage of "Onward Christian Soldiers"; a girl reading the Bible in the tub, dubbed "He Cleansed My Soul"; a cheerful white policeman writing a ticket under the moniker "Trust and Obey"; and a pilot in his patched-up single-engine "Heaven-Bound" plane urging us to "Have a Heavenly Christmas." The more expensive figurines—many of them representing current issues in annual, dated series—include a (most literally) fallen angel, halo askew, who looks rather startled as his bottom sinks into a cup of eggnog. In its title, this charmer assures us of yuletide cheer: our besotted angel is "Dropping In for the Holidays."

Such Christmas bibelots are tenderly described in the Precious Moments catalog:

> There is a tradition in most homes that certain ornaments on the family Christmas tree commemorate special times and special people we hold dear. Each exquisite, inspiring ornament reflects these wonderful times and loving people, and will create treasured memories for Christmases to come ... These are moments to cherish, moments to reflect, and each is very precious.
>
> (Martin 1994, 247, 225)

Precious Moments are intended to hallow domestic rituals, traditions, and gift exchanges, which are presumed to multiply around the Christmas season. Yet there is a contradiction here: the items have been designed, produced, and put up for sale prior to the events they are meant to commemorate. The mass marketing of intimate gifts, embedded in the very name of the Precious Moments, means that your most personal moments have already been cast in porcelain, ahead of your experience of them. This is openly acknowledged in the description, which states that the ornaments *"will create* treasured moments." This is not merely a question of linear time: it represents the nearly imperative (and commercially marketable) demand for sentimentalization.

Such contradictions, embedded in the calculating creation of "needs" in consumerist society, has been apparent since the beginnings of the domestic Christmas in the United States (Schmidt 1995; Nissenbaum 1996). Shunned by the Puritan authorities of early New England because of its connections to pagan seasonal celebrations and to sexual[3] and alcohol excesses, the colonial Christmas was celebrated mainly by the working class as an occasion for public revelry and carnival. The eighteenth-century Christmas often became riotous; it was decidedly *"not* centered around the family or on children or giving presents" (Nissenbaum 1996, 38; emphasis added). The transformation of Christmas into a domestic holiday coincided with the growth of consumer culture in nineteenth-century America. This process created a new set of holiday rituals, such as stockings, the decorating of Christmas trees, gift wrapping, holiday card exchanges, and Santa Claus.

Such innovations obviously lacked direct biblical precedents and warrants. Indeed, Christmas has always been a difficult holiday for Christianity to baptize. The pagan seasonal connections, as well as the lack of biblical evidence for dating the birth of Jesus, led to rejection of the holiday by some branches of Christianity (such as the Puritan authorities mentioned above, and the Jehovah's Witnesses), and to an uneasy blessing from some other branches (Nissenbaum 1996, 3–9). The sometimes tenuous connection between Christian piety and Christmas celebrations suggests that in our own time, "Christmas represents a residual Christianity" (Bocock 1974, 114). It is this *residual* nature of religion in Christmas, in which the specifics of Christianity are replaced by a hazy nimbus to be invoked when convenient, that makes it a ripe target for exploitation by capitalist interests. Residual religion contributes a prestigious aura and, in a manner similar to how secular authorities have used the "higher" mandates of religion as a justificatory device for secular policies, advertising for religious products can invoke a religious aura to insinuate that they are above the base aspects of commercialism.

In contemporary America, residual Christianity is particularly promoted by the narrative specifics and family relations present in the Nativity mythology. These include the idyllic Holy Family, the vulnerability of the baby Jesus being born in a stable, the Magi as gift-givers, and the copious angelic appearances around the natal event. Schmidt refers to this constellation of narrative qualities as Christmas's "greater potential for consecration," in which the season's "dense symbols" play effectively "in the marketplace" (Schmidt 1995, 124, 126). Ironically, Christmas outpaces even Easter as a celebrated holiday in the United States, precisely because the marketplace can better appropriate the symbols and theology of the (innocent and cute) baby Jesus than it can the crucified adult. Theologically malleable, largely bereft of terror, the Christmas narrative is easily applied to placid, consumerist "family values."[4]

The culturally imposed gift-giving requirements of Christmas generate the seasonal ritual of Christmas shopping. The annual "official" beginning of the Christmas shopping season the day after Thanksgiving, the cheery newspaper announcements of the number of shopping days left, and the shared, mad rush of Christmas Eve shoppers—all these carry aspects of what scholars have termed "ritualization." While it is obvious that a coronation or a Catholic Mass are formal rites, there are many social activities that share the characteristics of ritual. Ronald Grimes has enumerated such qualities of ritual, maintaining that "when an activity becomes dense with them, it becomes increasingly proper to speak of it as ritualized" (Grimes 1990, 14). Drawing from Grimes' list of characteristics, the following are applicable to Christmas shopping, and especially to the ethos of Christmas shopping at the Precious Moments Chapel:

> performed, embodied, enacted, gestural (not merely thought or said), formalized ... stylized ... (not ordinary, unadorned) ... repetitive ... collective, institutionalized ... patterned ... standardized ... ordered ... traditional ... deeply felt, sentiment-laden, meaningful ... symbolic, referential ... perfected, idealized ... ludic ... religious ... conscious, deliberate.
>
> (*ibid.*)

This accretion of ritual characteristics renders holiday shopping into a prime example of ritualization, defined as "an activity that is not culturally framed as ritual but which someone, often an observer, interprets as if it were potential ritual. One might think of it as infra-, quasi-, or pre-ritualistic" (*ibid.*, 10).

Understanding the Precious Moments worldview requires such an "infra-ritualistic" approach, because its roots in evangelical Protestantism and its portrayal of quotidian scenes as reflections of biblical lessons do not invite formalized, sacramental rites. But the link between the Precious Moments theology and the capitalist consumer marketplace creates a formalized, institutionalized context for ritual-like activity in the buying and selling of Precious Moments articles. This institutionalized context supports both the activity of the marketplace itself, and the intended sentimental spiritual functions of the Precious Moments product line. The Precious Moments Chapel builds these elements into a holiday spectacle, where one can participate fully in consumer culture without feeling guilt about sullying the birth of Jesus with obeisance to Mammon. Billboards on the way to the chapel encourage us to "Celebrate the Spirit of the Holiday," and there's even an ornament of a tortoise, enjoining us to "Slow Down and Enjoy the Holidays" (Martin 1994, 254). This critique of the marketplace ritual of

Christmas shopping is itself not immune to co-optation and incorporation into the commodities for sale at the chapel.[5]

This co-optation occurs seamlessly because the Precious Moments Chapel, for all its religious sincerity and religious trappings, is actually a business, not a church, operated from the perspective of business interests. Its religious nature is already fully intertwined with the marketplace. But this raises larger theological and cosmological questions. In an essay in the *Atlantic Monthly* in March 1999, Harvey Cox relates how he detected theological patterns on the financial pages, once he saw how "The Market" had taken on the mystery, reverence, and omnipotence of God, to become "the only true God, whose reign must now be universally accepted and who allows for no rivals" (Cox 1999, 20). This insight reveals the universality of commodity logic; but this universality does not preclude the sham individualism of "niche marketing" the need to appear to treat us all as individuals:

> The Market already knows the deepest secrets and darkest desires of our hearts or at least would like to know them ... The Market wants this kind of x-ray omniscience because by probing our inmost fears and desires and then *dispensing across-the-board solutions, it can extend its reach.*
>
> (*ibid.*, 22; emphasis added)

One-hundred-and-fifty years earlier, in the *Communist Manifesto*, Karl Marx defined this dynamic of capitalism as a reduction of human relations, in which bourgeois society has "put an end to all feudal, patriarchal, idyllic relations ... and has left remaining no other nexus between man and man than naked self-interest, than callous 'cash payment.'" Marx adds that this reduction has, specifically, "drowned the most heavenly ecstasies of religious fervor, of chivalrous enthusiasm, of philistine sentimentalism, in the icy water of egotistical calculation" (Fernbach 1974, 70).

The subservient role of religion within capitalism, to which it contributes valuable luster and justificatory rhetoric, is aided by the manifold parallels between religious practices and structures of the marketplace.[6] Like much religious doctrine, the dynamics of the marketplace have a tendency to universalize themselves. Religions and economic systems are human creations that lull themselves (and others) with the brief authority of a false naturalism.[7] Maintaining the natural inevitability of a given religious or economic system entails masking or rationalizing not only its human construction but, even more urgently, the preventable harm it causes. Because the leveling, antihuman effects of the market have seeped into every corner of our sacred and secular lives, a great deal of effort must be poured into disguising this fact, in the realms of both exchange and production. Cox and Marx are correct that the mechanisms of capitalism have leveled human relations and drowned out competing cosmologies in a sea of coins. This ironically highlights the material ways in which religion lends its halo to obfuscating the machinery of capitalism.[8]

The Precious Moments Chapel contains many rooms in the castle of The Market, starting in the most literal sense of having more than half a dozen gift stores on site. The ritualization of the Christmas shopping season, in particular, plays on deep-seated desires for authentic human relations and friendships; but it uses these impulses to jump-start a (profitable) buying frenzy. Commercial culture lures us with promises that it can improve our human relations, if only we buy the right objects by the designated date. Precious Moments ratifies this by representing our human relations as reflections of a larger Christian cosmology.

The Precious Moments figurines present a world of domestic bliss in homologous relation to the heavenly realm. The private, domestic realm played a crucial role in the development of Christmas in the United States, as the celebrations moved indoors (Nissenbaum 1996, 132). Once inside, "little moments of familial ritual and gift giving were at the heart of the middle-class Christmas" (Schmidt 1995, 153). These very moments are now themselves iconocized by Precious Moments, evident in product lines emblazoned with "Baby's First Christmas," or "Our First Christmas Together," let alone more detailed representations of intimate scenes, such as the eggnog-drenched angel, or the mischievous, ribbon-unfurling puppy of "Tied Up for the Holidays" (Martin 1994, 225, 253ff).[9]

Precious Moments intends to celebrate the private and the personal. But it can only do so through the public mediation of the market. The chapel grounds does its best to hide this mediation while also keeping the cash registers jingling. One time-honored American method for achieving this is by sanctifying the stores themselves, and making them seem like a cozy home or a grand church. The Nativity scene on the front lawn, the roadside billboard "Celebrate the Spirit of the Holiday," and the Christmas shop's multiple thematic trees all point to the grounds themselves as a repository of holy holiday sentiment. When the "marketplace itself" is so "stunningly consecrated," there is "no clear line between church and mart, between the sacred and the secular" (Schmidt 1995, 159). The chapel also wants to blur the boundary between home and mart, between the domestic and the public, so that traveling to the chapel and buying Precious Moments merchandise become extensions of the domestic "family values" bliss they represent. The conscious coexistence of commercial concerns with the religious and social means of disguising them are evident (if not cynically so), in the admission of Howard L. Kratz, who designed similar displays in Philadelphia in the early decades of the twentieth century: "Christmas cathedrals were intended to present the store as 'above commercialism,' while at the same time winning big results for the business" (Schmidt 1995, 167).

This knowing wink, which acknowledges the simultaneity of commercial and noncommercial interests, has the further effect of masking (and iconocizing) production relations. This phenomenon is hardly limited to the Precious Moments products: the stepped-up demands of the holiday season require most workers today to labor harder and for longer hours during the holiday season than at other times, which hardly enables domestic idylls (Nissenbaum 1996, 310). Santa Claus delineates one effective means "to disguise the fact that most ... presents ... were commodity productions": he "mystified production and distribution" (*ibid.*, 172, 175).[10] But the elfin mythology of Santa Claus is too naïve for Precious Moments, which shows the actual production process in a series of storyboards (in the museum at the chapel), featuring pictures of the happy Thai workers who produce the figurines (Martin 1994, 35–38). Like the sanctification of the stores, this portrayal of the production process is meant to allay our fears about commercialization, but the attempt to glamorize the situation is easily doused, as it was by the icy water of *Forbes'* analysis: "Most of the figurines and decorative plates are manufactured cheaply in the Far East. They can be sold at a low price and still command handsome margins" (Schifrin 1995, 48).

These photos of the production process return us to another contradiction: the mass production of what are meant to be personal gifts. The earliest commercial Christmas gifts were often devotional in nature; the Bible itself was a popular item for commodification, variation, and price inflation (Moore 1994, 34–35; McDannell 1995, ch. 3; Schmidt 1995, 116, 128; Nissenbaum 1996, 147–48, 151–55). By marketing commodities that are religious and sometimes devotional in their ethos (including illustrated Bibles), and maintaining a neo-Victorian moral outlook, Precious Moments returns to the earliest manifestations of the commercialized domestic Christmas. But the primary mechanism by which Precious Moments (attempts to) avoid the "aesthetic of the serial, the machinic, the mass-reproduced" is in its very name, invoking the individual moment and its fragility (Morris 1993, 318). Each figurine is supposed to be individuated by each owner's "moment." But the moments are prefigured by the presuppositions of the Precious Moments world view.

This is where the ritualization plays its hand. The tension between American individualism and the interdependent nature of our economic system is mediated by the rhetoric of tradition. Commodity culture benefits by exploiting the balance between individuality and tradition. Consider, for example, the continual debates over traditional versus modern weddings. In the specific instance of that ritual, the need for props means that commodity capitalism can create, market, and sell an ever-proliferating panoply of goods for each discrete type of event, and for a range within them. Precious Moments is fully implicated in that logic: weddings, graduations, and birthdays are all occasions for which Sam Butcher has supplied baubles. But Christmas has a commercial density, calendric certainty, and religious patina that no other holiday can match. The presumption that "everyone" celebrates Christmas, that they will celebrate it annually, and that domestic gift-giving circles will increase through the generations, fuel the holiday and fuel the commercial need to reinforce its sanctity as insurance for future profits. The ritualization of Christmas shopping sidesteps contradictions in mass-produced gifts by flooding us with ever-increasing numbers and kinds of objects for sale. The Precious Moments line of products is also increasingly insistent on its projection of an intrinsic link between its goods and "tradition." The serial nature of the Precious Moments figurines intensifies that link in creating a desire to own a complete set, and to make the ornaments and figurines part of one's own family tradition.

Catherine Bell notes that "activities that are not explicitly called 'rituals' may seem ritual-like if they invoke forms of tradition" (Bell 1997, 145). Centering Christmas traditions squarely within sentimental domesticity, the Precious Moments Chapel gift stores proselytize participation in a public ritual of buying for time-honored private rites of gift exchange. Tradition is evident in all aspects of the figurines and of the chapel grounds. The teardrop-eyed characters support all planks of traditional family values ideology, albeit without explicit political engagement. The children are shown in patched-up homespun fashion, with the girls almost always in ankle-length skirts. Grandmothers knit, mothers bake, fathers and boys fish. Marriage commemoratives abound; same-sex commitment pieces don't exist. Workers ask for divine help—"Lord, Help Me Stick to My Job" shows an over-burdened secretary (Martin 1994, 188)—but they don't organize into unions.[11] The chapel's Christmas store broadcasts the message that the "traditional" Christmas is a quiet, domestic one, complete with snow, trees, gifts, and touching moments of personal connection. Tradition hallows the entire operation.

The traditions evoked here are nineteenth-century in tone and style. For instance, the ornament titled "Share in the Warmth of Christmas" features a bonneted girl, tightly bundled in a long-sleeve, high-neck top and a thick quilted skirt below (Martin 1994, 246). She strides toward us from a past time, which the artist and the corporation (with different degrees of sincerity, perhaps) want us to believe was "more 'in touch' than our own (time) with 'what really matters'" (Nissenbaum 1996, 316). But there are three problems with the projection. First, the unsullied traditional Christmas is a myth. Second, the representation of the unsullied Christmas is itself a commodity. Third, the projection of this myth of a more authentic past carries with it a desire for a cultural hegemony of religious moralism; while it is ironic that capitalism is achieving such universal hegemony instead of (and perhaps at the expense of) religion, both benefit by the projection of a closed cosmology.

Precious Moments creates a universe of sentiment, both at the chapel and in the world. An advertising display in one of the gift shops proclaimed the good news that "Precious Moments Are Your Passport to Loving, Caring and Sharing," invoking three themes of capitalism: universality, accessibility to all that you want, and commutability across differences. It may seem that the Precious Moments universe is harmless, a gentle apotheosis, as I termed it earlier. Yet this cosmology is hardly innocent of ideological underpinnings. Uncle Sam's patriotism links seamlessly with his support for the phone company as he jingle-istically reminds us to let "Let Freedom Ring" (Figure 7.1); ideologies of patriotism, patriarchy, respect for authority, and Christian exclusivism[12] undergird what appears to be an idealistic world of innocence. The contradiction between the charming children, who never appear to be

Figure 7.1 Precious Moments figurine titled "Let Freedom Ring." Photo by Jennifer Rycenga.

doing anything that would require severe chastisement, and the existence (and representation) of soldiers, policemen, and sermons, is not played out within the Precious Moments representations. It is enacted in the larger socioeconomic-political context outside of the chapel grounds. One decorates the family Christmas tree with "Trust and Obey" and "Onward Christmas Soldiers" ornaments not because the domestic ritual of familial togetherness is threatened by unruliness; rather, the function of the ornaments is to reinscribe familial and state authority, and chastise those who are not a part of the Precious Moments universe—those who stand outside of the warm cosmology of Christ, Christmas, and family.

This is made explicit by a Precious Moments collector, Judi Thomas, in a Fourth of July piece in *Precious Insights* magazine. She laments that

> while the *majority* of Americans still hold to a belief in the Judeo-Christian values on which this nation was founded, we find ourselves in a quagmire of lurid and disgusting art ... If America were a neighbor or friend, we would send "get well" cards and flowers ... because America is sick. If America were a toddler, we would spank her and put her to bed for a nap ... because she's stubbornly pushing the limits of reasonable authority.
>
> (Thomas 1994, 7; emphasis hers)

With the infantilization of the country and the use of reasonable authority to punish it, the actual world behind the Precious Moments facade emerges. These teardrop-shaped children are standing up for innocence, against the debasement of culture caused by actual diversity of opinion and diversity of people.[13] At Christmas, the chapel, in coalition with capitalism, can bring it all together—hearth and home, gift exchange and commodity exchange, tradition and innovation—and sustain this traditionalism like a talisman against encroaching evil. The Precious Moments universe, at least, is already purified: it depicts how joyous the world would be if everyone capitulated to "reasonable authority."

This, finally, explains why "domesticity and capitalism themselves, 'family values' and accumulative, competitive ones, have been deeply interlinked from the very beginning, even when they have appeared to represent alternative modes of feeling (or seemed to be in conflict with each other)" (Nissenbaum 1996, 318). The family realm represents a supposed haven from sordid competition, while the marketplace promises unlimited opportunity and abundance for individuals. Both the family and the market want us to believe that their existence is natural, their authority "reasonable." But, in strictly logical terms, capitalism doesn't need the family (capitalism "has torn away from the family its sentimental veil, and has reduced the family relation to a mere money relation" [Fernbach 1974, 70]), and the family, if it wants to be a location of genuine human relations, would reject the alienation created by capitalism. So why do they get along so well? Perhaps it is because they both want universal authority, but choose to mask it under the guise of love. They work hand-in-glove to sustain monotheism and monoculture, whether it is called God or the Market. As political theorist Barry Adam (1999) puts it, "a significant part of the success of the neo-conservative agenda has been due to their ... combining the neoconservative economic 'pill' with the promise of cultural hegemony for moralist author-itarianism" (*ibid.*, 26). This cultural hegemony joins with capitalism because they both participate in what Theodor Adorno (1998) calls mythical ever-sameness: "In the like-for-like of every act of exchange ... the balance of accounts is null. If the exchange was just, then nothing should really have happened" (*ibid.*, 159). While Adorno points out that this "doctrine of like-for-like is a lie," it is a powerful one, which can be materialized in the commodified, precious frozen moments of a nostalgic family idyll.

Where is the Christian God in these details? It will not do to doubt the subjective validity of people's faith. Perhaps, for some, a mass-produced fig-urine perfectly captures their hierophanic experience. But the presence of God in the foreground details, and the faith and intention of Sam Butcher, cannot loosen the grip of the commodity fetish. In fact, they lend it the per-fect justificatory cover. When the market says it is time to buy, the Christmas rush begins, basking in a hallowed glow. The chapel sets up the seasonal gift store, the light show, the Nativity, the holly and pine. The special Christmas figurines evoke tender memories: a boy in his pajamas standing by a coal-burning stove suggests "May Your Christmas Be Warm," while a girl is "Dropping In for Christmas" (Martin 1994, 226, 227), merrily skating, her old-fashioned scarf waving in the breeze above her folded hands. But the veneer of religion is thin; she is already tumbling through into the icy waters of capitalist calculation.

References

Adam, Barry D. 1999. "Moral Regulation and the Disintegrating Canadian State." In *The Global Emergence of Gay and Lesbian Politics: National Imprints of a Worldwide Movement,* eds Barry D. Adam, Jan Willam Duyvendak, and André Krouwel. Philadelphia: Temple University Press.

Adorno, Theodor W. 1998. *Critical Models: Interventions and Catchwords,* trans. Henry W. Pickford. New York: Columbia University Press.

Bell, Catherine. 1997. *Ritual: Perspectives and Dimensions.* New York: Oxford University Press.

Bocock, Robert. 1974. *Ritual in Industrial Society: A Sociological Analysis of Ritualism in Modern England.* London: George Allen & Unwin.

Cox, Harvey. 1999. "The Market as God: Living in the New Dispensation." *Atlantic Monthly,* March, 19–23.

Fernbach, David, ed. 1974. *The Revolutions of 1848: Political Writings,* Vol. 1. New York: Vintage.

Grimes, Ronald L. 1990. *Ritual Criticism: Case Studies in its Practice, Essays on its Theory.* Columbia: University of South Carolina Press.

Martin, Laura C. 1994. *Precious Moments Last Forever.* New York: Abbeville Press.

Marx, Karl. 1967. *Writings of the Young Marx on Philosophy and Society,* trans/eds Loyd D. Easton and Kurt H. Guddat. Garden City, NY: Anchor Books.

——. 1867/1977. *Capital, Volume One,* trans. Ben Fowkes. New York: Vintage.

McDannell, Colleen. 1995. *Material Christianity: Religion and Popular Culture in America.* New Haven, CT: Yale University Press.

Moore, R. Lawrence. 1994. *Selling God: American Religion in the Marketplace of Culture.* New York: Oxford University Press.

Morris, Meaghan. 1993. "Things to Do with Shopping Centers." In *The Cultural Studies Reader,* ed. Simon During, 295–315. New York: Routledge.

Nissenbaum, Stephen. 1996. *The Battle for Christmas.* New York: Vintage.

Schifrin, Matthew. 1995. "Okay, Big Mouth. Profile of Stanhome Chief Executive G. William Seawright." *Forbes* 156, 8 (October 9, 1995): 47–48.

Schmidt, Leigh Eric. 1995. *Consumer Rites: The Buying and Selling of American Holidays.* Princeton, NJ: Princeton University Press.

Thomas, Judi. 1994. "Happy Birthday, America." *Precious Insights* 7, 3 (June/July 1994), 7.

Wells, Rosalie J., ed. 1995. *Official 1995 Secondary Market Price Guide for the Enesco Precious Moments® Collection,* 13th edn. Canton, IL: Rosie Wells Enterprises.

Notes

1 Much of this information was gleaned from three visits to the chapel and tours of the grounds in June 1995, April 1996, and December 1998. My intent was to observe the structural workings of the mercantile and religious ideologies, and so I do not address questions concerning the subjective meaning of Precious Moments products to collectors, nor did I interview collectors for this essay. I wish to thank Kenneth Kramer, Michelle Gubbay, Elizabeth McAlister, Leonard Primiano, Kate McCarthy, and Deborah Dash Moore for their suggestions and critiques.

2 Many other pieces are "suspended," which increases their value on the secondary market. This is a deliberate strategy on the part of the parent company, Enesco, to generate interest and to trigger the desire for completeness among collectors.

3 Cotton Mather preached against sexual licentiousness at the solstice, and apparently with good reason: "There was a 'bulge' in the number of births in the months of September and October" in the early eighteenth century (Nissenbaum 1996, 22).

4 Consider, for instance, how the Slaughter of the Innocents doesn't get a great deal of commercial attention as a Christmas event. There is no Precious Moments figurine commemorating this horrifying episode from Christian mythology, despite its theological importance. Medieval representations of the slaughter were common; Giotto's work provides an exemplar of this. From one Christian era to another, the emphasis has shifted in the retelling of the narrative. The needs of capitalism explain this change of emphasis rather efficiently.

5 Schmidt notes the phenomenon of "nested commodities": "By the 1930s, in a series of hybridized fusions, chocolate bunnies drove cars, played the accordion, or golfed; they themselves, in other words, had become model consumers. Such goods are suggestive of the nested quality of modern shopping—one commodity

points to another commodity, which points to another, and so on" (Schmidt 1995, 224–25). What needs further development, and what I am trying to do here, is to show how religious commodities, in particular, feed on such nested structures and reinforce the fetish of the commodity form.

6 Cox notes that most religions have capitulated to market logic: "Most of them seem content to become its acolytes or to be absorbed into its pantheon, much as the old Nordic deities, after putting up a game fight, eventually settled for a diminished but secure status as Christian saints" (Cox 1999, 23).

7 Marx 1867/1977, 175, n. 35).

8 I am not opposing my analysis to Marx's, by the way. Another way of perceiving the halo provided by religion is to return to the second half of Marx's famous "religion is the opiate of the masses" quote, where he also opines that religion is "the heart of a heartless world" (Marx 1967). The world is heartless because of avoidable inequities, because of capitalism's dominance. Religion is a way of addressing the hunger for genuine human relations. But religion itself fails in this task because it, too, is so easily appropriated into the capitalist ethos and cosmos.

9 The use of puns in the names of the Precious Moments figurines reflect the public/ private dynamics of the keepsake marketplace. To "get" the names, one must participate in a shared community, because the names require a knowledge of idiomatic American English. But the "precious" aspect retains the flavor of an "inside" joke.

10 The Precious Moments universe does not dwell on the mythology of Santa Claus; instead it replicates the contradictions and tensions between commerce and obfuscation. Whether Santa Claus is left out of the domestic bliss of sharing Precious Moments because of theological uneasiness with his origins on the part of the evangelical Butcher, or because he represents a rival iconography, I cannot say with certainty. But it is likely a combination of the two. With almost no representations of Santa Claus in the Precious Moments world, Butcher's palette dwells on the domestic archetypes (Grandma in a rocking chair, children sneaking a look inside wrapped gifts, etc.).

11 I see this as a mollification of working-class culture, directed from above, rather than as an expression of job satisfaction or adaptability; it contrasts with the heartier attitude of country-western songs such as "Take This Job and Shove It."

12 Religious intolerance within the Precious Moments universe is muted by the *laissez-faire* tolerance of the marketplace. Thus there are both Catholic and King James versions of Precious Moments Bibles, and the president of Enesco, Eugene Freidman, does not hide his Jewish upbringing, gladly proclaiming the universality of emotions evoked by the Precious Moments characters. But it is hard not to see Christian exclusivism in pieces like "I Believe in the Old Rugged Cross" and "Happy Trails Is Trusting Jesus" [*sic*] (Martin 1994, 250).

13 I say actual diversity of opinion and people because Butcher is a past master at repainting his works to include children of color. His representations of Native Americans are especially stereotypical, though he claims to have grown up "among the Pit River Indians in Big Bend, California" where he "formed a fondness for Indian people" (museum exhibit, Precious Moments Chapel).

Chapter 8

Desert Goddesses and Apocalyptic Art

Making Sacred Space at the Burning Man Festival

Sarah M. Pike

A sculpture composed of mud and chicken wire and dedicated to the Vedic god Rudra burned spectacularly in the Nevada night sky on Labor Day weekend 1998. The fire sacrifice to Rudra consisted of a two-hour-long "opera," during which professional opera singers and classically trained musicians, as well as dozens of costumed dancers and drummers, paid homage to the god, while thousands of participants at the Burning Man festival sat watching in a circle on the prehistoric lake bed of Black Rock Desert. And this was only a warm-up for the festival's main event the following night, when a forty-foot-tall wooden effigy—"the Man"—also went up in flames to the drumming and cheers of 10,000 festival-goers. As I left behind the burning remains of the man and walked toward the lights of our temporary city of 10,000, I saw artists torching sculptures that I had wandered by many times over the past several days. Then suddenly, along the distant horizon, a galloping horse (a bicycle cleverly covered with electro-luminescent strips) appeared, followed by a huge dragonfly with flashing wings.[1] A feast for the senses, Burning Man merges the enchantment and playfulness of children's worlds with adult content, and it is this mix of elements that draws participants of all ages from across the country, from New York to nearby Reno.

As many commentators note, Burning Man started in 1986 as a small gathering of friends on a San Francisco beach. When it became too large and wild to escape the attention of city police, it moved to the desert (see Gilmore and Van Proyen 2005). Larry Harvey burnt a wooden effigy at the end of a relationship, and the "Burning Man" soon became an important rallying point for a small community of artists, musicians, and interested onlookers. Burning Man first came to the Black Rock Desert in 1990. Every year the festival attracted more participants, and as this happened, the organizers began to describe their vision for this event and established a few rules, such as "leave no trace." By 1997, the first year I attended Burning Man, it had become a week-long festival involving weeks of advance preparation and cleanup afterward, mostly done by volunteer crews. A "Public Works" crew creates "streets" that mark out the half-moon-shaped city—"Black Rock City"—that comes to life as festival-goers arrive with camping gear, pavilions, art installations, and a range of temporary desert homes. The city borders the "playa" as a real city might develop along a lakefront. Out on the playa are large sculptures, including the Man himself, and installations, but no campers. Concerts, performance art, and other events are scheduled every day and night of the festival, but most festival-goers spend their hours wandering around the temporary city looking at art and visiting "theme camps," which are a blend of campsite and interactive art installation. The first year I attended, the festival attracted around 10,000 men and women, but in 2008 attendance had grown to 48,000. Many, but by no means all, participants were white, middle-class, "twentysomething ravers, fiftysomething hippies and thirtysomething computer whizzes" (Lelyveld 1998).

Seeking their dispersed community on the Burning Man internet bulletin board several days after the festival was over and they had returned home, participants mourned the end of Burning Man and discussed its impact on their lives: "It was life-changing and the most spiritual experience I've ever had," wrote Shannon (b.b., September 2, 1997).[2] And another message promised, "In the dust I found my family, In the dust I found my clan, In the dust I found hope for us all. Until we burn again I will hold my screams inside, I will keep the ashes burning until again I join my tribe" (Kaosangel, b.b., September 2, 1997). Peri agrees that Burning Man is a place of belonging: "In the Black Rock Desert, I've found a new hometown, where my imagination can sail without limits and bounds … where the aliens and the child-adults find common ground" (b.b., September 28, 1998). Another bulletin board participant called Burning Man "the enactment of the city of the heart" (September 2, 1997). In the *Black Rock Gazette*, Burning Man's official newspaper, artist Charlie Gadeken said: "Sometimes I feel like my real life exists for 10 days a year and the rest is a bad dream."[3] In his poetic tribute to the festival, I Shambat declares: "When life returns to the desert Humanity is rejuvenated/with dew on our lips and paint on our bodies we enter the kingdom of god" (b.b., September 11, 1998).

This charged language contrasts sharply with journalists' accounts of the festival. While participants focused on the sacred or life-changing experiences that they brought home, *U.S. News and World Report* called it "the anarchist's holiday of choice" (Marks 1997); *Life* reported it as "the largest weinie roast ever" (Dowling 1997); *Wired* editor Kevin Kelly, writing in *Time*, designated Burning Man a "meaningless but mesmerizing ritual" (Kelly 1997); *Print* called it a "preapocalypse party" (Kabat and Ivinski 1997); and the *San Francisco Chronicle* described it as an "eccentric six-day art festival in the Nevada desert" (Whiting 1997). News stories tended to focus on the art and elements of debauchery: "measured in terms of artistic and sexual freedom, there is no place else like Black Rock City," Sam Whiting wrote in his *San Francisco Chronicle* article. However, what most intrigued me about the festival was that, for many participants, Burning Man was an event of *religious* significance, characterized by powerful ritual, myth, and symbol; experiences of transcendence or ritual ecstasy; experiences of personal transformation; a sense of shared community; relationship to deity/divine power; and, perhaps most important, sacred space.

Burning Man is open to anyone who will pay the gate price (from $160 for those with a low income to $300 in 2009) and follow a few rules, such as "Do Not Drive Your Car in Camp" and "All Participants Are Required to Remove Their Own Trash and Garbage." It provides a locus where cultural problems, and especially problems of ultimate meaning, are expressed, analyzed, and played with. This festival is an important cultural and religious site that exemplifies the migration of religious meaning-making activities out of American temples and churches into other spaces. Scholars of American religion have judged the decline in church attendance to signal a disestablishment (Hammond 1992), or the increasing personalization of religion (Bellah *et al.* 1985; Roof 1993), while others have noted the shift from mainline churches to conservative, experiential forms of Protestantism such as Pentecostalism and independent evangelical churches (Cox 1995). I want to first situate the festival in its historical context on the American religious scene, and then explore the ways in which festival participants create the sacred space that makes transformative and intense experiences possible. Finally, I will explore the ways in which Burning Man reveals crucial tensions in contemporary American life that emerge because of the unique space that the festival creates. In so doing, I want to suggest that popular religious sites like the Burning Man festival are essential to an understanding of contemporary issues and future trends in American cultural and religious life.

The Festival as a Place Apart

Burning Man is hailed as the "new American holiday," "a circus of chaotic behavior," "a Disneyland in reverse," and "an arena of visionary reality."[4] It belongs to a growing trend (since the late '60s) of large-scale cultural and religious events that offer alternatives or place themselves in critical opposition to ordinary life—neo-pagan festivals, raves, women's music festivals such as "Lilith Fair," and Rainbow gatherings, all of which offer participants sacred space and ritual.[5] Burning Man and these other events fit David Chidester's characterization of American sacred space: "sacred meaning and significance, holy awe and desire, can coalesce in any place that becomes, even if only temporarily, a site for intensive interpretation" (Chidester 1995, 14). It also belongs to a tradition of collective occasions which (to borrow historian Jon Butler's phrase) first flourished in the "spiritual hothouse" of the nineteenth century. Chautauquas, outdoor revivals, camp meetings, lyceum programs, and Spiritualist conventions were all intended to transform the minds and spirits of nineteenth-century men and women (Moore 1994).[6] I want to turn briefly to look at these earlier American religious events in order to place the Burning Man festival in a tradition of American worship that has provided alternatives to mainline churches and other established religious institutions. An understanding of how Burning Man becomes religiously meaningful to participants may also shed light on this stream of American religiosity.

Like contemporary festivals, these events of earlier eras were consciously experienced apart from the rhythms of daily life, and drew boundaries between their gatherings and the rest of society. They were occasions on which a multitude of meanings and desires converged on the beaches and wooded areas where these gatherings were held. They served as vacation retreats and as opportunities for conversion experiences, and exposed their participants to new and radical ideas. Historian of American religions R. Laurence Moore notes that nineteenth-century evangelical camp meetings and revivals were "theatrical" and "carnivalesque." "Critics complained," Moore writes, "but the setting of the revival, for the space of the few hours or days, often protected practices that were elsewhere forbidden." Camp meetings were occasions for indulging the senses as well as seeking conversion (*ibid.*, 45–46; see also Schmidt 1995).[7] Likewise, Burning Man participants come looking for spiritual enlightenment, artistic pleasure, sensual indulgence, and "radical self-expression," to borrow one of founder Larry Harvey's favorite phrases. Evangelical camp meetings and festivals like Burning Man have very little in common in form and appearance with religious gatherings in mainline Protestant or Catholic churches. Historian Nathan O. Hatch says critics of camp meetings "perceived a manifest subversiveness in the form and structure of the camp meeting itself, which openly defied ecclesiastical standards of time, space, authority and liturgical form" (Hatch 1989, 50). Because their wild surroundings heightened the contrast to everyday life, controversial behavior like ecstatic dancing was exaggerated in these settings. Burning Man's site in a barren desert, like camp meetings in the hills of Kentucky, makes it strange and wild to city dwellers because it provides a sensual and aesthetic contrast to the everyday world. These nineteenth-century attractions for religious seekers prefigured celebrations like Burning Man, where embattled Silicon Valley employees escape from "the world of engineers and clocks" to spend a week in Black Rock City (Ed, b.b., September 10, 1998).

As in descriptions of their nineteenth-century forebears, accounts of Burning Man have in common the impression that festivals are *not* like the everyday world in which most of us live and work. Black Rock City comes to be a place of powerful and transformative experiences that cannot be had elsewhere. What is it about this festival that produces such powerful impressions in participants? How does Burning Man come to be imagined and experienced as such a different place from the world outside? Or, in the words of geographer Yi-Fu Tuan (1977, 6), how does a "space" which is "open and undefined" become a "secure and familiar ... place" for festival-goers?[8] The festival is transformed into a sacred space that contrasts to the outside world in a number of ways. Festival participants create what cultural theorist Rob Shields calls "placemyths," composites of rumors, images, and experiences that make particular places fascinating. Burning Man participants tell stories designed to locate the festival in what Shields describes as "an imaginary geography vis-à-vis the placemyths of other towns and regions which form the contrast which established its reputation as a liminal desti-nation" (Shields 1991, 112).[9] Participants work before, during, and after festivals at making an experience set apart from their lives "back home."[10]

Much of the advance planning and networking, as well as post-festival discussions, take place on the internet, where contact information, festival journals, photographs, and short videos are shared. Cyberfiction writer Bruce Sterling notes in his report from Burning Man that the festival has evolved into "a physical version of the internet" (Sterling 1996, 198). An extended festival narrative of words and pictures exists through links from website to website, allowing festival participants to keep their community alive across the country. The World Wide Web, notes Janet Murray in her study *Hamlet on the Holodeck: The Future of Narrative in Cyberspace*, "is becoming a global autobiography project ... pushing digital narrative closer to the mainstream" (Murray 1997, 252; see also Turkle 1995). Burning Man is just one of many real-world events that are extending their life through the internet and creating new forums for narrative. At the ninth Annual Be-In in January 1997, Larry Harvey discussed the similarities and differences between Burning Man and cyberspace: "on the one hand, says Harvey, Burning Man is a compelling physical analog for cyberspace" because "it is possible to reinvent oneself and one's world aided only by a few modest props and an active imagination," but on the other, Burning Man, unlike cyberspace, is an experience that heightens awareness of the body (Burning Man website, www.burningman.com).

Its life on the internet contributes to the sense that Burning Man is not like the churches and homes of ordinary life; it is a marginal site, or "heterotopia," to borrow Michel Foucault's term. There are places in every culture, says Foucault, "which are something like counter-sites, a kind of effectively enacted utopia in which ... all the other real sites ... are simulta-neously represented, contested, and inverted" (Foucault 1986, 24).[11] At Burning Man, Mark writes to the bulletin board, "I felt as if I BELONGED somewhere, a sensation that is curiously difficult to maintain in the Mid-west" (September 12, 1998). Like many others, Pan-o'-Playa regrets his return to ordinary life: "I'm trying not to let the tar, nicotine and sludge of this, the Outer World, drag me down" (b.b., September 15, 1998). Festival-goers reject and vilify the outside world in order to heighten their sense of the festival as a more important reality. I noticed this when I returned from

Burning Man '98 and began reading messages on the Burning Man bulletin board, many of which expressed a longing to return to Burning Man and contempt for normal life: "Buddy, this is our church, this is our respite from suffering through 358 days of Christian-inspired, bore-me-to-death society with all its mind-numbing institutions, corporations, and television. This is where we pray, this is our sacred place," wrote Mark (b.b., September 2, 1997). Like Mark, many festival-goers describe their Burning Man experience in such a way as to protest the ordinary world outside festival bounds. After Burning Man '98, I Shambat described the contrast between being in the outside world and being at the festival in a long poem he wrote to the bulletin board: "Come, disaffected/suburbanites/Souls like oil-splattered rags/ Minds torn up in the clock:/Come, take your mind-rags/and heart-rags/And let desert/Cleanse them/With Holy Fire" (b.b., September 11,1998). In this view, the outside world has corrupted and oppressed the men and women who arrive at Black Rock City to be cleansed, renewed, and initiated into a different reality.

The festival is conducive to powerful experiences because it is imagined as a blank canvas, a frontier of possibilities and unrealized potential—"the vacant heart of the Wild West" as one observer put it.[12] Larry Harvey instructs festival-goers to "imagine the land and the looming lakebed of the playa as a vast blank screen, a limitless ground of being."[13] And *Piss Clear*, one of Black Rock City's two newspapers, reminds festival-goers: "All that lays before us is the wide open playa floor. It is our palette and canvas, to create the world we can't enjoy at home." The land is thought of as something passive that human imaginings can be projected upon and, at the same time, as a living force that must be dealt with. In "Burning Man and the Environment," Harvey explains the relationship between Black Rock Desert and the festival: "We have discovered a new land; it is a place, a home, a living earth we can possess. And just as surely as our sweat will saturate this soil, it will possess us" (Burning Man website). The construction of Burning Man as a place apart is aided by its remote location in a desert about 110 miles north of Reno, near the tiny town of Gerlach. Black Rock country, a small portion of the Great Basin, is surrounded by the Granite, Calico, Black Rock, and Selenite mountain ranges. In the Nevada desert, survival is an issue; scorching sun, sandstorms, and sudden rain make the environment challenging for city dwellers. Storms wreak havoc on campsites and art work at the same time that they bring together festival-goers in the common project of keeping their tents up and sheltering each other from the elements.

One of the most effective ways that Burning Man establishes itself as a "church" of sorts is through anti-religious art and the subversive appropriation of familiar symbols. One example of festival-goers' playful irony is the Temple of Idle Worship at Burning Man '98. A sign at the temple instructed visitors: "You can light candles and prostrate yourself all you want, but your prayers won't be answered: the Deity is napping."[14] In the "What, Where,

When of Burning Man '98," a guide to festival events and exhibits, the Temple of Idle Worship is described as a "spiritual power point on the playa," but visitors to the temple are warned that "it makes no difference in what way you recognize this power as all forms of ritual and observance are meaningless here." In "Festival: A Sociological Approach," Jean Duvignaud writes that "all observers agree that festival involves a powerful denial of the established order" (Duvignaud 1976, 19). Folklorist Beverly Stoeltje explains that "in the festival environment principles of reversal, repetition, juxtaposition, condensation, and excess flourish" (Stoeltje 1992, 268). These principles are everywhere apparent at Burning Man, and help to give participants memorable experiences through contrasts between everyday life and the festival.

Figure 8.1 Interactive ritual art at Burning Man 1998. Photo by Sarah M. Pike.

Although festival-goers contrast their Burning Man experience to life in the outside world, they borrow the idioms of that world in order to criticize organized religion, consumerism, and social mores. During Burning Man '98 I came upon a confessional in the shape of a large wooden nun painted colorfully with flames coming up from the bottom of her robe, and words along her head reading "Sacred Disorder of the Enigmata!?!" and "Confess Your Conformities!" In front of the nun confessional a framed sign, "the Enigmatic Psalm of Eural," was written in biblical language, but its meaning was intentionally obscured. When I walked through the confessional's curtains I was faced by a round mirror decorated and painted with the message: "Be Your Own Messiah." The appropriation of religious symbolism—messiah and confession—both reifies and critically comments on Catholic practice.

Figure 8.2 Interactive ritual art at Burning Man 1998. Photo by Sarah M. Pike.

It is a playful display, yet serious in its underlying critique, an attitude mimicked in dozens of other festival appropriations of religious symbolism. On my first day at Burning Man '97 I noticed a two-foot statue of the Virgin Mary squirting out a stream of water for thirsty festival-goers. In the Burning Man world, all religions and traditions are up for grabs, and authenticity, authority, and purity are not at issue. In the eclectic world of Burning Man, artists and performers also borrow from non-Christian religions and cultures that are foreign to most Americans. An advance notice of "performances," published on the Burning Man site two weeks before the 1997 festival, described the "daughters of Ishtar," a lavish production of opera, music, dance, and ritual: "This ritual of death and resurrection is a revival of an ancient Sumerian cult, after 3,000 years of latency." Another announcement, this one for "Blue Girl," promises: "The intergalactic Fertility Goddess from the 16th Dimension will arrive to seduce you with eerie multilingual arias; her ship is fueled by drummers and such cult leaders as the Buddha, Krishna, L. Ron Hubbard and the Easter Bunny." Here futuristic thinking— "intergalactic"—is grounded in the ancient notion of a fertility goddess and juxtaposed with cultural figures as serious as the Buddha and as marketable as the Easter Bunny. Many theme camps included signs with religious references like "Buddha's Seaside Den of Iniquity," "Confess Your Sins!" and "Repent!" If sin is not exactly celebrated at the festival, its meaning is called into question by festival-goers' playful irony and an atmosphere of revelry.

Religious idioms are decontextualized in order to make fun of and protest religious institutions of the outside world, but they can also be appropriated for constructive purposes and made to serve the festival community. On my first afternoon exploring the playa by bike, I spotted a series of signs with sketches of churches on them that directed people to an orange tent called "The Cathedral of the Wholly Sacred." In front of the tent opening was a hand-painted sign that read, "Offer something, leave anything, anything sacred to you, your dog, our time here on the playa, the desert, Jewel, Leo Trotsky, whatever. (Sanctity is Contingent.)" I stepped inside the carpeted tent, glad for some relief from the desert heat. An altar, covered with Indian-print cloth and candles as well as a variety of objects left by visitors, served as the cathedral's centerpiece. Offerings left in front of the altar included good luck candles, incense, a basket with chilli peppers, Chapstick, tobacco, a conch shell, silver sandals, a mother goddess statuette, clay figures fashioned of clay left out for visitors to use, sunglasses, and necklaces. Visitors had written messages in a small notebook left out for that purpose: "free to be you and me," "Death, abandonment, pain, sorrow—Burning Man show me happiness again," "the desert exposes us—shows our true nature and forces us to learn lessons. I pray that I am strong enough to endure even when there is despair. Love, freedom, life"; "I give thanks to the ancestors"; and other notes. Like a traditional church or shrine, the "cathedral" offered a space of contemplation in which festival-goers could share with each other their thoughts about the festival, and the altar within the shrine created a focal point for visitors' reflections.

Altar art is one of the most ubiquitous forms of expression throughout the festival, and the smallest of sacred spaces. Public altars invite participation by the whole community and are specifically designed to contribute to the festival experience. One of the altars I saw in 1997 was covered with photos, a plastic skull, bottles of beer, candles for saints, and other odd objects; a sign instructed people to "alter the altar." This community altar made possible a conversation between participants who might never meet each other face to face. It also gave them an opportunity to help create the meaning of Burning Man with their shared prayers and confessions. Participation is a key festival theme: "No Spectators" is one of Burning Man's slogans, and festival-goers are constantly reminded that they are responsible for the production of festival space. Altars and other sacred places are self-consciously designed to bring together individual and community. They serve diverse purposes and accumulate meanings over a short period by providing points of focus in the midst of the visual complexity of festivals.

Sculptures, shrines, altars, and installations become the focal points of ritual performances, usually scheduled at night. Burning Man '97 and '98 featured lavish Saturday-night performances that converged on temple/ sculptures which festival-goers had photographed, admired, and worked and climbed on over the past few days. These sculptures were created by Bay Area artist Pepe Ozan out of playa mud and chicken wire, and filled with dry wood. Professionally trained opera singers, dancers, and musicians combined with festival volunteers to create the late-night spectacles. The 1998 Sacrifice to Rudra, the Vedic god of fire, began at around 3 a.m. and opened with an invocation to Rudra in Sanskrit. The dark expanse of desert was illuminated by a full moon and flaming batons spun through the air by fire dancers. A hundred costumed dancers split into groups representing earth, water, air, and fire. Watching from the temple sculpture, a priest and priestess stood in long gowns that flowed over stilts. Other characters circled the Rudra sculpture with the dancers: drummers marched with their drums strapped over their backs, and a man with a lizard mask rode in a chariot. At the end of the performance, the temple was torched by performers, and thousands of spectators danced around the fire. Ritual organizers evoke powerful emotional responses from festival participants by borrowing elements of ancient cultures, but providing their own interpretations rather than trying to duplicate other cultures' ritual practices.

Since 2001, the focus of collective ritualizing at Burning Man has been the huge memorial temples that are burnt at the end of the festival. These occasions are more solemn than the festive burning of "the Man." After artist David Best created the Temple of the Mind in 2000, the temples, which Best and other artists have shaped differently each year, have been visited every year by tens of thousands of festival participants, who leave memorials and write on all of the temple's surfaces. Altars, shrines, messages, and mementos have become more numerous and more elaborate, and the temple increasingly has become a focus of contention over the meaning of mourning and the proper ritual experience at Burning Man (Pike 2005).

Sacrifice and Transformation

If Burning Man art and ritual feel apocalyptic or post-apocalyptic, as many observers and participants have remarked, this is because fire and sacrifice are their central idioms.[15] One news story recounted, "Nevada's sixth-largest city was torched Sunday night as the Burning Man spit sparks and fell over backward onto the desert floor" (Whiting 1997). Crosses dot the Burning Man landscape, and are played with and redefined by festival-goers. The *San Francisco Chronicle* reported that before the actual burning of the man, "a man named Highway Hal stood naked on a motorized cross" (Whiting 1997). A festival-goer named Fred describes his experience this way: "The man burnt and so did my outer skin giving me space and movement to grow into another year" (b.b., September 2, 1997). Fire symbolically strips off the self at the same time that it is physically felt, furthering the purification the festival is expected to bring about. Shady Backflash explains the symbolism of the Burning Man: "It felt like the collective fears, rage and frustrations of everyone there were going up in smoke" (b.b., September 11, 1998). The Man, writes Bruce Sterling, "becomes a striking neon symbol of pretty much everything that matters." It is ironic that the sacrificed Man stands at the center of the festival, a community that celebrates its opposition to organized Christianity. The sacrificial meaning of Burning Man varies from person to person. It may aid the cause of personal renewal, cleanse self and community, or provide a means of creating a new self and world out of the ashes of the old.

Festival-goers embark on a kind of pilgrimage as they leave behind the ordinary world and travel to the desert to be transformed—"pilgrims to a new land," the 1997 web guidelines called them. Festival-goers travel toward Black Rock City with expectations built up in earlier conversations about the festival, and then maintained by festival rituals and works of art that affirm that their lives will be changed by the festival experience. "As pilgrims to a new land, each of us becomes a founder," notes Larry Harvey.[16] These festival-goers' accounts of their preparations and trips to festivals are similar to the stories of other religious people described in studies of pilgrimage.[17] Burning Man, George points out on the bulletin board, is "what today's faithful experience in Mecca or Rome, only without all that burdensome dogma" (b.b., September 2, 1997). In his introduction to a collection of essays on pilgrimage, Alan Morinis explains that what is essential to pilgrimage is a quest for what is sacred, especially the valued ideas and images of communal and personal perfection (Morinis 1992, 18–21). Burning Man participants set off from home hoping to experience ideal communities and to discover new selves at the festival, which then becomes for them a sacred space of unlimited possibilities.

The journey is often described by festival-goers as one of personal transformation and healing. Because identity is malleable in festival space, self-transformation comes more easily. Hanuman tells other bulletin board readers: "My old self has been torched! I am reborn!" (b.b., September 2, 1997). Participants create the festival with art, dance, and ritual, but Burning Man also acts on them in ways that open up the possibility for natural and supernatural experiences otherwise unavailable: "I can't believe the power that all of you have helped me see within myself," writes Pamela (b.b., September 2, 1997). Many reports from Burning Man mention the ways in which it is a life-changing and initiatory experience. During the festival, participants mark these changes on their bodies. Sam writes to the bulletin board: "I got my head shaved while I was there ... and emerged a new person" (b.b., 6 September 1997). Some festival-goers wish for friends and community to be renewed as well as for self-transformation. In the journal where visitors to the "Temple of the Wholly Sacred" put down their thoughts about the festival, one person wrote: "May men find their gentleness as they rise phoenix-like from this fire here. The new face of power." Self-transformation is mirrored in the hybrid art forms that abound at Burning Man, such as art cars and bicycles masquerading as giant insects or horses, or the lifelike figures that seemed to be emerging out of the playa dust (or sinking into it). "Cars morph into bugs and software programmers into painted pagans," reported Jennifer Kabat in *Print* (Kabat and Ivinski 1997). The boundaries between human and nature, as well as between human and machine, are open to question and experimentation during the festival.

Festivals promote creative self-expression and sensual enjoyment, and in so doing, enable festival-goers to go beyond their usual ways of carrying themselves and acting toward others. In order to create a "superreal" festival world of meanings absent from the workplace and urban landscape, festival-goers highlight what is lacking for them outside, such as sexual freedom. Moving more slowly helps festival-goers to forget the fast pace of their everyday lives. They speak of the festival as a place of enhanced sensory perceptions or altered awareness.[18] Even time is lived differently at the festival, as Pan-o'-Playa points out in a diary-like message to the bulletin board: "I am very quickly slowing down to a Playa clock and mindset" (b.b., September 23, 1998). This slowing down, the sense that festival space and time are different from ordinary life, is experienced through the body, and it is the body as much as the mind that is changed by Burning Man. One participant, in her third year of law school, remarks on the contrast: "After spending the year in the oppressive confines of a rigorous brainwashing, soul-crushing enterprise like law school, Burning Man brings me back to myself. I remember what it feels to laugh until I cry! … to dance until I fall down … to make friends with people I have no immediate reason to distrust … to walk around naked and love it, never feeling ashamed of my body, but rather being fully present in it" (Julie, b.b., September 5, 1997). Layney, a first-time festival-goer, gives thanks for "the chance to be part of something that really makes sense … i have it in my bones." She describes the heightened awareness of being in her body and moving differently from her usual ways of moving that resulted from dancing around a fire late at night: "i danced myself into a new existence … i ground myself into the sweet desert earth and set free to a blazing fire" (b.b., September 2, 1997). The body is simultaneously liberated and constrained. The hot and dry festival environment constantly reminds festival-goers of their embodied existence. But nudity, dancing, body paint, and costuming can liberate the body as well as insist on its presence.

Burning Man as Home and Family

Festivals are not only places of "anarchy" and unlimited self-expression; transformative experiences are possible because Burning Man is at the same time "home," "tribe," and "family." It is a place where men and women say they experience an ideal community and where they create anew familiar concepts like neighborhood and church. Annual journeys to festivals are simultaneously adventures to exotic "uncharted shores" and to familiar, homelike, memory-laden places. The world that festival-goers represent as being on the fringes of "mainstream" culture becomes the center of their most meaningful activities. Soon after leaving the festival, Kaosangel calls Burning Man "the place we all call home, in the place we are alone, together under a firelit sky" (b.b., September 2, 1997). Some participants describe a sense of oneness with other festival-goers and the feeling of belonging to an extended family, while others speak of it as a tribe: "I walked alone for twenty years, I have screamed since I was born, this world had almost killed me, before I found my home. We are all one tribe" (Anonymous, b.b., September 2, 1997). For many participants, festivals are an ideal way of being with others, and for this reason they relate more intimately to each other at festivals than in other social environments. Mistress Cinnamon reminisces a month and a half after Burning Man '98: "i've felt misplaced ever since i got back, brc [Black Rock City] is my home and the citizens are my people" (b.b., October 18, 1998). Festivals become home-like places where participants can be the kind of children they want to be, can share intimate secrets and play in the ways schools, parents, and religions in the outside world deny them. "Got 'Home' Tuesday morning. How fucked up is that? BRC is my HOME dammit! … I believe I'll relocate to my home on the playa … I'm dreading the commute to LA daily but it beats suburbia."

Over email, festival-goers share with each other their reluctance to return to normal life after the heightened experience and welcome sense of community at Burning Man. References to village, home, family, church, and tribe attest to festival-goers' desire for an experience of community that is lacking in daily life.

Even more than a spiritual home or substitute for church and family, Burning Man symbolizes utopian hopes: "That's what Burning Man brings back to my heart: Hope," says Migwitch, who continues: "We are the ones who create the world that we all long for, the imaginary community to which we constantly compare the one in which we live" (b.b., September 11, 1998). "Remember," writes another festival-goer to the bulletin board, "THERE IS ANOTHER WAY" (Ranger Thumper, b.b., September 9, 1998). "Dark Angel of Black Rock" puts it this way: "The beauty of Black Rock City is powerful. It is stronger than the world we have escaped from ... Burning Man is no longer merely a festival. It has metamorphosed into a way of life for the new millennium" (b.b., September 15, 1998). Festival-goers believe they are the vanguard, visionaries who will usher in new ways of making art and living life.

Conclusions

In the many ways I have suggested, Burning Man participants establish— through narrative, ritual, and fantasy—a contrast between the festival world and everyday society, in which the former takes on a heightened reality and represents for participants a world made over by festival-goers' views of economics (barter system), law enforcement (tolerance and self-policing), gender, ecology, and the nature of the divine. Mike explains that for him Burning Man was "idol worship in the purest sense," rather than "a media-created god or goddess" (b.b., September 2, 1997). Anthropologist Margaret Thompson Drewel, building on the work of Victor Turner and Clifford Geertz, writes that in Yoruba culture, "rituals operate not merely as models of and for society that somehow stand timelessly alongside 'real' life. Rather they construct what reality is and how it is experienced and understood" (Drewel 1992, 174). Burning Man works hard to represent itself as a new reality. Festival organizers' website statement, "Building Burning Man: The Official Journal of the Burning Man Project," begins by explaining that the festival is a critical response to corporate America and an antidote to con-sumerism, then asks rhetorically, "Where else, but in America, would people be invited to pack their belongings, journey into a desert wilderness, and there create the portrait of a visionary world?"[19] There is an expectation and excitement in the festival atmosphere that makes participants feel that they are contributing to a powerful social force. Festival literature and art instal-lations underscore this aspect of the festival with their apocalyptic language of sacrifice and redemption.

The themes of sacrifice and redemption, death and rebirth, disintegration and creation suggest that for many participants the festival's impact is profound. But the symbolic significance of the Man's demise is still up for grabs: "'Meaning' is dog meat in the face of experiment and experience" is how *Village Voice* writer Erik Davis sums up festival-goers' attitudes toward interpretations of Burning Man (Davis 1995). In fact, festival-goers debate the festival's meaning before, during, and after Burning Man. The most striking characteristic of bulletin board discussions about Burning Man and Burning Man literature are the conflicts that emerge as participants and organizers create festival space, experience the festival, deconstruct their experiences after the fact, and plan for next year's festival. In a multipart message to the bulletin board called "A Newbie's Perspective-or-THIS is community?" Gomez Addams described nasty neighbors who stole tools and water, harrassed people, played over the sound level restrictions, and sabotaged other camps (b.b., September 11, 1998). Criticism as well as praise of the festival appeared on the bulletin board and fueled debates over intrusive photographers, "gawkers," neighborliness, and environmental issues. Concerns about the festival's environmental impact have threatened its future at this site.[20] In the many years that I have attended Burning Man, the theme "leave no trace" has appeared on all email messages from the organizers and on all other festival literature. Trash continued to be an issue in the messages of horrified festival-goers who saw debris dumped along the roads leading away from the festival site when they traveled home.[21] Other bulletin board readers responded by urging everyone to focus on the positive, life-affirming aspects of Burning Man, rather than its failures. By emphasizing first their separation from the outside world, and second their unity as tribe and family, the Burning Man community tries to downplay inner differences and contradictions.

Participants expect Burning Man to embody their ideals, but the festival does not always live up to such expectations. In fact, it may perpetuate the social problems festival-goers say they want most to change, such as wastefulness and rigid organizational structures. "Like it or not, Burning Man is not about survival. At its most *extreme*, it's about projecting our God-fearing red-blooded American values of waste, greed and debauchery on an empty canvas of dust and air. And at its most innocent, it's an *escape* valve from the societal rules that bear down on us daily."[22] Thus the opposition between festival and outer worlds is often complicated by the many differences *among* festival-goers, and the realization that instead of leaving the outer world behind, they have brought its problems with them. Tripper, for instance, understands Burning Man somewhat differently than the "many airheads" who "gush on about what a utopian experience Black Rock City is, when all it really is is an amalgam of twisted reflections, magnifications, and rejections of the culture we purport to leave behind" (b.b., September 23, 1998). Controversies at Burning Man follow a pattern described in an extensive literature by folklorists and anthropologists on festivals as places where conflicts are worked on and resolved. In "Shouting Match at the Border: The Folklore of Display Events," Roger D. Abrahams argues that public events provide opportunities for "perilous play": confrontation, negotiation, and creative responses to social tensions. Festivals and fairs, explains Abrahams, "in part dramatize and reinforce the existing social structure," but they also, as in the case of Burning Man, "insist ... that such structure be ignored or inverted, or flatly denied" (Abrahams 1982, 304).

An uneasy dynamic develops at Burning Man, which reveals the tensions between individual and community that the festival is intended to harmonize. Festival-goers gather to share a common experience, but in so doing they may discover the many differences that separate them and threaten their efforts at community building. Of all the tensions and contradictions that characterize Burning Man, none is as charged as the relationship between self and community. In "The Year of Community—You Are a Founder," Larry Harvey describes his understanding of Burning Man: "Ours is a society of activists and your experience of our community will be defined by two essential elements: radical self-expression and a shared struggle to survive."[23] Burning Man participants engage in self-exploration and commune with nature at festivals, but they also establish important friendships and intimate relationships with other festival-goers. Observers of the relationship between self and community in the contemporary United States have argued that Americans tend to emphasize the needs of the self over those of the community. Robert Bellah and his colleagues point out in *Habits of the Heart* that when Americans describe their spirituality, they talk most about personal empowerment and self-expression, rather than the requirements of community (Bellah *et al.* 1985; see also Anderson 1990; Roof 1993). In contrast, Burning Man emphasizes both the needs of the self and the creation of community. Self-expression is encouraged but must be constantly tempered by consideration for one's neighbors.

If the festival is a site for life-changing experiences of self and community, for the creation of new religious and cultural visions, then, for these reasons, it is a contested site. The festival works its transformative magic on participants because of a set of contradictions that exist within it: festival-goers escape their home life when they journey to the festival, and at the same time expect festivals to be the location of "home" and "family"; they imagine the desert as a "blank canvas" as well as a "living land"; the language of "tribes" and "villages" coexists with advanced electronic technologies; festival-goers constantly negotiate between self-expression and the needs of community; in festival art and ritual they express desire for both sacrifice and salvation; and Burning Man's apocalyptic overtones are meant to both describe the disenchantment and decay of American life today, and envision a future that is rejuvenative as well as destructive. It is the creative work that characterizes Burning Man—playing with symbolic meanings and creating new rituals from old—in response to these contradictions that transforms the festival into places of meaning.

References

Abrahams, Roger D. 1982. "Shouting Match at the Border: The Folklore of Display Events." In *"And Other Neighborly Names": Social Process and Cultural Image in Texas Folklore,* eds Richard Bauman and Roger D. Abrahams, 303–21. Austin: University of Texas Press.

Agnew, John A. and James S. Duncan, eds. 1989. *The Power of Place: Bringing Together Geographical and Sociological Imaginations.* Boston: Unwin Hyman.

Anderson, Walter Truett. 1990. *Reality Isn't What It Used to Be: Theatrical Politics, Ready-to-Wear Religion, Global Myths, Primitive Chic, and Other Wonders of the Postmodern World.* San Francisco: Harper & Row.

Bachelard, Gaston. [1958] 1964. *The Poetics of Space,* trans. Maria Jolas. New York: Orion Press.

Bellah, Robert N., Richard Madsen, William M. Sullivan, Ann Swidler, and Steven M. Tipton. 1985. *Habits of the Heart: Individualism and Commitment in American Life.* San Francisco: Harper & Row.

Buttimer, Anne. 1993. *Geography and the Human Spirit.* Baltimore: Johns Hopkins University Press.

Chidester, David. 1995. "Introduction." In *American Sacred Space,* eds David Chidester and Edward T. Linenthal, 1–42. Bloomington: Indiana University Press.

Cox, Harvey. 1995. *Fire from Heaven: The Rise of Pentecostal Spirituality and the Reshaping of Religion in the Twenty-First Century.* Reading, MA: Addison-Wesley.

Crumrine, N. Ross and Alan Morinis, eds. 1991. *Pilgrimage in Latin America.* New York: Greenwood Press.

Davis, Erik. 1995. "Terminal Beach Party: Warming Up to the Burning Man." *Village Voice,* October 31, 31–34.

Dowling, Claudia. 1997. *"Life* Goes to the Burning Man Festival." *Life,* August, 16–18.

Drewel, Margaret Thompson. 1992. *Yoruba Ritual: Performers, Play, Agency.* Bloomington: Indiana University Press.

Duncan, James and David Ley, eds. 1993. *Place/Culture/Representation.* New York: Routledge.

Duvignaud, Jean. 1976. "Festivals: A Sociological Approach." *Cultures* 3, 1: 13–25.

Falassi, Alessandro. 1987. *Time Out of Time: Essays on the Festival.* Albuquerque: University of New Mexico Press.

Foucault, Michel. 1986. "Of Other Spaces." *Diacritics* 16: 22–27.

Gilmore, Lee and Mark Van Proyen, eds. 2005. *Afterburn: Reflections on Burning Man.* Albuquerque: University of New Mexico Press.

Gregory, Derek. 1994. *Geographical Imaginations.* Oxford: Blackwell.

Griffith, James. 1992. *Beliefs and Holy Places: A Spiritual Geography of the Pimeria Alta.* Tucson: University of Arizona Press.

Haberman, David L. 1994. *Journey through the Twelve Forests: An Encounter with Krishna.* New York: Oxford University Press.

Hammond, Phillip E. 1992. *Religion and Personal Autonomy: The Third Disestablishment in America.* Columbia: University of South Carolina Press.

Hatch, Nathan. 1989. *The Democratization of American Christianity.* New Haven, CT: Yale University Press.

Hiss, Tony. 1990. *The Experience of Place.* New York: Knopf.

Kabat, Jennifer and Pamela A. Ivinski. 1997. "Operation Desert Swarm." *Print,* September/October, 4–5.

Kelly, Kevin. 1997. "Bonfire of the Techies." *Time,* August 25, 60–62.

Lefebvre, Henri. [1974] 1992. *The Production of Space,* trans. Donald Nicholson-Smith. Oxford: Blackwell.

Lelyveld, Nita. 1998, "Wild Westfest." *The Philadelphia Inquirer* (September 9): E01.

MacAloon, John J., ed. 1984. *Rite, Drama, Festival, Spectacle: Rehearsals Toward a Theory of Cultural Performance.* Philadelphia: Institute for the Study of Human Issues.

Manning, Frank, ed. 1983. *The Celebration of Society: Perspectives on Contemporary Cultural Performance.* Bowling Green, KY: Bowling Green University Press.

Marks, John. 1997. "Burning Man Meets Capitalism." *U.S. News and World Report,* July 28, 46–47.

Moore, R. Laurence. 1994. *Selling God: American Religion on the Cultural Marketplace.* New York: Oxford University Press.

Morinis, Alan, ed. 1992. *Sacred Journeys: The Anthropology of Pilgrimage.* Westport, CT: Greenwood Press.

Murray, Janet H. 1997. *Hamlet on the Holodeck: The Future of Narrative in Cyberspace.* New York: Free Press.

Myerhoff, Barbara G. 1974. *Peyote Hunt: The Sacred Journey of the Huichol Indians.* Ithaca, NY: Cornell University Press.

——. 1982. "Rites of Passage: Process and Paradox." In *Celebration: Studies in Festivity and Ritual,* ed. Victor Turner, 109–35. Washington, DC: Smithsonian Institution Press.

Niman, Michael I. 1997. *People of the Rainbow.* Knoxville: University of Tennessee Press.

Orsi, Robert A. 1991. "The Center Out There, In Here, and Everywhere Else: The Nature of Pilgrimage to the Shrine of Saint Jude 1929–65." *Journal of Social History* 25, 2 (winter): 213–32.

Pike, Sarah M. 2001. *Earthly Bodies, Magical Selves: Contemporary Pagans and Search for Community.* Berkeley: University of California Press.

——. 2005. "No Novenas for the Dead: Ritual Action and Communal Memory at the Temple of Tears." In *Afterburn: Reflection on Burning Man,* ed. Lee Gilmore and Mark Van Proyen, 195–213. Albuquerque: University of New Mexico Press.

Rinschede, G. and S. M. Bhardwaj, eds. 1990. *Pilgrimage in the United States.* Berlin: Reimer Verlag.

Roof, Wade Clark. 1993. *A Generation of Seekers.* San Francisco: Harper.

Schmidt, Leigh Eric. 1995. *Consumer Rites: The Buying and Selling of American Holidays.* Princeton, NJ: Princeton University Press.

Scott, Jamie and Paul Simpson-Housley, eds. 1991. *Sacred Places and Profane Spaces: Essays in the Geographies of Judaism, Christianity and Islam.* Westport, CT: Greenwood Press.

Sears, John. 1979. *Sacred Places: American Tourist Attractions in the Nineteenth Century.* Oxford: Oxford University Press.

Shields, Rob. 1991. *Places on the Margin: Alternative Geographies of Modernity.* New York: Routledge.

Soja, Edward W. 1989. *Postmodern Cartographies: The Reassertion of Space in Critical Social Theory.* New York: Verso.

Sterling, Bruce. 1996. "Greetings from Burning Man." *Wired* November 4, 196–207.

Stoeltje, Beverly. 1992. "Festival." In *Folklore, Cultural Performances, and Popular Entertainments: A Communications-Centered Handbook*, ed. Richard Bauuran, 266–69. Oxford: Oxford University Press.

Tuan, Yi-Fu. 1977. *Space and Place: The Perspective of Experience.* Minneapolis: University of Minnesota Press.

Turkle, Sherry. 1995. *Life on the Screen: Identity in the Age of the Internet.* New York: Simon & Schuster.

Turner, Victor. 1974. *Dramas, Fields, and Metaphors: Symbolic Action in Human Society.* Ithaca, NY: Cornell University Press.

Turner, Victor and Edith Turner. 1978. *Image and Pilgrimage in Christian Culture: Anthropological Perspectives.* New York: Columbia University Press.

Whiting, Sam. 1997. "A Blaze of Glory." *San Francisco Chronicle,* September 2, E1-E2.

Wojcik, Daniel. 1997. *The End of the World as We Know It: Faith, Fatalism, and Apocalypse in America.* New York and London: New York University Press.

Notes

1 Photographs of some of these were on the Fruit of the Lumen website (www. scumby.com/~wesBman98/), which is no longer active.

2 The hundreds of messages on the bulletin board were one of main sources for this essay. All bulletin board messages (designated as "b.b." and a date) were originally read at http://bbs.burningman.com/index?14@^8013@/ and were available through the archives at this address. The URL is no longer active. I first heard about the festival in 1996 when one of my students told me about his experience there. I then attended the festival in 1997 as a participant-observer, and returned almost every year for the next ten years. Over these years the festival experienced tremendous growth and increased publicity, but the issues I address here have remained remarkably consistent from year to year. Other sources I used were two newsletters published during the festival: *The Black Rock Gazette*, and *Piss Clear*; informal conversations with other festival-goers during the festivals and with several of my students back in ordinary life; and the Burning Man website and other websites of participants. I also read through a variety of media accounts of the festival, both in print and online.

3 Interview by Lee Gilmore, September 5, 1998.

4 Sterling 1996, 1; Scotty, Burning Man b.b., September 11, 1998; Kelly 1997, 62 (quoting Larry Harvey); Harvey, "Radical Self-Expression," Burning Man website, 1998 (www.burningman.com).

5 During two years of reading through the Burning Man bulletin board, I saw mention of raves, Lilith Fair, Lollapalooza, pagan festivals, Grateful Dead shows, Rainbow gatherings, and the original Woodstock. Pike (2001) is a study of ritual and sacred space at contemporary pagan festivals across the United States. For an in-depth description of national Rainbow Family gatherings, see Niman 1997. Information about raves is easily available on the internet; for example, a rave network with many links is at http://hyperreal.org/raves.

6 R. Laurence Moore discusses Chautauqua Sunday School Institutes (Moore 1994, 151). The essays in *The Celebration of Society* cover a wide variety of festivals, sporting events, masquerades, and other celebrations in the United States and elsewhere (Manning 1983).

7 Schmidt discusses "the peddling of festivity" at church festivals and hawkers waiting on the outskirts of camp meetings to sell "food, liquor, patent medicines, books, ballads, shoe polish, and daguerreotypes" (Schmidt 1995, 21).

8 Also see Bachelard [1958] 1964; Lefebvre [1974] 1992; Soja 1989.

9 G. Rinschede and S. M. Bhardwaj describe "place mythologies" as narratives of the virtues and sanctities of specific sites (Rinschede and Bhardwaj 1990, 11). But the sites they identify, like Burning Man, probably have negative associations as well. Other studies of place mythologies that have helped me understand festivals as "places apart" include Agnew and Duncan (1989); Buttimer (1993); Duncan and Ley (1993); Hiss (1990); Sears (1979). For some good examples of place myths see Griffith (1992); Scott and Simpson-Housley (1991).

10 Anthropologist Victor Turner contrasts flexible, egalitarian liminal events to the stratified, normal world (Turner 1974, 200–01).

11 Much of Foucault's work is taken up with issues of power and space. My understanding of festivals as "places apart" has also been helped by Duvignaud (1976); Falassi (1987); Gregory (1994); MacAloon (1984); Stoeltje (1992).

12 Darryl Van Rhey, "The New American Holiday" in "Building Burning Man: The Official Journal of the Burning Man Project" (Winter 1998).

13 Larry Harvey, "Radical Self-Expression," Burning Man website, August 1997.

14 *Black Rock Gazette* 1997.

15 Scholars disagree on the meaning and appropriate usage of the terms *apocalypticism* and *apocalyptic.* I follow folklorist Daniel Wojcik's suggestion that *apocalypse* "refers to the catastrophic destruction of world or current society, whether attributed to supernatural forces, natural forces, or human actions" (Wojcik 1997).

16 "The Year of Community—You Are a Founder" (August 7, 1997).

17 For instance, see Crumrine and Morinis 1991; Haberman 1994; Morinis 1992; Myerhoff 1974; Orsi 1991; Rinschede and Bhardwaj 1990; Turner and Turner 1978.

18 There is much discussion about drug use and abuse at Burning Man. From festival-goers' own descriptions of their festival experiences, it would seem that drugs play a part as often as not. However, perhaps as a result of a visible law enforcement presence, drugs are not as common as alcohol.

19 Winter 1998.

20 In February 1999 I received an issue of "Jack Rabbit Speaks," urging festival-goers to write letters to the Bureau of Land Management, which oversees Black Rock Desert. This was the most recent request for help from festival organizers in several years of negotiating with local authorities and other groups concerned about the festival's effects on the land. The Burning Man website has links to more information about these issues.

21 A heated and contentious discussion of trash on the bulletin board lasted for months after Burning Man '98.

22 Stewart McKenzie, "Bitch Bitch Bitch about Burning Man," *Piss Clear* 1997 (the "other" Burning Man newspaper).

23 Burning Man website, 1997.

Part III

Popular spirituality and morality

Those of us who work in the field of religious studies have occasion to talk about religion with a wide variety of people, and conversations with colleagues suggest that we often encounter a similar sentiment. "I'm not really religious," we hear from students, strangers on airplanes, and long-lost relatives at family reunions, "but I consider myself a very spiritual person." Sometime in the past generation, it seems, a rift has developed between "religion," which appears to connote for many institutional affiliation, rigid dogma, medieval metaphysics, and a kind of mindless obedience to authority, and "spirituality," which seems to betoken an individualized, eclectic, and free-form personal engagement with the transcendent, however an individual may understand it.

We hear the word "morality" much less often in these encounters, yet the moral decision-making that people do on a daily basis is inevitably bound up with (though not necessarily always in concert with) the wider spiritual (or religious) world view within which they operate. In this section, we look at popular culture with an eye not so much toward specific behaviors and narratives that invite religious interpretation, but rather toward those places where Americans seem to be turning (or being led) for resources in the day-to-day task of building spiritual and moral life.

Margaret Miles' effort at defining spirituality is a good point of departure: "Spirituality is a consciously chosen set of beliefs, attitudes, values, and practices that the person selecting them anticipates will serve the purpose of more life by providing orientation and specifying responsibility" (*Seeing and Believing* 1999, 15). These beliefs, attitudes, values, and practices were once subsets of overarching and comprehensive religious world views: one prayed the rosary because one was a Catholic; one didn't eat pork because one was a Jew. In the United States today, however, secularization, the decline of institutional religious affiliation, and widespread knowledge of and interaction with diverse religious traditions have meant that spirituality now exists for many in American culture as a free-floating entity unto itself, the eclectic product of exposure to multiple religious, psychological, and other interpretive frameworks. The chapters that follow collectively argue that the popular culture products we encounter casually as daily entertainment are an increasingly important source in that mix. At the same time, traditional religious moral systems are developing creative strategies to make themselves visible and relevant in this complex mix.

Sara Moslener's study (Chapter 10) of the Faith Based Abstinence Movement (FBAM) offers a close-up look at one such effort. Represented by such organizations as True Love Waits and Silver Ring Thing, the FBAM, Moslener argues, has successfully positioned itself as a kind of brand in the consumer-oriented culture of American teenagers. By recognizing its target audience as media-savvy consumers whose identity is often derived from the products they consume, the FBAM presents sexual abstinence as a "lifestyle product" that offers both long-term romantic happiness and stylish consumables – purity rings and niche Bibles, among other things. This analysis highlights both the significance and the malleability of counter-cultural rhetoric; groups like True Love Waits and Silver Ring Thing have co-opted the language of the sexual revolution for decidedly socially conservative purposes. Moslener notes, for instance, that college students' use of the language of "coming out" as virgins allows them to position themselves as counter-cultural while affirming the values of a conservative social mainstream.

As much as traditional spiritual and moral patterns are branded in the currency of commercial culture, they are also, as Lisle Dalton, Monica Siems, and Eric Mazur demonstrate (Chapter 12) with respect to the animated television series *The Simpsons*, the stuff of incisive (and hilarious) parody. The authors show that swipes against traditional religious morality and spirituality are a mainstay of *The Simpsons*' humor; the Evangelical Christian neighbor is an insufferable milksop, the mainstream Protestant minister a faithless mouther of liberal platitudes, the only regularly featured Jew a greedy, chain-smoking, child-loathing professional clown. The absence (at least officially) of religious hegemony in the United States means that all traditions are fair game for ridicule, though the viciousness of *The Simpsons*' humor seems to increase proportionally with the level of power and influence wielded by the group in question. That is, Protestants come off especially badly; the Hindu convenience store operator, if a caricature, is generally handled sympathetically.

Plainly, *The Simpsons* does not represent a re-emergence of forms of moral and spiritual discipline like those the authors of Chapters 9 and 10 see in their subjects. What this show does represent, the authors claim, is a place where the tensions of a multireligious society—in which innumerable (and universally flawed) moral meaning systems come into conflict—get humorously, and perhaps cathartically, aired. For all the irreverence of *The Simpsons*, its characters reckon with real moral dilemmas and their resolutions reflect real moral insight.

Elijah Siegler makes a similar case for the moral significance of another television genre, the ensemble police drama, in Chapter 9. In his updated review of television cop dramas, Siegler argues that television dramas, especially police series that trace characters' development over time, can "communicate religious possibilities, explore religious issues, and ask religious questions." Whether religion functions primarily as a social identity marker, as in *Law & Order*, as an aspect of personal, private dramas, as in *NYPD Blue*, or as an opportunity for explicit theological reflection, as in *Homicide: Life on the Street*, these shows all stimulate debate about religious moral issues. The police officers in all of these shows, each coming from a distinctive religious or nonreligious background and working in morally complex situations, face the often conflicting claims of what is right and what is just.

Drawing on the work of Michel Foucault, Siegler sees a kind of confessional display in "the box," the police interrogation room, which he contends is "the best example of sacred space on prime-time television." What makes that space sacred is the fact that in the interrogation, before the defense attorneys and prosecutors have arrived, the police have an opportunity to wrest justice from bureaucracy, the criminal has the opportunity to confess and thereby find redemption, and the audience is afforded "an opportunity to grapple with the same moral ambiguities explored during each episode, and to 'confess' its sins vicariously." In *The Simpsons* and these police dramas, the authors claim, a popular entertainment product becomes a venue for consideration of serious moral and spiritual issues. The time viewers spend with these products, even though they may be passing the time before dinner or bed, may also be valuable moments in which to reckon with the complexity and ambiguity of moral life in contemporary America.

Another kind of spiritual experience may be occurring in a social space more known for its incessant updates of personal trivia. Buddhist scholar Daniel Veidlinger's investigation of the "social web"—social networking sites like Facebook and MySpace, and messaging utilities such as Twitter (Chapter 11)—makes the case that such sites are fulfilling many of the spiritual functions of traditional religions in their interpretive, interactive, and integrative roles, hypothesizing that recently reported high levels of religious switching among Americans may be linked with the high levels of "social trust" created by these online networks, making institutional religious affiliation less vital in meeting that need. Reviewing the content of spiritual conversation occurring on these sites, Veidlinger is also impressed, and concludes that, inanities notwithstanding, "substantial discussions about issues of ultimate importance" occur on these sites, and that the depth of insight in MySpace and Facebook discussion groups is "surprisingly good."

Veidlinger's analysis of the religious significance of the internet goes farther than most, though, in its claim that these sites not only serve common religious functions, but that they may actually have specific consequences for users' spiritual world views, "the beliefs, attitudes, values, and practices" that provide orientation, according to Miles' definition cited above. Specifically, his computerized analysis of nearly three million user profiles suggests that frequent use of social networking sites and messaging functions promotes a Buddhism-friendly, de-centered view of the self, one on which users see themselves "as standing within a complex nexus of causes and conditions rather than as embodying an individual personal soul."

Few would argue that Facebook is turning the world Buddhist, that Homer Simpson's Everyman is as spiritually instructive as his counterpart in medieval morality plays, or that vicarious entry into "the box" of the *Homicide* squad room is as fundamentally transformative as the ritual of confession was and remains for many Roman Catholics. And yet, these analyses insist, these are not the trivial time-wasters they might initially appear to be. If indeed, in our information-soaked and overwhelmingly diverse society, moral and spiritual identities are patchworks of beliefs, attitudes, values, and practices culled from everything from traditional religions and family custom to internet chat rooms and popular song lyrics, it makes sense to examine those places in our culture where the idiocies, ambiguities, and insights of that eclectic process are surfacing. Even those who are affiliated with traditional religious institutions are drinking, consciously or not, from these spiritual wells, especially as these groups make more and shrewd use of popular culture forms. In the end, perhaps the most interesting thing these popular culture products can tell us about spirituality in America today is how powerful and endlessly mutable religious patterns are in a multi-cultural society that has (so far) resisted religious homogenization. In such a world, these examples demonstrate, an apparently limitless number of world views can come into contact, conflict, and, in fascinating ways, confluence.

Chapter 9

Is God Still in the Box?

Religion in Television Cop Shows Ten Years Later

Elijah Siegler

Sometime around 1996, I realized something about my television viewing habits: three out of the four TV dramas that I watched regularly (some might say "religiously") were cop shows (the other was *The X-Files* [Fox, 1993–2002]). This was striking because I never previously cared for the genre. The formulaic car chases; the right-wing "lock 'em up and throw away the key" mentality; the overall cheesy production values; and the hyper-macho leading men paired with super-sexy female partners: none of it gave me a reason to watch. Two examples should suffice—*T.J. Hooker*, which ran from 1982–86 on ABC and later on CBS; and *Hunter*, which ran on NBC from 1984–91—but the list is endless.

But the shows that caught my attention in 1996 were different. *Law & Order* (NBC, 1990–present), *NYPD Blue* (ABC, 1993–2005), and *Homicide: Life on the Street* (NBC, 1993–99) were all exceptionally well written, directed, and acted. As I wrote in "God in the Box: Religion in Contemporary Television Cop Shows" for the first edition of *God in the Details* (199–216), they embodied the "quality television" that was a hallmark of "a golden age of TV, second only to the 1950s" and had the Emmys and critical accolades to prove it. But more than that, all three regularly featured religious-themed episodes, and dealt "consistently, seriously, and self-consciously with religious and moral concerns."[1]

I argued in my original essay that television can be and is a locus of real thought about serious religious issues. As the strongest examples I could find, I used *Law & Order*, *NYPD Blue*, and *Homicide* as my case study. This updated essay summarizes the argument of the original, but also looks at the three original shows in the 10 years since the first edition was published. Naturally, I focus on *Law & Order*, which has had the most successful career of the three—it has been on the air continuously since 1990 and been spun off several times. In the conclusion, I will suggest a new hypothesis about who is responsible for religious themes on television.

How Television is Religious

After 60 years of regular broadcasting, we can stipulate that television broadcasting is a distinct art form. Actually one could say it is several art forms: the talk show, the situation comedy, and the dramatic series. But what is TV's religious genius? Clearly, secular television programming does not aid in prayer or meditation, and in fact is often seen as a distraction from these activities. Television programs may involve the audience in ritual through congregating to watch "appointment shows." (For an embarrassing example, in the early 1990s, my friends and I ritualistically gathered around the dorm room TV set to watch and laugh over *Beverly Hills 90210* [Fox, 1990–2000]. But this is ritual of the most profane sort—unlike the sacred quality of theater performance [Schechner 1993].)

Do TV and film communicate religious ideas in the same way? On the surface, these two media may share many characteristics (both consist of moving images that most often construct a "realistic" narrative with identifiable characters) and borrow from each other (movies are shown on TV; TV shows are based on movies, and *vice versa*). In fact, the religious genius of each is very different. To use an architectural metaphor, movie palaces are (or were, before the rise of megaplexes) cathedrals of the image, where we partake in shared experiences. Televisions are home shrines, personalized and comfortable. If it has only been a decade or so since the field of religious studies finally recognized that important religious work goes on at home, then it is now time for the field to recognize television as a source of religious meaning (for example, see Iwamura 2003; Salvo *et al.* 1997).

While the specific religious genius of film continues to be debated (indeed, theorizing the intersections between film and religion is a major pastime within the scholarship), all agree film's power seems to owe much to myth. Films often recapitulate the structure of myth, most famously in the case of George Lucas self-consciously borrowing both specific visual references and the narrative pattern of the "hero" myth, articulated by the popular theorist of myth Joseph Campbell (Campbell 1973; Cambell and Moyers 1991, 177–79; for a critical analysis, see Gordon 1995).[2] These new filmed myths then become part of people's personal "everyday" mythology.

By contrast, the television series does not recapitulate myth so much as complexify it. If, at its best, film-as-myth has the possibility to communicate a religious truth, then the television drama, at its best, can communicate religious possibilities, explore religious issues, and ask religious questions. Thanks to its multiple characters and plotlines, television—more than film, and perhaps more any other art form—can represent and provoke religious debate. This debate may be literal—an argument between two characters—or it may be in the form of stories or themes that stimulate internal debate among the viewers.

Television is also particularly good at charting long-term religious transformation in its characters, whether depicted as conversion, salvation, or disenchantment.[3] To best appreciate how religion operates in a television series, one must first understand that a television series is not a collection of discrete moments. Television drama is an open narrative; the audience gains pleasure from viewing regular characters operating in predictable ways. So if a character on a TV series is shown to have a certain religious outlook on life in episode 3, regular viewers can interpret that character's actions in future episodes as informed by that outlook, even if that outlook is never explicitly acknowledged. Then if, in episode 25, the same character has a crisis of faith, the audience can reflect back to the previous episodes that led up to that.

Three Cop Shows

The three cop shows on which I'll focus stimulated debate about religious and moral issues and show religious change in characters, but each did it differently. *Law & Order* follows a single criminal case, from investigation (the "order") by New York City Police to prosecution (the "law") by the District Attorney (DA). Even though each episode takes place over several months' time (indicated by titles announcing the date and location of each scene), each one invariably begins with the police called to a crime scene (usually a murder), continues through the investigation and prosecution, and ends with the verdict. In my original article, I argued that *Law & Order* was concerned mostly with the social aspect of religion. Religion was a marker of identity—much like race, economic status, or gender—and was one more way violence might erupt, one more way the precarious urban peace could topple.

NYPD Blue, also set in New York, followed a format associated with series co-creator Steven Bochco and his seminal 1980s cop show *Hill Street Blues* (NBC, 1981–87), and also used in another series he created, *L.A. Law* (NBC, 1986–94). The "Bochco" format involves an ensemble cast of characters in a well-defined location with many intertwining storylines that combine the personal and professional, the serious and the comic, some storylines ending after one episode, some lasting a few episodes, some continuing for the year. *NYPD Blue* occasionally used religion for local color or comic relief, but principally explored the personal, private aspect of religion. Its exploration of the lower register of human emotion—despair, rage, and anxiety—was so unrelenting that its occasional moments of grace were all the more poignant and cathartic. These themes of spiritual despair and occasional grace can be attributed to the other co-creator, David Milch, a former doctoral student in English at Yale. The detectives, recovering from grief, addiction, damaged lives, sought redemption, forgiveness, second chances. Sometimes they found their salvation (though it usually proved to be sadly temporary). Much of this religious content remained unsaid for most of the *NYPD Blue* season. But the final episodes of *NYPD Blue*'s first three seasons directly addressed religion. The season finales, in typical Bochco style, resolved some key storylines of the season while ending on a "cliffhanger" that kept viewers eagerly awaiting the next season in the fall. At the end of the first season, a "beat" cop confesses to a priest that she murdered a gangster who was blackmailing her. The second season ended with Detective Andy Sipowicz, originally conceived as the show's alcoholic, racist anti-hero, marrying Greek-American Assistant DA Sylvia Costas in an Orthodox ceremony. The third season ended with the same priest who married Andy and Sylvia "churching" their newborn son. Priests have played pivotal roles only at the end of the season; at the end of the day, when his work is done, a cop must reckon with God.

Homicide: Life on the Street was a squad-room drama set in Baltimore. It took the most formal risks of the three programs. Some episodes followed a standard Bochco format; some were focused on a single storyline. Several shows took extreme narrative risks—entire episodes were set in one room; or were told from perspectives other than that of police protagonists: the families of the murder victims, for example, or a stalker. The series was based on a book by journalist David Simon, who spent a year with the Baltimore "murder police," and later went on to create the acclaimed cop show *The Wire* (HBO, 2002–08).

Homicide asked the toughest religious questions. What are the root cause(s) and consequence(s) of evil? What is the nature of death? Detectives test their faith, while criminals must look for confession and absolution. *Homicide* was the most self-consciously theological of these three "quality" cop shows of the 1990s. One reason is that the show's theology was overwhelmingly given expression by one set of partners, Detectives Frank Pembleton and Tim Bayliss. Frank Pembleton, the brilliant African American detective, is the moral and dramatic center of *Homicide*. He has become a homicide cop "to speak for those who cannot." He is a speaker for the dead. His motives are not the only things that are explicitly religious; his skill at interviewing murder suspects in the interrogation room is attributed to Jesuit schooling. Bayliss, Pembleton's partner, is the audience stand-in—eager, naïve, one step behind Pembleton's detective work. Bayliss's "religion *à la carte*" is a foil for Pembleton's rigorous religious training and moral insight, while also serving as well as representative of the average viewer. One example of this is the following exchange, taken from one episode ("Nearer My God To Thee," October 14, 1994) out of a trilogy largely given over to religion.

PEMBLETON: What religion were you raised?

BAYLISS: You know, I was a mutt. My mother was a Methodist. My father he believed in the Colts. I was baptized by the Presbyterians, confirmed by the Episcopalians, and my girlfriend in college, she was a knockout, a Unitarian, so I joined. How about you, Frank, still Catholic?

PEMBLETON: You know the Jews have Orthodox, Conservative and Reform.
There are two kinds of Catholic, devout and fallen. I fell.
BAYLISS: What's up with the three hour mass? I was at a wedding and I got
up to receive the host. I had to ask for two I was so hungry.
PEMBLETON: You're not Catholic and you took communion?
BAYLISS: Is that wrong?
PEMBLETON: If my God wins, you're screwed.

Bayliss, the modern, sees religion as a convenience to be changed or dis-
carded as needed. Pembleton, the pre-modern, however facetiously, sees
religion as divine warfare. Later conversations that I had with *Homicide*
head writer and producer Tom Fontana confirmed that it was his intent to
have their relationship form the heart of the series; their "double character
arc." As Fontana said:

> We decided first season that Frank would go from no belief to belief.
> Bayliss would go from belief to no belief. When Pembleton left *Homi-
> cide*, he had achieved an understanding of his real place in the universe.
> [...] Bayliss was a seeker – he went through a journey. In the course of
> the series they pass each other. They love each other because they each
> knew they were seeking. Yelling at each other was all about "help me
> know what it's about."
>
> (Tom Fontana, personal interview, September 26, 2005)

God in the Box

Both *NYPD Blue* and *Homicide* featured prominent scenes in the interrogation room. Between the investigation and prosecution, there is one moment,
limited in both time and space, where an act both good and lawful, both fair
and just can take place. This moment occurs in the interrogation room—
known in *Homicide* as "the box." From a structural (narrative) point of
view, this moment is important because, if a skilled interrogator can obtain a
written confession from the suspect before the law dictates that the suspect
must be let go (usually 24 hours after making an arrest), the cop does not
have to "waste time" proving the suspect committed the crime by gathering
evidence. A trial is not necessary if the defendant pleads guilty. From a
dramatic point of view, the interrogation is the turning point of the story, not
to mention a showcase for "award-winning" acting. From our religious perspective, this is a moment where communion between the police and the
criminal is possible, where the former can find the truth and the latter can
seek absolution, and where the audience can find meaning.
    The box admits only one or two cops and the suspect. But often a third
party may be present, standing on the other side of the two-way mirror—the

silent watcher or listener. The box turns into a display, what French philosopher Michel Foucault called the panopticon (Foucault 1977, especially 195–228) that permits those watching to exert a form of power over those being watched. Therein, the police work becomes a performance: the detectives know they are being observed; the suspects may or may not (depending on how many times they have been in the situation before). Who watches? Usually people in authority. The commanding officer watches to make sure the detective does not beat or abuse the suspect ("crossing the line"). The district attorney watches to see if there is enough to warrant an arrest. Other detectives watch to see "how it's done." Or, in a plot device used by all three shows, suspects are made to watch their partners-in-crime being questioned from behind the mirror. The observed suspects readily pin the blame on the others to cut better deals for themselves.

The box, then, is a place where the normal rules are suspended. With no clocks and no windows, the box has no time. The box is the site of the enacted ritual of confession. The police usually prevail because they are clever and good, of course, but also because the suspects *want* to confess. "Giving it up" produces a sense of relief for the criminal, the cop, and audience alike. In fact, the box (often used as a slang for the television itself) provides the most meaningful moments of revelation and experience for the viewers, who are themselves watching the interrogations. This voyeurism transcends simple audience–actor relationships, but in fact provides the viewer with an opportunity to grapple with the same moral ambiguities explored during each episode and to "confess" its sins vicariously.

Foucault locates our desire for confession in power relations:

> The obligation to confess is now relayed through so many different points, is so deeply ingrained in us, that we no longer perceive it as the effect of a power that contains us; on the contrary, it seems to us that truth, lodged in our most secret nature, "demands" only to surface.
>
> (Foucault 1980, 60)

Indeed, Foucault historicizes the beginning of the confessional mode in the West, dating it from the Lateran Council's codification of the sacrament of penance in 1215. This, he argues, eventually led to changing procedures in criminal justice that "helped to give the confession a central role in the order of civil and religious powers" (*ibid.*, 58).

The box on *NYPD Blue*, *Homicide*, and *Law & Order* is a confessional located at the intersection of several different discursive fields: the prosecutorial and investigative, the public and the private, the civil and religious, and the audience and actors. It turns the loosely moral and ethical issues of the crime drama into larger religious dramas. In that sense, the box is the best example of sacred space on prime-time television.

After 1999

Homicide had just ended when the original "God in the Box" went to press in 1999, but a made-for-television movie one year later (aired February 2000) not only reunited every regular and recurring character from the show's past, but also made *Homicide*'s implicit theological concerns (the importance of forgiveness, the nature of evil, the meaning of death) even more explicit, almost obvious. The quality of *Homicide: The Movie* was not up to the level of the best seasons of the series, but it provided a satisfying resolution of the theological jousting between Bayliss and Pembleton (Siegler 2009).

When the first edition went to print, *NYPD Blue* was at the end of its sixth season. There were major cast changes in the succeeding years, but the changes only reinforced the show's dynamics. The attractive white female detective Diane Russell was replaced by attractive white female detective Connie McDowell; earnest Hispanic junior detective Martinez was replaced by earnest African American junior detective Jones; hard-nosed yet sympathetic African American boss, Lt. Fancy, was replaced by hard-nosed yet sympathetic Hispanic boss, Lt. Rodriguez.

The show repeated the same religious tropes of the earlier years: Sipowicz losing a loved one, and finding redemption through suffering, only with new cast members and, one may argue, ever decreasing viewer impact. *NYPD Blue*'s twelfth and final season concluded in February 2005 on a deliberately anti-climatic note: Sipowicz, who had just been promoted to squad lieutenant, working late, alone in his new office. For a man whose spiritual journey was marked by loss (of loved ones, of self-control) and whose only solace came from the daily grind of "the job," this final fade-out was perfect; it seemed Andy achieved a measure of peace at last, shuffling papers. (Though did it have to take 12 years to get there?)

At the end of the 1998–99 television season, *Law & Order* was going strong. Its ninth season was the highest rated yet, the thirteenth most watched show on American television. (The show would peak during its twelfth season, with a ranking of #7 before dipping down in the ratings.) By the summer of 2009, *L & O* had finished its nineteenth season. It has continued with its rotating cast of characters and its unbendable format of investigation followed by prosecution of a crime. In 1999, it debuted its first spin-off, *Law & Order: Special Victims Unit* (known as *SVU*), about a police squad that deals with sex crimes and child victims. Another successful spin-off, *Law & Order: Criminal Intent* (*CI*) about "the major case squad," followed in 2001.[4] These multiplying series seemed to dilute the quality, originality, and importance of the whole franchise. One can now find reruns of the three *Law & Order* series at virtually every hour of every day, causing it to lose its impact as "quality television."

All three *L & O* franchises continue to use plots "ripped from the headlines," including stories involving religion. In the past 10 years, it is likely that there have been more episodes featuring religion because there have been more "headlines" featuring religion in our national consciousness than in the 1990s: the 9/11 attacks, the sex abuse scandals in the Catholic Church, and recurring debate over the teaching of evolution, just to name a few "big stories." *L & O* finds issues that push people's buttons and gives them something to talk about around the water cooler. Religion stories are particularly juicy. All three *L & O* series aired episodes based on the story of Rev. Ted Haggard, noted megachurch pastor and former president of National Association of Evangelicals, who preached against homosexuality but was caught with a male prostitute in November, 2006. A few months after the story broke, the original *L & O* aired "Church" (February 9, 2007); *CI* aired "Brother's Keeper" (February 20, 2007)—which also fictionalized Haggard's public altercation with noted atheist author Richard Dawkins—and *SVU* aired "Sin" (March 27, 2007).

Besides the "ripped from the headlines" plots, the three shows all feature a preponderance of Catholic characters. From the first season of *L & O*, the two main characters—the primary detective, Mike Logan (played by Chris Noth) and Assistant District Attorney (ADA) Ben Stone (played by Michael Moriarty)—were identified as Catholic. Currently, the main character on *SVU* (Det. Elliott Stabler) and the two main characters on *CI* (Det. Goren and Det. Logan, who was added to the cast of *CI* after leaving the original *Law & Order* series) all identify as Catholic.[5] Despite these similarities, however, each of the three series offers a different perspective on religion.

Law & Order: No Essence to Religion

L & O continues to feature two or three plots per season in which religious issues feature prominently, usually in a very topical way. A complete list is not necessary; two examples from 2005 should suffice. The first, "Sects" (March 30, 2005), fictionalizes the murder–suicide of Ricky Rodriguez, who suffered sexual abuse as a child raised by the controversial religious movement known originally as the Children of God, but more recently known as the Family International. The second, "Age of Innocence" (October 12, 2005), is loosely based on the case involving Terri Schiavo and the ethics of euthanizing a woman in a vegetative state.

There are several templates used on *Law & Order* to deal with religion. Notably, the "cult scare" template—first seen in the early episodes "God Bless the Child" (October 22, 1991) and "Apocrypha" (November 3, 1993)—still has currency. The plots of those episodes concern, respectively, parents belonging to "the Church of the Brethren" (a religion clearly modeled on Christian Science) who let their daughter die rather than seek medical help, and a charismatic cult leader who is charged with murder and whose followers commit ritual suicide after his conviction.

"Sects," of course, borrows the same "cult scare" template. More recent examples include "Bogeyman" (April 20, 2008), which features a litigious self-help religion—called Systemotics, but instantly recognizable as Scientology—that practices controversial birthing rituals. "Lost Boys" (November 19, 2008) involves "The Church of True Path," which is referred to as a fundamentalist Mormon church, but not the actual Fundamentalist Church of Jesus Christ of Latter Day Saints. Nonetheless, the character Prophet Wyatt, the group's scheming, polygamous leader, is clearly based on Warren Jeffs. In these two examples, as with "Church of the Brethren" in the earlier episode, *L & O* uses thinly veiled pseudonyms of actual religious groups. The fictionality is all the better to frame the terms as negatively as possible.[6]

One important exception to the "pseudonymous cult" rule is the episode "The Wheel" (December 11, 2002), about a recent immigrant from China found burned to death in front of the Chinese Vice-Consul's apartment. The victim's religion is not identified as a made-up "cult," but as Falun Gong, an actual religious/physical cultivation group banned by the Chinese government since 1999 (Ownby 2008; Palmer 2007). What is more significant is that *L & O* portrays Falun Gong far more sympathetically than it does "cults" with American origins. Of course, "The Wheel" features the usual anti-cult arguments, complete with references to the leader of the People's Temple, Jim Jones, and the leader of the Branch Davidians, David Koresh. And the dramatic centerpiece of the episode—a silent protest on the courthouse steps, where dozens of Falun Gong members hold frozen qigong poses—seems designed to have a chilling effect.

But over all, Falun Gong is depicted with unusual sympathy and even-handedness. Its spokesman in the episode, an affable white man who runs practice sessions in Central Park, claims Falun Gong "fills a spiritual void." Its chief attacker is the duplicitous Chinese Vice-Consul. A character in the episode portraying a Chinese-American human rights lawyer offers a balanced discussion of the Chinese government's treatment of Falun Gong practitioners. The last word of the show (typically an ironic comment by the DA or ADA meant to sum up the major theme of the episode) is delivered by McCoy; referring to someone who would commit murder rather than be returned to China, he comments: "Makes me realize why people are finding religion in China." By *L & O* standards, this is practically an endorsement of Falun Gong. Why are Fundamentalist Mormons and Scientologists not accorded the same respect?

The answer gets to the heart of *Law & Order*'s treatment of religion. Religion is acceptable when it is normal as defined by law and government. As Walter Davis, Teresa Blythe, Gary Dreibelbis, Mark Scalese, Elizabeth Winslea, Donald Ashburn, Kimberly Ayers, and Lonnie Voth write:

> *L & O* functions as a myth that reinforces confidence in the existing social system ... Aimed at an upscale audience ... this show turns

horrendous crimes of passion into intellectual puzzles. This transformation gives the audience and those who control society reassurance that in spite of all the threats to social order, we need not lose our rational equilibrium ... *L & O* portrays the American criminal justice system as a workable moral guide that restrains and punishes evil and thereby provides security for law-abiding citizens.

(Davis *et al.* 2001, 127–36)

L & O comforts the viewer by showing evil—including "abnormal" religion—as being punished. In "The Wheel," however, a particular religion is defined as abnormal by the Chinese government—itself a suspect entity in *L & O*'s universe.

After the "cult scare" trope, the next most common and consistent religious template for all of *L & O* might be referred to as the "God told me to do it" episode. An early iteration of this theme is seen in the episode "Angel" (November 29, 1995), in which an observant Catholic woman cremates her baby; she wanted her daughter to be with God in heaven, she explains on the witness stand. Variations on this theme include "Under God" (February 5, 2003), featuring a Catholic priest who claims God told him to kill a neighborhood drug dealer, and "Good Faith" (March 30, 2007), in which a fundamentalist father kills his daughter's evolution-teaching science teacher and claims he was motivated by a legitimate fear of divine retribution.

These episodes feature ADA McCoy, now the longest-running major character in the *L & O* universe, functioning as a mouthpiece for an unsympathetic view of religion. McCoy argues with a rotating cast of assistants and bosses, who take more sympathetic views—or at least more pragmatic ones, based on divining the jury's own religious beliefs. For most of the history of the series, McCoy has been portrayed as a lapsed Catholic, but recent seasons have seen him turn increasingly "anti-religious." (In "Under God," ADA Southerlyn asks him: "what did those nuns do to you?")

Another religious theme on *L & O* is the threat of radical Islam. Obviously this theme has become prominent since the terrorist attacks of September 11, 2001. "American Jihad" (October 2, 2002) is based on the John Walker Lindh case. Greg Landon is an obnoxious, rich teenager who converts to Islam and murders a feminist professor who had organized protests in front of an Islamic bookshop. More recently, in "Angelgrove" (March 19, 2008), a woman is found stoned to death and, although suspicion falls on her Muslim boyfriend or his associates, it turns out that her son murdered her because she had committed adultery. (Her son attended a fundamentalist Christian summer camp, based on the one in the 2006 documentary *Jesus Camp*.) Interestingly, in both cases, the immigrant Muslim community is shown in a generally positive light.[7]

SVU: Sex not Salvation

L & O: Special Victims Unit features much the same representation of religion as its progenitor, though with its focus on sex crimes and child victims, religion naturally comes across even more negatively. *SVU* draws the contrast between the "normal" and the "deviant" more strongly than *L & O*. This should come as no surprise; deviancy could be considered the overall theme of *SVU*. One representative episode is "Abomination" (November 11, 2003), in which the two deviant religious groups featured are not the focus of the murder investigation (though both are "ripped from the headlines"). The first, "Re-Genesis," is an evangelical movement that helps gays recover their heterosexuality; the second, led by Reverend Shaw and his protestors from Nebraska, is based on Fred Phelps of Westboro Baptist Church of "God Hates Fags" fame. Both are seen as deviant when contrasted to the normal Det. Stabler, known as a church-going family man concerned for his daughters, who reveals in this episode that he attended Catholic school for 12 years.

More deviant religion is seen in the episode "Ritual" (February 3, 2004), when a Nigerian boy is murdered in New York's Central Park in what appears to be ritual human sacrifice, and suspicion briefly falls on a local Santeria group. The most substantive treatment of religion in *SVU* is found in the episode "Charisma" (November 16, 2004), which actively plays upon all the cult stereotypes in the moral panic playbook: a "cult" leader lives on a compound with "brainwashed" women and their children, most of whom he is sleeping with, despite being their father. Even more than in the original series, words like "cult" and "brainwashing"—which most scholars dismiss as having no descriptive value—are used unreflectively, and comparisons with David Koresh and Charles Manson are regularly made.

Criminal Intent: The "Cult" Leader as Con Artist

L & O: Criminal Intent, on the other hand, has treated religion somewhat differently from its two sister shows. It has always been more of a character-based show, focusing on the personality of its lead detective, Robert Goren (played by Vincent D'Onofrio) and of the criminals he outwits.[8] This allows for a more substantial depiction of religion.

Much of the series is predicated on Detective Goren's eccentric personality and brilliant detective skills. These qualities are manifested in his broad knowledge of many subjects, including religious ones. In one episode, he identifies a text written in Aramaic. Like *L & O*'s McCoy, he is a lapsed Catholic and, also like McCoy, an "ex-altar boy" (first revealed in the fourth episode of the series, "The Faithful" [October 17, 2001]). But unlike McCoy, Goren's "lapsed" status doesn't translate as a disdain for religion: one of Goren's dominant personality traits is empathy for those with strong (though "normal") beliefs. For example, in the episode "The View From Up Here" (January 2, 2005), a naïve housekeeper (her naïveté is explained by her being brought up on "a farm in Vermont") is tricked into believing God is telling her to kill her employer. When Goren convinces her she has not been receiving divine guidance, she moans, "I'm so stupid." "You're not stupid to have faith," Goran replies.

"The Pilgrim" (November 17, 2002)—broadcast a month after the L & O episode "American Jihad"—deals with Islamic terrorism on a superficially similar level: the perpetrator of violence is a white convert to Islam, from a privileged background. However, in "The Pilgrim," Ethan Edwards is depicted much more sympathetically than is Greg Landon in "American Jihad." For one, Edwards shares his name with John Wayne's character in 1956 classic Western *The Searchers*, a possible allusion to the American Muslim character's legitimate, though misguided, search. The title of the episode refers to his radicalizing trip to Egypt, but also, as Goren puts it, "looking to a connection to something bigger than himself." Edwards was a theology major at college and now works as a substitute teacher. Why is this attempted mass murderer rendered sympathetically? For one, by doing so it allows Goren to demonstrate his knowledge (arguing the Koran with Edwards) and empathic personality.

If Goren's status as an ex-Catholic manifests itself not as disdain for religion, it does manifest as disrespect for institutional authority. This allows for dramatic tension with his boss—Captain Deakins (Jamey Sheridan), portrayed as politically savvy and very conscious about not offending any powerful institution in New York, including the Catholic Church. As he tells Goren: "You just enjoy beating up on the Catholic Church" (from "The Faithful") or later, "if the Church gets another black eye I'll never hear in the end of it" ("Acts of Contrition," October 23, 2005).

The "cult scare" trope exists, but is handled differently in *CI* than in *SVU* or *L & O*. Of course, discourse about "cults" and "brainwashing" is used as unreflectively here as in the other two shows. But the purpose is different— less to invoke a "ripped from the headlines" shiver of recognition in the audience, and more to give Goren's eccentric, charismatic personality a criminal of similar stature with whom he can match wits. Goren needs a sparring partner in the box. Thus the show has given him recurring nemesis Nicole Wallace (played by Olivia d'Abo), a master manipulator—Moriarty to Goren's Sherlock Holmes. Most of the show's villains are seen as con artists—and some of those con artists have qualities associated with the "cult leader."

For example "Con-Text" (January 5, 2003) features "Gracenote," a self-help program that bears a resemblance to Landmark Forum, the personal development company, often described as quasi-religious, that grew out of Werner Erhard's est movement. This dialogue quickly links it to cult scares:

ADA CARVER: Is it a cult? Mind control?

DETECTIVE GOREN: Yes.

DETECTIVE EAMES: No.

ADA CARVER: How reassuring.

DETECTIVE GOREN: They use the same psychological coercion as cults.

The founder of "Gracenote," Randall Fuller, manipulates participants in his seminar to commit murder, but is himself manipulated by Goren into admitting his crimes.

Aired only three months later, "Legion" (April 6, 2003) features the unlikely character of a charismatic sound engineer, JoJo Rios, who brainwashes neighborhood kids through the philosophy of Marcus Aurelius. Broadcast a few months after that, "Sound Bodies" (November 16, 2003) portrays a budding cult leader—an adolescent named Conroy Smith—who convinces three girls to murder for him using the "recycled philosophy" (as Goren calls it) of Herman Hesse, Carlos Castaneda, and Khalil Gibran.

Detective Logan's personality is less flamboyant than Goren's. His genotype is less the eccentric detective à la Sherlock Holmes, and more the cynical urban cop trying to manage tensions of the city, like on the early days of L & O. In "The Healer" (April 23, 2006), the villain is, yet again, a manipulative con artist—in this case, a phony voodoo healer. Her hypocrisy is contrasted with a genuine voodoo practitioner, Mama Louise, who Det. Logan and his partner visit in her Brooklyn apartment.[9] This seems to be a fairly standard depiction of religion in a CI episode; had it featured Goren, he might have demonstrated his own surprising knowledge of voodoo healing. Instead, Logan must negotiate between the various constituencies—poor African Americans, wealthy cancer patients seeking alternative cures, and part-time home nurses. Logan performs even more delicate negotiations in "World's Fair" (January 2, 2007) when a Muslim woman is killed by the family of her Catholic boyfriend.

Religion as Red Herring

What ultimately do we make of this constant use of religion on L & O? The show has been on the air for almost 20 years, but there has been little scholarly analysis of its depiction of religion. One exception is an article in The Journal of Religion and Popular Culture, whose main argument is that the "show again disparages hyper-religiosity in favor of more mainstream views of religion and morality" (Clanton 2003). This is a fairly inarguable point. To give an example, in "American Jihad," Landon (the Lindh character) wants his attorney to be a Muslim. It turns out to be Anwar Mohammed, a moderate Muslim and an old friend of McCoy's ("Don't confuse his politics with my faith" he tells McCoy about Landon). He is almost completely irrelevant to the episode's themes and narrative.

Over all, the most important use of religion in *L & O* is that of the red herring, a narrative device used to distract the audience from the real motivation for murder. Often that motivation revolves around sex. For one example, let us return to "American Jihad." Why did Greg Landon convert to Islam and change his name to Mousah Salim? In the final scenes of the episode we find out the reason is sexual impotence and unrequited love. In "Good Faith," we find out that the father really killed his daughter's biology teacher because he believed she was having an affair with him, not because he was in fear for his daughter's soul.

In the previously discussed *SVU* episodes "Abomination" and "Ritual," despite the initial evidence, the murders turn not on religion, but on the jealousy or depravity of university professors (always an easy target for television cop shows, they are usually depicted as pompous, effete liars). In "Abomination," a professor kills his gay son's lover because his son's homosexuality disproves his psychological theories about homosexuality. In "Ritual," the Nigerian boy's death is made to look like a Santeria ritual by a professor of art history who had raped and killed him after buying him as a sex slave. Even in the *SVU* episode "Charisma"—which from beginning to end deals in "cult scare" rhetoric—the cult leader Abraham's motive is ultimately not religious, but financial: his 12-year-old pregnant bride will inherit a trust fund worth two million dollars if she gives birth and has no living relatives.

Criminal Intent clearly has a different view of religion, but even here, red herrings abound: in "The View From Up Here," the "God told me to kill" plot is a second-act distraction—the murders are about an obsessed lover and real estate. As S. Elizabeth Bird puts it, "individual choice, although hypocritically framed as faith, is identified as the evil, not faith itself" (Bird 2008, 37).

With rare exceptions, what I wrote 10 years ago still holds true: *L & O* "admits no essence, no substance to religion." In many ways, the *L & O* creators recognize that religion is beyond the show's purview.[10] Clearly, no police drama has taken on the mantel of *Homicide* and the early seasons of *NYPD Blue* in being deeply concerned with religious issues. So, then, what police drama shows do substantively address religion?

The most popular cop shows over the past 10 years have been *CSI* (CBS, 2000–present), its various spin-offs (set in Miami [CBS, 2002–present] and New York [CBS, 2004–present]), and its imitators (*NCIS* [CBS, 2003–present] and *Bones* [Fox, 2005–present]). Bird has argued that, like *Law & Order*, the *CSI* franchise (or at least the original Las Vegas-set series, which is the subject of Bird's analysis) respects "normal religion." Even more, the main character, Gil Grissom (played by William Petersen), keeps his mother's rosary in his desk and speaks of a need for both science and religion (Bird 2008, 25–30). However, despite Bird's argument, it seems that the popularity of forensic cop shows represents a move away from the spiritual concerns of *NYPD Blue* or *Homicide*. Forensic evidence is a physical puzzle, not a theological one. Main characters have eccentricities instead of moral positions; visual style substitutes for ethical questioning; and plots revolve around physical evidence rather than the "desire to confess." The visual pleasure gained from elaborate computer graphic sequences—seeing in great detail a bullet enter a body, or the effects of poison on a lung, for example—displace the moral pleasure gained from character development and discussion.

As we have already seen, it is the interrogation room—the "box"—that is the most sacred site in the police drama television genre, certainly in *NYPD Blue*, but especially in *Homicide*. In this windowless, clock-less room, normal rules of time and space are suspended, and the drama is compressed and intensified. Both the police and the suspects engage in ritual performance. Police use a variety of techniques to extract a confession without "crossing the line" into brutality. Suspects begin by lying, but in the end generally offer a public confession, if only to "free" the conscience even as the confession leads to a bodily imprisonment. (Michel Foucault famously theorized that confession was not liberation at all, but a "ritual of discourse" that is produced by "a power that constrains us" [Foucault 1980, 60–61].)

Of course, even today, interrogation-room scenes are a mainstay of cop shows. We have already seen how this is the case with *CI*. Even the *CSI* shows feature—however unrealistically—crime-scene technicians questioning suspects and witnesses. Another example of a current cop show in which "the box" features heavily in each episode is *The Closer* (TNT, 2005–present); getting confessions through empathy is where Brenda Johnson (Kyra Sedgwick) excels. But there is no moral complexity at work—the box is the place where she uses her guileless Southern charm to obtain a confession from the guilty party. In other words, not since *Homicide* and *NYPD Blue* have we seen the box as a sacred space, as a space for absolution and transcendence.

Even one of the most critically acclaimed cop shows of the past 10 years, *The Wire*—often called one of the best television shows of all time—is resolutely secular. Often compared with the nineteenth-century social novel—in its panoramic view of the city, featuring finely drawn portraits of criminals, cops, kids, politicians, the working class, and the links between them—*The Wire* critiques failing urban institutions, but religion is rarely mentioned (Detweiler 2009).[11]

Auteurs Trump Genre

So where are the heirs of *NYPD Blue* and *Homicide*? If not amongst the current crop of TV cop shows, where are we to look for religious meanings on TV? We must look to TV series created by those responsible for imbuing

NYPD Blue and *Homicide* with their religious complexity. In other words: follow those most responsible for the quality of the series, the *auteurs*. (As I have noted elsewhere, a "creative individual who works mostly in TV can be considered a religious artist" [Siegler 2009, 401].) After *Homicide*, Tom Fontana (its head writer and producer—and the person most responsible for its high-quality writing and theological themes) created the prison drama *OZ* (HBO, 1997–2003) (Siegler 2009, 416). *OZ* inherited much of *Homicide*'s moral concern about retribution and redemption, as well as its theological complexity.

David Milch was the heart of *NYPD Blue*. Alan Sepinwall, a television critic for the New Jersey *Star-Ledger*, who maintained an exhaustively complete *NYPD Blue* website, wrote: "For the first seven seasons of the show, Milch either wrote or rewrote nearly every line of dialogue in every episode" (Sepinwall 2006). After Milch left *NYPD Blue* at the end of the 2002–03 season, he created *Deadwood* (HBO, 2004–06), set in the eponymous mining town in the Dakota Territory in the 1870s. At first glance, *Deadwood* seems to conform to the western genre (shootouts, stagecoaches, outlaws) as well as historical drama (most of the characters are historical figures). In fact, *Deadwood* is about how community is formed, how a lawless town develops law and order (see Newcomb 2009). As Milch said: "What had interested me was the idea of order without law" (Havrilesky 2005). In some ways, then, *Deadwood* is the classic cop show in reverse: how the America depicted in *NYPD Blue* (and other cop shows) got that way in the first place.

David Milch is responsible not just for the continuities of theme between his two shows, but of language as well. The unique language patterns of early *NYPD Blue*, which simultaneously masked and revealed a character's moral intentions, migrated to *Deadwood*, where outrageous profanities and nineteenth-century colloquialisms made these speech patterns even more distinctive. Sheriff Seth Bullock, like Sipowicz, speaks with gritted teeth and barely suppressed rage, because both men are under incredible strain trying to do good in a corrupt world.

OZ and *Deadwood* went off the air in 2003 and 2006, respectively. While they were on the air, they were TV's most religious "cop shows," even though they were neither on network TV (both on HBO), nor overtly concerned about religion *per se*, nor traditional cop shows. As of mid-2009, both Milch and Fontana are developing new series; and of course new TV *auteurs* are developing new ways to express the sacred in the secular, and to put God in the box.

References

Bird, S. Elizabeth. 2008. "True Believers and Atheists Need Not Apply." In *Small Screen, Big Picture: Television and Lived Religion*, ed. Diane Winston, 17–41. Waco, TX: Baylor University Press.

Brown, Karen McCarthy. 1991. *Mama Lola: A Vodou Priestess in Brooklyn.* Berkeley: University of California Press.

Campbell, Joseph. 1973. *Hero With a Thousand Faces.* Princeton NJ: Princeton University Press.

Campbell, Joseph and Bill Moyers. 1991. *The Power of Myth.* New York: Anchor Books.

Clanton, Dan W., Jr. 2003. "These are Their Stories: Views of Religion in *Law & Order.*" *Journal of Religion and Popular Culture* 4 (Summer). www.usask.ca/relst/jrpc/art4-lawandorder.html

Davis, Walter T., Jr., Teresa Blythe, Gary Dreibelbis, Mark Scalese, Elizabeth Winans Winslea, Donald L. Ashburn, Kimberly Ayers, and Lonnie Voth. 2001. "Law & Order: The Cop Show Prescription for Containing Evil." In *Watching What We Watch: Prime-Time Television through the Lens of Faith*, 127–36. Louisville, KY: Geneva Press.

Detweiler, Craig. 2009. "*The Wire*: Playing the Game." In *Small Screen, Big Picture: Television and Lived Religion*, ed. Diane Winston, 69–97. Waco, TX: Baylor University Press.

Foucault, Michel. 1977. *Discipline and Punish: The Birth of the Prison*, trans. Alan Sheridan. New York: Pantheon Books.

——. 1980. *The History of Sexuality, Volume I: An Introduction.* New York: Vintage Books.

Gordon, Andrew. 1995. "Star Wars: A Myth for Our Time" in *Screening the Sacred: Religion, Myth, and Ideology in Popular American Film*, ed. Joel W. Martin and Conrad E. Ostwalt, Jr, 73–82. Boulder, CO: Westview Press.

Havrilesky, Heather. 2005. "The Man Behind Deadwood." *Salon.com* (March 5). http://dir.salon.com/story/ent/feature/2005/03/05/milch/index.html

Iwamura, Jane. 2003. "Altared States: Exploring the Legacy of Japanese American Butsudan Practice." *Pacific World: Journal of the Institute of Buddhist Studies* 3, 5: 275–91.

Jihad Watch and Dhimmi Watch. 2008. "Law and Order Shills for Islam." (March 20). www.jihadwatch.org/archives/020390.php

Newcomb, Horace. 2009. "In the Beginning ... *Deadwood.*" In *Small Screen, Big Picture: Television and Lived Religion*, ed. Diane Winston, 43–68. Waco, TX: Baylor University Press.

Ownby, David. 2008. *Falun Gong and the Future of China.* New York: Oxford University Press.

Palmer, David A. 2007. *Qigong Fever: Body, Science, and Utopia in China.* New York: Columbia University Press.

Salvo, Dana *et al.* 1997. *Home Altars of Mexico.* Albuquerque: University of New Mexico Press.

Schechner, Richard. 1993. *The Future of Ritual: Writings on Culture and Performance.* London: Routledge.

Sepinwall, Alan. 2006. "Frequently Asked Questions (FAQ) about NYPD Blue." www.stwing.upenn.edu/~sepinwal/faq.html#newwriters

Siegler, Elijah. 2009. "Television Auteur Confronts God: The Religious Imagination of Tom Fontana." In *Small Screen, Big Picture: Television and Lived Religion*, ed. Diane Winston, 401–26. Waco, TX: Baylor University Press.

Notes

1 Much of the material in this chapter (and to which I will refer hereafter without further citation) is drawn from my chapter in the first edition of *God in the Details* (2001, 199–215).
2 Later editions of Campbell's 1973 work have a picture of Luke Skywalker on the cover.
3 Obviously, film also often depicts a character's religious change, but this change is often manifested as the journey of the film's protagonist—the famous "hero quest," a "monomyth" that has a set pattern (Campbell diagrammed it as "departure, initiation, return") and in which other characters function as aids or obstacles to the quest (Campbell 1973).
4 Several other spin-offs were unsuccessful: *Crime and Punishment* (2002–04), a reality show; *Trial by Jury* (2005–06); and *Conviction* (2006).
5 Logan's final episode of *CI*, "Last Rites" (August 17, 2008) features a priest who convinces Logan to resign from the police force.
6 Often at the end of the show a title card proclaims: "The preceding show was fictional."
7 Particularly in the case of "Angelgrove," this positive portrayal of Islam bothered some conservative Christians (see *Jihad Watch and Dhimmi Watch* 2008).
8 Beginning in its fifth season (2005–06), Chris Noth—who had been part of the original cast of *L & O*—joined *CI* as Det. Mike Logan and became an alternating lead detective, giving D'Onofrio a less demanding schedule. In early 2009, Jeff Goldblum (as Det. Zach Nichols) replaced Noth as the every-other-week lead.
9 This is surely a reference to Karen McCarthy Brown's classic ethnography *Mama Lola* (Brown 1991).
10 For exceptions, see Clanton's (2003) analysis of definitions of good and evil in "Angel"; Bird's (2008) defense of original series' episode "Bible Story" (December 7, 2005). Like Bird, I find that this episode is full of biblical allusions and genuine religious themes.
11 The thrust of the article is that viewing *The Wire* gave Detweiler a moral imperative to recommit to a life of public service.

Chapter 10

Don't Act Now!

Selling Christian Abstinence in the Religious Marketplace

Sara Moslener

With the rise of the Religious Right in the late 1970s, the general public became aware of evangelical concerns regarding the nation's religious and moral integrity. Targeting abortion, homosexuality, divorce, sex education, pornography, and sexual promiscuity as symptoms of national decay, the Moral Majority mobilized conservative evangelicals and solidified a budding alliance between conservative politics and evangelical Christianity (Freedman and Freedman 1988, 327, 333). Evangelical denominations and para-church groups, committed to restoring the moral status of the country, focused their efforts on the adolescent population. Leading the way, the Southern Baptist Convention launched True Love Waits in 1993. Developed by the Reverend Richard Ross, a Southern Baptist youth minister, True Love Waits is a Christian sexual education program with the sole purpose of promoting premarital sexual abstinence.[1] A year after its founding, True Love Waits held a national rally in Washington DC, introducing the movement onto the national scene and confirming its position within the evangelical–Republican alliance. Shortly thereafter, numerous other religious groups endorsed the movement, and young people of all Christian faith traditions found themselves attending True Love Waits rallies and signing pledge cards committing themselves to sexual abstinence before marriage.[2]

That same year, Denny and Amy Pattyn, youth ministers from Yuma, Arizona, discovered that their county's rate of teenage pregnancy was among the highest in the nation. In conjunction with the nondenominational John Guest Evangelistic Team, they began a local program that encouraged church-going youth to adopt abstinence until marriage as a central element of their Christian faith commitment. Amy Pattyn even traveled to Mexico to purchase silver rings for the young people to wear as signs of their commitment. In 2000, the Pattyns relocated their organization to Pittsburgh, Pennsylvania, developed a multimedia stage, and began touring locally with a group of young abstinence evangelists. Despite his initial reticence to accept federal funding, Pattyn and his organization, Silver Ring Thing, accepted a significant grant from the federal government in 2003, allowing them to establish the organization as an independent nonprofit organization with the resources to extend it into a national campaign.[3]

The Faith-Based Abstinence Movement (FBAM), represented by True Love Waits and Silver Ring Thing, stands as a beacon for young people who desire to live "in, but not of the world," as they believe is biblically mandated. However, when viewed in the context of US political life, popular media culture, and most significantly the market economy, this "purity revolution" (as it is sometimes called) reveals a deeper complicity with mainstream cultural values. The FBAM strategically situates itself at the center of US politics and culture, while at the same time it maintains rhetoric that is consciously counter-cultural. By doing so, the leading organizations of the FBAM—Silver Ring Thing and True Love Waits—effectively code themselves as relevant, counter-culturally, even as they are interwoven in the dominant culture of conservative Protestant religion and politics. With numerous strategies for negotiating modernity and religion, the secular and sacred, Silver Ring Thing and True Love Waits offer a type of socially conservative evangelical Christianity, a product or "brand" that is especially packaged and marketed for adolescent consumers. The maintenance of the movement's counter-culturally relevant position within the North American religious landscape is best understood as an attempt to gain prominence within this religious marketplace, in competition with other products for the attention of its consumers.

Building the Brand: The Emerging Political Relevance of Sexual Abstinence

As we see in the current debates raging over same-sex marriage, influencing the definition of sexually normative practices in the United States remains one of the primary efforts on the agenda of socially conservative evangelicals, and the marriage of conservative Christian sexual morality and a Republican political agenda has been a hearty and long-lasting one, even if, like all marriages, at times it suffers from various strains and pressures. It is an alliance to which the FBAM remains highly indebted for establishing and maintaining its political relevance as it has worked to define its product for a particular niche market.

A year after its founding in 1993, True Love Waits constructed a national display in conjunction with a national Youth for Christ conference in Washington, DC. As part of the weekend's events, numerous young abstinence pledgers deposited 211,163 pledged cards attached to stakes onto the lawn of the National Mall (Goodstein 1994). While most of the 20,000 young people attending the rally were enjoying the frivolity of dancing and socializing at the weekend's concerts, 150 white-ribboned attendees made their way to the White House. According to *The Washington Post*, the students were welcomed by President Clinton, who offered full political and moral support (McCarthy 1994). However, True Love Waits founder Richard Ross was disappointed with the President, who cited government's limited ability to influence people's behavior. President Clinton remarked that personal morality, not government policy, was more appropriately suited for shaping an individual's sexual decision-making, and commended the students for their commitment to premarital sexual abstinence. With no time for questions or discussion, the group left feeling less than satisfied with their efforts to bring their movement to national prominence (Goodstein 1994).

Despite its inability to curry favor with the commander-in-chief, True Love Waits eventually found support in the Republican-controlled Congress. In 1996, the Reverend Robert Turner, a support coordinator for True Love Waits, was invited to testify at a Senate Appropriations Committee chaired by Pennsylvania Senator Arlen Specter (at that time still a Republican). Reverend Turner challenged abstinence efforts that focused primarily on the amelioration of pregnancy rates and sexually transmitted diseases. He claimed that this approach neglected the emotional and moral consequences of premarital sexual activity, the governing values of True Love Waits (Turner 1996, 87–91). Though numerous other groups were represented at the hearings, the particular concerns of Reverend Turner and True Love Waits emerged later that year in the language of a provision added to the much-anticipated "Welfare Reform" bill amending the *Social Security Act* (P.L. 74–271 [49 Stat. 620]). Section 710(b) of this bill provided funding to organizations offering abstinence-only education that was defined, in part, as education that (1) teaches the social, psychological, and health gains of sexual abstinence, and (2) teaches that sexual activity outside the context of marriage results in harmful psychological effects (see Title V, §510(b) [42 U.S. Code 710]).[4]

Denny Pattyn was initially quite hesitant to accept government funding. As he explained:

> I became disgusted with what they said I had to do to get this money. You know, here's what you have to take off the walls of your room. You couldn't have any religious symbols up. I was disgusted because the idea of abstinence is a religious idea. That's where it comes from. You can't really make sense of abstinence without faith.
>
> (Interview with Denny Pattyn, October 31, 2006)

Fortunately for Pattyn, President George W. Bush's first official act was to expand the Charitable Choice Act to create the Faith-Based Initiative. Under these new guidelines, Pattyn no longer felt constrained by the possibility of federal funding, and contacted the other Pennsylvania Senator, Rick Santorum, to help him apply for a Maternal and Child Health Special Programs of Regional and National Significance (SPRANS) Block Grant.[5] Silver Ring

Thing was awarded the grant and received $700,000 for 2003. The grant was renewed the following two years, with Silver Ring Thing receiving total federal funding of $1,400,000.

Pattyn remained wary—having witnessed other organizations lose their religious focus when tied to government regulations—but made adjustments necessary to receive federal funds. These adjustments, however, proved insufficient for some, and in May 2005 the American Civil Liberties Union filed a law suit against Secretary of the Department of Health and Human Services Mike Leavitt, Assistant Secretary of the Administration for Children and Families Wade Horn, and Associate Commissioner for the Administration on Children, Youth, and Families Harry Wilson.[6] Acting in their official capacities, they were accused of neglecting to "sufficiently monitor or audit the use of funds" by a faith-based group (American Civil Liberties Union 2005a, 2–3). Another key complaint of the suit concerned Silver Ring Thing's live show; although the organization began providing an alternative secular event for students not wishing to attend the faith-based part of the show, the American Civil Liberties Union (ACLU) claimed the provisions separating the faith-based portions from the secular components were insufficient. Furthermore, the ACLU contended that Silver Ring Thing used abstinence education as an evangelistic tool, funding of which was a clear breach of the First Amendment's "No Establishment" clause, a claim that seemed to be supported by Silver Ring Thing's federal tax filings, which were listed under the name of another organization: the John Guest Evangelistic Team (*ibid.*, 4).

Pattyn asserted his organization's compliance by pointing out that 75 per cent of the Silver Ring Thing program contained no religious content. With guidance from the federal government, the organization was permitted to apply for federal funding for that portion of its work. Thus Pattyn's organization offered two alternatives at the same event—one faith-based and one not—and at a certain point in the program, the audience was offered the option of continuing with a nonfaith-based alternative in another part of the event facility. This, as far as Pattyn and his colleagues understood, kept them in full compliance with the government's regulations for the use of federal funds for abstinence education (interview, October 31, 2006).

The ACLU, however, claimed that these efforts were not enough. The complaint claimed that Pattyn strongly encouraged the entire audience to stay for the faith-based portion of the show, and that students attending felt pressure to participate in the religious part of the program. Furthermore, students who chose the secular programming were expected to leave the main presentation hall, while the rest were able to stay. As a result, only a few responded to the offer of a secular program (American Civil Liberties Union 2005a; Pattyn interview, October 31, 2006). In this way, the ACLU claimed, Silver Ring Thing was able to coerce students to remain at the main presentation hall to hear testimonies and a sermon, and to participate in the organization's purity ritual, in which the young people made a commitment both to sexual abstinence and to Jesus Christ. Media studies scholar Mara Einstein describes the ACLU's concerns more directly. She contends that the relationship between the Department of Health and Human Services, Silver Ring Thing, and the Bush Administration was a deliberate attempt to maintain the influence of an evangelical–Republican agenda on national policy at the expense of neglecting policies that more adequately expressed the needs and concerns of the general population (Einstein 2008, 187–89).[7]

Despite these shortcomings, Silver Ring Thing made several attempts to prove its compliance with federal law shortly after the legal complaint was filed. Pattyn issued a statement acknowledging that his organization was faith-based, but insisted that federal funds had always been used properly (Connoly 2005). However, clandestine attempts to alter the religious content of the organization's website caught the attention of the ACLU, who noted in a press release that Silver Ring Thing's attempt to "sanitize" it only proved its culpability. According to Julie Sternberg, senior staff attorney for the ACLU's Reproductive Freedom Project, the organization's keen concern for its web-based content revealed its true intent: "They are going to great lengths to paint a picture of an organization that does not use tax payer dollars to promote religion. Unfortunately, altering their website will not be enough to hide the overtly religious message that they have been promoting for years on the public's dime" (American Civil Liberties Union 2005b).

Despite Silver Ring Thing's best efforts, on August 25 a letter from Assistant Commissioner Harry Wilson, one of the defendants in the case, alerted the organization that its funding had been suspended. By mid-September 2005, Silver Ring Thing had been informed that reallocation of the remaining $75,000 would be dependent upon the organization's submission of a "Corrective Action Plan" that provided an adequate course of action for maintaining a distinction between the religious and secular components of its programming (Wetzstein 2005). Pattyn and his organization seemed unconcerned by this injunction and announced to the media that the lawsuit had in fact aided the organization by generating enough private donations to offset any eventual loss of federal funds (Rittmeyer 2005).

The suit was settled in February 2007 after Silver Ring Thing, in conjunction with the Administration for Families and Children, terminated the grant effective January 31, 2007, forfeiting the remaining $75,000 (American Civil Liberties Union 2005a; Pattyn interview, October 31, 2006). The settlement laid out stipulations that regulated Silver Ring Thing's future application for, and use of, federal funding. In order to apply for funding, the organization would be required to comply with federal laws regarding the use of funds for religiously based activities.

Interpretations of the settlement varied depending on the reporting source, giving each side the ability to claim a small victory. The ACLU claimed victory because the court found that Silver Ring Thing in its current configuration was not legally able to procure funds, and could not do so in the future without radically altering its organization and submitting to government oversight, an arrangement into which Pattyn was not eager to enter (American Civil Liberties Union 2006; Pattyn interview, October 31, 2006). According to Pattyn, however, the court's dismissal of the case worked entirely in favor of his organization. Pattyn identified his organization's three goals with regard to the case: that it would be dismissed, that the organization would not lose any funding already received, and that the organization would not lose the privilege of applying for funding in the future (interview, October 31, 2006). Since each of these goals was met, Pattyn claimed that he was victorious. Furthermore, he accused the ACLU of sending out an "erroneous" press release that skewed the settlement stipulations:

> It was actually very deceptive how they said it because we didn't lose one dime. They said we lost our funding. They said we lost our grant. What we decided to do was ... we decided to forego the remaining two months of our grant because we didn't want to have to make any changes in how we did our program. They assumed that because we gave up our grant, that we lost funding. What they didn't understand was that we had already received all of our funding at that point and we had already spent it. So we weren't receiving any funding. So that's how that was deceptively sent out to the media.
>
> (Pattyn interview, October 31, 2006)

Though both sides claimed victory in this case—Pattyn's narrative inconsistencies notwithstanding—the tensions between the ACLU and Silver Ring Thing recall the rhetoric of the so-called "culture wars," a theory of conflict developed by James Davison Hunter to describe what he perceived to be the irreconcilable dispute between "progressive" and "orthodox" camps in the North American political and religious landscape. These conflicts, according to Hunter, are based on incompatible and immutable views of moral accountability that, when institutionalized, create a polarized political landscape with particular implications for North American family life (Hunter 1991, 43). Though Hunter's thesis has been challenged by subsequent studies, the media certainly had no difficulty using the model to sell this story. Curiously, as soon as the court decision was announced, the mainstream media lost interest in the story, possibly because of the limitations of the culture wars theory to provide explanations for compromise.

Finding the Market: The Cultural Relevance of Sexual Abstinence

The FBAM's adept and prolific use of popular culture and advanced media technology as meaning-making devices invites an inquiry into the implications of the close relationship between the abstinence movement and mainstream media culture. Availing itself of the most sophisticated media technology, both True Love Waits and Silver Ring Thing spread their message of faith and purity through the internet, published print and, most conspicuously, live performance. In these contexts, the groups adapt images, films, songs, themes, and narratives from mainstream media culture and "recast" them according to the strictures of their abstinence message.

Recasting is the process by which beliefs and practices are adapted to meet the perceived needs of individuals. By doing so, religion becomes a commodity unifying symbols and practices that often advance a particular identity marker (Roof 1999, 69–70). For advocates of abstinence, this identity marker is sexual purity, which is posited as central to the Christian faith commitment and commodified through the use of popular culture and multimedia technology, thus making it highly attractive to potential consumers.

For an organization like Silver Ring Thing, recasting is a process applied to both religious beliefs and popular entertainment. Many of their skits are sophisticated replications of sketches from the long-running late-night program *Saturday Night Live*. Although alike in characterizations, costumes, and style of humor, the narratives for each sketch are re-scripted to accommodate the abstinence message. Early on in the Silver Ring Thing show, audiences are entertained by a round of *Jeopardy*, but with celebrity contestants such as Johnny Depp, Paris Hilton, and Jack Black, one quickly determines that this is *Jeopardy* as known to fans of *Saturday Night Live*. Alex Trebeck insults his alternatively absent, insane, and vain guests by mocking their inability to answer simple questions regarding not great works of literature, architecture, or art, but sexually transmitted diseases. It is clear that these celebrities represent everything that Silver Ring Thing advocates against—self-indulgence, irresponsible living, and the sexual *ennui* that members of the organization believe inebriates North American popular culture. Strangely, this message, delivered under the guise of caustic humor, sarcasm, and insult, does not transmit the moral superiority one would expect. Rather, its use of an easily recognizable context and its mega-stars provide a level of comfort for the audience.

Many portions of the Silver Ring Thing event function as signifiers of other cultural events or themes. The skit—as an imitation of a *Saturday Night Live* sketch, which itself is an imitation of the game show *Jeopardy*—simultaneously draws upon popular culture references while reiterating those references according to the abstinence message, in this case the "jeopardy" of promiscuous sexuality and ignorance of sexually transmitted infections.

Silver Ring Thing's use of popular culture gains it immediate trust among its media-saturated audiences. This design is intentional, the group's former program coordinator "Tracy" told me.[8] If students can connect with a piece of popular culture, she explained, they begin to feel that Silver Ring Thing is a group that understands their experiences as adolescent consumers of popular culture, and later find themselves more open to embracing the more serious message of the evening: abstaining from sexual activity before marriage is God's design for your sexual life. Embrace God's intention and you will be blessed relationally, physically, emotionally, and spiritually; reject God's plan and you will be sentenced to a future of bitter memories, emotional turmoil, disease, unwanted pregnancy, and separation from God (Interview with "Tracy," October 18, 2006).

Within this core message reside several hints about the group's struggle to negotiate its abstinence message in light of the pull of popular culture, and American culture in general. Some bits of humor throughout the evening reflect the group's anxieties concerning race, gender roles, and sexual orientation. One video is a "commercial" that touts a false *Time-Life* series titled *There for the Breakup.* The *Time-Life* operator cheerfully explains that this series offers recordings of vicious break-up fights exacerbated by the couple's sexual histories, crises that students committed to abstinence would be able to avoid. Among the audio clips used to entice potential customers is one in which an actor notes: "I'm a black man, this child is white. I'm pretty sure it's not mine." The perpetuation of a negative stereotype of black men being unwilling to take on parental responsibility is either ignored or neglected by the organization. As for the all-white audience, they respond to the joke in the same vein as all the others—with uproarious laughter.

Racial stereotypes are not the only labels perpetuated in the evening's performance. Immediately following this "commercial," another video begins—one in a series that run intermittently throughout the evening— titled *The Laws of the Father.* In each of these clips the hyperbolic words of an overprotective father chastise the potential suitors of his daughter, issuing insults and potential death threats. These video segments draw heavily upon the gender stereotype that a girl's sexuality is passive and thus vulnerable to attack. As a result, her father, as chief protector of her chastity, must control his daughter's dating relationships and sexual experiences. Without an accompanying video sequence directed toward young men, this series of videos suggests that Silver Ring Thing has yet to overcome a sexual double standard.

At first blush, this "girls only" message is inconsistent throughout the show. The organization's literature does not single out young women to heed the message, nor does it define purity in particularly gendered terms. In fact, "Tracy" explained that Silver Ring Thing works diligently to make its message relevant to men. During her purity talk, in which she frankly discusses her own sexual history, she informs the audience that currently young women are as sexually aggressive as young men. Each of her explanations, however, assumes a particular construction of masculinity and femininity reminiscent of that found in secular abstinence curricula (Doan and Williams 2008, 104). These gender constructions assert young women as the natural arbiters of sexual purity and young men as the natural purveyors of sexual aggression. Women who are sexually aggressive are not "myth-busters"—the title of Silver Ring Thing's 2008/09 live performance—as a feminist interpretation would presume, but evidence of an out-of-control sexual ethic. However, young men who defy their natural inclination for sexual aggression are not sexual deviants but role models and heroes, according to Silver Ring Thing. Defined in opposition to one another, young men and young women are expected, respectively, to resist and embrace their "natural" inclinations, an observation that Heather Hendershot also makes of True Love Waits (Hendershot 2004, 90).

This assumed heterosexism is evident in yet another "commercial" for a medication that promises to cure all ailments associated with sexually trans-mitted diseases. The commercial lists a host of silly and unbearable side-effects in order to show the audience that sexually transmitted diseases are a life-altering affliction. Among the list of side-effects is a "desire to see *Brokeback Mountain*," followed shortly thereafter by a "desire to be *in Brokeback Mountain*." As a reference to a popular film depicting a life-long love affair between two men, the anti-gay inference reinforces the heterosexism of their message.

Silver Ring Thing's ability simultaneously to enjoy and criticize popular culture gains it immediate trust among the media consumers in its audience. It perceives the need of its audience to feel like they belong, and it uses popular media as a way to communicate its recognition of that need. By acknowledging its audience as media consumers in a culture that values consumer identities, Silver Ring Thing is able to ascribe significance to those in attendance and gain their trust by creating its own media discourse.

"Branding" the Product: Sexual Abstinence as the New Counter Culture

Despite its deliberate positioning at the center of political and cultural life in the United States, the sexual abstinence movement works to maintain a stance that is distinctly counter-cultural, particularly as it relates to main-stream beliefs and values regarding human sexuality. With assistance from media outlets such as *The Washington Post* and *The New York Times*, the movement has garnered a reputation for advocating resistance to perceived cultural norms of sexual promiscuity and experimentation. This pattern—according to historian R. Laurence Moore (1986), a consistent and long-standing one in American religious history—earns the organizations in the FBAM the ability to critique the dominant culture even as they speak from within it, to benefit from all of the advantages of being a part of the main-stream even as they play the role of prophets, warning society of its failures.

In an article in *The New York Times*, 17-year-olds David Medford and Lara McCalman use the language of the gay rights movement as they pro-claim their virginity as its own kind of "coming out." Notes Medford: "It's awesome to be a virgin. I want to give that as a gift to my wife. I want it to be special, not something I do just to fit in. I feel there's a lot of people that are virgins, but they're afraid to come out" (*New York Times* 1993). By invoking the metaphor of the closet, Medford articulates an interesting connection between the abstinence commitment and the assertion of sexual identity. The article offers McCalman the opportunity to reiterate her own claim as she reflects on the importance of peer influence: "Once you know 100 kids can do it, you know another kid can do it. It's positive peer pressure.[...] So many of us are coming out of the closet. I'm a virgin and proud of it." The article presumes connection between sexual rights and sexual abstinence.

In the 1960s and 1970s, when sexuality became deeply tied to one's personal identity, the "sexual revolution" provided culturally marginalized sexual communities—women, gay men, and lesbians, particularly—with a canopy under which to organize for political rights. Not surprisingly, leaders in the FBAM identify this sexual liberation movement—an era marked by increased sexual freedoms—as the indisputable origin of the current moral and social crisis. It is strange, then, that many media outlets, including those sponsored by the Southern Baptist Convention, use the rhetoric of the sexual revolution.

And yet, according to these media reports, sexual abstinence is more than a personal choice; it is the declaration of a sexual identity akin to coming out of the closet. As members of a self-proclaimed counter-culture, these students boldly assert a marginalized sexual identity in the face of pressure to conform to the accepted standards of sexual behavior, which they perceive as sexual experimentation and promiscuity. The process they replicate—that of gay, lesbian, bisexual, and trans-gendered individuals publicly claiming their sexual identity—is one not sanctioned by the subset of evangelical Christians who ascribe to sexual abstinence.

This discrepancy was cleverly (if unwittingly) resolved in 1994, when *Washington Post* editorialist Colman McCarthy, writing on the True Love Waits rally in Washington, DC, labeled the group who met with President Clinton "sexual revolutionaries." McCarthy's piece lauded the efforts of the students by referring to the sexually abstinent young people as courageous—even rebellious—individuals moving against the tide of social expectations. By doing so, McCarthy effectively reframed them in the terminology of the sexual liberation movement of the 1960s. Of this newest sexual revolution, McCarthy wrote:

> If that sounds as though debauchery were the agenda, it's only because such notions of sexual liberation have come to be equated with reckless hedonism. A current and growing revolution differs from the conventional one: Its goal is abstinence, for teenagers to be liberated from peer and commercial pressures that push or cajole the young into premarital sex.
> (McCarthy 1994, A19)

With these words, McCarthy recast the latest chapter of the sexual revolution against a socially conservative agenda.

The adaptation of the radical rhetoric of the sexual revolution to the FBAM is initially a curious proposal. However, we have already seen examples of the FBAM's use of media-generated technologies to render identities flexible and open to the transformative influence of mediated discourses. More than media subjects, the constituent parties within the FBAM reinforce their media portrayals by posting favorable articles on their websites, or even incorporating news items into their own publications. By doing so, they open themselves up to the same media-generated technologies they employ to transform audiences at their live shows. As a result of entering into this flexible, media-generated discourse, the FBAM, and the media that portray it, can adapt some of the rhetoric of sexual liberation previously so despised by social conservatives, and recast it according to the traditionalist parameters of the abstinence movement.

For Silver Ring Thing, being the latest incarnation of the sexual revolution is a call to be counter-cultural. "Tracy" explains that being "counter-cultural" means

> ... wanting to create in a sense a reverse peer pressure whereas standard peer pressure [claims that] when you are a teenager you have sex. Whether it's on your prom night or sometime in college the standard expectation is that you would have sex.
>
> (Interview, October 18, 2006)

But Silver Ring Thing's sexual revolution is not merely rhetorical, since it also implements a well-planned strategy for penetrating its consumer market. As "Tracy" continues, the process

> ... takes some version of a majority of students who are going against that message to reverse that message. And so that's why our target number is to reach 20 per cent of America's youth with our message.
>
> (*ibid.*)

These numbers are not just vague figures, but the result of a strategic business plan that emerged once the group received its nonprofit status. According to Silver Ring Thing's website, its "National Rollout Plan" is based on its desire to create a "culture shift" among teenagers whereby sexual abstinence becomes the norm (Silver Ring Thing n.d.). The organization specifically targets the most densely populated areas of the country, some of which house satellite branches. As "Tracy" explains, according to Silver Ring Thing's market assessment, it will take the commitments of 20 per cent of North American youth to affect this shift. (The group recently added shows in Mexico and Canada.)

Drawing on Pattyn's pre-ministry successes in the business world, Silver Ring Thing has transformed the project with market analysis and strategic planning, making a business of "creating" a counter-culture. Even as journalists like Colman McCarthy have established the movement's image as revolutionary, the leadership of organizations like Silver Ring Thing has successfully altered a once-revolutionary movement using methods more akin to Wall Street than to the grassroots movements of the 1960s.

Whatever cynicism this invokes, not all abstinence adherents view the counter-cultural aspirations of the movement as an attempt to "market" abstinence. Daniel Stowe, a youth minister from the Mid-West whose church has hosted a Silver Ring Thing event, thinks the increased visibility of sexual purity as a counter-culture option has in fact helped stem the tide of sexual promiscuity that would otherwise run rampant. One of the values of this cultural opposition, according to Stowe, is the notion of deferred gratification. Students he observes are immersed in a society of "immediate fulfillment" that provides them with numerous goods, services, and relationships to fulfill every need with greater and greater speed and efficiency. He teaches abstinence to his rather sizeable youth group in an attempt to help them understand that sexual and emotional intimacy are not commodities quickly and easily obtained, while he is keenly aware of the challenges he faces in opposing a culture that offers young people numerous forms of immediate gratification (interview with Daniel Stowe, December 3, 2006).

Whether rooted in the rhetoric of sexual revolution, a strategic business plan, or a concern for reinstituting the value of deferred gratification, the counter-cultural foundations of sexual abstinence would appear quite different without the precedent of the counter-cultural movements of the 1960s. However, the ability of the movement to weave language of that period together seamlessly with scriptural proclamations, which they claim are culturally transcendent, allows abstinence advocates to universalize their message beyond the contemporary moment.

Selling the Goods: Sexual Abstinence in the Religious Marketplace

As a functionary within the religious marketplace, participants in the FBAM are prepared to advance their cause according to the stipulations of that market. Namely, they are prepared to compete for the attention of adolescents, a consumer market whose favor is highly prized by secular purveyors of popular culture. Recognizing this, the FBAM has positioned itself as the natural antagonist of secular media discourse, not by eschewing popular media, but by creating an alternative discourse that uses the attention-getting aspects of these media in which to encode its own counter-cultural message. This strategy is hardly new to evangelicals who, since the nineteenth century, have readily adapted and even innovated mass media, market research

analysis, popular culture, and technological advancement in an attempt
to reach the widest audience possible. However, recent scholarship in the
field of religion, media, and marketing argues that this strategy is not
merely about creating consumers of a particular religious product, but is
about utilizing postmodern theories of destabilized identities in order to
reshape consumer consciousness according to particular mandates (Hoover
2006, 85; Lyon 2004, 94; Roof 1999, 69–70). By acknowledging their audiences as consumers of popular culture and utilizing the flexibility of media-
generated identities, organizers of Silver Ring Thing are able to effectively
shift a participant's self-understanding within the course of the organization's
two-and-a-half hour presentation.

The most recent inquiry into the persuasiveness of religious marketing
contends that evangelicals in particular are highly concerned with the
decreased numbers of young believers. Youth pastors and other leaders
employ marketing strategies that attempt to establish "brand" loyalty at an
early age. In order to do so, religious leaders must compete with the numerous alternatives youth have for filling their leisure time. Unless their message
matches the popular trends in the market, evangelical initiatives will be
rendered irrelevant. Furthermore, in the age of sound bites, pixels, and fast-
moving media, the core message must be presented in a compact, simplified,
and easily digestible manner to have any impact at all (Einstein 2008, 194).

Denny Pattyn's wife, Amy, has helped shape Silver Ring Thing so that it
targets adolescents as young as 11-years-old. As she noted in a recent BBC
documentary,

> I think that it is the perfect age to start because you're capturing a pure
> mind and you are rallying friends around them, that is the time to cap-
> ture a mind and a heart because it's not already experienced sexual
> activity, it's not going down the road, it's not facing the same kind of
> peer pressure you are at a high school level.
>
> (BBC 2004)

Though couching her concern in spiritualized, therapeutic rhetoric, Amy
Pattyn recognizes the necessity of an impressionable consumer identity
among her targeted audience. As a result, the FBAM is a particular brand of
Christianity, a way of marketing socially conservative evangelicalism for
adolescents.

As a brand of evangelical Christianity, sexual abstinence functions effectively as a commodity largely because the FBAM is not attempting to turn
adolescents away from their primary religious communities. Rather, the
movement encourages individuals and communities to invest in their product
as a supplement, an "add-on" to an already established faith system. While
some individuals come to sexual abstinence from a nonreligious background,
most are already active as Christian believers. The challenge then is to create

a brand that offers benefits to Christian believers that they are not already receiving.[9] In order to set itself apart from the plethora of offerings available to evangelical adolescents, the FBAM offers a lifestyle product—one that promises a great deal. As a brand name, True Love Waits offers both a promise and the condition of that promise. Not only does it promise that true love exists and is waiting for you (yes, you!), it promises that if you wait to have sex, your marriage will be blessed by the otherwise elusive gift of authentic romance.

The two central material products—the brand's "anchors"—available under the abstinence brand are purity rings and Abstinence Study Bibles. Along with T-shirts, key-chains, buttons, Bible studies, music, films, and websites, these items provide material evidence of one's membership in this select group of young people. Of course, anyone is invited to become select. The process of branding presumes the malleability of identity. Thus an average student enters a Silver Ring Thing event and leaves with a newfound sense of meaning, a community, an Abstinence Study Bible, and a ring. All of this is done by showing the audiences that their identities as consumers of mainstream media are acknowledged and affirmed.

As an evangelical organization that adapts themes from popular culture and relies upon the most up-to-date technology, Silver Ring Thing is hardly unique. Adapting, advancing, or even inventing media outlets has long been a characteristic strategy of the evangelical movement for transmitting the gospel message to the widest audience possible. Whether transforming technologically sophisticated theatrical venues into worship spaces, or utilizing mass production and creating the prototype for the modern-day corporation, Protestant evangelicals have never hesitated to make the most of mass media, consumer market analysis, popular culture, and technological advancement (Brown 2004; Gutjahr 1999; Kilde 2002; Nord 2004).

The most recent examples of evangelicals adapting to consumer tastes and market trends is the phenomenon of culturally relevant niche Bibles. Due to the technological shifts that occurred in the publishing industry starting in the 1980s, niche Bibles are now the norm for Bible publishing. By adapting to the digital revolution in secular publishing, Bible publishers began exploiting the ease with which they could add extra-biblical content to their products. They are currently able to produce endlessly diverse sets of specialized Bibles marketed to specific readers who fall into a variety of categories: newlyweds, mothers, adolescents, dieters, single parents, and those addicted to drugs and alcohol, to name only a few (Gutjahr n.d., 4).

Without a doubt, this phenomenon has aided the FBAM in promoting its own moral agenda. The *True Love Waits Study Bible* and Silver Ring Thing's *Abstinence Study Bible* rely strongly on the niche-Bible phenomenon to ascribe sacred status to abstinence teachings. Silver Ring Thing, for instance, inserts over 60 pages of nonbiblical material that is based on the content of its live show (interview, October 18, 2006). Students who purchase a Silver Ring are provided a copy of this text developed especially for new adherents to sexual abstinence and new Christian believers. With a detailed introduction to studying the Bible and a topical reference guide, Silver Ring Thing's Bible readers are introduced to a form of Christianity in which sexual abstinence stands as a key tenet of the faith.

But by far the most widely acknowledged symbol of the FBAM is the purity ring. The numerical success of the purity ring is only one small indication of its significance to those who wear it. Even though students are not just instructed to wear it, but must purchase it first, the ring is nonetheless imbued with sacred status as a sign of the pledger's commitment to oneself, God, and one's future spouse, and it symbolizes the wearer's sexual and spiritual transformation. The ring is also more than ritually significant; adolescents who purchase one at a Silver Ring Thing event are provided with ring-care instructions in the *Abstinence Study Bible* that include information on cleaning it, what to do when you need a new size, and what to do if you lose it. Beyond these practical instructions, this introductory section of the Bible implores the wearer to wear the ring every day. "Wear this ring like you'll wear your wedding ring—it is a promise to the person you will marry" (Silver Ring Thing 2000, 3). After participating in the ritual, students are also advised on what to do if they are tempted to break their promise. One of the Silver Ring Thing evangelists ends the evening by instructing members of the audience to flush their ring down the toilet if they do end up breaking their promise.

Despite the impression given by its moniker, Silver Ring Thing did not originate the idea of the purity ring. Nor did that task fall to the founders of True Love Waits, the earliest of the FBAM organizations (Richard Ross, email, November 18, 2006). Though True Love Waits certainly popularized the use of the purity ring, Richard Ross explains that they were simply picking up on a trend that was already occurring among church families.

> Parents might take a 12-year-old to a nice restaurant, give a gentle nudge toward purity, and then present the ring. As True Love Waits emerged, it made more sense to most parents to present the ring after making the promise—often in a beautiful church ceremony.
>
> (*ibid.*)

Extending a family-based ritual, True Love Waits became the first organization to mark a commitment to sexual purity with a purity ring ceremony. Started as a sex education program for Southern Baptist youth, True Love Waits formally launched its campaign in Tulip Grove, Tennessee, when 51 teenagers participated in the first purity ring ceremony at Tulip Grove Baptist Church (*St. Petersburg Times* 1993, 6). Ross presided at the event that was intended to encourage already chaste young people, providing them with peer support and a symbol that reminded them of their commitment to sexual abstinence before marriage. Unlike Silver Ring Thing, True Love Waits does not focus its energies on a live performance. As an organization, True Love Waits has launched numerous campaigns focusing on church, family, school, and neighborhood involvement. In each of these contexts, hundreds of thousands of students have participated in purity ring ceremonies that vary according to the creative outlets at their disposal. True Love Waits assists in these events only to the degree that it provides a template for the purity ring ceremony that can be downloaded from its website. It also provides a detailed set of instructions for before and after the ceremony.

True Love Waits encourages leaders to include the entire family, or to provide a "significant adult" for those whose families will not be involved. Adults are responsible for purchasing a ring for the youth to bring to the event; in some cases churches commission rings for the group. The ceremony itself begins with a prayer and continues with a litany in which students, parents, adults, and the ceremony leaders read responses proclaiming their rejection of corruption and their commitment to purity (LifeWay n.d.).

Churches and other groups hosting True Love Waits' ring ceremonies are not obligated to use these resources, and they often employ their own creative energies to stage a more unique event. Most of these events retain elements that resemble weddings; most are held in church sanctuaries—sometimes with pledgers wearing white—and although there is no *exchange* of rings or vows, the inclusion of these elements is crucial for communicating the import of the event. In 2003, the youth of Greater Starlight Baptist Church in New Orleans participated in a True Love Waits Debutante Ball. Having run a True Love Waits program for three years, the church decided to create a more elaborate event to follow the 12-week study program. Dressed in formal wear, the young people were introduced, made their pledge, and were presented with purity rings by their parents (E. Moore 2004). A church in Bartlett, Tennessee, displayed its ingenuity by performing a wedding ceremony, but instead of making vows to one another, the two young people involved made vows of purity. Accompanied by a wedding entourage, they wore attire appropriate for a wedding ceremony as they received their purity rings. Following the ceremony, everyone was invited for punch and cake to celebrate the happy occasion (Keith 2005).

As this last example illustrates, the purity ring ceremony is not an isolated event. It functions as a prenuptial agreement that extends the wedding ritual into a series of events that require self-control and deferred gratification. The only way to participate in this extended ritualization of adolescent sexual development is to maintain the commitment. Though not every young person who practices this extended premarital rite wears a ring to symbolize their commitment, those who do are hardly unique in the movement.

Daniel Stowe has long incorporated abstinence education into his own ministry. He was especially impressed with the Silver Ring Thing event sponsored by his church, though he shared some doubts about the symbolic effectiveness of the ring. For Stowe, the ring is a nice reminder to youth, but as an accountability system it lags far behind a sincere relationship to Jesus Christ and accountability to peers. He sees little value in an "outward symbol" compared to "what God's doing on the inside." In other words, the ring itself functions only to signify a commitment, not to perform that commitment. Confirming the ring's symbolic potency—as well as the potency of the rituals performed in the ring's transmission—he compares the purity ring to his own wedding band that he slips on every morning. The ring itself, he claims, does not keep him faithful to his wife. His love of God and his wife, not the act of wearing the ring, are the enactment of his wedding vows (interview, December 3, 2006).

Despite the skepticism of youth leaders such as Stowe, major media outlets have recently reported that sales of purity rings have increased dramatically in the past five years (Fantz 2005; see also Riddle 2007; Rosenbloom 2005). Though the trend of wearing purity rings began in the context of a family ritual, young people and their parents can now find purity rings at most major jewelry outlets. Some people purchase simple and inexpensive bands, others opt for more ornate versions, and some receive custom-made rings with inscriptions, religious symbolism, or scriptural notations.

As a central symbol of the extended prenuptial agreement, the purity ring is often incorporated later into wedding ceremonies. Both Silver Ring Thing and True Love Waits promote this practice, with True Love Waits even providing liturgical resources that can be included in the wedding ceremony. This text tells the couple of the many benefits they will receive as they approach the challenges of marriage. It honors them as an example to many who demand instant gratification, and blesses them for choosing to "prioritize God's ways." Though there is no way to know how many weddings incorporate the True Love Waits wedding liturgy, the organization's website offers one report of a couple who melted down their purity rings in order to make the bride's wedding band (LifeWay 2001). Other reports indicate that couples exchange purity rings at the altar, and Silver Ring Thing founder Denny Pattyn often officiates at ceremonies in which the purity ring plays a central role in the wedding ritual. For many adolescents, the silver ring functions as a "placeholder," anticipating the day when it will be exchanged for an engagement ring or wedding band (Rosenbloom 2005).

In a survey I conducted between September and December 2006, 21 out of 31 Christian college students indicated that they previously wore, or currently wear, a purity ring.[10] A fair number of these students have attended abstinence events, and most of the girls had received their ring from either their parents or boyfriend, while the boys received them primarily from their parents. Others had purchased a ring themselves, either before or after attending an abstinence event, suggesting the ring's significance to students who participate in the FBAM at their college. Many of these students articulated their decision to wear the ring as a form of witnessing their faith, as a reminder of their commitment, or as a mark of their ritualized identity. One student commented that the ring functions as a "door-opener," which allowed her to share her Christian faith with non-Christians. "Lydia," a student at "Midwestern Christian College," recognized the ring's multi-functionality:

> I wear it as a symbol of my commitment and also as encouragement to others who are waiting and a tool for witnessing about Jesus Christ and how important sexual purity is. I find it very encouraging when I see other people about my age wearing purity rings because I know that I'm not alone in this.

For "Lydia," the ring communicates various things to different viewers. To a non-Christian, it testifies to her Christian faith, while also communicating the importance of sexual abstinence.

Though it is unclear from "Lydia's" response whether or not she perceives non-Christians as individuals in need of both messages, her ring also communicates a message to her fellow Christians, and seeing other rings reminds her that she is not alone in her commitment. She intimates her hope that her ring provides the same encouragement to others. Though "Lydia" attended a Silver Ring Thing event, her comments reflect the strategies of True Love Waits, which seeks to provide support for students already committed to abstinence.

For "David," a student at "Southwest Christian College," the decision to wear the ring occurred within the confines of his family. At the age of 15, he selected a ring with the help of his mother and sister, who then presented it to him on his sixteenth birthday. Surrounded by his extended family, he received the ring as a sign of their support. For him, the commitment to abstinence was a foregone conclusion, to the degree that this family ceremony felt more like a "celebration" and a "time of support." As most do, "David" wore his ring on his left ring finger, indicating a parallel to the marriage commitment. However, when he went away to college outside of his evangelical subculture, he switched the ring to his right hand so potential dates would not be confused as to his marital status.

Another student at "Southwest Christian College" had very different feelings toward purity rings. "Andrew" was quite critical of ring-wearers, even if he understood their purpose. Though he shares a commitment to sexual purity, he feels rather dubious about "showing off" to others.

> I have many friends with purity rings and question them on the purpose of their rings at times. It seems to be only worn for the reason of showing off to others the commitment you have made. I suppose there is a value. Like tattoos as modern-day baptism. It shows to the world what

you have decided and what your life means to you. The only problem is that I am the most abstinent person I know and would tell people about my decision, but only if asked. I do not want to offer this information out to show my "holier than thou" attitude.

"Andrew" understands the ideals behind the symbolism of the ring. However, his observations have shown him that the real function of the ring is quite distinct from its ideal. For him, the flaunting of one's commitment is a contradiction to the modesty mandated by that commitment. He is not afraid to share his commitment, and seeks to maintain the "rule of ring," which prioritizes humility and obedience, not pride.

As a central symbol of the FBAM, purity rings communicate three critical messages. Specifically, the ring is primarily an expression of the wearer's commitment to sexual purity and sexual abstinence before marriage. However, it also signifies the assumption that it will one day be replaced by another ring representing a marriage commitment. The ring communicates participation in an extended prenuptial ritual laden with expectations for the ritual's consummation, and as such, it symbolizes a heterosexual marriage free from sexual regret, emotional distress, and relational complications, the ultimate product offered by the FBAM. But as a material commodity, the ring represents something else: like Nike shoes or shirts from Abercrombie & Fitch, the ring "labels" the wearer as a consumer in the commodified world of religious, political, and cultural ideologies.

Conclusion

As a player in both consumer and religious marketplaces, the FBAM marks itself as both a natural extension of—and a radical departure from—the *status quo*. Happy to employ marketing strategies and branding capabilities, organizations like True Love Waits and Silver Ring Thing provide their consumers with both material and nonmaterial products. Students who purchase rings and abstinence study Bibles buy into a plan for their lives based on a particular understanding that God has designed their sexual and romantic lives with their best interest in mind. Like all lifestyle media on the market, buyers must agree to maintain that lifestyle if they wish to receive the benefits it promises.

Participants in the FBAM, as a brand that utilizes its political position and adapts multimedia technology and entertainment to maintain its market presence, maintain themselves as culturally relevant. However, their use of counter-cultural rhetoric—rhetoric that they draw from the sexual revolution even as that revolution has come to be the norm—situates the movement as transcendent of contemporary trends, values, and identities. Together, these components create a seamless brand of Christianity in the form of the FBAM that effectively negotiates the sacred and the secular, the religious and the modern, to become more than relevant, but even prominent within the religious marketplace.

References

American Civil Liberties Union. 2005a. "American Civil Liberties Union Brief in Complaint." *American Civil Liberties Union of Massachusetts v. Leavitt, Horn, & Wilson* (16 May). www.aclu.org/FilesPDFs/teeneducomplaint.pdf

American Civil Liberties Union. 2005b. "In Light of ACLU Lawsuit Charging the Federal Government with Funding Religious Activities, the Silver Ring Thing Removes Religious Content from Website" (19 May). www.aclu.org/religion-belief_reproductive-freedom/light-aclu-lawsuit-charging-federal-government-funding-religion

American Civil Liberties Union. 2006. "ACLU Announces Settlement in Challenge to Government-Funded Religion in the Abstinence-Only-Until-Marriage Program the 'Silver Ring Thing'" (23 February). www.aclu.org/reproductiverights/sexed/24246prs20060223.html

BBC. 2004. "American Virgins." *This World Documentaries*, British Broadcasting Company (25 January).

Brown, Candy Gunther. 2004. *The Word in the World: Evangelical Writing, Publishing and Reading in America, 1789–1990*. Chapel Hill: University of North Carolina Press.

Connoly, Cecil. 2005. "ACLU Sues HHS over Abstinence Aid." *The Washington Post.* (17 May): A10.

Crary, David. 2005. "ACLU Lawsuit Alleges that Abstinence-Only Program uses Federal Funds to Promote Christianity." *The Associated Press.* May 16. (Posted online at: [www.aegis.com/news/ads/2005/AD050944.html].)

Doan, Alesha E. and Jean Calterone Williams. 2008. *The Politics of Virginity: Abstinence in Sex Education.* Westport: Praeger.

Einstein, Mara. 2008. *Brand of Faith: Marketing Religion in a Commercial Age.* New York: Routledge Press.

Fantz, Ashley. 2005. "Teens Hot on Abstinence (But Cool on Sex)." *Herald News* (30 June): E05.

Freedman, John, and Estelle Freedman. 1988. *Intimate Matters: A History of Sexuality in America.* Chicago: University of Chicago Press.

Goodstein, Laurie. 1994. "Saying No to Teen Sex in No Uncertain Terms." *Washington Post* (20 July): A01.

Gutjahr, Paul. 1999. *An American Bible: The History of the Good Book in America.* Stanford: Stanford University Press.

——. 2008. "The Bible-zine *REVOLVE* and the Evolution of the Culturally Relevant Bible in America." In *Religion and the Culture of Print in Modern America*, eds Charles Cohen and Paul Boyer, 326–48. Madison: University of Wisconsin Press.

Hendershot, Heather. 2004. "Virgins for Jesus: The Gender Politics of Therapeutic Christian Fundamentalist Media." In *Shaking the World for Jesus: Media and Conservative Evangelical Culture.* Chicago: Chicago University Press.

Hoover, Stewart M. 2006. *Religion in the Media Age.* New York: Routledge Press.

Hunter, James Davison. 1991. *The Culture Wars: The Struggle to Define America.* New York: Basic Books.

Keith, Patsy. 2005. "Teens Walk the Aisle for True Love Waits." *Commercial Appeal* (13 February): BT6–7.

Kilde, Jeanne Halgren. 2002. *When Church Became Theatre: The Transformation of Evangelical Architecture and Worship in Nineteenth Century America.* Oxford: Oxford University Press.

LifeWay. 2001. "God Blesses Pledges With Happiness." LifeWay Student Ministry True Love Waits (February). www.lifeway.com/tlw/media/news_happiness.asp

——. n.d. "Ring Ceremony." LifeWay Student Ministry True Love Waits. www.lifeway.com/tlw/leaders/ring_ceremony.asp

Lupu, Ira C., and Robert W. Tuttle. 2005. "The Faith-Based Initiative and the Constitution." *DePaul Law Review* 55 (Fall): 1–118.

Lyon, David. 2004. *Jesus in Disneyland: Religion in Postmodern Times.* Cambridge, Mass.: Polity Press.

McCarthy, Colman. 1994. "No 'Safe' Teenage Sex." *Washing Post* (20 August): A19.

Moore, Elizabeth. 2004. "Teens Believe True Love Waits." *Times-Picayune* (9 October): 20.

Moore, R. Laurence. 1986. *Religious Outsiders and the Making of Americans.* New York: Oxford University Press.

New York Times. 1993. "True Love Waits for Some Teen-Agers." (21 June): A12. www.nytimes.com/1993/06/21/us/true-love-waits-for-some-teen-agers.html

Nord, David. 2004. *Faith in Reading, Religious Publication and the Birth of Mass Media.* Oxford: Oxford University Press.

Riddle, Sasha. 2007. "Chastity Jewelry Has Become Popular with Many Teens." Modesto Bee (26 April): D1.

Rittmeyer, Brian C. 2005. "Silver Ring Thing Says it Will Survive." *Pittsburgh Tribune Review* (24 August). www.pittsburghlive.com/x/pittsburghtrib/news/cityregion/s_366857.html

Roof, Wade Clark. 1999. *Spiritual Marketplace: Baby Boomers and the Re-making of American Religion.* Princeton, N.J.: Princeton University Press.

Rosenbloom, Stephanie. 2005. "A Ring That Says No, Not Yet." *New York Times* (8 December): G1.

Saltzman, Jonathan. 2005. "ACLU Suit Sees Religious Content In Abstinence Plan." *Boston Globe* (17 May): A1.

Silver Ring Thing. 2000. *Silver Ring Thing Abstinence Study Bible*, The New Living Translation. Wheaton, IL: Tyndale House Publishers.

Silver Ring Thing. n.d. "SRT's National Roll-Out Plan." www.silverringthing.com/images/SRTRolloutPlan.pdf

St. Petersburg Times. 1993. "Teens Pledge Abstinence." (1 May): 6.

Turner, Rev. Robert. 1996. *Abstinence Education: Hearings Before a Subcommittee of the Committee on Appropriations.* United States Senate Committee on Appropriations, Subcommittee on Departments of Labor, Health and Human, and Related Agencies. 104th Cong., 2nd sess. (11 July).

United States Code §710. 2006. *Personal Responsibility and Work Opportunity Reconciliation Act.* 42.

Wetzstein, Cheryl. 2005. "Nation Headline: Federal Funds Suspended for Abstinence Program." *Washington Times* (24 August): A06.

Notes

1 Although Ross still serves as one of True Love Waits' spokespeople, he now holds a faculty position in Student Ministry at Southwestern Baptist Theological Seminary in Fort Worth, Texas.

2 The True Love Waits pledge:

> Believing that True Love Waits, I make a commitment to God, my family, my friends, my future spouse and my future children to live a lifetime of purity including sexual abstinence from this day until I enter a biblical marriage relationship.

3 In 2003, Silver Ring Thing received a federal grant from the Department of Health and Human Services for $750,000, to be used in 2004. The next year they received another $750,000 to continue expanding their programming through 2005 (see Crary 2005).

4 Currently, the federal government provides over $140 million a year from three funding sources for abstinence educators, many of which parallel the True Love Waits model in order to be eligible for federal funds.

5 In 2005 this program was renamed Community Based Abstinence Education (CBAE) after the Administration for Children and Families took on its administrative responsibilities.

6 Legal and political conflicts over federal sponsorship for abstinence education have existed from the inception of the movement itself. As early as 1981, the ACLU filed a lawsuit against the government claiming that its actions violated the "No Establishment" clause of the First Amendment to the US Constitution.

7 According to legal scholar Ira Lupu, the Bush Administration did not adequately educate faith-based groups receiving federal funding regarding their constitutional use and, as a result, numerous lawsuits are now pending (Lupu and Tuttle 2005). Fellow legal scholar Melissa Rogers has also observed a great deal of confusion among faith-based organizations. Rather than providing adequate governance and instructions to groups in using federal funds, the Bush Administration emphasized the moral quality of the work generated under the initiative. As a result, faith-based groups were not prepared to understand how the strictures of the "No Establishment" clause affected their work (Saltzman 2005).

8 The names of all of the people interviewed or surveyed for this chapter—excluding Richard Ross and Denny Pattyn, who are public figures—have been changed to protect their anonymity.

9 The FBAM knows quite well that one's Christian affiliation does not automatically mark one as sexually pure, nor are Christian marriages free of mistrust, emotional trauma, and the threat of divorce. A sexually pure marriage, however, can offer these promises.

10 The names of the students and the colleges they attended have been changed to protect the identity of the survey participants.

Chapter 11

When "Friend" Becomes a Verb

Religion on the Social Web

Daniel Veidlinger

Technological millenarians have been prophesizing the salvation of humanity through the computational powers of those little electronic boxes on our desks for some time now (Kurzweil 1999). There are many compelling arguments to be made about the benefits and detriments of religious life in the digital age, and a major study titled *Faith Online*, conducted in 2003 by the Pew Internet and American Life Project, engages many of the seminal issues at stake here: Will people use the internet to pursue spiritual avenues that are outside the mainstream, leading to new forms of religious expression? Will the internet usher in a new Reformation, as did the printing press 500 years ago? Will the instantaneous and surface-level nature of much of the content on the World Wide Web impede truly deep contemplation? The Pew study reveals that at least 64 per cent of American internet-users employ the internet for overtly religious or spiritual matters, such as learning about holidays, sending email with religious or spiritual content, and seeking information on where to attend religious services (Clark *et al.* 2004). All indications are that this number has grown since the report was released in 2004, making it imperative that we attempt to understand the ways that religious ideas and behaviors are influenced by this new medium. This chapter, however, does not aim to chronicle the many specifically religious websites that are used by the faithful to participate in their religion. Rather, it examines one particular area of the internet that is not overtly religious, yet fulfills many of the functions commonly associated with religion, while also affecting the spiritual life of users. The area to which I am referring is the "social Web," the collection of social networking sites such as Facebook, MySpace, and Friendster; bookmarking sites such as Delicious and Stumble Upon; messaging utilities such as Twitter; social knowledge bases such as Wikipedia; publishing tools such as blogs; and other such applications that are all designed to foster multiple levels of interaction among users, who are encouraged to post a profile and share ideas, pictures, comments, and messages in an effort to create collaborative worlds of meaning.

These social features of the internet give rise to a number of functions that are fundamental to most successful religions. There are many ways to view

religion, as the contributions to this volume amply attest, and for the purposes of this chapter, following Mun-Cho Kim (who carried out early work
on religion and the internet), I will focus on how the social Web satisfies
three main functions of religion: interpretation, interaction, and integration.
The interpretive function, Kim argues, "has to do with the ability of religion
to provide meaningful answers to ultimate and eternal questions about
human existence," while the interactive function "has to do with the ability
of religious organizations to provide opportunities for some people to
associate with others with whom they can exchange ideas, benefits, lifestyles,
tastes, and so forth." He suggests that all people are looking for "friendship,
companionship, acceptance, and recognition," and that, for "some people in
modern society," belonging to a religious community "provides a sense of
community making it easier to cope with either loneliness or isolation" (Kim
2005, 140–41). As for the integrative function, sociologist Emile Durkheim
argued that religion is integrative because it involves "beliefs and practices
which unite into one single moral community called a Church, all those who
adhere to them" (Durkheim 1963, 47).

Once we establish the way the social Web affords these functions, we can
then explore the expansive effects wrought by this domain on the consciousness of frequent users. My own computerized analysis of almost three
million user profiles from a variety of social networks suggests that these
networks tend to promote a decentered view of the self that is in harmony
with the deepest insights of Buddhism. Scholars have debated intensely the
notion that different forms of communication technologies, from writing
through the printing press to mass media, produce a bias toward different
religious ideas; here we extend that discussion to the social Web.[1]

The Social Web as a Site for Interaction and Integration

Like other communities, religious communities constitute an arena through
which individuals can be integrated into a group and partake of the communal identity that accrues to that social state of being. At the same time,
through their dialogical interactions with others in the group, including their
exchange of ideas and so forth, they establish a sense of their own identity
within the group. As Alf Linderman and Mia Lovheim point out, "social
trust" is a crucial element in this construction of identity.

> From early childhood, the individual experiences interaction with par-
> ents and others, an interaction through which the individual can develop
> her/his conception of the self. Trust in the continuity and the coherence
> of the external social reality is essential to this process. Through a
> development based on trust in the social context in which individuals
> find themselves, they gradually find out who they are.
>
> (Linderman and Lovheim 2005, 122)

What normally occurs in modern life is that these networks, which have been built up over the years and within which one finds the comforts of identity and meaning, break down as their members—friends, schoolmates, co-religionists, neighbors, relatives—move on to pursue their lives in different locations, perhaps moving away to attend university, or to pursue a job opportunity or marriage. For a variety of reasons, in modern society a large number of people lose touch with those with whom they grew up. They are forced to establish new relationships with new people, who can be difficult (or liberating, depending on the way the person was socialized in the earlier stages of life). But what if all of those ghosts from the past were suddenly conjured up again and presented to the subject? That is the new reality with the social Web. Any reader who is on Facebook knows well the phenomenon to which I am alluding here. One is assaulted almost daily by requests to let old friends into the private world of the "profile." I have now gotten in touch with literally hundreds of people from my past that I was sure I would never meet again. Those parts of my life were, I had thought, closed and gone, only to be reopened again with a vengeance. Old pictures of myself in compromising positions at summer camp have been posted—and commented upon—by people I have not heard from in 20 years. In a stroke, my fears and insecurities, as well as happy memories, hopes, and wishes from those formative years of my life, have all come rushing back. But how can this experience affect the role of religion in our lives today?

Religion in its integrative function provides institutional continuity ensuring that, as members of a community following similar rituals, group identity and a feeling of belonging can be maintained even in the face of changing members of the group. It is the structure that is important, rather than the actual people who operate within it. But what happens if contact with the individual members of a group can be maintained easily over great distances through the social functions of the internet? Is there a need to identify with a formal group if communion with individuals can be maintained? A recent survey by The Pew Forum on Religion & Public Life revealed that Americans, while overwhelmingly claiming to be "religious," are not clinging to one particular religious identity, but rather are changing religious affiliation at a surprising rate. Roughly half of the people in a large study said that they changed religion at least once (Pew Forum 2009). Could this have anything to do with their ability to keep in touch with their circle of friends, those with whom "social trust" affords the security that static membership in a religious group used to provide?

The major currency of the social networks, such as MySpace and Facebook, is precisely the capital that emerges from social trust. The constant acquisition and classification of friends serves as the bedrock upon which these systems are built, and many of the applications revolve around "tagging," "poking," "winking," and otherwise interacting on basic levels with friends. The number of friends that one has can be quantified, allowing for one's social capital to be measured in concrete ways. But since the ultimate goal of these networks is to have friends, one's "friend count" could be seen as defining one's value in relation to the highest measure of "the good" according to the logic of the system. The acquisition by Ashton Kutcher of one million followers for his Twitter feed, for example, actually made the headlines (CNN.com 2009). Could he now be considered the high priest of Twitter? Just as in religious hierarchies such as the Indian caste system— where one's position is a function of one's degree of ritual purity or proximity to the sacred locus of the divine—so the size of one's list of friends or followers could be construed as a measure of the sanctity accruing to an individual, with the ultimate ideal, the *summum bonum*, being the state of having everyone on Earth as a "friend!" There is even an application called "FriendWheel" that produces a kind of *mandala* by arranging the names of friends along the perimeter of a circle and demarcating the connections amongst the friends using different colored lines. In laying bare the connections between members of this cyber-society and allowing also for instantaneous communication including audio and video interaction with each of them, the social Web displays some of the key interactive and integrative functions that have heretofore been associated with religious groups.

The Social Web as a Site for Interpreting and Making Sense of the World

Buddhologist and cultural critic Peter Hershock (1999) is not alone in arguing that the internet and modern technology in general lead to social isolation and encourage individualism, while weakening cultural diversity and damaging the very fabric of society along the way. Many people agree with the words of a well-known Texas broadcaster that,

> ... while all this razzle-dazzle connects us electronically, it disconnects us from each other, having us "interfacing" more with computers and TV screens than looking in the face of our fellow human beings.
>
> (Jim Hightower, quoted by Boase *et al.* 2006, 2)

However, these fears have not been borne out by recent studies of internet behavior, most of which have shown that heavy internet users have a very rich social life replete with extensive engagement with other people—albeit through the medium of the internet rather than in face-to-face situations. One of the largest such studies, conducted for the Pew Internet and American Life Project, concludes that

> ... the internet is not destroying relationships or causing people to be anti-social. To the contrary, the internet is enabling people to maintain existing ties, often to strengthen them, and at times to forge new ties.

> The time that most people spend online reduces the time they spend on ... relatively unsocial activities ...
>
> *(ibid.,* 3)

More than ever before, people are sharing ideas, thoughts, and feelings with each other on the internet and in particular via socially-oriented websites such as MySpace, Facebook, and Twitter. Humanity has never had tools that facilitate this kind of inclusion of others in one's own experience, certainly not when those others are dispersed to the four corners of the globe. But more than this, the mass of exchanged messages, blogs, and chat-group postings in which questions are posed and answered, debated, and discussed constructs a realm of shared meaning and interpretation of the world that can stand in for the corpus of ideas that have generally been associated with religious doctrine.

It is often assumed that because a lot of chatter on social networks is inane, one cannot have substantial discussions about issues of ultimate importance in this medium. I have found, however, that the depth of insight and discussion on MySpace and Facebook groups is surprisingly good, and that many substantive discussions can be had in this environment. Sherry Turkle has also noted that the internet users she interviewed found that they were not just able to have good conversations through the internet, but that in many cases they were able to communicate *more* effectively and get more information across to their interlocutor than in person (Turkle 1995, 226). One young woman said that

> she finds it easier to establish relationships online and then pursue them offline. She has a boyfriend and feels closer to him when they send electronic mail or talk in a chat room than when they see each other in person. Their online caresses make real ones seem less strained.
>
> *(ibid.,* 227)

In fact, many social network profiles are so detailed that they tell more about the person than many of their "real-life" friends already know. I have looked at a number of profiles and found out information about friends and relatives in five minutes that I was not aware of after three decades of live encounters—details such as what their favorite television shows are, what books they loved to read as a child, which of their friends they think would make the best politician, and which the best actor.

In the "groups.myspace.com" domain there is a list of the MySpace groups that exist in each of 36 categories. Interestingly, the category "Religion & Beliefs" is the seventh most popular category (excluding "Other"), with 125,408 different groups (as of April 20, 2009). The only categories more popular are "Entertainment," "Music," "Fan Clubs," "Activities," "Schools & Alumni," and "Recreation & Sports." "Religion & Beliefs" has nearly twice as many groups as "Family & Home," and three times as many as "Pets & Animals," "Hobbies & Crafts" and "Business & Entrepreneurs." This is a very significant development, suggesting that people do see the internet as a site where the most fundamental existential conditions can be seriously discussed, even though this occurs outside traditional relationships with professional religious counselors.

Let's take a look at a discussion thread that was found on the first page of topic listings from the MySpace group *Buddhism*. That it involves authentic expressions of religious sentiment on the part of the contributors becomes obvious as one reads through it. The *Buddhism* discussion group (groups. myspace.com/Buddhism) has over 4500 discussion topics with over 1400 members actively posting and responding to topics ranging from meditation and karma to the eternal fallibility of language, Tibetan politics, vegetarianism, and a whole host of other issues.

"Overdose" is a 29-year-old male located in Minnesota who started a discussion thread in a post from April 20, 2009, titled "Meditation in empitness [*sic*] state of mind":[2]

> ... beliefs are really only exist in the surface of our awaken state of mind. Pratice empty the mind in meditation and you'll see that in certain state of meditation where the mind is empty that all these ideas really have no meaning or values. Right and wrong, good and bad all these dualities and ideas about this and that no longer matter. When mind is empty from rationalized subjects, everything we talk about in this blog hold really little or no meaning, no values or should I say it doesn't affect who we really are ... How can one be free when he/she is the one who is attach to the words and ideas? The measure of one own spiritual growth and obtainment is the absent of one mind from rationalizing.
>
> (MySpace.com 2009a)

Here is an attempt to deal with one of the core questions in Buddhism, the relationship between the conventional world (in which our ideas and experiences have meaning) and the ultimate reality (that is beyond any dualities). What role can an awareness of this ultimate reality play in our lives? How can we function in both realities? These are the kinds of question with which Buddhist thinkers have grappled for centuries. How does the group respond to this profound (but admittedly poorly worded) inquiry? "Garyszone," a 70-year-old male from Virginia, recognizes the conflict inherent in trying to live a regular life while striving for Buddhist ideals:

> Overdose, what you say is clear.—The empty mind is a mind at peace (if i can paraphrase your viewpoint).—Sometimes (perhaps) we can ease our troubles by taking time out to enjoy the peace of an empty

mind.—However, (imo),[3] we cannot live our daily lives with an empty mind.—(Even if we simply want a drink of water.)

(imo) One should not even "try" to have an "empty mind" in daily life.—Rather, we need to develop and refine our ways of thinking so that our thoughts are less likely to cause suffering within us ...

"Been" (male, 35, from Santa Cruz, California) points out that a nonliteral interpretation of the notion makes it easier to digest:

> "Empty mind" is not about being empty of thoughts ... it is the understanding that those thoughts and what those thoughts are about, are empty of self-essence. "Empty mind" is empty of our false assumptions and our malformed prejudices. It is like eyesight without wearing colored classes that throws a tint onto everything we see ...

The next posting is an interjection by a male teenager named "Diesel" from North Carolina, who brings the discussion down from the metaphysical heights of Buddhist philosophy and toward the kind of problems experienced by many young adults:

> I have gotten to a state where i no longer see good and evil, i don't have any feelings and i lost all concept of time and i am just here. i don't know if this is the right way of seeing things but i cant get out of it now and it was scary at first but i have gotten used to it because even my feelings and emotions are inside of my head. fear, happiness and everything else. whats the next step if there is one or can i bee wrong somehow.

This posting highlights a perennial problem in Buddhism and other religions that focus on withdrawal from an emotional and desire-driven engagement with the world: are the spiritual states being advocated psychologically healthy for human beings or, in stripping away the hopes and fears around which we build our lives, has something essential been lost? Is "Diesel" experiencing the flat effect that is associated with depression in western medicine, or is he beginning to attain deep spiritual insights—or both? The next post, by a 35-year-old male from Chicago going by the name "Hughfus Happenstance," veers in the direction of trying to help Diesel understand his situation:

> Things will come back. I mean, things like good and evil ... or rather harmful and beneficial. but when they do, you will now see the interdependence and impermanence of them. the diamond sutra goes on about this. you may find it useful for you right now.

At this point, "Treading Water" (male, 28, Canton, Michigan) brings up a classic Buddhist observation:

> ... Clinging to ideas is just like craving sweet candy. We don't get better by banning candy from the world, although temporarily removing ourselves from the temptation may be helpful at first. We get better by overcoming the craving. Overcome the craving and you could open a candy shop.

"Treading Water" then supplies a standard Buddhist reply:

> The world is full of things to delight in. It would be foolish to try and rid the world of pleasurable things when the real problem is our insatiable thirst for them ... We believe certain things about the objects of our passion that those things do not really possess. One way to overcome craving is to do what you suggest. Bring spaciousness to the mind and observe the process of craving. We can then break its hold over us.

Clearly the participants are dealing in a serious and sustained manner with topics of great importance both to them personally, and to Buddhism and religion generally. It is also noteworthy that the contributors appear to have a high degree of facility with the difficult concepts of emptiness, desire, and interconnection, and deploy them ably to explain how to balance the experience of ultimate reality with the realities of human psychology. Many critics feel that the World Wide Web is structurally incapable of supporting meaningful and nuanced engagement with serious issues, but in fact the foregoing discussion, culled at random from the first of many pages of topics on the Buddhism group, agrees in substance with what one would expect an educated person who is knowledgeable in Buddhism (but not a trained Buddhologist) to write. If we compare some of the above statements with the writings of well-known scholars, we can find very similar statements. For example, prominent philosopher of religion John Hick writes:

> ... in the experience of *satori* the human mind finally transcends egoity and with it the entire apparatus of concepts developed in the ego's dealings with its environment. It is then able to enjoy a unitive intuition of ultimate reality ... [O]ur ordinary experience is a function of the dualistic consciousness in which the ego affirms itself over against a world of objects. But this dualistic structure is transcended in the moment of enlightenment in which the Real (*śūnyatā*) and our unitive awareness of it (*prājña*) become one. For the Real is beyond all human conceptions and distinctions; and the mind in the state of *prājña* has emptied itself of those same concepts and distinctions.
>
> (Hick 1989, 292)

Hick presents the argument much more artfully, of course, and with fewer (but still some) mistakes,[4] yet our MySpace contributors can hold their own here. They appear to have hit on the key points and to have expressed them in a way that would pique the interest of a typical social network user.

Many other religiously-oriented discussion groups on MySpace can become remarkably personal in tone and take on the air of a confessional. Here, closely held opinions and deep personal problems are expressed often in a surprisingly candid manner. For example, from the group "Spiritual Awakening," we find a discussion thread about "Helping depressed/anxious friends," where 20-year-old "Cain" offers that:

> im going through depression … i find that my martial arts is helping me both spiritually and physically, but as far as mentally im still in that state of mind … i also have an addictive personality … i feel ashamed of myself to the point where i dont want to live anymore. Its a vicious never ending cycle. I feel helpless in a way, but i feel like when i talk to people about my problems it helps me.
>
> (MySpace.com 2009b)

Twenty-year-old "Aiyana" begins a series of replies to this posting, saying

> Hey I agree, as I was very depressed and also went through a stage of schizophrenia/psychosis when smoking weed and other drugs (as have alot of other people I know). Some people will go through their lives never having a problem, whereas alot of people suffer from metal problems.

"Cain" then adds:

> i think i am slightly bipolar … i am anti-social to people i dont know … and im also a self conscious person, i always worry what someone else is thinking, and im afraid of rejection, which prevents me doing alot of things … i wasnt exactly fed with a silver spoon in my mouth, i grew up poor, my mom is bipolar and schizophrenic and used drugs that my brother sold to her, she would beat the hell out of my brother if he didnt get her any …

"Doodles" (a 46-year-old male) says:

> I've suffered through severe depression most of my life, and am still struggling with it. First of all, Cain, you have to realize that pot actually contributes to depression if you're doing it on a regular basis. I know this from personal experience. So you really have to do what you can to stop. Finding a local support group is probably your best bet.

In a similar vein, on the group "Day of Prayer and Fasting," a 21-year-old female who goes by the moniker "Love not the World" is clearly having difficulties as she writes in the forum "I need some mercy, some prayer":

> I feel like a wretch ... Going to fail 2 of my classes out of laziness ... Got a speeding ticket ... Boyfriend is thinking about breaking up with me ... Mom alternates between wanting me home and telling me to move out, constantly reminding me of this ... I'm too comfortable in my low paying job to try to switch ... I feel like spiritually I am in a waste-land. I don't even feel like I care enough about myself to bother. What the heck is wrong with me?
>
> (MySpace.com 2008)

Twenty-five-year-old "Tovah Lyfe" assures her that she will indeed be in her prayers and opines that "hope and confidance should't be in [oneself] but in the all mighty. Thruough him nothing can go wrong."

Social networks in these examples are sites where truly meaningful issues can be presented and worked out as a group—where lively debate, insightful advice, compassion and, dare I say, wisdom can be found in abundance. More intimate even than this, we can clearly discern a process of communal confession emerging, through which the penitent is cleansed of the burden of her sins by means of forgiveness and/or understanding on the part of this community of strangers.

What accounts for the tendency witnessed amongst members to discuss with complete strangers their feelings about these issues? Perhaps there are here echoes of Victor Turner's conception of *communitas* as a group defined by its shared experience of undifferentiated and hierarchically flat commu-nion amongst the members who exist in a liminal state. Liminal entities are "neither here nor there; they are betwixt and between the positions assigned and arrayed by law, custom, convention and ceremonial" (Turner 1969, 95–96). Certainly, when logged into a social network, one enters a highly fluid environment located within the nebulous region known as cyberspace, in which contact can be made with anyone at any time, and the regular rules of society are for the most part suspended while identity itself becomes highly mutable, depending on the culture of the particular network being used.

There is a crucial difference between the way these conversations are car-ried out in the online discussion forums and the way they would unfold in face-to-face encounters. They leave a trail of information that would not have remained during an oral exchange other than in the (not so reliable) memories of the participants. The written format has the advantage of keeping a record of the discussion, and nudges people into expressing them-selves in more detail and putting more thought into their statements (if not into their spelling) than they would if they were having an oral discussion. The continuing record of the conversation also allows people to quote exactly what was said by their interlocutors so that a more precise discussion can ensue. Furthermore, these conversations entice the reader to enter into the fray by posting comments that endorse or challenge the views presented, leading to a much deeper engagement with the text. The knowledge that many members of the community emerging around the text will be reading the postings from their computers around the country and even the world also creates an excitement that is not present in more traditional, fixed modes of discourse. The "electronic word," as classicist Richard Lanham terms it, provides us with a dynamic canvas upon which to present, contest, and consolidate our deepest spiritual concerns in an open and fluctuating environment that conforms well to the postmodern ethos. Out of this arises "a body of work active not passive, a canon not frozen in perfection but volatile with contending human motive" (Lanham 1993, 51).

The Social Web and the Expansion of Consciousness

Besides fulfilling the interpretive, interactive, and integrative functions of religion, there are strong reasons to believe that frequent usage of the social Web inclines users towards an understanding of themselves that is in accord with specific insights from Buddhism and other religions that deny a unitary self. Monistic traditions have long recognized the problematic nature of individuation as commonly conceived. Buddhist meditation, for example, was developed to help weaken the idea of a personal, unchanging self through insight into the interconnected and ever-changing ecological system of personal identity. The radical interconnectedness of all things was emphasized in the later Mahayana forms of Buddhism, which took an even more deconstructive view of the self to counteract what they believed were latent essentializing tendencies in earlier forms of Buddhism. The Mahayana thinkers, especially of the Madhyamika school, insisted that all things exist only in relation to other things, that they are defined and reified through a complex network of causes, language, and ideas that enfolds the entire cosmos into an interdependent web. The problem inherent in this view of the human condition is that in our normal state we do not see this web of interconnections, and we fall into the belief that we are independent egos existing in and for ourselves. There is a famous image called the Jeweled Net of Indra that says that all of reality is like a network of jewels carefully arranged so that each one reflects all the others. Therefore every object in existence actually contains every other object. One can see a million Buddhas in every particle of dust, and you in me and me in you.

   Like modern-day mystics, there is evidence that people who spend a lot of time using the social features of the internet are more open to seeing themselves as standing within a complex nexus of causes and conditions rather than as embodying an individual personal soul. A brief analysis of how our sense of personhood arises and where in our body it appears to be located will help to explain how this might be so. Most people will insist that "they" are located in their head, and believe that this perception arises because that is where the brain is situated. However, if the brain were in the feet, consciousness would still be experienced as in the head, because that is where four of the five senses are located. "We" are where our senses are.[5] Marshall McLuhan famously asserted that the power of the media and technology in general lies in their ability to extend the human senses. For example, the telephone can be viewed as an extension of the ear such that someone speaking into a phone at the other end can be thought of as actually speaking into your ear. Likewise, television is an extension of our visual capabilities, and so forth. Thus,

> after more than a century of electric technology, we have extended our central nervous system itself in a global embrace, abolishing both space and time as far as our planet is concerned. Rapidly, we approach the final phase of the extensions of man—the technological simulation of consciousness, when the creative process of knowing will be collectively and corporately extended to the whole of human society, much as we have already extended our senses and our nerves by the various media.
> (McLuhan 1964, 3–4)

It is still remarkable that McLuhan made these statements a generation before the internet was developed, but they are truer now than they were 40 years ago, as socially oriented communication technologies resituate the locus of the perceived self and extend or displace consciousness beyond the individual body. As technology has evolved through the printing press into the internet and other electronic media that enable instant communication, it has fostered the ability to break down the spaciotemporal barriers that bind embodied beings by vastly extending the senses through which we experience the world, leading to a growth in consciousness of each other and the world. With heavy use of the internet, consciousness itself begins to be located as much in cyberspace as in the body. We are located—or better, the sense of "I" is located—where our senses tell us we are located, so if one's eyes and ears are locked onto the internet for hours a day, it is likely that the sense of self will begin to drift beyond the body, that there will be a blurring of the point at which the self ends and the other begins. Nineteen-year-old "Diesel," a MySpace member who often posts his thoughts in the MySpace "Buddhism" discussion group, articulates this phenomenon well in a recent statement about his spiritual evolution:

> gradually the ego begins to weaken and in time it dissolves completely, as does the sense of i, me and mine. no sense of self or ownership. that is how i feel of course now i wouldn't use the word feel to describe it either.
> (MySpace.com 2009a)

This often happens when we watch a good movie—we begin to forget about the real world outside, and become a part of the action. Consciousness migrates to the screen. This affects our whole state of mind: we feel relaxed when there is levity on the screen and tense when something bad is happening to the characters. "We" have left the theater and moved into the movie. On the internet, the penetration of ideas—such as radical interdependence and the mutability of personal identity—into the ways that many in the online population at large construe the world may advance along with the cognitive changes that occur due to the vast extension of human senses forged by the unparalleled power of this communication technology.

As a scholar of Buddhism, I naturally relate the phenomena that I detect emerging on the internet to salient aspects of Buddhist philosophy, but as Brenda Brasher, the author of a pioneering study of spirituality on the internet artfully titled *Give Me That Online Religion*, points out, people from a wide variety of traditions

> see the Web, the Internet, the entire phenomenon of computer-mediated communication as a tremendous advance in human solidarity and oneness. Christian theologian Jennifer Cobb claims that in building these communicative technologies, we have merely hardwired our preexisting interconnectedness. Cobb contends that in cyberspace, we have externally actualized our evolving psycho-spiritual ties with one another.
>
> (Brasher 2001, 40)

It is notable that postmodern theorists of subjectivity have also suggested that the unitary self lacks a foundation in reality, that what we think of as our one, true self is illusory, and that in fact we should think in terms of decentered selves with hybrid identities. Sherry Turkle, a pioneer in the study of the psychological effects of the internet, admits that she did not grasp these ideas well when she was first introduced to them in college, but then announces:

> I am meeting them again in my new life on the screen. But this time, the Gallic abstractions are more concrete. In my computer-mediated worlds, the self is multiple, fluid, and constituted in interaction with machine connections; it is made and transformed by language.
>
> (Turkle 1995, 15)

But is there any empirical basis for the claims being made here? The social features of the internet allow users continually to create a large amount of "user-generated" textual content that represents an unprecedented corpus of information on how people across wide segments of society think about almost any issue imaginable. Religious views and ideas are a very common subject in this corpus, and a lot can be learned about how religion is actually developing on the ground from analyzing this text. Computing has also developed to the point where pattern-recognition algorithms can operate efficiently over inconceivably large amounts of data to recognize trends and constellations of ideas that would not be readily visible to a human researcher. I have recently completed an analysis of 2,948,000 user profiles downloaded randomly from a representative sample of popular social networks, which can be used to tell us a lot about the direction in which religious ideas, mores, and attitudes are moving in this population.

It is very difficult for a computer to assess the degree of penetration of complicated psycho-philosophical notions such as the denial of a unitary consciousness, but what can be done is to look at the degree of popularity of a religion such as Buddhism that focuses on these kinds of ideas. If we exclude Asians with a traditional Buddhist background from the data set, people in all age segments who are heavy users of social media on the internet are about ten times more likely to identify themselves as Buddhist than are people in the offline population as a whole.[6] Comparisons with online believers in other religious traditions, such as Judaism and Catholicism, show that the numbers of adherents of these religions are much more in keeping with the overall proportion of the offline population who identify as belonging to these traditions. A raw count of terms such as "technology" and "internet" in profiles shows that they occur more often in close conjunction with the term "Buddhism" than with any other religion. Specifically, whereas someone interested in "technology" and "internet" is no more likely to identify as Christian, or have an interest in Christianity, than an average person, they are respectively 4.5 and 2.4 times more likely to identify as Buddhist, or be interested in Buddhism, than an average person using the social networks examined for this study. Similarly, heavy use of applications that involve extensive and prolonged interaction with others, such as massively multiplayer online role-playing games, is also associated with Buddhism and spirituality, as suggested by the clustering of these terms together in user profiles. The Pew study around faith online concurs that "there is a tendency for those who describe themselves as 'spiritual but not religious' to be among the heaviest Internet users" (Clark *et al.* 2004, iii). This is significant for my research because spirituality is itself very strongly associated with Eastern religions such as Buddhism in the profiles I examined: people describing themselves as "spiritual" were over 25 times more likely to also describe themselves as Buddhist than as belonging to any of the Western religions.

More suggestive data can be garnered by examining the discussion groups on social networks. A count of the members of the main religious discussion groups on MySpace reveals that the "Buddhism" group has 22,241 members, whereas the "Christianity" group has 106,529 members, and "Islam" has 13,161. As most members of MySpace are American, one would expect the ratio of members in the Christian group to those in the Buddhism group to be somewhere around the same as it is in the population, about 80:1. Here it is just under 5:1. The number of Muslims in the United States is approximately the same as the number of Buddhists, so one could expect these numbers to be similar as well, but in fact there are almost twice as many members of the Buddhism group. An analysis of the content of the groups shows that there is a noticeable difference between the relatively anonymous profiles on MySpace and those with personally identifiable information found on Facebook. In the former, we would expect to more readily find the ethos of Turner's *communitas*, and it is very possible that this is connected to the presence of a lot more discussion about the expansion of consciousness on MySpace religion forums than on similar Facebook forums. Further study needs to be done in this direction, but having looked through hundreds of group forums on both Facebook and MySpace, those on Facebook appear to deal far more with questions of proper ritual behavior, as well as affirmations of identity. Among the most popular groups on Facebook are those that tend to affirm a specific identity—"100,000,000 Christians worship God," "I'm a Muslim & I'm Proud," "Let's find 1,000,000 Christians," and "To Prove that there are more than 1,000,000 people who Worship ALLAH!!!," "Six Million to Remember the Six Million"—whereas those on MySpace are less constrained and more philosophically speculative. For example, postings such as the following are much more common on MySpace than Facebook:

> We say that we are one with the universe, but each one of us saying this still has the illusion of separate human existence and because of it doesn't truly see. The very word "We", or "I" is an implication of separateness and personality. We have to behold that the universe itself is one, first of all, and then transform our soul to become this universe— make a fusion with universal "consciousness."
>
> (MySpace.com 2009c)

Could it be that internet technology itself, especially its social features, can stimulate those who spend a significant amount of their time living within its infinite nexus of connections to accept Buddhist ideas such as interdependence more readily than the rest of the population?

Many critics will say that heavy use of social websites actually stimulates the inclination towards individual ego and self-importance. A social network profile has many of the attributes of a shrine, but in this case it is a shrine to oneself. It mimics in essential ways memorials made for the dead, but the subject is still living and is the main creative force behind the enterprise. Profiles are typically adorned with electronic glitter and tinsel, shimmering with a thousand spots of light. The profile-maker's favorite music emanates from the site and a series of pictures scrolls through an eternal loop. These shrines, however, are also communal affairs, as the content is not produced solely by the owner, but is also the product of many wall postings and additions by friends, who add pictures, videos, greetings, comments and artwork to this living testament to the owner. If the subject does die, however, these do become actual memorial shrines such as "Justice for Miranda."[7] Will some incarnation of MySpace exist in a thousand years, still bearing the profiles of those who lovingly built their online persona today?[8]

Another ego-enhancing common feature of the social Web is the ability to "update" friends about what one is doing moment to moment, for who other than a complete narcissist would think that the world cares about what he or she ate for breakfast? Getting a response like "sounds delicious" from a friend in Singapore only stimulates self-important people to write more and record their every move. Ashton Kutcher, who has over a million people subscribing to his Twitter feed, has said

> At the end of the day, we all have ego, we all have some level of ego … But if we can use our ego to actually create good charitable things in the world in some way, and use our ego—originally, I defined Twitter as an ego stream when I first saw it. But then what I realized is if we can transform that into something that's positive that can actually effectively change the world, that can be a really valuable tool.
>
> (CNN.com 2009)

And indeed it turns out that one of the most popular applications on Facebook is "Causes," with over 26 million users.[9] This application sees in the Facebook platform an unprecedented opportunity for "seizing the future and making a difference in the world around us." It allows people to "create a cause, recruit their friends into that cause, keep everybody in the cause up-to-speed on issues and media related to the cause, and, most importantly, raise money directly through the cause for **any** U.S. registered 501(c)(3) nonprofit or Canadian registered charity" [emphasis in the original].[10] So there is no reason to think that these features necessarily impede a user's march towards spiritual insights and holistic thinking.

References

Boase, Jeffrey, Lee Rainie, and Barry Wellman. 2006. *The Strength of Internet Ties.* Washington: Pew Internet and American Life Project.

Brasher, Brenda. 2001. *Give Me That Online Religion.* San Francisco: Jossey-Bass.

Clark, Lynn, Stewart Hoover, and Lee Rainie. 2004. *Faith Online.* Washington: Pew Internet and American Life Project. www.pewinternet.org/Reports/2004/Faith-Online.aspx

CNN.com. 2009. "Oprah, Ashton Kutcher Mark Twitter 'Turning Point'" (18 April). www.edition.cnn.com/2009/TECH/04/17/ashton.cnn.twitter.battle

Dennett, Daniel and Douglas Hofstadter, eds. 1981. *The Mind's I*. New York: Basic Books.

Durkheim, Emile. 1963. *The Elementary Forms of the Religious Life*, trans. Joseph Swain. London: George Allen & Unwin.

Harrington, Ashley. 2006. "MySpace Purgatory." *Urban Dictionary* (September 18). www.urbandictionary.com/define.php?term=MySpace+purgatory

Hershock, Peter. 1999. *Reinventing the Wheel: A Buddhist Response to the Information Age*. Albany: SUNY Press.

Hick, John. 1989. *An Interpretation of Religion*. New Haven, CT: Yale University Press.

Kim, Mun-Cho. 2005. "Online Buddhist Community: An Alternative Religious Organization in the Information Age." In *Religion and Cyberspace*, eds Morten Hojsgaard and Margit Warburg. London: Routledge.

Kurzweil, Ray. 1999. *The Age of Spiritual Machines*. New York: Viking Penguin.

Lanham, Richard. 1993. *The Electronic Word: Democracy, Technology, and the Arts*. Chicago: University of Chicago Press.

Linderman, Alf and Mia Lovheim. 2005. "Constructing Religious Identity on the Internet." In *Religion and Cyberspace*, eds Morten Hojsgaard and Margit Warburg. London: Routledge.

McLuhan, Marshall. 1964. *Understanding Media: The Extension of Man*. New York: McGraw Hill.

Myspeace.com. 2008. "I need some mercy, some prayer." http://forum.myspace.com/index.cfm?fuseaction=messageboard.viewThread&entryID=58776155 &groupID=106361788&adTopicID=27&Mytoken=785D7A50–0A2B-4E90–92A57824207F9CB675857067

——. 2009a. "Meditation in emptiness state of mind." http://forum.myspace.com/index.cfm?fuseaction=messageboard.viewThread&entryID=73398392&adTopicID=27&categoryID=0&IsSticky=0&groupID=100000602&Mytoken=B2CE55CA-869A-4D79–90C0207DA8DA10B564182568

——. 2009b. "Helping depressed/anxious friends." http://forum.myspace.com/index.cfm?fuseaction=messageboard.viewThread&entryID=73407327&adTopicID=27&categoryID=0&IsSticky=0&groupID=100111317&Mytoken=26CC8C1F-B185–46C7–9121057C221BEF991807911

——. 2009c. "Beyond Separateness (and relativity)." http://forum.myspace.com/index.cfm?fuseaction=messageboard.viewThread&entryID=73411483&adTopicID=27&categoryID=0&IsSticky=0&groupID=100111317&Mytoken=D579DE3D-1092-4F02-AE9B460F164A900E23690576

Ong, Walter J. 1982. *Orality and Literacy: The Technologizing of the Word*. London: Routledge.

Pew Forum. 2008. "U.S. Religious Landscape Survey." Washington, DC: The Pew Forum on Religion & Public Life. http://religions.pewforum.org/affiliations

——. 2009. "Faith in Flux: Changers in Religious Affiliation in the U.S." Washington, DC: The Pew Forum on Religion & Public Life. http://pewforum.org/docs/?DocID=409

Turkle, Sherry. 1995. *Life on the Screen: Identity in the Age of the Internet*. New York: Simon & Schuster.

Turner, Victor. 1969. *The Ritual Process: Structure and Anti-Structure*. Chicago: Aldine Publishing.

Notes

1 The best place to start an investigation into issues related to the idea that different media promote different modes of consciousness, which then affect our social and cultural expressions, is Walter Ong's celebrated book *Orality and Literacy: The Technologizing of the Word* (Ong 1982).
2 Some selections are presented here exactly as they appear on the online bulletin board, so the reader is urged to ignore the somewhat irregular grammar and spelling.
3 In the fast-paced language of online communication, "imo" stands for "in my opinion."
4 Hick's passage is not error-free. In the Sanskrit word *prajñā*, it is the terminal syllable that is supposed to be long rather than the first one as he has written, and he might better have said "the ego affirms itself over *and* against a world of objects" rather than allowing the conjunction of two prepositions. These errors might well be oversights on the part of the publisher's copy-editor, but, as the contributors to the MySpace discussion have no similar editorial assistance, this seems only to strengthen my point.
5 Daniel Dennett deals with the topic of where the self is located in a fascinating chapter of his *The Mind's I*, called "Where Am I?" In that chapter he undergoes a fictitious operation to remove his brain from his body and place it in a vat with radio receivers connecting it to his body's nervous system. After the operation, he naturally expects to feel as if he is in the vat, because he assumes that "he" is basically his brain, but in fact he finds himself in his body looking at his brain in the vat. He tries to perceive his consciousness as being located in the brain, but cannot generate the sensation of being anywhere other than in his body, even though intellectually he is pretty sure that "he" is in the vat (Dennett and Hofstadter 1981, 217–31).
6 These figures are based upon the latest Pew research survey on religious identity in America, which suggests that 0.7 per cent of the American population (or approximately 2,100,000 people) identify themselves as Buddhist (Pew Forum 2008).
7 www.myspace.com/justice_for_miranda.
8 The online *Urban Dictionary* addresses this issue in its entry "MySpace Purgatory":

> This is the level of Internet Purgatory dedicated to old myspace profiles. A profile found here will most likely never be updated again but is also unlikely to get deleted. This may happen when a user forgets their password, is hacked, goes to prison, dies, or even when they simply abandon their myspace profile ... The original owner of a myspace profile located in Purgatory is themself [*sic*] also considered to be in Purgatory for as long as the profile is there (Harrington 2006).

9 An application on a social network is a program built by software developers that operates within the environment of the social network, and members can choose to use it and allow it to interact with their profile if they wish. Many of these applications allow people to play games with their friends through the social network, or to share music or photographs.
10 501(c)(3) is the US tax code-related designation for a nonprofit organization to which one can make a donation and deduct that donation from one's income tax.

Chapter 12

Homer the Heretic and Charlie Church

Parody, Piety, and Pluralism in *The Simpsons*

Lisle Dalton, Eric Michael Mazur, and Monica Siems

Most of the family shows are namby-pamby sentimentality or smarmy innuendo. We stay away from that.

Matt Groening

The story goes like this: Marge and Homer take some time for themselves and leave Bart, Lisa, and Maggie with Grandpa. Agents from child welfare discover the children running amok and place them into foster care with the neighbors. The new foster father, Ned Flanders, faints upon hearing that the children have never been baptized, so he packs up the children and his own family and heads for the Springfield River. Homer, missing the point, panics because "in the eyes of God they'll be Flanderseses." At the river, Homer pushes Bart out of "harm's way," and the baptismal water falls on his own head. When Bart asks him how he feels, Homer responds, in an uncharacteristically pious voice, "Oh, Bartholomew, I feel like St Augustine of Hippo after his conversion by Ambrose of Milan." When Ned Flanders gasps, "Homer, what did you just say?" Homer replies nonchalantly, "I said shut your ugly face, Flanders!" The moment of spiritual inspiration has passed, and the children are back with their parents, unbaptized and safe ("Home Sweet Home-Diddily-Dum-Doodily").[1]

The prominent role of religion and the attitude toward it are not unique to this episode. Once a week for nearly the past two decades (and more in syndication), *The Simpsons* has proved itself unafraid to lampoon Evangelicals, Hindus, Jews, and religion generally. The frequency of religious plots and subthemes would itself be enough to distinguish this show from other prime-time fare. Not since the Lutheran program *Davey and Goliath* has a cartoon addressed religion so forthrightly. But while that Sunday morning program carried moral lessons of faith, this Sunday evening program ridicules the pious, lampoons the religious, and questions traditional morality. Instead of sermonizing at the audience, this program speaks with them, and possibly for them as well.

This half-hour series emerged as one of the most popular shows of the 1990s, and it regularly addresses issues involving institutional religion—including representations of religious traditions, discussions of moral and religious themes, and portrayals of mythological figures—as well as that which is often labeled "spirituality." Regular characters include a Hindu convenience store manager, a Jewish entertainer, an Evangelical neighbor, and a Protestant minister. Evil, morality, sin, the soul, and other religious themes are openly discussed. In terms of the genres associated with the show—the situation comedy and the animated cartoon—*The Simpsons* represents quite a departure from traditional fare in which religion is rarely if ever addressed. The writers' treatment of religion might even be construed as a heresy of sorts. Yet it is often an insightful heresy, for although the program thrives on satire, caricature, and irony, it does so with a keen understanding of current trends in American religion. *The Simpsons* implicitly affirms an America in which institutional religion has lost its position of authority and where personal expressions of spirituality have come to dominate popular religious culture.

"Don't Have A Cow, Man!": Reactions to *The Simpsons*

The Simpsons were the brainchild of Matt Groening, who developed the characters in short cartoons on the *Tracey Ullman Show* in the late 1980s. When *The Simpsons* aired in January 1990, it was the first animated prime-time series on American television in more than two decades. An immediate success, within a year it was the highest-rated show on its network and was often among the top ten shows on television. It occasionally outperformed *The Cosby Show*, a family-oriented situation comedy that dominated the ratings in the late 1980s. Over time, its weekly ratings have declined, but the program still consistently ranks as one of the network's top shows. Its success has continued in syndication, ranking first among reruns during the 1994–95 season (Freeman 1995, 14).[2] The program has become so popular that it is able to attract popular cultural icons (including actors, comedians, musicians, athletes, and talk-show hosts) as guest "voices."[3]

The Simpsons has also been a merchandiser's dream. During its first season, more than a billion dollars' worth of licensed Simpsons merchandise was sold in the United States. In 1991, licensed manufacturers shipped up to a million T-shirts per week. In an example of the show's cultural impact, some school principals banned a shirt featuring Bart and the slogan "Underachiever and Proud of It" (Riddle 1994, A5), and unlicensed merchandise (including one with Bart depicted as an African American) is commonplace despite millions spent to enforce copyright (Lefton 1992, 16).

This popularity also brought intense scrutiny from critics. Emerging amid the family values debates of early 1990s, *The Simpsons* has undergone close examination for its portrayal of family life. One famous jibe came from President George H. W. Bush in a 1992 speech before the National Religious Broadcasters association, in which he called for "a nation closer to *The*

Waltons than *The Simpsons*."[4] Other critics have damned *The Simpsons* as a symptomatic expression of the contempt for traditional values that permeates American culture. In his critique of the entertainment industry, Michael Medved catalogs instances of religious characters portrayed as duplicitous, hypocritical, insincere, and even criminal (Medved 1992). He cites one scene from *The Simpsons* in which Bart utters an irreverent prayer ("Two Cars in Every Garage, Three Eyes on Every Fish") as proof of the industry's pattern of religious insensitivity. Another media critic, Josh Ozersky, places *The Simpsons* in a wider critique of "anti-families" that included 1990s-era programs *Roseanne* and *Married ... With Children*, noting that while "the playful suppression of unhappiness has always been one of TV's great strengths," this breed of sitcom also deflects public concern away from social disintegration related to the decline of the family. As such, the irony and sarcastic humor of these shows—though he admits *The Simpsons* often tends toward "witty and valid social criticism"—serve to extend television's unhealthy influence over the American public's self-image. "TV," he laments, "has absorbed the American family's increasing sense of defeat and estrangement and presented it as an ironic in-joke." And while this mocking might temporarily placate the dysfunctional tendencies of our times, it does not "lift the spirits." Ozersky argues that the deployment of irony in the face of domestic discontents is an "assault on the family and on all human relationships" since it acts as the "antithesis of deep feeling," "discourages alarm at the decline of the family," and disparages the "earnest, often abject bonds of kin" that lie at the heart of family life. He urges readers to reject "the soullessness of TV's 'hip, bold,' anti-life world" (Ozersky 1991, 11–12, 14, 93).

Despite such condemnations, reactions to *The Simpsons* have not been entirely negative. Many writers (in secular and religious periodicals) praise the show's clever writing and, oddly enough—considering this is a cartoon—its realism. Danny Collum praises *The Simpsons* for "grasping the complexity and ambiguity of human life." He credits it for its insightful, even realistic portrayal of an American family that is frequently abrasive, argumentative, and beset by financial problems. Collum notes that—at the time he was writing—the Simpsons were among the few TV families that went to church or consulted a minister. And while he recognizes their religiosity tends toward "pretty lame K-mart evangelicalism," it merits consideration because it shows characters striving for a "moral anchor" and a "larger sense of meaning" in the midst of otherwise chaotic and aimless lives (Collum 1991, 38–39). Chiding religious groups and educators who have denounced the series as promoting bad behavior, Victoria Rebeck praises it as sharp satire that shows how parents are often ill equipped to cope with their children's (and their own) problems. For her, this comes as a welcome departure from the "pretentious misrepresentation of family life that one finds in the 'model family' shows" (Rebeck 1990, 622). Similarly, Frank

McConnell notes that *The Simpsons* "deconstructs the myth of the happy family" and "leaves what is real and valuable about the myth unscathed ... They are caricatures not just of us, but of us in our national delusion that the life of the sitcom family is the way things are 'supposed' to be" (McConnell 1990, 389). He praises the show's humanism and rapid-fire humor, which he considers "profoundly sane."

"Gabbin' about God": Scholarly Viewing of Religion and Television

That *The Simpsons* generates such divergent reactions from critics suggests that it has struck a sensitive nerve that lies close to the heart of the public debate over the portrayal of religious values in the media. In an ambitious 1994 study of religion on television, researchers conducted a five-week analysis of religious behaviors on prime-time shows. After cataloging the activities of 1462 characters in 100 episodes, the study found that religion was "a rather invisible institution" in prime time; fewer than six per cent of the characters had an identifiable religious affiliation, and religiosity was rarely central to the plots or the characters. The report concluded that "television has fictionally 'delegitimized' religious institutions and traditions by symbolically eliminating them from our most pervasive form of popular culture" (Skill *et al.* 1994, 251–67, especially 265). The study may have been biased; other explanations for the "symbolic elimination" of religion in prime-time television range from skittishness about offending religious adherents to alleged irreligiosity within the entertainment industry.[5] Nonetheless, as Medved claims, the result is programming that often seems an "affront [to] the religious sensibilities of ordinary Americans" (Medved 1992, 50).

On the other hand, other scholars argue that it is better to analyze television using broader conceptions of religion. For them, the very act of watching television serves as a religious event—a domestic ritual of devotion to stories that would function like religious narratives in other cultures and eras. Gregor Goethals, borrowing from sociologists Peter Berger and Thomas Luckmann, asserts that television provides a symbolic universe that serves as an overarching framework for ordering and interpreting experience (Goethals 1981, 125; see also Greeley 1987). Hal Himmelstein analyzes television programming in terms of various persistent "myths," including "the sanctity of the ordinary American family," "the triumph of personal initiative over bureaucratic control," and "the celebration of celebrity." He further argues that these myths sustain the political and economic needs of various social institutions (Himmelstein 1994, 3, 10).

These debates over religion on *The Simpsons* reflect what anthropologist Clifford Geertz called the "intrinsic double aspect" of cultural products that are both models of and models for reality. Does *The Simpsons* reflect our attitudes—particularly toward religion—or does it shape them? Does television act as mirror to show us ourselves as we really are, or as we ought to be? As the reactions to *The Simpsons* suggest, it is an important debate. Geertz argues that such cultural patterns "give meaning ... to social and psychological reality both by shaping themselves to it and by shaping it to themselves" (Geertz 1973, 93). The reaction to *The Simpsons*, mirroring broader debates about America's values and morality, suggests that the show serves as a model of contemporary belief and behavior in American life; the show is a microcosm of what Americans currently do and do not hold sacred. This picture of America delights some, and appalls others. And although *The Simpsons* targets many social institutions, myths, and presumptions, religion inspires some of the show's sharpest satire, and correspondingly some of its best insights into contemporary America.

"Home Sweet Home-Diddily-Dum-Doodily": Welcome to Springfield

It is the world of the Simpson family that feeds the recriminations and fears of those who despise it, while offering humor, irony, succor, and a subtle morality play for those who adore it. Through the television lens (or more appropriately, its mirror), viewers see the mundane lives of the Simpsons, and themselves in the reflection—an odd but often uncannily accurate portrait of Americana. The cast represents a cross-section of ages, genders, races, and religions; it includes police officers, teachers, entertainers, clergy, bartenders, and janitors. The Simpson family includes Homer (a dim employee at a nuclear power plant), his wife Marge (a devoted but overworked housewife), and their children: Bart (a good-natured but mischievous boy), Lisa (a precocious, sensitive girl), and infant Maggie.

The fact that the characters are cartoons presents an interesting dynamic, separating the "reality" of our lives from the "pretend" world of the Simpsons. Even so, the family presents noble truths, painful realities, and ironic depths in a very "real" way, enabling viewers to identify with the sentiments and to be altered by them. This two-way relationship invites viewers to enter the Everytown of Springfield,[6] to visit the Simpsons' world and perhaps comprehend how it informs their own. While they rarely "mug" for the camera, the self-reflexive actions of the characters help by constantly acknowledging their television status. From the show's opening sequence that depicts the characters racing home to watch their own opening credits, to the frequent subreferences to other television shows, networks, and personalities, viewers are reminded of television's importance in the lives of the Simpson family and—since we are watching them watch—our own. Indeed, as if to mock our own viewership, the Simpsons' television is often alluded to as the sixth (and most appreciated) member of the family. The Simpsons watch television and are conscious of its influence over their lives, while we watch them and ponder, fret, and complain about how they are reflecting and shaping our thoughts and attitudes.

In Springfield, representatives of religious communities are rendered as stereotypes, easily identifiable to viewers and easily objectionable to adherents. The only regularly appearing Jewish character, Herschel Shmoikel Krustofski (Krusty the Clown), is the star of Bart and Lisa's favorite television program. He is anything but devout. A gross caricature of a stereotypically secularized Jew corrupted by wealth and fame, Krusty is addicted to cigarettes, gambling, and pornography. He dislikes children, finances his lavish debt-ridden lifestyle by over-marketing his own image unabashedly, and fakes his own death to avoid paying taxes. In an episode that parodies *The Jazz Singer*, Krusty recites a Hebrew prayer while visiting the Simpsons, and later admits that as a youth he disappointed his father by abandoning rabbinical studies to become a clown. The rest of the episode involves the attempts by Bart and Lisa to reconcile the estranged father and son. Using advice from various Jewish sources, they eventually succeed ("Like Father, Like Clown").[7]

Another character, Apu Nahasapeemapetilon, is manager of the local "Kwik-E-Mart" and one of the few identifiable Hindus on network television. Apu practices vegetarianism, maintains an in-store shrine to the elephant-headed deity Ganesha (quite plausible insofar as Ganesha's connection to prosperity appeals to the ambitions of the Hindu diaspora), and marries according to Hindu ritual. In Springfield, however, Apu must endure the slights of his incredulous customers; Homer belittles Apu's diet, throws peanuts at the shrine, and suggests that Apu "must have been out taking a whiz when they were giving out gods" ("Homer the Heretic"). More problematic is the inference that South Asians manage all convenience stores; Homer joins Apu on a Himalayan pilgrimage to visit the high "guru" of Kwik-E-Marts, and during a visit to a seaside town, the Simpson family stops at a local convenience mart managed by another South Asian ("Homer and Apu"; "Summer of 4 ft. 2").

The subjects of the most mockery, however, are the Simpsons' evangelical Christian neighbors, the Flanders family. Exceedingly cheerful, Ned, his wife Maude, and their "goody-goody" children Rod and Todd provide the perfect foil to the Simpson family. They are polite, well-liked, righteous, generous, peaceful, and neighborly—all qualities the Simpsons seem to lack. They are also extraordinarily pious: spotting escaped zoo animals running through town, Ned exclaims that he has seen the elephants of the apocalypse. Maude reminds him that the Bible describes four horsemen, not elephants. "Gettin' closer," he replies ("Bart Gets an Elephant"). Bart uses a special microphone to fool Rod and Todd into thinking that God is communicating with them over the radio. On another occasion they bounce on a trampoline and exclaim, "Each bounce takes us closer to God," and "Catch me Lord, catch me," before crashing into each other ("Radio Bart"; "Homer Alone").

Stereotyping is not the only way institutional religion is lampooned; religious leadership is the butt of much of the program's humor. Though other religious figures appear on the program (most notably in an ecumenical radio program titled "Gabbin' about God" with a minister, Krusty's father the rabbi, and a Catholic priest ["Like Father, Like Clown"]), there is no doubt that the Reverend Timothy Lovejoy represents all clergy—to their general misfortune. When ever-righteous Ned Flanders telephones Lovejoy upon learning that the Simpson children were never baptized, Lovejoy—clearly annoyed by Flanders' intrusion—suggests that Ned consider another religious tradition: "They're basically all the same," he notes before hanging up. When Marge asks if a particular activity is a sin, Lovejoy picks up the Bible and exclaims, "Have you read this thing lately, Marge? Everything's a sin" ("Home Sweet Home-Diddily-Dum-Doodily"). He encourages Marge to seek a divorce during a weekend retreat she and Homer attend to fix their marriage ("War of the Simpsons"). And when a comet threatens to destroy Springfield—and immediately after Homer laments not being religious—Lovejoy is seen running down the street yelling, "It's all over, people, we don't have a prayer" ("Bart's Comet").[8]

Lovejoy's anemic approach condemns all religious leadership, and is part of a larger critique of religious traditions consistent with the other stereotypes and the actions of the regular characters. After eating potentially poisonous sushi, Homer prepares for death by spending his last moments listening to the Bible on tape. Unfortunately, the "begats" put him to sleep, causing him to miss the sunrise he had hoped to die watching ("One Fish, Two Fish, Blowfish, Blue Fish"). (He survives.) Bart responds to a request for grace with a somewhat irreverent prayer: "Dear God: We paid for all the stuff ourselves, so thanks for nothing" ("Two Cars").[9]

The program also uses familiar supernatural religious figures for comic effects. Both Satan and God have appeared on the program, and their portrayals mix the sublime and demonic with the ridiculous, presenting them as much human as they are supernatural. Satan is a familiar visitor to Springfield; in various episodes he offers Homer a doughnut in exchange for his soul; holds appointments with Montgomery Burns, the devious owner of the local nuclear plant; and uses a personal computer to keeps tabs on lost souls. Satan manifests in different forms, and typical of the program's use of irony, he is portrayed in one episode by Ned Flanders ("Treehouse of Horror IV"). In contrast, God is a cross between Mel Brooks' "Two-thousand-year old man" character and Charlton Heston's aged Moses—a familiar stereotype with a humorous and not-too-blasphemous sting. As might be expected of an anthropomorphic God, however, certain divine attributes (omniscience, omnipresence) seem lacking; in a meeting with Homer, God inquires whether St Louis still has a football team (at the time, it did not) and later excuses himself to appear on a tortilla in Mexico ("Homer the Heretic").

The depictions of God and Satan reinforce the morality play qualities of the Simpson characters. Homer, as Everyman, is a poorly educated working man. He is simple, well-meaning, loving, and committed to his family, regardless of how much they annoy him. Marge, as Charity, is always doing for others, particularly her family, while neglecting herself. In the few cases where she is self-indulgent, she ends up plagued by guilt, and though tempted by vices, she always returns to care for her loved ones. The eldest child, Bart, as Temptation, is the animated Tom Sawyer. He is an irascible boy who never studies, serves detention, plays pranks, yet loves his sister, obeys his mother, and occasionally respects his father. The eldest daughter, Lisa, as Wisdom, is the smart student and teacher's pet, the child who dreams of Nobel prizes and presidential elections, and who relies on her saxophone and the Blues to release her from her torment. The youngest child, Maggie, represents Hope, the embodiment of innocence and vulnerability.

Juxtaposed with the dubious portrayals of institutional religion are nuanced and intricate examples of admirable and noble behavior. Krusty, Apu, and Ned are volunteer fire-fighters who help put out the burning Simpson home after Homer falls asleep on the couch smoking a cigar (and skipping church) ("Homer the Heretic"). Ned, despite Homer's frequent ribbing and abuse, adheres closely to the Christian ideals of turning the other cheek and practicing charity. He invites the Simpsons to his barbecues, shares football tickets with Homer, offers to donate organs (without solicitation), lets the town come into his family's bomb shelter to avoid a comet's destruction, and agrees to leave it and face near-certain doom when it becomes too crowded ("Homer Loves Flanders"; "When Flanders Failed"; "Homer's Triple Bypass"; "Bart's Comet"). Even the Simpsons, "America's favorite dysfunctional family" (Rebeck 1990, 622), often overcome their John Bunyanesque characterizations. Marge and Homer reject opportunities to be unfaithful, attend a retreat to save their marriage, and drag the family to a seminar to improve their communication skills. Homer attempts to improve his relationship with his father, hunts down his half-brother, and tolerates his annoying sisters-in-law. Though constant rivals, Bart and Lisa share genuine affection and occasionally work together; when Lisa becomes the star goalie of Bart's rival ice hockey team, the two put down their sticks and exit the rink arm-in-arm rather than compete for their parents' love. Bart even solicits the assistance of a Michael Jackson sound-alike to help write Lisa a birthday song ("Life on the Fast Lane"; "The Last Temptation of Homer"; "Colonel Homer"; "War of the Simpsons"; "Bart's Inner Child"; "One Fish, Two Fish"; "Grandpa vs. Sexual Inadequacy"; "Oh Brother, Where Art Thou?"; "Lisa on Ice"; "Stark Raving Dad").

The diverse attitudes toward religion come together in the episode titled "Homer the Heretic." Refusing to attend church, Homer embarks on a journey of personal spirituality, encounters Apu's Hinduism and Krusty's Judaism, and ultimately comes face-to-face with God. During a dream, God grants Homer permission to miss church, and when he awakens he is a changed man: calm, peaceful, and able to commune directly with nature. The following week, while asleep on the couch, Homer sets the house alight, and the volunteer fire department (Krusty, Ned, and Apu, or as Reverend Lovejoy puts it, "the Jew, the Christian, and the miscellaneous") rushes to put it out. Homer questions the value of attending church, since the Flanders' house is also on fire. "He's a regular Charlie Church," Homer notes, suggesting that religious faith did not protect the Flanders' home. But just as Homer utters these words, a providential cloud forms over the Flanders' home and rain extinguishes the blaze—but leaves the fire burning the Simpson home. Asked by Marge if he has learned anything, Homer notes that God is angry and vengeful. The Reverend Lovejoy replies that it is the charity of the pluralistic volunteer fire department and not God's anger that is the lesson to be learned. The house is saved, and so is Homer's faith—in humanity, if not in God.

And so, perhaps, is the viewers', if the focus shifts from the show's content to its context, to what is happening on this side of the glass. Reverend Lovejoy's sentiment—that "God was working in the hearts of your friends and neighbors when they came to your aid"—represents the sort of generic Christianity prevalent in today's mainline Protestant churches and in most television portrayals of religion. Against the backdrop of declining religious authority, increasing personal choice, and "flattening" of doctrines into more palatable themes, television presents revamped morality plays such as this in which personal piety, religious pluralism, and sincere goodness rate higher than denominational adherence and church attendance. The show's coda reinforces this point: having promised to be "front row center" in church the next Sunday, there is Homer, snoring through Lovejoy's sermon, dreaming of another *tête-à-tête* with God (in which God informs Homer not to be upset, since "nine out of ten religions fail in their first year").

"Send in the Clowns": Analyzing The Simpsons

It is helpful to take a step back and remember that this is (after all) a cartoon, written by comedy writers and drawn by comic artists. Several episodes feature gestures that highlight the characters' traditionally animated hands: three fingers and a thumb. Indeed, whatever "reality" is posited in the program is of the viewers' making. By working both sides of the reality mirror, the show engenders feelings of both identity and difference—the characters are both "us" and "not us." They are "us" in the sense that they are not ideal, but "not us" in the sense that—their cartoonishness aside—they fall far shorter of the mark than we think we do. The television mirror here is a funhouse one, which provides an exaggerated, distorted, yet still recognizable image of ourselves. Ozersky notes this, and criticizes the show not only for failing to provide a positive model, but for rewarding an attitude of superiority and ironic smugness in its viewers. Closer to the mark, however, might be Rebeck's observation that such critics "have missed the point. *The Simpsons* is satire," and as such its characters "are not telling people how to act" (Rebeck 1990, 622).

Interestingly, Rebeck illustrates her point with a religious-themed episode; she compares *The Simpsons'* detractors to a minor but recurring character in the show, the Sunday school teacher. Beleaguered by the children's questions about whether their pets will go to heaven—particularly Bart's inquiries about an amputee's leg and a robot with a human brain—she finally blurts out, "All these questions! Is a little blind faith too much to ask for?" ("The Telltale Head"). At best, some critics want proactive television that encourages viewers to maintain a level of "blind faith" in certain cherished ideals and values. At worst, they lambast *The Simpsons* because it fails to reinforce our society's "dominant ideology" with its cherished myths of eternal progress and traditional authority structures.

But exposing a myth to ridicule and debunking it are two different things. Recall that McConnell's highest praise for *The Simpsons* was that "it deconstructs the myth of the happy family wisely and miraculously leaves what is real and valuable about the myth unscathed" (McConnell 1990, 390). Rebeck notes that the Simpsons are not characters to be emulated, but "if anything, they are giving people an outlet so they won't have to act out" (Rebeck 1990, 622). Herein lies another paradox; it is precisely *because* the program fails to offer us any sustained ideals of its own—least of all desirable ideals that challenge the majority—that it serves as a negative model for mainstream ideals of family and religion, if only by default, and offers instead a catharsis generated by a good laugh.

If many of television's early sitcoms were little more than thinly veiled presentations of the "American dream," *The Simpsons* and shows like it come much closer to actually representing "comedy" than most of its predecessors. Himmelstein notes that, to those having difficulty handling "the chaos of daily life," comedy represents "the logical order of the ideal" by revealing the "ludicrous and ridiculous aspects of our existence." It is most powerful, he concludes, "when it is possible for both the artist and the spectator to note the contradictions and value conflicts of society." Comedy shades into satire when it deals with what he calls "traditional and everpresent irritations which people know as evils but which they also find themselves powerless to eradicate" (Himmelstein 1994, 77).

On *The Simpsons*, the disjunction between the way things are and the way they ought to be persists, and any bridge across that gap proves temporary and largely unrecognized by the supposedly victorious Simpsons themselves. At the end of an episode, the family often debates the "lesson" they've learned, with none of them seeming to get the point. Thus, if the inclusion of humor at the expense of institutional structures marks *The Simpsons* as satire, this recurring failure to offer true resolutions distinguishes it as irony.

Defined by literary critic Alan Wilde, irony in our era is "a mode of con-sciousness, a perceptual response to a world without unity or cohesion" which nonetheless bears "the potential for affirmation" of both the world's absurdity and its "unfinished" nature (Wilde 1981, 2, 6). Here it seems that the models "of" and "for" society coalesce. Rebeck notes, "The Simpsons show us ... what it was about our upbringing that made us brats as kids and neurotic as adults" (Rebeck 1990, 622). They do not show us how to remedy those conditions, implying that they don't need fixing. In an imperfect world one fares best by behaving imperfectly.

Ozersky sees *The Simpsons* functioning this way, with profoundly negative implications for society. He argues that the show makes viewers "less inclined to object to the continuing presence of unsafe workplaces, vast cor-porations, the therapy racket, and all the other deserving targets of *The Simpsons'* harmless barbs" (Ozersky 1991, 92). But Ozersky fails to see another side to the "irony" coin. For segments of society who *cannot* object to those failings, *The Simpsons* reminds them that they are not *completely* powerless as long as they can laugh at the forces that oppress them. James Chesebro identifies irony as the "communication strategy" of the disen-franchised that reassures an audience because it presents characters who are "intellectually inferior and less able to control circumstances than is the audience" (Chesebro 1979, quoted by Himmelstein 1994, 79). In other words, the character's life is more absurd than the viewers'—a funhouse mirror. This is especially true in cases of what Chesebro calls "unknowing irony" in which the character's "ignorance and social powerlessness" are not feigned. Archie Bunker, the somewhat pitiable and perennially unredeemed bigot of *All in the Family*, is a perfect example of "unknowing irony" from the pre-*Simpsons* television era. In order for ironic programming to serve as a model "for" society, he had to remain unredeemed. Otherwise the show would have been something substantially different from what it was. As Himmelstein notes, self-knowledge and self-criticism in Archie would "sacrifice" the show's "unknowing irony" and turn it from "a biting artistic revelation of bigotry in a contemporary social milieu" to a "a popularized group-therapy session thrown in the audience's face" (Himmelstein 1994, 125). And while *The Simpsons* contains far fewer "serious" moments than *All in the Family* did—Homer is clearly more absurd and less pitiable than Archie ever was—the two proceed in a decidedly "live and don't learn" manner.

Not surprisingly, Homer's lack of intellectual and moral progress is expressed most powerfully in the religious-themed episodes. The accidental baptism in the Springfield River mentioned earlier elicits in him only tem-porary piety. He becomes a messianic leader for the "Stonecutters" (a men's organization modeled on Freemasonry), but his attempts to get the members to dedicate themselves to charitable acts causes the group to disband ("Homer the Great"). In the "Homer the Heretic" episode, not even a face-to-face encounter with the Almighty can change Homer's character. At every turn the opportunity for redemption passes, and Homer is back where he started: marginal, powerless, and unenlightened. In all these episodes, it is not unbelief that is counseled, but rather belief in basic values (for example, charity, camaraderie, and support) in a different way—within the family rather than outside it. In the end, Homer realizes the folly of striving too hard to "belong," and instead ends most episodes proud and confident of who he is, warts and all. As Richard Corliss notes, "Homer isn't bright, but he loves his brood." He is also a faithful husband and father who "will do anything—go skateboarding off a cliff, defy his boss, buy Lisa a pony—if the tots scream loud enough and if Marge gives him a lecture" (Corliss 1994, 77). In other words, Homer's progress (or lack thereof) in each episode reveals a character who can be counted on to do the right thing, if accidentally or begrudgingly. This conveys a sense of an underlying human goodness, however many layers of ineptitude one might have to penetrate to find it.

"All The World Loves a Clown": The Simpsons as Religious Archetypes

And thus we return to the notion of the Simpsons—especially Homer—as "us" and "not us." He has the same values and desires, but expresses them in a buffoonish style. This is the key to discerning the significance of *The Simpsons* not only as satire of religious phenomena, but also as a religious phenomenon in itself. The history of religions has many examples of clowns who convey messages to the faithful. Historian Don Handelman describes the linguistic connections between "buffoon" and "fool" and notes the "affinities" between the fool in medieval drama and the clown as religious performer. According to Handelman, "Clowns are ambiguous and ambivalent figures ... The clown in ritual is at once a character of solemnity and fun, of gravity and hilarity, of danger and absurdity, of wisdom and idiocy, and of the sacred and the profane" (Handelman 1987). A character such as Homer Simpson oscillates between knowing and not knowing, between knowing that he knows and not knowing that he knows. He approaches the divine but simultaneously defames it, and thus embodies the irony of a character who knows no real resolution.

In some religions, the identity and difference between clowns and their audiences is an immensely significant dialectic—that paradox of "us" but "not us." In the Hopi tradition, ritual clowns perform actions backward, upside down, or in an otherwise ridiculous fashion—for example, entering a plaza by climbing head-first down a ladder. They may engage in exaggerated simulated intercourse and perform other activities that violate Hopi social norms. Interpretations have stressed two aspects: entertainment value, and the pedagogic value of illustrating the foolishness of misbehaving. In this sense, Hopi clowns foster a sense of superiority among the audience members who know more and are more sophisticated than the clowns. However, as Emory Sekaquaptewa notes, clowns, while parodies of the society, must be recognizable in order to have an effect. It may be a funhouse mirror, but it's still a mirror, and clowns show that the way *not* to behave is precisely the way we often behave in an imperfect world. As Sekaquaptewa explains, clowns show that people "have only their worldly ambition and aspirations by which to gain a spiritual world of eternity ... We cannot be perfect in this world after all and if we are reminded that we are clowns, maybe we can have, from time to time, introspection as a guide to lead us right" (Sekaquaptewa 1989, 151).

Thus sacred clowns, through their mockery of norms, serve to reinforce a tradition's values. They "contradict the laws of society to remind people of distinctions between the sacred and profane. They cross ordinary boundaries in order to define them" (Bastien 1987). *The Simpsons* represents both a model of and a model for contemporary American society, not only because it reveals contemporary attitudes about religious institutions, morality, and spirituality, but also because it functions in the time-honored way of religious satirists. As Joseph Bastien notes, "Traditionally, religions have employed humor and satire to bring people together and dissolve their differences. Clownish antics ... [are] not intended to desecrate the sacred but to dispel some of the rigidity and pomposity of the church-goers" (*ibid.*). The targets of *The Simpsons*' ridicule are hardly malevolent forces, but rather exponents of what Victoria Rebeck calls a "sincere but useless" form of religion, teaching us that the most ridiculous thing a person can do is take anything in life too seriously (Rebeck 1990, 622). "The laughter of fools," Bastien says, is "praise to a God who disdain[s] pride among his people" (Bastien 1987). But surely such a God would permit us to be proud of ourselves for getting the joke.

Conclusion: "A Noble Spirit Embiggens the Smallest Man"

In a cartoon universe that thrives on irony, satire, and endless subversion, there can be no heresy save an unreasonable dedication to convention. In Homer's world, and perhaps in our own, there is no longer a well-defined orthodoxy against which a meaningful heresy might be mounted. This does not diminish the fact that the Simpsons fulfill the important function of the sacred clowns—sustaining what is important by poking fun at religious conventions. What is important to believe and do, however, defies description. In keeping with the show's insight into the contemporary religious scene, there is a persistent message of a loss of institutional authority (although institutional practice and loyalty linger) coupled with diverse forms of personal and noninstitutional religiosity. In this light, the would-be "heretic" Homer fulfills the role of the American spiritual wanderer; though linked culturally (if unsteadily and unenthusiastically) to biblical tradition, he regularly engages a mosaic of other traditions, mythologies, and moral codes. In the face of these ever-shifting layers of meaning, he stumbles along, making the most of his limited understanding of their complexities. His comic antics remind us that the making of meaning (religious or otherwise) is ever an unfinished business, and that humor and irony go a long way toward sweetening and sustaining the endeavor.

Post-Script: The Hoary Heresy

In February of 2009 *The Simpsons* surpassed *Gunsmoke* as the longest-running prime-time series in American history. Well into its twentieth season, over 438 original episodes have been aired, and the show has won virtually every award given out by the television industry. Add to this a successful feature film, a wide-ranging Web presence, comic books, video games and toys, and *The Simpsons* arguably has as large and diverse a footprint in American popular culture as any television series in history. A generation of Americans has now grown up with the show, and it runs continuously in syndication around the world in over a dozen languages. Although rumors about cancellation have circulated for years and ratings have fluctuated, it has been renewed through 2011 and the principal cast members have signed contracts to continue their roles.

Our original intent with this chapter was to examine critically the religious dimensions of the show, particularly where these afforded insights into contemporary American religion. In doing so, we believe our efforts helped set the tone for subsequent writing about religion on the Simpsons. Over the past decade, other scholars, journalists, and even theologians have taken up the religious dimensions of the show. Probably the best known book-length study is Mark Pinsky's *The Gospel According to the Simpsons* (2001), which drew judiciously on our work in the first edition of *God in the Details*. More recently, other texts have argued for a "systematic theology" embedded in the show and promoted its use for pastoral purposes (Heit 2008). Some of our original insights are now dated—for example, the prime-time "taboo" against religious topics and characters found in content analyses of the 1980s lifted in subsequent decades. In part this was due to the expansion of cable networks, some of which began to pursue niche religious audiences. Another factor was the higher public profile of religion in American public life that corresponded to the political potency of conservative Protestantism. But certainly the innovative approach to religious topics developed by *The Simpsons'* creative teams deserves some credit for opening the door to more religious content on television. In our estimation, the show's "core religious values"—a playful mixture of subversive satire, irony and subtle affirmation—that emerged in the early seasons have been sustained. Thus our analysis of early-season favorites like "Homer the Heretic" and "Homer vs. Lisa and the

Eighth Commandment" resonates with religiously themed episodes in later seasons.

The show has continued to explore the religious lives of its main characters, and even some minor characters, in considerable depth. Usually this has involved forays into the varied dimensions of American Christianity. Episodes have looked at faith healing ("Faith Off"), missionary work ("Missionary Impossible"), apocalypticism ("Thank God Its Doomsday"), prayer ("Pray Anything"), and denominational switching ("The Father, the Son and the Holy Guest Star," aired 2005). The public debates about religion and its place in society—often identified as the "culture wars"—get regular airing on the show, including two episodes on the evolution debate ("Lisa the Skeptic" and "The Monkey Suit") and another on the rise of Christian theme parks ("I'm Goin' to Praiseland"). Of course, the most persistent religious dimension of the show has been the relationship between the Simpsons and their evangelical neighbor, Ned Flanders. Although Ned undergoes a significant crisis of faith in one episode ("Hurricane Neddy"), and loses his wife in another ("Alone Again, Natura-Didily"), his character typically is shown as a committed Christian, struggling to maintain his cheerfulness and ethical ideals in the face of the frequent taunts and tribulations perpetrated by his less devout neighbors. That he sustains his faith, more or less, throughout, perhaps helps explain the show's broad appeal. Shrewdly, its creators hit upon a formula that secular fans can read as sharp religious critique of narrow-minded scriptural literalism. At the same time Christian viewers (who have embraced Ned) can find parables of patience and forbearance.

In addition to its limning of the Christian mainstream, the Simpsons' spiritual curiosity often wanders down the varied paths of American religious pluralism. Noteworthy episodes include one where Lisa, upset at the "megachurching" of Springfield, adopts Buddhist ethics ("She of Little Faith"), and another in which Apu, owner of the local convenience store, gets married in a Hindu ceremony in the Simpsons' backyard ("The Two Mrs. Nahasapeemapetilons"). In "The Joy of Sect," the Simpsons join a cult called the Movementarians. Although ostensibly satirizing groups like Scientology and intentional communities like Rajneeshpuram, the episode simultaneously skewers mainstream misunderstanding and moral panic in response to new religions. Krusty the Clown, a rueful lapsed Jew in early seasons, finally becomes a bar mitzvah in season 15 ("Today I am a Clown"). Islam, perhaps the most challenging tradition for an American comedy show, finally gets a Simpsons treatment in 2008 ("Mypods and Broomsticks"). As the range of traditions covered has expanded, so has the criticism—often with the same ambiguity that we found in our survey of critics from the show's early years (these were mostly from Christian and Jewish writers). Thus, for example, Pinsky finds that while some American Hindus see Apu as an offensive stereotype and dislike the show's flagrant distortion of doctrinal issues, others recognize that the primary target of the show's satire is mainstream ignorance of Hindu traditions (Pinsky 2001, 128–29).

Why the persistent emphasis on religion and religious characters? Perhaps the obvious answer is the longevity of the show, which has afforded (even demanded) explorations of every facet of American culture, religion included. Add to this the economic advantages enjoyed by cartoons; one actor can voice multiple characters, hence the affordability of having lots of them, including the spiritually inclined. More qualitatively, why has the show maintained a relatively consistent tone in its treatment of religion? For all their mockery and satire, the creators seem genuinely affectionate toward their main characters and their spiritual striving. Our original essay argued that *The Simpsons'* humor, particularly its use of irony, was a strategic response to a sense of powerless and disenfranchisement that had crept in American life in the late twentieth century. Thus it was pitch-perfect for a media-saturated society whose religious sensibilities had strayed from traditional institutions, but not entirely disappeared. The George W. Bush-era assertiveness of "strong religion" notwithstanding, this ironic stance remains potent. By some measures, Americans waver and wander in their beliefs as much as ever, and institutionalized religions (alongside most other major social institutions) have suffered sharp declines in public confidence (Silver 2009). The recognition of this trend as a rich vein for comedy is among *The Simpsons'* greatest strengths—as invigorating today as it was innovative at the show's conception. Early on, its creative teams found their religious path, and, despite occasional twists and turns along the way, have kept the faith. Homer's spiritual pratfalls and confusions endure, in part, because they help leaven enduring anxieties about the eclectic and irresolute condition of American religious life.

References

Bastien, Joseph. 1987. "Humor and Satire." In *Encyclopedia of Religion,* ed. Mircea Eliade. New York: Macmillan.

Chesebro, James. 1979. "Communication, Values, and Popular Television Series – A Four-Year Assessment" In *Television: The Critical View,* 2d edn, ed. Horace Newcomb, 16–54. New York: Oxford University Press.

Christianity Today. 1992. "Prime-time Religion." 36 (March 9): 60.

Collum, Danny Duncan. 1991. " … Because He Made So Many of Them." *Sojourners* 20 (November): 38–39.

Corliss, Richard. 1994. "Simpsons Forever!" *Time* 143, 18 (May 2), 77.

Freeman, Michael. 1995. "The Official End (1994–95 Syndication Season Led by *The Simpsons*)." *Mediaweek* 5, 35 (September 18), 14.

Geertz, Clifford. 1973. "Religion as a Cultural System." In *The Interpretation of Cultures,* 87–125. San Francisco: Basic Books.

Goethals, Gregor. 1981. *The TV Ritual.* Boston: Beacon Press.

Greeley, Andrew. 1987. "Today's Morality Play: The Sitcom." *New York Times* (May 17), 1, 40 (Arts and Leisure).

Handelman, Don. 1987. "Clowns." In *Encyclopedia of Religion,* ed. Mircea Eliade. New York: Macmillan.

Heit, Jamey. 2008. *The Springfield Reformation: The Simpsons, Christianity, and American Culture.* New York: Continuum International.

Himmelstein, Hal. 1994. *Television Myth and the American Mind,* 2nd edn. Westport, CT: Praeger.

Lefton, Terry. 1992. "Don't Tell Mom: Fox Looks to a Degenerate Clown and a Violent Cat-and-Mouse Duo to Revitalize 'The Simpsons' Merchandise Sales." *Brandweek* 33 (August 10): 16–17.

McConnell, Frank. 1990. "'Real' Cartoon Characters: *The Simpsons.*" *Commonweal* 117 (June 15): 389–90.

Medved, Michael. 1992. *Hollywood vs. America: Popular Culture and the War on Traditional Values.* New York: HarperCollins.

Olive, David. 1992. *Political Babble: The 1,000 Dumbest Things Ever Said by Politicians.* New York: John Wiley and Sons.

Ozersky, Josh. 1991. "TV's Anti-Families: Married … with Malaise." *Tikkun* 6 (January/February): 11–14, 92–93.

Pinsky, Mark. 2001. *The Gospel According to the Simpsons: The Spiritual Life of the World's Most Animated Family.* Louisville: Westminster John Knox Press.

Rebeck, Victoria A. 1990. "Recognizing Ourselves in *The Simpsons*" *Christian Century* 107 (June 27): 622.

Richmond, Ray and Antonia Coffman, eds. 1997. *The Simpsons: A Complete Guide to Our Favorite Family.* New York: HarperCollins.

Riddle, Lyn. 1994. "A Rascal Cartoon Character Sets Off a Controversy in South Carolina." *Los Angeles Times* (March 1), A5.

Rosenthal, Andrew. 1992. "In a Speech, President Returns to Religious Themes." *New York Times* (January 28), A17.

Sekaquaptewa, Emory. 1989. "One More Smile for a Hopi Clown." In *I Become Part of It: Sacred Dimensions in Native American Life,* ed. D.M. Dooling and Paul Jordan-Smith. San Francisco: Harper San Francisco.

Silver, Nate. 2009. "American Losing Their Faith in Faith … And Everything Else." *FiveThirtyEight: Politics Done Right,* March 12. www.fivethirtyeight.com/2009/03/americans-losing-their-faith-in-faith.html

Skill, Thomas, James D. Robinson, John S. Lyons, and David Larson. 1994. "The Portrayal of Religion and Spirituality on Fictional Network Television." *Review of Religious Research* 35 (March): 251–67.

Wilde, Alan. 1981. *Horizons of Assent: Modernism, Postmodernism, and the Ironic Imagination.* Baltimore, MD: Johns Hopkins University Press.

Notes

1 Title names are taken from Richmond and Coffman (1997) and are rarely used on the air.

2 In February 1997, the program passed *The Flintstones* to become the longest running prime-time animated series.

3 See Richmond and Coffman (1997).

4 See Rosenthal (1992, A17). Writers for *The Simpsons* responded. In one episode Bart quips, "We're just like the Waltons. We're praying for the Depression to end, too." In another incident, Bush administration "drug czar" William Bennett noted he would "sit down with the little spikehead [Bart]" and "straighten this thing out." The show's producers replied: "If our drug czar thinks he can sit down and talk this out with a cartoon character, he must be on something" (Olive 1992, 61).

5 The American Family Association commissioned this study, often highlighting opinions compatible with its criticism of television programming. However, the article eventually appeared in a refereed journal. The study took place during the first year *The Simpsons* aired, and probably included several episodes in its sample. None of the explicitly religious episodes discussed here aired until 1991. There is little quantified research to challenge its basic findings (see *Christianity Today* 1992, 60).

6 Every device is used to obscure Springfield's location. The fact that *Father Knows Best* was located in a "Springfield" seems only to reinforce *The Simpsons'* contrasting image of traditional American television families.

7 Jackie Mason, who trained for the rabbinate before entering show business, provides the father's voice.

8 The comet disintegrates in the thick layer of smog permanently settled over the town, making Lovejoy's rantings that much more ridiculous. However, Ned's personal religiosity is redeemed; he selflessly offers his family's fallout shelter to the unprepared townspeople and leaves it when it fills beyond capacity. The shelter collapses just as everyone—moved by Ned's generosity and singing "*Que sera, sera*"—exits to face down the comet with him. Flanders has, in effect, saved the town twice: once by generosity and once by selfless example, both motivated by his religious sensibilities.

9 This scene inspired Michael Medved's criticism noted above.

Part IV

Popular "Churches"

Polls show that most Americans consider themselves either religious or spiritual (and occasionally both), but more and more are likely to mix and match religious ideas and practices, while fewer are likely to spend their entire lives within one religious tradition. A 2009 Pew study, in fact, found that 44 per cent of Americans no longer belong to their childhood religious faith tradition. This phenomenon has its roots in a variety of factors, including the level of freedom with which Americans may select among religions with minimal social repercussions (see Hammond, *Religion and Personal Autonomy*, 1992; Roger Finke and Rodney Stark, *The Churching of America*, 1776–1990, 1992). But also instrumental has been the breakdown of the monopoly enjoyed by religious institutions in contemporary culture. Wade Clark Roof (*A Generation of Seekers*, 1993) argues that more and more people—particularly those born since the beginning of the "baby boom" generation—prefer experimenting with religion/spirituality, and as a result are often seen as less loyal to the religious communities of their birth.

This freedom to move among religions according to one's conscience has produced a culture in which people are not only increasingly mobile among religious traditions, but also increasingly nontraditional. Younger Americans, especially, are increasingly likely to satisfy their religious/spiritual needs in unconventional ways. Because of the lessons they learned from observing their parents' and grandparents' generations, many now do not feel a need to go to churches or other religious institutions to get whatever it was that they might have gotten there. And because of a variety of cultural events in their collective memories, from Vietnam to the public disgrace of high-profile Christian leaders, they often don't trust institutions—religious or otherwise—to serve them anyway.

This does not mean that religious institutions are useless, but that they apparently have lost their monopoly in the construction and maintenance of meaning and community in contemporary America. Feeling a need to congregate but a suspicion toward institutions, many Americans reconstitute their own popular "churches" that provide those elements once monopolized by the church. Whether it is in a message from Jimmy Buffett or a hip-hop artist, in a virtual community or a celluloid one, many people have relocated their religious impulses and come together in seemingly nonreligious settings that serve them in a seemingly religious capacity.

The chapters in this section share this theme of distancing from traditional religious institutions. In some cases, it may take the form of suspicion of—or disdain for—familiar cultural institutions that no longer reflect the community. Robin Sylvan, exploring the spiritual implications of rap and hip-hop (Chapter 15), notes the difficult economic and social conditions from which many of the artists emerged. He argues that the music runs "directly counter to the religious world view of the mainstream culture it has come to permeate" and that it "refuses to take refuge in the hope of otherworldly salvation." Painfully direct and grounded in the lives of its performers, hip-hop communicates ancient styles and symbols in a new, often anti-institutional venue. Representing an entirely different world, Julie Ingersoll (Chapter 13) examines "parrotheads" and identifies an anti-religious people who are quasi-institutional in their desire for community, ritual, mythology, and meaning found at Jimmy Buffett concerts. Ingersoll concludes that they are "irreverent toward institutional religion and yet often draw analogies between the way Buffett philosophy shapes their views of the world and 'spirituality'."

In other cases, distance can be created symbolically rather than by suspicion, and can result in parallel institutions that, intentionally or unintentionally, replace institutions like the church. For example, Rachel Wagner (Chapter 14) details the diverse and intricate forms of religious activity available in the online virtual community *Second Life*, where one can attend an Anglican service, visit a Mayan temple, or listen to a dharma talk from a virtual Buddhist monk. Wagner argues that the quality of such religious experiences, and the religious aspects of participation in *Second Life* itself, raise challenges for our understanding of some basic religious studies category lines—sacred and profane; real and unreal. In the process, she says, *Second Life* highlights "the constructed nature of all religion" and the "element of play that always has been part of religious life."

Eric Mazur and Tara Koda (Chapter 16) argue that the Walt Disney Company, with its product line of symbols and its mass marketing of meaning, is unintentionally competing with traditional religious institutions. Rather than labeling Disney a religion, Mazur and Koda argue that, because of the shifting role of religious institutions in America, "Disney's products ... fill many of the roles often filled by religion." In a culture where religious/ spiritual needs can be met outside of religious institutions, cyberspace and Disney seem acceptable providers for the religious/spiritual needs of their consumers.

The possibility that institutions can earn a profit in the religious world illustrates another powerful—and seemingly inevitable—element of the popular "churches": commercialism. Three of the four following chapters describe experiences based on a commercial exchange—the production and distribution of music, attendance at a concert, or admission to a theme park or theater. And although salvation always has a price—your soul, your heart, or your wallet—these popular "churches" distinguish customers from bystanders (in what Mazur and Koda call the "religification" of a commodity). All are welcome at a Buffett concert or at Walt Disney World, as long as they pay for admission. In the world of rap and hip-hop, the commercial conditions that produced the experience—economic hardship—still provide an important backdrop against which the art form has developed. Without money to record and distribute the message, or to buy and play the CD, one cannot participate fully. Even in the case of *Second Life*, one needs at least the wherewithal to access the internet. With the price of salvation measured in dollars rather than piety, class must surely play a part in the popular "churches." As Ingersoll notes, parrotheads are "predominantly middle and upper middle class" and "invariably white"; Mazur and Koda point out that Disney is not much more diverse. However, participation in either Jimmy Buffett's world or Walt Disney World is not explicitly restricted to those groups, and the attraction of rap and hip-hop to the larger non-African American population has made it one of the most powerful movements in contemporary music. And as anyone knows who has ventured online, in cyberspace no one needs to know what you look like. Anyone who plays by the rules can participate.

The commercial and seemingly egalitarian qualities of many popular "churches" can mask the fact that more than economics is at the heart of these alternative institutions. Though the ideology is grounded in consumerism, it can still provide meaning in a commercialized world. These quasi-religious institutions combine elements of ritual, myth, morality, and spirituality, and provide instruction that is transforming, prescriptive, and elevating for participants. The world view that they provide often appears this-worldly, narcissistic, and manipulated for the financial benefit of the corporation. But as Mazur and Koda point out, it is pervasive, in tune with the times, and even satisfying to those who accept it, even if it isn't necessarily consistent with traditional religious ideology.

In the end, we are left with the impression that these popular "churches" are not altogether different from traditional churches, though they complicate many conventional conceptions of collective religious life. The significance here is not that the popular "churches" are unlike anything ever seen, but rather that they are consistent with social patterns for relocating the religious impulse. As we noted earlier, everything connected with the search for meaning is ripe for comparison with those elements usually reserved for institutional religion. This includes the act of institutionalization, and as the following chapters show, John Calvin's notion—that the "visible church" is different from the "invisible church" of the saved—has not been abandoned, but instead has been reapplied by those searching in new places for their own salvationary community.

Chapter 13

The Thin Line between Saturday Night and Sunday Morning

Meaning and Community among Jimmy Buffett's Parrotheads

Julie J. Ingersoll

The sea of people dressed in brightly colored clothes surrounds me as I walk the rows between the thousands of cars. Lyrics from different Jimmy Buffett songs blend together as I move out of range of one stereo system and into another. Everyone I pass is singing one song or another. But the parking lot partiers wearing beach clothes and tropical attire are not as surprising as the makeshift beaches, portable resorts, and volcanic islands they have brought with them. More than one group of cars has parked in such a way as to leave room for the sand they brought with them in pickup trucks. On the mounds of sand they have set up beach chairs and blankets, beach balls, and other inflatable toys. There is even a volleyball net.

One group of parrotheads[1] has rented a flatbed to transport a generator that provides energy for the Jacuzzi that bubbles and steams beneath the group's *papier-maché* palm trees. Another parrothead club has set up an island-themed bar complete with a pencil-thin mustached bartender (in a Ricky Ricardo jacket) and blenders for the frozen margaritas that members share with passers-by. And finally—my favorite—an enormous volcano has been erected in the center of the parking lot; the attached parrotheads in Hawaiian shirts and grass skirts sing, "I don't know, I don't know, I don't know where I'm gonna go when the volcano blows ... "

The party was held at Irvine Meadows Amphitheater in the fall of 1995. The annual Irvine Buffett Shows run for two nights each year, and (at least according to parrothead lore) this is one of the biggest parking lot parties at any of the shows. It starts about noon on Friday and runs until the wee hours of Sunday morning, when the last of the long line of cars drives out of the lot.[2]

While one might be surprised at the level of creativity here, on the surface, at least, this is pretty much what one would probably expect of fans of Jimmy Buffett, whose two best-known songs are "[Wasted Away Again in] Margaritaville," and "Cheeseburger in Paradise." There's no seriousness here; and if there is anything resembling religion it is just pure unadulterated hedonism, right?

The rationale for a religious analysis of parrothead life[3] is unlike the typical rationale for scholarly undertaking; interest in the topic cannot be attributed to its uniqueness. On the contrary, this topic is academically interesting because it clearly illustrates an under-recognized influence of "religion" in our everyday world. Two basic questions frame this inquiry. First, in this apparently irreligious phenomenon, how many parallels with aspects of traditional religions can we find? And second, can our positing this seemingly irreligious phenomenon as "religion" give us theoretical insight into questions about the nature of religion and its role in modern "secular" society?

The Parrotheads

According to the *60 Minutes* interview that aired on May 11, 1997, Buffett had 30 concert dates scheduled for the season—all of which sold out—with more than one million people attending his shows annually. Buffett himself has called the parrotheads cult-like (in an affectionate sort of way).[4] Many parrotheads know the words to all his songs—and since playlists are readily available on the World Wide Web well before the shows, pretty much everyone in the audience knows the lyrics to each of the songs played at any given

Figure 13.1 A typical parrothead at a pre-concert party in Nashville, February 1999. Photo by Wanda Stewart.

show. It is not unusual for the fans to drown out the band in their "hymn" singing.

Perhaps most surprising, though, is the broad age span of fans. Parrotheads range in age from children of seven or eight years old to retired folks. I sat next to a couple in their sixties (in lawn seats, no less) at their first show in San Francisco two years ago. I have played guess-the-song lyrics with a nine-year-old (and nearly lost), and I have had a critical mass of self-described parrotheads in several of the undergraduate courses I have taught. While parrotheads include people of all levels of education and economic status (I know at least three religious studies PhDs who consider themselves part of the phlock[5]), they are predominantly middle and upper middle class. The sociological characteristic that seems most constant among them is race: they are invariably white.

The Antireligious Stance of Buffett, His Music, and His Fans

By all accounts Jimmy Buffett has led a life that flouts traditional religious sensibilities.[6] He glorifies sex and drugs, he seemingly advocates irresponsibility in the name of freedom, and he openly derides traditional religion. In one of many possible examples, on one album this former Catholic altar boy sings: "Religion, religion. Oh there's a thin line between Saturday night and Sunday morning." Poking fun at both Catholics and Protestants, the same song from the *Fruitcakes* album goes on to include the "Mea Culpa" and then to lampoon the simple-mindedness of televangelists. As Buffett puts it, "Religion's in the hands of some crazy ass people" (Buffett 1994).[7]

On another album he parodies the "Seven Deadly Sins" (Buffett 1995), while an older album includes a song titled "My Head Hurts, My Feet Stink, and I Don't Love Jesus" (Buffett 1976a). In another example, this self-proclaimed Calypso poet tells us more than we may want to know when he sings about his aversion to church, haircuts, and underwear (Buffett 1976b).

Parrotheads are equally irreverent toward institutional religion, and yet often draw analogies between the way Buffett philosophy shapes their views of the world and "spirituality."

Parallels between Parrotheadism and Traditional Religion

Despite its irreverent tone and occasional hostility toward religion, there are many ways in which parrotheadism functions in the lives of Buffett fans that parallel aspects of traditional religion.[8]

The first parallel, which helps make sense of many of the others, is the parrotheads' notions of utopian paradise. Parrotheads are considered citizens of Margaritaville. (Before performing the hit song "[Wasted Away Again in] Margaritaville," Buffett often begins: "Please rise for the national anthem.") A website titled "Bubba [a nickname for Jimmy] for Beginners" includes a

"Survival Guide for New Parrotheads /or/ Where is Margaritaville Anyway?"

> So, where IS Margaritaville, anyway?! Well, that's a tough one to answer. For some it's a paradise island in the Caribbean; for others it's a powder white beach along the Yucatan; and for some, sleeping along a gentle river as their rod bends at a biting fish. It's as much a state of mind as anything.[9]

Margaritaville is the community of parrotheads that is not geographically bound. It exists across space and time in the hearts and minds of Buffett followers. These parrotheads measure the here and now against their conception of mythic sacred space: a tropical island and a sailboat; a world characterized by freedom, good friends, and time to play (fishing and flying, especially). This is not escapism. On the contrary, parrotheads strive to make this paradise part of their everyday lives, and look upon those who put off the enjoyment of life in favor of drive and ambition with derision as, at best, hopelessly misguided or, at worst, lacking in real humanity. Many Buffett songs celebrate this orientation toward life, but one that lays it out most clearly is Buffett's 1978 "Cowboy in the Jungle." It talks about out-of-place tourists who "try to cram lost years into five or six days" because it "seems that blind ambition erased their intuition" (Buffett 1978).

Forget suburban homes. Even trailers are a bit too pedestrian in Buffett ideals. In "Migration" (1974a), Buffett worries about the mobile homes that were "smothering" the Florida Keys. Wishing a storm would blow them up to the "fantasy land" of Orlando, he concludes that all that metal would look better as beer cans.

For parrotheads, the limits to our ability to live in this mythic paradise (sin) are our materialism and lack of appreciation for the simple things in life. "Life Is Just a Tire Swing," Buffett sings in one song of the same name (1974b), while in another he longs for the days before he put "quarters in his [penny] loafers" (1983a). And he confesses: "Now times are rough and I've got too much stuff" (1983b), and critiques a world overrun by self-storage units and lacking in poets. But sacred space does exist in real time, and not just as mythic imaginings of Buffett and his flock of parrots. New Orleans, Louisiana, and Key West, Florida, are two places that have had a great impact on Buffett and his music, and these places loom large in the minds of parrotheads; many have visited the sacred sites and many more long to do so. When devotees pull out a photo album of their travels to Buffett shows, the albums often also include pictures from trips to either of these pilgrimage sites.

Recreational use of alcohol and drugs is celebrated and elevated to the point of ritual that transports parrotheads from their everyday existence.

Other ritual aspects include an annual pilgrimage to shows and participation in the preconcert gatherings. The Head Parrot himself has pointed to the ritual aspect of the events: "It's a tribal celebration—a rite of summer passage no different than the kinds of parties thrown by our primitive relatives in the cave days."[10] Sacred time is marked off from profane time as parrotheads participate in the madness surrounding a show. According to Buffett's interpretation, "They transform into Parrotheads ... they come to the show with their own personal Mardi Gras attached to them." They have "their feeding frenzy [a song reference] and return to normal life."

Just as Mardi Gras precedes Lent, the preshow party prepares devotees for the transcendent experience to come. There is a revival-like atmosphere inside the concert venue, in which concertgoers sing lyrics to songs, many of which they consider profoundly poetic and meaningful. When Buffett sings about a friend of his who, upon reaching the age of 40, reflects on somber realizations of midlife in "A Pirate Looks at Forty" (which he performs at every show now), it is not at all uncommon to see middle-aged men, eyes closed, sitting and quietly singing along. I have even seen them join hands and sway together in what seems clearly to be a shared experience of something transcendent.

On a website that asked parrotheads to write on the topic "Why I Love Jimmy Buffett Music," fans posted comments that sounded decidedly like descriptions of mystical experiences. One said that "Jimmy's music is a drug; the best kind of drug." Another wrote, "His music is medicine for my mind. It clears out all the stress and anxiety. He takes us to our own Margaritaville ... He gives me my only peace of mind ... My world revolves around his music. I've left the planet for a minute."

At least two contributors to this site actually made the comparison between Buffett and the transcendent. One noted that he loved Buffett's music because "he [Buffett] makes life seem not so threatening ... he's like a god because he creates parrotheads wherever he goes." Another wrote, "Jimmy knows how to spell life out in simple terms. What he writes about is [sic] those issues that we all have to deal with on a daily basis. If I thought god had a brother it would be Jimmy for sure. He speaks the Truth!"[11]

But most parrotheads would see Buffett as more of a prophet than a savior, a religious leader rather than a god. Buffett espouses a philosophy of life and a value system[12] that parrotheads are drawn to, but the community of parrotheads has taken on a life of its own. The clearest way to illustrate this is to point to the concert/preconcert party experience. While the concert is the ostensible reason for gathering, in many ways the real event is the preconcert party. I have been to shows where the venue officials squelched the preconcert party by opening the parking lot only a couple of hours before the show and by prohibiting (and enforcing the prohibition of) barbecue grills and alcoholic beverages there. The atmosphere at such shows is decidedly different.

Irvine Meadows, on the other hand, seems to encourage the parrothead gathering. According to parrotheads, a key official at that venue is a member of the phlock—and indeed, I have seen a parking lot security cart (resembling a golf cart) decorated with crepe paper and parrots, cruising the aisles of cars and parking lot partiers. Parrotheads who don't manage to get tickets to the Irvine show sometimes come to the parking lot party anyway. They often do manage to buy tickets from someone once they are there, but I have heard people say that if they didn't get into the show, the party itself was worth coming for. In some ways, the show itself is just the icing on the cake. Parrotheads gather to renew old friendships; to sing and dance; to drink margaritas, rum drinks, and Coronas; and to renew their Caribbean souls. Then they go to the show.

And while Buffett lampoons traditional religion, the fact that he sees the mythic element to his work is made clear with his dedication of the album *Off to See the Lizard* to Joseph Campbell. A song line specifically refers to a comment made by Campbell to Bill Moyers. Campbell told Moyers that he pitied people with "no invisible means of support," a phrase that became a line in a Buffett song.[13]

But there are more parallels between parrotheadism and traditional religion than these philosophical, mystical, and ritual comparisons. There is also a sociological similarity in terms of the way membership as a parrothead contributes to both an individual sense of identity and a sense of community. As explained earlier, a group of parrotheads is referred to as a flock (phlock), and while the intended reference is clearly to a flock of birds, in the case of the argument at hand it is notable that the term "flock" also commonly refers to the members of a church congregation. One has to wonder if the multiple meanings might not be intentional. Parrotheads make friends at concerts and meet up again with the same people year after year, but they also connect with each other in a nationwide network of parrothead clubs and a multitude of websites and chat rooms on the internet.

Parrotheads in Paradise is the officially recognized club network, which in 1995 boasted 15,000 members in 81 clubs.[14] The network's annual convention, called "The Meeting of the Minds," drew 750 participants in that same year. Clubs typically meet on a monthly basis for "fellowship" (their term) and to work on the ongoing community service and environmental projects they undertake. According to *Coconut Telegraph*, the national club newsletter, "Civic minded parrotheads in cities across the country have voluntarily gathered under the Buffett banner to promote peace, justice and the American way." Clubs have provided volunteers for the Red Cross, UNICEF, and the Children's Wish Foundation. They have organized to help flood victims, participated in "adopt-a-highway" programs, and joined environmental cleanup efforts. According to local club newsletters, a parrothead club in Massachusetts organized a Special Olympics, and the Left

Coast Parrotheads in Southern California work for Habitat for Humanity and the area's Ronald McDonald House.[15]

Parrothead club members not only meet regularly during the year, but also have special events, including concert trips, camping trips, and fishing trips. One northern California couple invited parrothead friends from around the country to their parrot-themed wedding.

But Buffett fans also connect with one another over the internet. There are innumerable websites, but one in particular seems most suited for discussion in this paper. The Church of Buffett, Orthodox invites visitors with this greeting: "All ye faithful believers enter our hallowed halls. Those who believe in Jimmy Buffett the musician, not Jimmy Buffett the entertainer ... Please, kick the dust off your sandals and enter these holy pages by clicking on the menu."[16]

While most parrotheads consider their sacred text to be the entire canon of Buffett lyrics, the Church of Buffett, Orthodox argues that the "revered chief poet" has succumbed to the influence of commercialism and that his music has suffered. They mark *Changes in Latitudes, Changes in Attitudes* as the turning point, with some including it in the "holy writ" (their term) and others not. In particular they label "Margaritaville" as "apostasy."

Counterculture or Mainstream?

The Church of Buffett, Orthodox is the prophetic voice in Margaritaville calling the parrotheads (and the Head Parrot) to be faithful to the anti-materialism of Buffett philosophy, calling them to be mindful of what they trade for their material success. But the larger segment of parrotheads looks a lot like the rest of the American middle class. They are lawyers, corporate employees, entrepreneurs, nurses, and teachers.

A quick look around the parking lot party confirms this social and economic status of the parrotheads. There are few BMWs and Mercedes (even at a southern California concert), but there are also very few older cars. Parrotheads drive Hondas and Toyotas; they drive late-model small pickups and sport utility vehicles. Many own expensive motor homes in which they travel to Buffett shows (which is not easily done without some financial means). Also, the annual trek many parrotheads make to the Meeting of the Minds in New Orleans, as well as the trips to the Caribbean and Key West, also indicate a certain degree of financial stability.

Parrotheads' position in the middle class is nowhere more clear than in the social service/reform efforts of the parrothead clubs. Members who have logged sufficient participation in these activities get first crack at concert tickets (which can often be hard to get, as the shows sometimes sell out in the first few hours of ticket sales).

Voluntary societies that work to help victims of tragedy, bring joy to terminally ill children, and build houses for the poor (and most recently to preserve the environment) are quintessentially of the American middle class.

Voluntarism, as we know it, developed concurrently with the middle class in the nineteenth century. The willingness to organize to "better the lot of the less fortunate" was a badge of social status that came with material success sufficient to allow time for such activities (Albanese 1992, 402–24; Roof and McKinney 1987, 40–71).

Yet parrotheads revere those who would make themselves free by throwing away the trappings of materialism and wealth. They recognize that out-of-control consumption in our society diminishes freedom, but, by all appearances, they join enthusiastically in America's acquisitiveness. Buffett himself is a case in point. A man of tremendous wealth, Buffett owns boats, planes, and real estate; he does not live the vagabond lifestyle about which he sings. While in many ways parrotheads put forth an incisive critique of the values embraced by the American middle class, in other ways they embrace those values.

So what can we make of this paradox? Are the parrotheads merely idealizing one value system and living an opposing one? Are they insincere? Are they hypocrites? Or is there something more going on here? Our positing parrotheadism as a religion raises parrothead activities to the level of ritual, and points us to Victor Turner's work on ritual to explain how we might be able to take seriously both sides of this paradox.

In his seminal work *The Ritual Process* (Turner [1969] 1995, especially "Liminality and Communitas," 94ff), Turner explores various dimensions and characteristics of ritual. He writes, specifically, about liminality and *communitas* as they function—and are created—in rites of passage, but his observations also fit well the parrothead ritual attached to the annual pilgrimage to a Buffett show, and help to explain how parrothead values make sense in the context of the realities of parrothead lives.

With concert ritual, parrotheads detach from their everyday lives. They enter what Turner calls a liminal stage. And finally they are reincorporated into the structure of their old lives, but exist in that structure in a new way.

The detachment consists of shedding the order and reserve of their everyday lives (what Turner calls "structure"): making preparations, including buying tickets, planning costumes, decorating the car, and making the trip. Such detachment is the precursor to the liminal phase, in which the transformation of character takes place. Turner points to the ways in which the liminal phase creates an "intense comradeship and egalitarianism," where "distinctions of rank and status disappear or are homogenized" (*ibid.*, 95). (It is hard to tell a doctor from an electrician when both are barefoot on a portable "beach" wearing straw hats and Hawaiian shirts and drinking shots of tequila.)

It is in the egalitarian moment, according to Turner, that *communitas* emerges: "communitas emerges where social structure is not" (*ibid.*, 126). Turner even points to the paradox of *communitas* and structure existing side by side:

It is as though there are here two major "models" for human inter-
relatedness, juxtaposed and alternating. The first is of society as a
structured, differentiated, and often hierarchical system of politico-legal-
economic positions with many types of evaluation, separating men in
terms of "more" or "less." The second, which emerges recognizably in
the liminal period, is of society as an unstructured or rudimentarily
structured and relatively undifferentiated comitatus, community, or even
communion of equal individuals.

(*ibid.*, 96)

Turner then goes on to apply the label "communitas" to this second type of
community. He explains that the egalitarian values espoused as part of the
ritual process are carried back into the structure to maintain a tension
between hierarchy and egalitarianism in the larger society: "There is a dialectic here, for the immediacy of communitas gives way to the mediacy of
structure ... Men are released from structure into communitas only to return
to structure revitalized by their experience of communitas" (*ibid.*, 129).

Turner's focus is on the value of this dialectic for society as a whole; he
goes so far as to argue that no society can function adequately without it
(*ibid.*, 129). But what does this process mean for the individual? How are
parrotheads transformed when they make their pilgrimage from their
middle-class lives, through the "carnival" that is a Buffett concert, and
back again? Instead of one competing value system undermining the other
(middle-class consumption versus anti-materialist freedom), the ritual process actually allows the competing value systems to exist in creative tension
with each other. Parrotheads may dream of giving it all up to live on a sailboat in the islands, but parrothead ritual gives them just enough time in that
"one particular harbor" to allow them to keep it all together in the structure
of the real world. They can keep the vision of Margaritaville alive in their
hearts and minds while living their lives in Los Angeles, New York, or Cin-
cinnati. And the nongeographical utopia has an added advantage over the
geographical one: it can more readily survive the forces of history.

A Return to our Initial Theoretical Questions

Granted, many of the analogies to religion, drawn by Buffett and the parrotheads themselves, are made as tongue-in-cheek remarks; they are drawn
with irony and a sense of humor. But I contend that they make sense, and
indeed are funny, only because there is more to them than the irony alone.
So how does our playing with categories of religion and applying them to a
seemingly irreligious phenomenon aid us in the study of religion?

First, this examination shows us something important about an issue that
has occupied sociologists of religion in recent years. Proponents of secularization theories have posited the "decline of religion" coinciding with the rise

of modernity. According to secularizationists, in an older society where a single religious tradition dominated, the plausibility of that tradition was maintained by the fact that most everyone in the society subscribed to it. With modernity has come increasing exposure to a plurality of world views that has, in turn, undermined the plausibility structures of these once-dominant religions.

Critics of this theory point to several apparent flaws. First, they note the vitality of religion in North America, where a significant degree of pluralism and religious competition has been the norm. Second, they call attention to the worldwide increase in conservative religiopolitical movements (often called fundamentalisms). Third, they argue that new religious movements are flourishing. Fourth, and probably greatest in significance, they point to the rise of what people prefer to call "spirituality" (personalized, individualized religion).

They argue that religion hasn't declined; it has been reshaped, and may no longer be recognizable to those who define "religion" in terms of churches and other institutions. Most recently, they have focused on whether this increased individualism is a thing to be mourned or celebrated. "Sheila," a research subject who appeared in *Habits of the Heart* (Bellah *et al.* 1985), has become the classic example of individualism run rampant as she coined her own term for her individual personal religion, "Sheilaism." Bellah and his colleagues expressed their concern over our society's loss of a sense of community (plausibility structure). Wade Clark Roof, on the other hand, has celebrated the diversity and creativity he found in the often individualistic "spirituality" of his research subjects in *A Generation of Seekers* (Roof 1993). He concludes that the renewed emphasis on "spirituality" in the 1990s is actually a more "mature expression" of "the quest for a spiritual style" that took hold of baby boomers nearly three decades ago (*ibid.*, 242). Roof sees this new spirituality as being sophisticated in its grappling with questions of meaning and its embracing of the multi-layeredness of belief and practice. He is hopeful about the ways in which he sees this new spirituality embracing authentic pluralism, calling people to live as transformed individuals while at the same time committed to a new sense of community.

Secularizationists have rejoined the debate, asserting that their theory had been mischaracterized, and that what was meant in the phrase "decline of religion" was a decline of the cultural authority of religious institutions; that the decline predicted by secularization theory in no way refers to the elimination of religious sensibilities altogether (Yamane 1997). If these latest contributions to the debate by secularizationists are correct, then what we have is merely a disagreement of the definition of secularization, with both sides agreeing that religion (outside of institutions) may still be thriving.

The case of Jimmy Buffett's parrotheads adds to the discussion of the role of religion in contemporary American life because, as we have seen, parrotheadism is not merely an individual phenomenon; it has a profoundly communal character. It is precisely the transcendent sense parrotheads have of being connected to something bigger than themselves that gives meaning to this experience. There are probably many people who buy Jimmy Buffett CDs, and even attend a concert or two, who never make the move to identifying themselves with the collectivity.[17] Being a parrothead is, by definition, seeking to align yourself with others who connect with Buffett's music and philosophy in a similar way. We may not have to choose, theoretically, between seeing religion as institutionally focused and seeing it as individually focused. It seems there may be a third form of religion and religious experience that is nontraditional, noninstitutional, but at the same time shared and communal.[18]

The second theoretical consideration that is illuminated by this examination engages an older debate in religious studies over the very nature of religion. Often scholars have focused on religion and asked if there was something about the religious experience that drew people to it. The question has made religion seem to be a "thing" out there that automatically attracted adherents. I would propose that an examination of the religiosity of a particular group of music fans such as this one shows us that this traditional framing of the question misses the mark. What we have, it seems, is not necessarily something essentially religious that draws people in, but something essentially human that makes them seek it, whatever its form.

Essential human needs for meaning, purpose, ritual, community, and "transcendent" experience (in which I include any experience that satisfies our need to feel a part of something bigger than ourselves, whether it is an Eastern mystical oneness with the universe or Christian communion), have been met in different ways in different societies. Most recently in the West, those needs have been met by institutional religion. For this reason, institutional religion has functioned as our benchmark. However, these needs are so essentially human that human beings will always find ways to fulfill them. Parrotheads, who live in a secular world in which institutional religion has lost its cultural clout, and which is imbued with skeptical cynicism about institutions generally, will create a sense of community where they find the necessary tools to do so. Let me close with a parrothead benediction from Buffett's "Growing Older but Not Up" (1980) that might serve as that community's motto: "I'd rather die while I'm livin' than live while I'm dead."

References

Albanese, Catherine L. 1992. *America: Religions and Religion*, 2nd edn. Belmont, CA: Wadsworth.

Bellah, Robert N., Richard Madsen, William M. Sullivan, Ann Swidler, and Steven M. Tipton. 1985. *Habits of the Heart: Individualism and Commitment in American Life*. Berkeley: University of California Press.

Buffett, Jimmy. 1974a. "Migration." *A1A*. MCA Records.

——. 1974b. "Life is Just a Tire Swing." *A1A*. MCA Records.

——. 1976a. "My Head Hurts, My Feet Stink, and I Don't Love Jesus." *Havana Daydreamin'*. MCA Records.

——. 1976b. "Pencil Thin Mustache." *Livin' and Dyin' in 3/4 Time*. MCA Records.

——. 1978. "Cowboy in the Jungle." *Son of a Son of a Sailor*. MCA Records.

——. 1980. "Growing Older but Not Up." *Coconut Telegraph*. MCA Records.

——. 1983a. "One Particular Harbour." *One Particular Harbour*. MCA Records.

——. 1983b. "We Are the People Our Parents Warned Us About." *One Particular Harbour*. MCA Records.

——. 1994. "Fruitcakes." *Fruitcakes*. MCA Records.

——. 1995. "Bank of Bad Habits." *Barometer Soup*. Margaritaville Records.

——. 1998. *Jimmy Buffett: A Pirate Looks at Fifty*. New York: Random House.

Roof, Wade Clark. 1993. *A Generation of Seekers: The Spiritual Journeys of the Baby Boom Generation*. San Francisco: HarperCollins.

Roof, Wade Clark and William McKinney. 1987. *American Mainline Religion*. New Brunswick, NJ: Rutgers University Press.

Turner, Victor W. [1969] 1995. *The Ritual Process*. Hawthorne, NY: Walter de Gruyter.

Yamane, David. 1997. "Secularization on Trial." *Journal for the Scientific Study of Religion* 36, 1 (March): 109–22.

Notes

1 The label "parrotheads" refers to fans of musician Jimmy Buffett. As with most aspects of these folk, there is no uniformity in the appellation; it is written as Parrot Head, Parrothead, parrot head, or parrothead. I have opted, for the most part, to use the latter, but when citing someone else's use of the term (or the name of a club, for instance) I have retained the form used.

2 The data for the above description and the material that follows were gathered over the course of many years of participant observation. Having been a parrothead myself for nearly 25 years, I have attended 11 shows in six venues, visited Margaritaville in New Orleans, Louisiana, several times, and am a member of the Left Coast Parrot Heads. I wish to thank Jon Reese of Santa Barbara, California, for his assistance with song lyrics and citations, and Rasa Lemmond, a religious studies major at Millsaps College in Jackson, Mississippi, for her help with research and analysis.

3 While Buffett himself, as "Head Parrot," and the lyrics of his songs are discussed insofar as they are relevant, the focus of the paper is specifically on the culture of the parrotheads.

4 "Parrot Head Phenomenon," https://www.msu.edu/~gibbensr/jimmy/phenom.htm (originally at http://pilot.msu.edu/user/gibbensr/jimmy.phenom.htm).

5 Birds commonly travel in flocks, and parrotheads often exchange an "f" at the beginning of a word with a "ph" (parrothead). Thus, a group of parrotheads is referred to as a phlock.

6 Born Christmas Day in 1946 (Pascagoula, Mississippi), Buffett was raised as a Catholic—a tradition he resoundingly rejected. His first album, *Down to Earth* (1970), included three songs highly critical of religion and religious people whom he saw as hypocritical ("The Christian," "The Missionary," and "Truck Stop Salvation").

7 Copyright restrictions forbid lengthier use of lyrics.

8 www.cobo.org/about/index.html. I first saw the term "parrotheadism" on the Web page for the Church of Buffett, Orthodox, which is discussed later in this chapter. (Originally at www.homecom.com/mhall/cobo/aboutbct.html)

9 http://galenalink.com/~parrothd/buffettBubba.htm (9/12/97; this page no longer exists).

10 "Feeding Frenzy," interview with Buffett, www.msu.edu/~gibbensr/jimmy/feeding.htm (originally at http://pilot.msu.edu/user/gibbensr/jimmy/feeding.htm).

11 www.suresite.com/cgi-bin/WebX.cgi?l3@2I0@.ee6bcOf (7/16/97; this page no longer exists).

12 This philosophy of life and value system are perhaps most clearly spelled out in Buffett's (1998) autobiographical bestseller, written as he reached his fiftieth birthday, *Jimmy Buffett: A Pirate Looks at Fifty.* (The book title is a reference to his much loved song, "A Pirate Looks at Forty.") It is also readily apparent in song lyrics too numerous to reproduce here.

13 Taken from a list of literary references found in Buffett's work on a parrotheads Web page: http://homecom.com/cobo/FAQ/litrefs.html#1 (9/11/97; this page no longer exists).

14 By 2009, these numbers had grown to 237 chapters in the United States, Canada, and Australia, and a membership of more than 26,000.

15 In the nineteenth century, the rise of the middle class was marked by an increase in social "do-gooder" societies. Catherine Albanese has argued that the "moralism" that gave rise to the volunteerism was (and is) a central component of American civil religion (Albanese 1992).

16 www.homecom.com/mhall/cobo/ (9/11/97; this page no longer exists).

17 Actually, articles in magazine such as *High Times* and *Rolling Stone* belie this point and argue that Buffett's following is relatively small, but so loyal that it will snap up any record he makes (or novel he writes). This is interesting and, if true, would bolster my argument, but I do not have the resources to evaluate its accuracy.

18 I am not claiming that this finding is opposite those of Bellah or Roof. It is merely a refocusing on a different aspect of the various forms of religion uncovered by these and other researchers.

Chapter 14

Our Lady of Persistent Liminality

Virtual Church, Cyberspace, and *Second Life*

Rachel Wagner

Can someone desecrate a virtual church? Is it possible to commit a "virtual" sin? Who would have thought, a few decades ago, that we'd ask what it means to "really" perform a religious ritual, or whether we need our bodies to do so? But given the recent proliferation of deeply immersive online experiences, these are exactly the questions we now ask. In the online virtual community *Second Life*, for example, one can find a "Catholic" church run by a nonpriest in priest's digital garb, and people attending (and even sleeping through) services; a real-life Buddhist monk spreading the dharma; a replica of a Mayan temple with a real-life donation feature; and recently, a "prim" (a digital representation of a piece of wood, manufactured randomly) that some claim displays a miraculous image of the Virgin Mary. Clearly, there is religion in *Second Life*. But what kind of religion is it?

In 2006, I co-led a team that conducted a series of interviews in *Second Life*.[1] Based on the responses it is clear that, in online environments, distinctions between sacred and profane, virtual and real, play and ritual break down, challenging our sense of what is "here" and what is "there." Boundaries of all kinds—between play and ritual, between virtual reality and material reality, between the physical body and the digital body—are disrupted in online spaces like *Second Life*, raising questions about some of the most pertinent issues at stake in today's discussion of virtual religion. What is happening today may seem strange, new, and fascinating for the study of religion and what it means for people to come together in a collective experience, but it also highlights the notion that religious experience has always been a form of imaginative "play."

Virtual Religions: Churches in *Second Life*

What makes a space sacred? This question seems easier to answer in real life than in virtual space—one either enters a sanctuary or one doesn't. The physical space of a church or synagogue demarcates it as different from the surrounding world. However, in *Second Life*, one can see an erosion of the distinction between sacred and profane space.

Mark Brown is an Anglican priest who was ordained by the Bishop of Wellington, New Zealand, with the charge of "overseeing the virtual ministry instead of one based in a church built of bricks and mortar" (Hamilton 2008). Brown ministers exclusively in *Second Life*, and in his *Christian Mission to a Virtual World*, a missive about ministry in *Second Life*, he offers readers directions about how to download the software, log in, create an avatar (a digital representation of oneself), locate the virtual Anglican Cathedral, and then "teleport" to the Cathedral grounds:

> You would then be welcomed by the service leader and given the liturgy by clicking on a book located on a table near the entrance. You then click on a virtual pew and select "sit." The service leader will then either type the liturgy, or say it for all to hear or offer both ... When it comes to the sermon the message has been prerecorded and at the appropriate time is streamed into *Second Life*. Following the service people [avatars] congregate around the Cathedral for fellowship and discussion. Wherever you are in the [real] world, if you have a good internet connection and a reasonably powerful computer you can attend church.
>
> (Brown 2008, 6)

Another SL resident called "Alwin Alcott" could be channeling religious theorist Mircea Eliade when he remarks that *Second Life* "can help with understanding the untouchable divine world."[2] Eliade defines the distinction between sacred and profane as "two modes of being in the world, two existential situations assumed by man in the course of his history" (Eliade 1957, 14). He says that "[r]evelation of a sacred space makes it possible to obtain a fixed point and hence to acquire orientation in the chaos of homogeneity, to 'found the world' and to live in a real sense" (*ibid.*, 23). Despite the impossibility of absolutely identifying sacred and profane in *Second Life*, these categories enable us to examine how users see their own spaces, and how this illuminates the erosion of the distinction between sacred and profane in cyberspace.

In particular, Eliade helps us understand the impulse to build, which the religious person does as a means of staving off chaos, and in apparent imitation of an unchanging sacred realm that is inaccessible in his present life. Entering a space that has not been given order well matches Eliade's description of chaos as "an uncosmicized because unconsecrated space, a mere amorphous extent into which no orientation has yet been projected, and hence in which no structure has yet arisen" (*ibid.*, 1957, 64). In *Second Life*, churches and temples establish for their builders a hierophany—"an irruption of the sacred" that makes an area "qualitatively different" from those around it, and as such "reveals an absolute fixed point, a center" in undifferentiated (chaotic) space (*ibid.*, 26; 21). By building in the profane spaces in *Second Life*, residents "symbolically transform [them] into a cosmos through a ritual repetition of the cosmogony" (*ibid.*, 31). Since, for the religious person, profane space represents absolute nonbeing, this gives a sense of order and predictability to a chaotic realm, and permits for the performance of ritual as it is authenticated by it. It is, for Eliade, a singularly religious act.

However, Krystina Derrickson argues that representation of the sacred in virtual space is not the same thing as the construction of sacred space in real life. Considering the online *hajj*, Derrickson (2008) points out the "ambiguous" nature of sacred space in *Second Life*, where the simulated Mecca "may be considered a form of sacred virtual space," because of the "detailed reconstructions of spiritually-charged physical loci," and the "behavioral regulations encouraged by sim owners in the treatment of those virtual spaces."[3] For Derrickson, when sacred space is constructed in a virtual context, its sacredness is endowed by intent. The sacredness that any virtual building exhibits is thus contested, reflexively constructed, and subject to simultaneous multiple interpretations. We can see this in the opinions of *Second Life* resident "Beauman Hargson," who built a virtual replica of a well-known cathedral, and one day discovered a digital penis on its altar. As "Hargson" noted, rather nonchalantly: "one mouse-click and it is deleted so I don't mind too much about that."

Due to their virtual nature, sacred structures in *Second Life*, unlike real-life sacred structures, are infinitely malleable. Digital pollutions are momentary; sanitation is as easy as a click of the mouse. The ambiguous quality of "sacredness" in *Second Life* became apparent to me in the spring semester, 2008, when students in one of my classes explored the online *hajj*, and I was uncertain whether one of their avatars should "enter" the digital *hajj* in his Batman costume. Such questions are the hallmark of the contested nature of sacred space in a virtual context.

The ambiguity of the sacred means that certain traditional religious rituals are generally acceptable in *Second Life*, such as lighting Shabbat candles, praying, or meditating. However, for those with *bona fide* religious credentials who engage in ritual activity within *Second Life*, there are some limitations to online ritual performance. You can enact an animation to "kneel" while you pray (Hamilton 2008), but you cannot engage in the traditional sacraments. You will find no marriages, baptisms, or eucharists performed in the Anglican Cathedral. The Catholic Church affirms this proscription, and has banned any consideration of virtual eucharist. Rabbi Yosef Y. Kazen argues that the embodied, physical aspect of religious identity is crucial for certain religious practices. Kazen, who manages a number of online resources for Orthodox Jews, claims that rituals such as a bar mitzvah ceremony or a prayer service with a *minyan* (ten adult males) cannot be conducted in a virtual environment. "We don't necessarily see the spiritual reality of what is happening [when we engage in embodied rituals]," he says, "but certain things have to be done with physical people, just as food has to be eaten by physical people" (quoted by Zaleski 1997, 19). Latter-day Saint and Second Lifer "Mo Hax" agrees: "Even though we Mormons take the sacrament (communion) and don't believe in literal transubstantiation, the rite seems out of place in SL, to me at least ... priestly ordination is done 'by the laying on of hands.' Such things require physicality."

Rev. Brown explains that online, the Anglican Church offers only "non-eucharistic services" along with Bible study and discussion groups; that is, those things that help to build a sense of community, but which do not require any sense of physicality or verification of religious authority. This sentiment is echoed by New Zealander Anglican theologian Bosco Peters, who explains his view with implicit references to theological arguments about the relationship between "inner" and "outer" signs of grace:

> Baptism, immersion into the Christian community, the body of Christ, and hence into the nature of God the Holy Trinity may have some internet equivalents—for example, being welcomed into a moderated group. But my own current position would be to shy away from ... having a virtual baptism of a *Second Life* avatar. Similarly, I would currently steer away from eucharist and other sacraments in the virtual world. Sacraments are outward and visible signs—the virtual world is still very much at the inner and invisible level.
>
> (Peters 2009)

Peters disapproves of performing the sacraments online precisely because he claims they depend upon physicality. The traditional church-administered sacraments, he says, rely upon the "outward" (their physicality). He quips: "Baptism uses water, Eucharist uses bread and wine. We cannot pour a jar of jelly-beans over someone and say they are baptized. We cannot consecrate a bicycle and say this is the Eucharist ... Hence, we cannot baptize an avatar in the virtual world—as there is no water there, nor is an avatar a person on whom we can confer baptism" (*ibid.*). The efficacy of *Second Life* activities, says Peters, are too "inner" and "invisible," meaning, it seems, that they are too symbolic.

Such claims seem a bit odd when one considers the "inner" and "invisible" activity of the Holy Spirit hoped for by Christians through the performance of the sacraments, and when one observes that the sacraments themselves are "virtual" in that they merely represent something deeper, namely, the work of grace. Mark Brown also insists that his missionary work in *Second Life* is based on the Anglican commitment to an "incarnational mission," an equally problematic assertion for a group that sees physicality as a hallmark of authenticity. It seems that the real problem here is the confusion of what "real" means in a world of increasing representation and replication, and the way that this discussion highlights the "virtual" nature of symbolism already inherent in the most traditional aspects of ritual.

Accompanying the question of physicality is the related question of identity in *Second Life*, which allows people to decide, in some cases, who religiously they would like to be and which religious mask (or masks) they would like to wear. On the one hand, Lisa Hamilton argues that virtual church "offers the safety of anonymity," in that "[n]othing prevents members from creating avatars in the opposite gender, or even ones resembling animals more than humans ... there are no name tags in the virtual church" (Hamilton 2008). *Second Life* faith communities can invite diverse groups to mingle, as in *Second Life* mosques where Sufi, Salafi, Sunni, and Shia Muslims all congregate, and where, as one Muslim in *Second Life* remarks, "they all talk to each other, which might not be the case in real life, I regret to say" (Crabtree 2007).

On the other hand, questions of identity create new problems in the performance of online rituals. In an interview with "Omega," who read the liturgy and led the mass in *Second Life*, James Wagner Au learned that not all who seem to be priests online really are. As "Omega" explains, he wanted the experience to be "like an actual mass," even though he is not Catholic and even though he is "certainly not a real minister, nor do I do this sort of thing in real life ... I wanted to bring more real-world things into SL so people could experience them if they couldn't in real life" (Au 2004). At the end of a service conducted by "Omega," a woman asked for a blessing of her unborn child. "Omega" replied that the blessing wouldn't be "legit" or "hold much value" since he was not a "real priest." In classic reflexive posture, the woman claimed "it would count to me."

Sacred (Cyber)Space: The Church of *Second Life*

What if we examine *Second Life* itself as a sacred space, entered into from the profane realm of our own ordinary lives? The computer defines its space (at least with current technology) with a window into which we peer—and into which we are invited to project our selves in some way or another. As Jennifer Cobb puts it, virtual reality is "a place that feels removed from the physical world" (Cobb 1998, 31), just as the sacred space of a church or synagogue "feels removed" from the profane space of the physical world. One enters *Second Life*. One leaves *Second Life*. One shifts one's "appearance" when one enacts one's avatar. One forgoes the ordinary needs of daily life when one enters—there is no eating, no sleeping, and no aging in *Second Life*. Some have even considered the possibility of inhabiting virtual space as a sort of digital heaven, or perhaps, as Cobb describes it, "the Platonic realm incarnate" (*ibid.*).

Passage into *Second Life* involves ritualized behavior set in motion by the log-ins, clicking procedures, and teleporting that allow one to "enter" into the virtual environment. This ritual—what theorist of ritual Victor Turner might have called a rite of passage—is typically the place or time within which a participant crosses from one mode of being into another, typically via a symbolic *limen* or "threshold." According to Turner, rites of passage involve admission into the community at new levels. The initiant "passes through a cultural realm that has few or none of the attributes of the past or coming state," and, once in this stage, stands outside of "the network of classifications" that traditionally organize and confer status. "Liminal entities" are therefore "betwixt and between the positions assigned and arrayed by law, custom, convention, and ceremonial" (Turner 1969, 94–95).

The notion of the threshold resonates well with the boundary where the hardware of the body meets the hardware of the computer that houses a virtual "space," and if there were any place where we might be able to observe the presence of distinctive realms, it would be in the threshold between them. When my avatar first entered *Second Life* in 2006, it appeared on "Orientation Island" which was, at one time, the place where all new avatars were spawned. When one appeared in this digital environment, it exhibited what the *Second Life* developers call the "default avatar look." Everyone's avatar looked exactly the same, with the exception of basic gender patterns. As soon as you learned how to use the controls, however, you could make changes to your avatar's appearance, including its body shape, skin color, and hair and eye color, as well as "attachments" (clothes, objects, etc.). You could also quickly acquire animations, or mini-programs that allow specified movements (Rymaszewski *et al.* 2007, 80). Experienced Second Lifers could easily recognize a "newbie" by the quality of his or her avatar, and by his or her agility using animations.

The parallels between the rituals performed in *Second Life* and Turner's academic description of rites of passage suggest an important relationship between them. Of the liminal entities engaging in a rite of passage, Turner says: "It is as though they are being reduced or ground down to a uniform condition to be fashioned anew and endowed with additional powers to enable them to cope with their new station in life ... Secular distinctions of rank and status disappear or are homogenized." Turner notes that "as liminal beings they have no status, property, insignia, secular clothing indicating rank or role, position in a kinship system—in short, nothing to distinguish them from their fellow neophytes or initiands." In a rite of passage, a "neophyte," says Turner, must "be a *tabula rasa*, a blank slate, on which is inscribed new knowledge and wisdom of the group ... in order to prepare them to cope with their new responsibilities" (Turner 1969, 103). New initiants into *Second Life*, too, are "ground down," in that their real-life selves are shorn away in some respects, leaving only a digital visage that represents them in the "new" world.

Even for those who are long-time Second Lifers, the experience of liminality is refreshed in some ways with each new session, suggesting that the user indeed experiences what Krystina Derrickson (2008) calls "a profound sense of entry." She describes the experience of logging on:

Once the user enters her password, her avatar begins to materialize, coalescing from a gray mass into a patchwork of flashing colors, and finally into her ultimate form, every time awakening into the sim where she ended her previous session. The sim itself loads, flickering into existence, and bodies begin to appear moving around and beyond her at various distances though she cannot move. There is a sense of immersion in an immaterial but materializing landscape.

(*ibid.*)

This moment of transition, or passage through a ritual portal, has been aptly described by Arnold van Gennep in his more individual look at liminal rites: "the door is the boundary between the foreign and domestic worlds in the case of an ordinary dwelling, between the profane and the sacred worlds in the case of a temple." Therefore, says van Gennep, "to cross the threshold is to unite oneself with a new world" (van Gennep 1996, 532). In the case of *Second Life*, the "door" is the process of logging on: the series of mouse-clicks and intentional digital interactions that constitute the "passage" from one "world" to the next.

Turner's description of the rite of passage extends into the new *Second Life* resident's ongoing orientation into the new world, where the shared nature of the experience is again apparent. Users in new online environments usually must spend some time in what T. L. Taylor calls "newbie zones," where they spend time with other "low-level" players and "learn the initial skills required for the game and the ways to coordinate with other" (Taylor 2006, 31). Gradually, users "undergo a socialization process" that helps them go beyond initial training and become participants in a "community of practice" (*ibid.*, 32). In *Second Life*, everyone begins with the same status but gradually accumulates animations, customized hair, professionally rendered "skin," and group associations that help them to be recognized as "insiders" or true Second Lifers.

Beyond the point of orientation, *Second Life* is itself a liminal space that affords initiants the freedom to do otherwise unacceptable things, prompting a temporary disruption of social order that helps maintain the *status quo* in real life. In such rituals, liminality temporarily grinds all participants down to the same level, so that the most powerful are subjected to the playful derision of the least powerful, representing what Turner calls *communitas*. Thus we have an explanation for the popularity of an event like the grid-wide winter holiday snowball fight, in which the "Lindens" (the only institutionalized power structure in *Second Life*) are pelted by "everyone else." According to Turner, liminality focuses on the "ritual powers of the weak" (Turner 1969, 102). People are permitted to "revile" the chief-elect "and most fully express [their] resentment, going into as much detail as [they] desire." The chief-elect must simply listen in patience and humility (*ibid.*, 101).

This sense of *communitas* offers some people—those who are typically without power—experiences of temporary potency. Among the topics discussed in connection with video games—and, one could argue, *Second Life*—notes Miroslaw Filiciak, are "[e]scapism, getting away from everyday life worries, and deriving satisfaction in doing things that we could never do in the real world" (Filiciak 2003, 99). "Roger Junchke," a self-proclaimed *Second Life* "terrorist," spends his time blowing up virtual churches. The act is excusable, however, since, as "Junchke" claims, "nothing actually gets destroyed in SL so all it really does is lights and smoke." For "Junchke," his actions have a liminal function, in that they are his "benign and petty way of expressing my dislike of Christian fundamentalists."

Not all examples of liminal experimentation—from "naked avatars sitting on the Koran to a swastika painted on the synagogue" (Crabtree 2007)—are well received in *Second Life*. According to *Second Life's Community Standards*, certain areas are designated as appropriate for "offensive" and/or sexual activities and others are not. Upon joining *Second Life*, each resident agrees to a code of conduct that includes a statement about not engaging in "assault" in a "Safe Area"; that is, not "shooting, pushing or shoving another Resident ... [or] creating or using scripted objects which singularly or persistently target another Resident" (*Second Life* n.d.). According to the authors of *Second Life: The Official Guide*, in the online world you can participate in all the "virtual hedonism" that you want—"having as much virtual sex as possible" or "shooting at other people, possibly while piloting a spaceship" (Rymaszewski *et al.* 2007, 13). You can even purchase animations and identify partners willing to enact virtual rape within *Second Life*, or find avatars who look like children to engage in animated pedophiliac pornographic fantasies. Obviously, the ethical implications of these virtual acts require serious scrutiny. This demands that we take seriously the problem of defining just what kind of "space" *Second Life* is, and who "we" are when we inhabit it.

In *Violence and the Sacred*, Rene Girard argues that societies periodically need a disruption of social order. After establishing his case that society by its very nature is invested with a desire for violence and retribution, Girard argues that, through selecting a sacrificial victim, "society is seeking to deflect upon a relatively indifferent victim, a 'sacrificeable victim,' the violence that would otherwise be vented on its own members." Thus violence is "not denied," but is "diverted to another object, something it can sink its teeth into" (Girard 1977, 4). If this is how things work in *Second Life*, then we can understand the violence in it to be functioning within a broadly religious framework.

One such violent area is the "Death Pit" in *Second Life*. According to Second Lifer Warren Ellis:

A mechanical Death Pit has been constructed on the Potato Farm, a parcel on the north road. A square caged floor. The floor is made out of metal panels. The idea is that people don the Wastelands Combat

Head-Up-Display—a piece of software that turns your avatar into a videogame character that can deal and receive damage—pull one of the local, horribly primitive weapons, and slash each other to death in the cage. But the metal panels are tricked out. Some flip under your feet and drop you down a hole. Some pop out, I swear, buzzsaws that are coded to do your avatar damage, complete with squirting-blood animation. If the designer wasn't on *Second Life*, he'd be working at [US military prison] Abu Ghraib. Or for Dr Evil.

(Ellis 2007)

Clearly, the claim that this violence is not "real" contributes to its appeal. The case of the non-player character (NPC) in *Second Life* (and other virtual reality contexts) pushes the question of virtual violence even further. In the Buddhist hells of *Second Life*, one can see crudely-crafted human NPCs perpetually burning, being impaled, and thrown about by huge and loathsome horned creatures. In light of Girard's analysis, it would seem that the NPC victims in the Buddhist hells "can be exposed to violence without fear of reprisal" (Girard 1977, 13) precisely *because* they are permanently liminal, looking like, but not being, fully human. Had these NPCs been programmed with more human-like characteristics or interactive scripts, the problem of liminality in virtual reality would be even more sharply defined.

However, the victims need not be NPCs to fulfill a violent urge in a liminal environment. Girard argues that society is bloodthirsty by nature, and that by offering a sacrifice, people in a given society are appeased, and thus the sacrifice "serves to protect the entire community from its own violence" (*ibid.*, 8). This form of violence, Girard argues, is functional because it is "a form of violence that will put an end once and for all to violence itself" (*ibid.*, 27). The ritualizing of violence, including both actual sacrifice and rituals merely remembering sacrifice, functions for society precisely to "keep violence outside the community" (*ibid.*, 92). The sacrificial ritual, in fact, is "designed to function during periods of relative calm" because it is "not curative, but preventive" (*ibid.*, 102). This may help us to understand the remarks of resident "Thadeus Kalig," who describes a *Second Life* group that was "impailing [*sic*] themselves one night," complete with "blood pools and all." He describes this event as "ritualistic." "Rex Dars" says that the activity in *Second Life* is "a role play and not intended to [be] real." It is "like acting out a sceen [*sic*] from a movie." For "Dars," "what happens online is totally sep[a]rate [from real life in most cases] ... if it [is] play acting and somebody gets 'killed' I see nothing wrong with that."

Game studies theorists Katie Salen and Eric Zimmerman argue that games can "play with meaning" and create a sort of "social contract" within which "forbidden play" can occur. Games can "create social contexts in which, very often, behaviors take place that would be strictly forbidden in society at large." In this "forbidden play" space, the player is "always in danger of [really] overstepping the social boundaries of play, jumping the gun, and breaking the magic circle" (Salen and Zimmerman 2003, 479). Cindy Poremba calls such experiences "brink games." Brink games "use their status as 'only a game' as a strategic gesture." Poremba is interested in those types of "forbidden play" that most intensely play with the boundary between game and reality, games that use the conceit of "it's just a game" with "a knowing wink" (Poremba 2007, 772). "Brink" games exploit the relationship between the real, the virtual, and the taboo, and are exciting precisely because of "the tangible threat of [a] breach" (*ibid.*, 776). Although most *Second Life* users claim that it is not a "game," it does exhibit the qualities of "forbidden play" by inviting its users to find that place where virtuality and reality meet. Of course, none of this answers the question of whether *Second Life* is a place of "play" or a space of shared human community and thus subject to certain standards of decency. The ability to engage in what I call "persistent liminality" means that some people will see their bad behavior as "play" anywhere online, and others will insist that the online world be subject to the same ethical standards as real life.

Not surprisingly, the authors of *Second Life: The Official Guide* explain that in *Second Life*, we can experience powers we might otherwise not: "*Second Life* works as if you were a god in real life. Not an almighty god, perhaps—more like one of those mythological minor gods, who tended to specialize in certain areas, get drunk, have sex, fight, and [most important] cast spells left, right and center ... And just like a mythological god, you're able to fly, and teleport wherever you like in an instant" (Rymaszewski *et al.* 2007, 7). But just as believers today can imagine Heaven but not enter into it in this life, so those who dwell in the real world can never fully inhabit the "sacred" space of *Second Life*. Game theorists have recognized the yearning induced by virtual reality. Miroslaw Filiciak says that the experience of interacting in virtual reality is characterized by intense desire: "We make the screen a fetish; we desire it, not only do we want to watch the screen but also to 'be seen' on it" (Filiciak 2003, 100). Ken Hillis expresses precisely such a sentiment about virtual reality's ability to induce a sense of longing and transcendence:

> There is a widespread belief that space (understood variously as distance, extension, or orientation) constitutes something elemental, and VR [virtual reality] reflects support for a belief that because light illuminates space it may therefore produce space a priori. As a result, VR users may experience desire or even something akin to a moral imperative to enter into virtuality where space and light ... have become one immaterial "wherein." The ability to experience a sense of entry into the image and illumination enabled by VR's design, coupled with both esoteric and pragmatic desires to view the technology as a "transcendence machine" or subjectivity enhancer, works to collapse distinctions

between the conceptions built into virtual environments by their developers and the perceptive faculties of users.

(Hillis 2006, 349)

Although writing before the advent of *Second Life*, Brenda Brasher makes a similar point: "That cyberspace is taken for a materialized instance of eternity may explain in part our passionate obsession with it ... To the true believers, cyberspace is a temporal heaven. Except, of course, it isn't" (Brasher 2001, 53). The computer functions as a "transcendence machine," inducing in us what Margaret Wertheim calls "a longing for the annihilation of pain, restriction, and even death" (Wertheim 1999, 259), and making our desire to inhabit virtual space strangely akin to our desire for immortality.

Brasher observes in cyberspace what she calls "omnitemporality"—"the religious idea of eternity as perpetual persistence"—and says that cyberspace is "[c]ontinuously accessible and ostensibly disconnected from the cycles of the earth" (Brasher 2001, 52). It is no surprise that cyber-imagination and religious imagination are related:

> [Virtual reality] appeared to its first Western consumers to be a concrete expression or materialization of the monks' concept of eternity ... It is always present. Whatever exists within it never decays. Whatever is expressed in cyberspace, as long as it remains in cyberspace, is perpetually expressed ... the quasi-mystical appeal that cyberspace exudes stems from this taste of eternity that it imparts to those who interact with it.
>
> (*ibid.*, 52)

The desire for permanence is also easily seen in virtual memorials of the type Brasher discusses (*ibid.*, 54), and which have also cropped up recently in *Second Life*. Users who wish to mourn the loss (through re-entry into real-life) of a fellow *Second Life* resident can memorialize his or her avatar in *Second Life* with a complete burial and re-usable casket. Of *Memoris*, a virtual graveyard in *Second Life*, blogger Warren Ellis says that, when real-life people die, they are sometimes memorialized in *Second Life* in this new way because message boards, the previous mode of grieving, "makes such losses transient. The community rolls on, and tributes and remembrance get lost in the churn. It is, to say the least, an unusual idea, that in a virtual world a permanent space be erected in memoriam of the people we've lost" (Ellis 2007). An earlier web-page version of a cyber-memorial, *Cyber Heaven*, provokes what Brasher calls "the elusive tang of cyber-eternity" (Brasher 2001, 55), the longing for permanence that is expressed by some in their fascination with virtuality. This permanence remains tantalizingly out of reach in *Second Life*.

But aside from questions about ongoing memorials of the departed, can a soul or self survive the death of the physical body in *Second Life*? SL resident "Harry Bulder" thinks so when he describes the potential for "cybernetic afterlife." Eventually, he says, "people will be able to create what amounts to a 'clone of themselves that exists in the network." The virtual clone can "learn what it is like to be 'me' and gradually become indistinguishable ... but it will not be a mortal being, just a program, and thus without death." For Bulder, the intangible self that enters into *Second Life* could remain there, in digitized form, when the physical body is no longer an acceptable vessel for it. Margaret Wertheim aptly points out that "while the concept of transcending bodily limitation was once seen as *theologically possible*, now it is increasingly conceived as *technologically feasible*" (Wertheim 1999, 263; emphasis in original).

Considering the implications of such theories, Wertheim says that "[t]he idea that the essence of a person can be separated from his or her body and transformed into the ephemeral media of computer code is a clear repudiation of the materialist view that man is made of matter alone" (*ibid.*, 268). This transformation would make *Second Life* a *de facto* nonmaterial heaven, presumably amenable to a postmodern, post-Enlightenment, secular world. Wertheim remarks that cyberspace becomes, in such a view, "a place outside space and time, a place where the body can somehow be reconstituted in all its glory" (*ibid.*, 263). Were cybernetic afterlife to be achieved, the user, or some remnant thereof, would at last fully inhabit the sacred space of virtual reality, and—dare I say—heaven? Wertheim notes that were the "immaterial self" to "survive the death of the body and 'live on' forever beyond physical space and time," we would be "back in the realm of medieval Christian dualism" (*ibid.*, 268). In other words, the "transcendence machine" could enable a final resolution of the liminality of space, place, and person.

Despite its consistent function as a meaningful means of entry into the virtual world, the rite of passage into *Second Life* is not a stable one, and in this way contrasts with many traditional religious rites of passage, especially those that are integral and longstanding parts of a community's life. Early in *Second Life*'s development, upon entering the world, one's avatar was spawned looking just like the other avatars of the same gender. More recently, one was led through a series of fluency-building exercises, one of which was a series of challenges to appease the "volcano goddess" while learning how to chat with other users. Today, new avatars are spawned in various "Help Islands" around *Second Life*, and users can define a distinctive avatar before it ever walks in virtual space.

This fluidity is characteristic of the online experience in general; it is "ambiguous"; it resists normal social and cultural classifications; it places us "neither here nor there" but rather "betwixt and between the positions assigned and arrayed by law, custom, convention, and ceremonial" (Turner 1969, 95). In *Second Life*, one doesn't cross over from one state into the other in any kind of permanent way as, say, one might if one were a bar mitzvah or experienced some other coming-of-age rite of passage. Rather, all of *Second Life* invokes a state of persistent liminality and all the complexities that such a notion brings along with it. Such fluidity and persistent liminality also characterize the representation of self in *Second Life*. Sherry Turkle says that when people select avatars in virtual reality, they don't simply "become who they play." Rather, they "play who they are or who they want to be or who they don't want to be" (Turkle 1997, 192). As Elizabeth Reid puts it, in cyberspace identities are self-defined in that "virtual reality is a construct within the mind of a human being" (Reid 1995, 166). The effect of interaction with and through one's avatar can affect one's daily life, since players "sometimes talk about their real selves as a composite of their characters and sometimes talk about their screen personae as means for working on their RL lives" (Turkle 1997, 192). In this respect, virtual environments produce the possibility of "liquid identity" (Filiciak 2003, 92).

Of course, the notion of hybrid identity has always been a part of human experience in drama and in religious ritual. For example, hybridity of identity characterizes Turner's analysis of the function of masks in traditional African ritual. In assessing the role of masks in a ritual for boys' circumcision, Turner found himself uncertain how participants in the ritual viewed the relationship between mask-wearer, ancestor (shade) represented, and the *Mvweng'i* (divine spirit) inhabiting the wearer: "Some informants say that the shade is identified with Mvweng'i, others that shade and masker operate in conjunction. The latter say that the shade rouses Mvweng'i and enlists his aid in afflicting the victim" in the rite of passage (Turner 1969, 17). It is remarkable how the same questions could be applied to one's sense of self in *Second Life*: are you your embodied self, your avatar, the role your avatar is currently playing, or someone else entirely when you are online? Or are you all of these at once?

If the use of avatars in *Second Life* evinces a hybridity of identity, then the same complexity must accompany the deeds enacted by avatars. Indeed, in our interviews residents' opinions about the nature of sin in *Second Life* depended largely upon their views about the relationship between embodied self and avatar. For residents like "Chumov Rapunoch," behavior in *Second Life* is not related to real life at all: "it is less sinning if you do it in SL ... it's not like real SIN." If people engage in transgressive sexual acts, for example, they "get away with it because there is no harm to anyone ... even though it is a sin and against the law in RL, people do it in SL, so SL 'downgrades' these actions." For others, it has primarily to do with the intent of the performer. "Rex Dars" told us that "the person mak[es] the decisions [regardless of whether] it's a real-life or *Second Life* body carrying [a sinful action] out ... but ... some thing[s] are done [in] a role-play and not intended to be 'real' like acting out a scene in a movie or something ... it's all subject to interpretation I guess." Intent is also the deciding factor for "Boli Lurri": "If you believe that certain actions are sinful and yet act them out, either in RL or SL, then ... according to [one's] religion, that person has sinned." So is virtual sin nonexistent because we are not the same as our virtual representations? Or is it "real" sin because we are somehow intrinsically connected to our virtual selves? Can the answer be different for different people (and avatars)?

For other *Second Life* residents, there is a definite continuity between embodied self and avatar, such that acts engaged in within *Second Life* are claimed to be of real-life consequence. *Second Life* resident "Murdoch Moore" told us that "I am still Jewish even when I am in *Second Life* ... the idea of being someone else in *Second Life* makes me uncomfortable." SL resident "Jonah Song" claims that "*Second Life* is just an extension of RL [real life]. 'Real life' is made up of interactions, the outflowing of people's inner lives. *Second Life* is the same thing." When asked about the notion of the soul, "Song" suggested that the soul can inhabit virtual and real space equally as well: "Just like our physical bodies aren't us, but what our spirits wear to interact in a physical world, we're interacting in a digital world through 'digital bodies'." The views "Song" expressed about the soul as the seat of moral responsibility allow him to view the relationship between the real world and *Second Life* as morally continuous: "Jesus taught that if you look upon a woman lustfully, you've committed adultery in your heart; or if you harbor murderous thoughts, you've murdered in your heart. We just use our bodies to sin, but it's not our bodies sinning but US. And the same thing is true for a place like the virtual world." For residents like "Song," the self or soul transcends its inhabitation in either digital or physical vessels. One might even say that for "Song," it is the soul that is most real—and that it can, apparently, inhabit our bodies and our avatars simultaneously.

"Horace Max," a Latter-day Saint SL resident, agrees. If we engage in activities in *Second Life*, "the consequences are spiritual." "Max" describes a virtual romantic relationship in which "one friend and I flew around in the sunset, danced and such, but I was plagued with real mortal guilt after that." For "Max," though, the "spirit" resides only in RL: "there isn't a SL spirit." This means that the consequences of activities in *Second Life* can *only* have real-life impact. SL resident "Cloud Meade" concurs: "acting out the things we think—even though it may only be virtual—has [real-life] consequences— ones that can hurt others." "Richard Bartle" makes a similar argument when he advises would-be game designers that virtual worlds "are an extension of real life" because "the interaction between players gives rise to a real-life morality that makes virtual worlds more than the mere games they would otherwise be." Says "Bartle": "it's because *we're* real that virtual worlds must be treated in moral terms as if they were equally real" (Bartle 2003, 589; emphasis in original). In this case, "persistent liminality" calls for a consistent moral framework.

However, one need not believe in God to argue for continuity of meaning between real-life and *Second Life*. Atheist resident "Benji Midway" told us that "SL is no less 'real' than the rest of our lives. The people are 'real' ...

Both my physical body and my avatar's 'body' are actually just a persistent temporal organization of subatomic particles." For "Midway," an avatar is "similarly an extension of [the] body." Because he saw his *Second Life* self as identical to his real-life self, SL resident "Daniel Kendall" eloped virtually with another resident and they were married in-world (that is, within *Second Life*). When asked about the ceremony and its significance, "Kendall" said, "the intent counts. We didn't need the big ceremony. We are married, no matter the physical aspects included ... [and] it means the same to me as in real-life." When we spoke with "Kendall," he was about to meet his new "wife" in real-life in a few hours. So what are we to make of virtual sin? Unfortunately, there is no simple answer. Different people engage with their avatars in different ways—and how they view the actions of those avatars depends tremendously on the degree of immersion in the lives of their avatars; on the nature of the virtual space they inhabit; and on their view of the relationship between the physical body and the virtual one.

Play, Ritual, and the Virtual: Making Sense of the Sacred

It seems it should be easy to define *Second Life* as either play or ritual—but it isn't. What does it mean to "play" at something, and how does this compare with the performance of a religious ritual? Play and ritual have a long history of imitating one another. Johan Huizinga, a scholar of play and the author of the landmark study *Homo Ludens* (1949)—describes play as "a free standing activity quite consciously outside 'ordinary' life as being 'not serious' but at the same time absorbing the player intensely and utterly" (Huizinga 2006, 107). Huizinga argues that a sacred performance is "played or performed within a playground that is literally 'staked out' ... A sacred space, a temporarily real world of its own, has been expressly hedged off for it" (*ibid.*, 108). To Huizinga, "[t]he turf, the tennis court, the chess-board and pavement hopscotch cannot formally be distinguished from the temple or the magic circle." We should recognize, he says, "the essential and original identity of play and ritual" so we can "recognize the hallowed spot as a playground" (*ibid.*, 113). This suggests that play and ritual have a lot more in common than we might at first think.

Like the tennis court or the chessboard, *Second Life* is a space apart from everyday life, and can thus be viewed as a form of play. But participation in it also can be viewed as a ritual. To make matters even more complicated, within *Second Life* there are areas that some residents treat as "magic circles" of play, and others that are viewed as arenas for ritual, and how one defines the boundary between them fluctuates widely based on the varying perspectives of the Second Lifers. If we then introduce the boundary between the "virtual" and the "real" into this complex stew, the possibilities for a single ordering paradigm become increasingly unlikely.

Accordingly, T.L. Taylor questions whether identifying such a line between the virtual world and the real world—or between play and nonplay—is even reasonable. For Taylor, the magic circle of play "can hide (and even mystify) the much messier relationship that exists between spheres—especially in the realm of MMOGs [massively multiplayer online games]." If we look at how people have utilized online spaces, he says, "we find people negotiating levels of self-disclosure and performance, multiple forms of embodiment, and the importing of meaningful offline issues and values into online spaces" (Taylor 2006, 152). Calling for "non-dichotomous models," Taylor claims that "the boundary between online and offline life is messy, contested, and constantly under negotiation" (ibid., 153). This "messiness" can be seen in all aspects of theoretical analysis of religion and *Second Life.*

Virtual reality is liminal, fluid, and hybrid, as we are too when we interact with it, making the distinction between religion and media a harder one to draw than we might like. After all, religion and media are both about mediation and communication—how we receive important information, and how its transmission affects reception. Media theorist Stewart Hoover rejects the oversimplified assumption that "the media and religion are separate and competing spheres and that, on some level, they inhabit the roles of 'sacred' (religion) and 'profane' (the media) influences in contemporary life." Instead, what has developed is "a less definite space where those distinctions exist in a state of fluidity and flux" (Hoover 2001, 50). This fluidity is readily evident in what Second Lifers had to tell us in our interviews about five recurring topics: ritual, violence, identity, sin, and the afterlife. These categories cropped up again and again as the ones most important to residents and most pertinent to the discussion of what is really going on with religion in *Second Life.* The notion of persistent liminality is easily recognizable in the contested nature of religious experience in *Second Life.*

It's not just "Orientation Island" or some other initiation activity that produces a liminal state in *Second Life.* Rather, throughout the *Second Life* experience the sacred and profane meet—virtual and real collide—and people are at once here and there, but neither here nor there. *Second Life* seems to offer persistent liminality, the on-demand and consistently ambiguous experience of liminality, characterized by the ambiguities of game/real life, sacred/profane, ritual/play, and self/other. In other words, the dissolution of absolute categories is a hallmark feature of religion in *Second Life.*

So why should we care about *Second Life?* Because it makes us think about what we mean when we talk about sacred space, about ritual, about self and community, and of course about religion. *Second Life* invites what Krystina Derrickson dubs a "Baudrillardian blurring of the RL/SL [real-life/ *Second Life*] treatment of space" (Derrickson 2008). In *Second Life,* a place like the online mosque in Mecca is designated as sacred, "and yet it is a contentious designation" (ibid.). Does this mean that the distinction between the sacred and the profane has lost significance when applied to *Second Life?*

Not necessarily—it seems that what people believe when they enter a virtual context can help us understand what they believe about what happens within it. Remarking on the nature of personal intent in creating meaning in virtual contexts, Lorne Dawson asserts: "All that matter are the experiences that are experimentally generated and manipulated by the skilful understanding and use of words and the temporary worlds they create in the minds of individuals" (Dawson 2005, 25). Even if an easy distinction between the real and the virtual has collapsed in online worlds like *Second Life*, the category of the "sacred" may still have salience for those who utilize it: "In the classic postmodernist mode, the simulation can be substituted for the reality, yet there is not really a complete collapse of the sign and the signified since the focus is still on some seemingly 'authentic' experience" (*ibid.*, 26). In other words, the concept of the "sacred" can help us make sense of how people think about the sacred, even if it cannot point to something about which everyone will easily agree. It seems self-evident that a postmodern, Baudrillardian, reflexive perspective is required—whether we like it or not.

The situation is characteristic of religion-at-large in today's massively-mediated, complex, globalizing, multireligious world. Referring to the construction of religious identity, Wade Clark Roof defines what he calls "reflexive spirituality," seeing in today's world "a situation encouraging a more deliberate, engaging effort on people's part for their own spiritual formation, both inside and outside religious communities" (Roof 1999, 75). This may be the best news yet, since reflexive spirituality is often thinking spirituality, as people decide what to do with the vast menu of options before them. In today's world, "[r]esponsibility falls more upon the individual—like that of the bricoleur—to cobble together a religious world from available images, symbols, moral codes, and doctrines, thereby exercising considerable agency in defining and shaping what is considered to be religiously meaningful" (*ibid.*, 75). In *Second Life*, this "cobbling" may involve some new construction as well, making it possible to consider religious identity in *Second Life* not as deconstructive of identity, but as constructive and deliberate in a way that interaction with less immersive media—and with less virtual bodies—may not be.

Dawson asks if "the exercise of reflexivity, long a hallmark of detached rational thought, is becoming, by radical extension, a new means of legitimating religious practice or even inducing 'authentic' religious experience," so that "the experience of reflexivity is itself being sacralized" (Dawson 2005, 26). This is reflexivity at its most influential—reflexivity alone determines whether or not an individual's use of the internet for online religious experience is "real" or not, and what that means for users. Furthermore, reflexivity itself is subject to the persistent liminality of experience that requires that we decide for ourselves if we are here, there, or somewhere in between. Interacting with *Second Life*, it can be all of the above. Perhaps virtual ritual creates its own justification in the form of self-reflection on its createdness.

Stephen O'Leary seems to be saying something like this when he remarks that "ritual action in cyberspace is constantly faced with evidence of its own quality as constructed, as arbitrary, and as artificial, a game played with no material stakes or consequences" (cited in *ibid.*, 21). But the very notion that construction is a crucial component in interactive new media may cause people to acknowledge more openly the constructed nature of all of religion, and to recognize the element of "play" that has always been a part of religious life.

References

Au, James Wagner. 2004. "Where Two or More Are Gathered." *New World Notes* (April 19). http://nwn.blogs.com/nwn/2004/04/where_two_or_mo.html

Bartle, Richard. 2003. *Designing Virtual Worlds.* Indianapolis, IN: New Riders Games.

Brasher, Brenda. 2001. *Give Me That Online Religion.* San Francisco: Jossey-Bass.

Brown, Mark. 2008. "Christian Mission to a Virtual World." *Brownblog* (April). http://brownblog.info/wp-content/plugins/wp-downloadMonitor/user_uploads/ Christian_Mission_to_a_Virtual_World.pdf

Cobb, Jennifer. 1998. *Cybergrace: The Search for God in the Digital World.* New York: Crown Publishers.

Crabtree, Shona. 2007. "Finding Religion in Second Life's Virtual Universe." *Washington Post* (June 16): B09. www.washingtonpost.com/wp-dyn/content/article/ 2007/06/15/AR2007061501902.html

Dawson, Lorne. 2005. "The Mediation of Religious Experience in Cyberspace." In *Religion and Cyberspace*, eds Morten T. Højsgaard and Margit Warburg, 15–37. New York: Routledge.

Derrickson, Krystina. 2008. "Second Life and The Sacred: Islamic Space in a Virtual World." www.digitalislam.eu/article.do?articleId=1877

Eliade, Mircea. 1957. *The Sacred and the Profane: The Nature of Religion.* New York: Harper & Row.

Ellis, Warren. 2007. "The Island of Lost Souls." *Reuters.com* (March 30). http://secondlife.reuters.com/stories/2007/03/30/second-life-sketches-the-island-of-lost-souls

Filiciak, Miroslaw. 2003. "Hyperidentities: Postmodern Identity Patterns in Massively Multiplayer Online Role-Playing Games." In *The Video Game Theory Reader*, eds Mark J. P. Wolf and Bernard Perron, 87–102. New York: Routledge.

van Gennep, Arnold. 1996. "Territorial Passage and the Classification of Rites." In *Readings in Ritual Studies*, ed. Ronald L. Grimes, 529–36. Upper Saddle River, NJ: Prentice Hall.

Girard, Rene. 1977. *Violence and the Sacred*, trans. Patrick Gregory. Baltimore, MD: Johns Hopkins University Press.

Hamilton, Lisa B. 2008. "Worshipping Online: Is It Really Church?" *Episcopal Life Online* (October 6). www.cuac.org/81834_101368_ENG_HTM.htm

Hillis, Ken. 2006. "Modes of Digital Identification: Virtual Technologies and Webcam Cultures." In *New Media, Old Media: A History and Theory Reader*, eds WHK Chun and T. Keenan, 347–58. New York: Routledge.

Hoover, Stewart M. 2001. "Religion, Media, and the Cultural Center of Gravity." In *Religion and Popular Culture: Studies in the Interaction of Worldviews*, eds

Daniel A. Stout and Judith M. Buddenbaum, 49–60. Ames: Iowa State University Press.

Huizinga, Johan. 1949. *Homo Ludens: A Study of the Play-Element in Culture*, trans. R. F. C. Hull. London: Routledge & Kegan Paul.

——. 2006. "Nature and Significance of Play as a Cultural Phenomenon." In *The Game Design Reader*, eds Katie Salen and Eric Zimmerman, 96–120. Cambridge, MA: MIT Press.

Peters, Bosco. 2009. "Virtual Eucharist?" *Liturgy* (June 28). www.liturgy.co.nz/blog/virtual-eucharist/1078/comment-page-1

Poremba, Cindy. 2007. "Critical Potential on the Brink of the Magic Circle." *Situated Play: Proceedings of DiGRA [Digital Games Research Association] 2007 Conference* (September): 772–78. www.digra.org/dl/db/07311.42117.pdf

Reid, Elizabeth. 1995. "Virtual Worlds: Culture and Imagination." In *CyberSociety: Computer-Mediated Communication and Community*, ed. Steven G. Jones, 164-183. Thousand Oaks, CA: Sage.

Roof, Wade Clark. 1999. *Spiritual Marketplace: Baby Boomers & the Remaking of American Religion*. Princeton, NJ: Princeton University Press.

Rymaszewski, Michael, Wagner James Au, Mark Wallace, Catherine Winters, Cory Ondrejka, and Benjamin Batstone-Cunningham. 2007. *Second Life: The Official Guide*. San Francisco: Sybex.

Salen, Katie and Eric Zimmerman. 2003. *Rules of Play: Game Design Fundamentals*. Cambridge, MA: MIT Press.

Second Life. n.d. "Community Standards." http://secondlife.com/corporate/cs.php

Taylor, T. L. 2006. *Play between Worlds: Exploring Online Game Culture*. Cambridge MA: MIT Press.

Turkle, Sherry. 1997. *Life on the Screen: Identity in the Age of the Internet*. New York: Simon & Schuster.

Turner, Victor. 1969. *The Ritual Process: Structure and Anti-Structure*. Chicago: Aldine Publishing Co.

Wertheim, Margaret. 1999. *The Pearly Gates of Cyberspace: A History of Space from Dante to the Internet*. New York: W. W. Norton & Company.

Zaleski, Jeff. 1997. *The Soul of Cyberspace: How New Technology is Changing Our Spiritual Lives*. San Francisco: Harper Edge.

Notes

1 An earlier version of this paper (with Kim Gregson and Austra Zubkovs) was presented at the national meeting of the Popular Culture Association, Spring 2007. I deeply appreciate the substantial and invaluable assistance offered by Kim and Austra; their work managing the in-world collection of material made the interviews possible. The analysis of the data presented here is entirely my own.

2 An "SL resident" (also referred to here as a Second Lifer) refers to anyone who has created an avatar, passed through the orientation procedures, and become an online member in the world of *Second Life*. Many Second Lifers refer to the virtual world by its initials ("SL"), distinguishing it from the real (or nonvirtual) world, which they often identify simply as "RL." I have changed the usernames of all interviewees in *Second Life* to protect their anonymity. Because all Second

Lifers already have a username that masks their true identity, and I met them only via their usernames, I have changed those names to add another level of anonymity within the world of *Second Life.*

3 "Sim" is short for "simulation" and refers to any number of structures made by users in the *Second Life* world. In this case, the sim is the digital replica of Mecca.

Chapter 15

Rap Music, Hip-Hop Culture, and "The Future Religion of the World"

Robin Sylvan

When rap music and hip-hop culture first emerged from the South Bronx in the late 1970s, critics dismissed it as a superficial fad that would quickly fade and be relegated to the dustbin of history. Over the course of the past three decades, however, this kind of pejorative assessment has been proved wrong time and time again, as rap has consistently dominated the music industry and hip-hop sensibility has become part and parcel of mainstream American popular culture. A case in point is the enormous success of female rapper Lauryn Hill's album *The Miseducation of Lauryn Hill* (1998), which topped the charts at number one for weeks, sold several million copies, and won numerous Grammies. Or perhaps one might channel surf the television to find rap music and hip-hop styles in commercials for everything from McDonald's hamburgers to Pringles potato chips to Mervyn's department store. This is an extraordinary trajectory for an African-American musical subculture that began in what is arguably the most economically and culturally marginalized neighborhood of the country.

What is even more remarkable about the success of rap and hip-hop is that it still contains a powerful and distinctive African-American religious world view that runs directly counter to the religious world view of the mainstream culture it has come to permeate. Faced with the oppressive historical circumstances of African Americans' marginalized status, this religious world view refuses to take refuge in the hope of otherworldly salvation but, rather, tells the truth about the harsh reality of this oppression and transforms the impulse toward anger and violence into empowerment, creative expression, spirituality, and positive change. Here I will look at the contradictory dynamics of hip-hop's rise to mainstream success—its historical and cultural development, its West African and African-American roots, and its spiritual dimensions—and explore the important implications for the larger landscape of religion in American popular culture.

"Old School": Cultural and Musical History

Rap music emerged as one component of hip-hop, a new street culture that included graffiti and break dancing as important forms of expression. The music for rap was put together by DJs mixing stripped-down, bass-heavy, polyrhythmic beats from turntables and samplers, drawing heavily on roots in soul, funk, and disco. This new style of sonic collage quickly became the soundtrack for street parties and "ghetto blasters" (portable tape players) throughout the Bronx. But the term "rap" actually refers to the rhyming poetry that the lead vocalist would improvise on the microphone in rhythm to the beats. Raps were spoken as well as sung, and they featured the rapper's prowess in turning a phrase. This prowess could take the form of innovative rhyming, rhythmic dexterity, boasting, humor, narrative storytelling, or even preaching. The subjects of the raps reflected the grim reality of young African Americans' life in the ghetto: racism, poverty, broken families, substandard housing, unemployment, violence, drugs, gangs, police brutality, arrests, incarceration, and short life expectancy.

Innovative DJs like Kool Herc and Afrika Bambaataa used their turntable mixing skills to create the first beat-driven sonic collages that form the foundation of rap music. These were originally dance mixes for neighborhood parties in houses, parks, and community centers. These pioneering hip-hop DJs not only drew heavily on soul and funk recordings, but also used the new technologies of the cross-fade mixer, the sampler, and the drum machine. Songs were segued seamlessly into each other for a continuous dance mix. At the same time, the breaks in each song and between songs—those places where the instrumentation would pull back to highlight the rhythm section— were emphasized and extended in a collage of peak dance beats. These became known as "break beats" or "b-beats," and DJ Kool Herc was their acknowledged master. The wild athletic dancing that accompanied these break beats became known as "break dancing," and the male break dancers became known as "break boys" or "b-boys" for short. Hip-hop DJs also developed new skills on the turntables which strongly contributed to the distinctive rap sound. Foremost among these was "scratching," a technique in which the DJ used his hand to quickly spin the record back and forth under the needle, thus producing a quirky staccato rhythm. Another technique was "backspinning," in which the DJ isolated a short verbal or musical phrase on a record, and repeated it by quickly spinning back to the beginning. One of the early creators and masters of both the scratch and the backspin was Grandmaster Flash. Both of these techniques produced crossrhythms on one turntable while the other supplied the main groove, a clearly polyrhythmic approach to musical composition. Samplers also allowed DJs to bring a wide assortment of sound sources into their eclectic pastiches.

Kool Herc and Afrika Bambaataa each had his own group of neighborhood friends, known as their "crew" or "posse," who hung out with them and accompanied them to all their jams. Thus rap music grew out of specific neighborhoods and local communities, each developing its own distinctive style. Often, there were competitions between DJs and their crews for territory, both physical and sonic, in which DJs would exhibit their mixing prowess and b-boys would display their dance moves. These competitions closely paralleled the territoriality of street gangs, but with one notable difference—there was no violence. Instead, the crews channeled their competitive energies into artistic expression, choosing a creative outlet rather than a destructive one. Afrika Bambaataa was a pioneer in making explicit the connection between these hip-hop crews and a sense of African identity and spiritual pride. Bambaataa, whose name means "affectionate leader" in Zulu, called his crew "Zulu Nation," and created an extended family unified not only by hip-hop expression but also by a positive vision of African-American community.

The raps themselves began with the DJs calling out on microphones over the music to exhort the audience to dance harder, repeating phrases like "rock the house," "get down," or "you don't stop." Because DJ mixing is a demanding task requiring full concentration, however, soon they brought in friends to work the microphone full time. Here again, DJ Kool Herc was an innovator in being among the first to use an MC (microphone controller or master of ceremonies). The MCs not only gave the parties more of a live feel, but they also fulfilled the important task of crowd control, maintaining a positive feeling, and keeping potential violence at bay. Very quickly, the MCs developed their own creative styles, using the latest slang and hippest rhymes to supplant the DJ as the focal point of the music. The competitive aspect shifted over to the rappers as well, as MCs dueled on the microphone trying to show who was the best rhymer.

In these early days of rap, roughly 1974 to 1978, it was still primarily an underground party phenomenon. This changed with the successful release of three seminal rap records—the Sugar Hill Gang's "Rapper's Delight" in 1979, Grandmaster Flash and the Furious Five's "The Message" in 1982, and Afrika Bambaataa's "Planet Rock" in 1983—which quickly established the commercial viability of rap. In 1986, Run-DMC completed rap's crossover to mainstream popularity when their single "Walk This Way" hit number one on the charts. Articles on rap began to appear in bastions of mainstream journalism like *The New York Times* and *Time* magazine. Run-DMC's crossover paved the way for the commercial success of other rap artists like LL Cool J, Eric B. and Rahim, Public Enemy, and Salt 'n' Pepa, one of the few prominent women rap groups. At the same time, vibrant local rap subcultures emerged in other urban centers around the country, including Miami, Boston, Houston, Oakland, and Los Angeles, each with its own distinctive sound and style.

Artists like Public Enemy and KRS-One made a strong push toward a more hard-core musical sound and a more militant political message. In combining an unflinching critique of contemporary black oppression with a visionary call to resistance and liberation, Public Enemy and KRS-One continued and updated a long-standing African-American musico-religious tradition of truth telling, an approach hip-hop scholar Angela Spence Nelson has called "combative spirituality" (Nelson 1991, 59).

The hard-core sound was to attain its greatest success, however, with the ascendancy of the Los Angeles area "gangsta" rap subculture in the late 1980s and early 1990s. The word "gangsta" is a reference to the centrality of gang activities among African-American and Hispanic youth in Los Angeles, which includes some of the worst crime and violence in the country and an underground economy largely based on crack cocaine. In areas like South Central Los Angeles, gang violence is commonplace, and the panicked response of white authorities has resulted in the creation of a virtual police state with its own violent excesses. The 1991 brutal beating of Rodney King by Los Angeles police, the acquittal of the responsible officers, and the subsequent riots on the streets gave an indication of the high level of hatred and tension in the area. It was out of this tableau of economic despair, gang violence, the crack epidemic, and police repression that gangsta rap emerged. The seminal gangsta group was N.W.A. (Niggaz With Attitude), whose 1988 album *Straight Outta Compton*, with its in-your-face attitude, funky West Coast sound, and gritty tales of violent gang life, sold more than two million copies. N.W.A.'s stylistic and commercial breakthrough opened the door for a number of other Los Angeles-area gangsta rap artists to attain success, including Ice-T, Snoop Doggy Dogg, and original N.W.A. members Ice Cube and Dr. Dre as solo artists.

The post-gangsta rap era has seen a new generation of rap artists break through to mainstream success as the market share of rap music has more than doubled in the past two decades. In addition to Lauryn Hill, artists like Puff Daddy (Sean Combs), Wu-Tang Clan, DMX, Master P, Jay-Z, Mase, and Eminem, to mention just a few, all had their run at the top of the charts. Far from being a passing fad, rap music has proved its staying power over the course of the past three decades, and has steadily grown in influence to become a permanent fixture in the mainstream world of popular culture. The fact that hip-hop is a primarily African-American subculture with strong roots in West African practices and sensibilities makes its penetration of mainstream popular culture an even more significant development from a religious perspective.

Poetry, Polyrhythms, Possession, and Prophetic Tradition: West African and African-American Roots

We've been rapping forever. You know, there's nothing new under the sun. The griots were doing the same, the storytellers, oral tradition people ... And the drum's also the center of it. You can't have it without the drum. And now hip-hop is experimenting, trying new things, but really the beat is what's always. It's the drums, just like drums in any form. That's definitely African.

(Interview with Malcolm [no last name given], Oakland, July 12, 1997)

In the course of doing research in the San Francisco Bay area in 1997, I had the opportunity to spend some time in the East Bay hip-hop community known as the Oakland Underground, attending musical events and conducting interviews with aficionados. Time and again in these interviews, I was struck by the explicit recognition and conscious acknowledgment of the African roots of rap and hip-hop. These roots can be traced back more specifically to two West African geographical and cultural zones: the coastal forest belt cultures like the Ga, Ewe, Fon, and Yoruba of modern Ghana, Togo, Benin, and Nigeria; and the Sahelian cultures of the Manding, Wolof, and Peul of modern Senegal, Gambia, Guinea, Mali, and Burkina Faso.

One of the primary religious complexes in the coastal forest belt is that of possession dances, sacred ceremonies in which drum ensembles and singers supply beat-driven polyrhythmic music and the initiates dance themselves into ecstatic trance states in which the gods take possession of their bodies, becoming physically present among the community for the purposes of counseling, healing, divination, and so forth. Many of the distinctive elements of this complex made their way to the Americas through the slave trade and became important components of African-American music and religion, albeit in significantly changed forms. Rap displays strong continuities with a number of these elements. Musically, one finds the centrality of rhythm as an organizing principle, with the elements of harmony and melody stripped down almost completely. The groove is generated from interlocking polyrhythms, and even though the constituent parts are sampled or prerecorded, they operate in the same way as live drumming. As one rapper said: "That is what, to me, makes hip-hop. It's got the rhythmic conversation of the drum and the rhythmic conversation of the bass" (interview with Paris King, Oakland, July 3, 1997). Another musician put it this way: "I'm pretty much focusing on the groove … . If it's a great groove, then … that really is the bottom line" (interview with Keith Williams, San Jose, July 4, 1997). And this polyrhythmic groove provides a connection to the ancestors, expressed thus: "Our ancestors are still calling. And the break beats we used in the beginning are still from God, still ally [sic] your soul" (interview with Jorge Guerrero, Berkeley, August 6, 1997).

The interconnection between music and dance is also central, as is evident in the importance of break dancing in the early hip-hop subculture. Many of the hip-hop aficionados I interviewed said that break dancing was their initial entry point into the music: "I was taking the energy of the beat and then just amplifying it through my movement. Like making the music almost seem like it was coming more intensely by seeing what I'm doing, or by me feeling what I'm doing, it seemed like the music became more intense" (interview with Steve Gaines, Berkeley, July 20, 1997). Some of these intensified states contain strong echoes of the possession experience:

> What I felt as a kid was strictly vibration, rhythm, and that music has a rhythm that just called my soul. It would make my soul jump out of my body, literally, and I'd have to move to it ... It really calls me, it really does ... Sometimes my body does things I can't even control and it's like I'm not even here ... It's just a link. Something touches you one day, just sparks your whole consciousness, and shows your body you can. Time and space is all about the rhythm in your body ... It's the ancients. It's definitely the ancients.
>
> (Guerrero, interview, August 6, 1997)

Interestingly, the circular form of break dancing, and even some of its dance moves, shows a striking similarity to African-American musico-religious dances like the ring shout, the Afro-Brazilian martial art capoeira, and traditional West African dances. The movements can also take the form of call and response, another classic element of African music, with the rapper's calls to "put your hands in the air" evoking an audience response of enthusiastic hand waving. These interactions demonstrate the participatory nature of the medium as well, another important principle of African music.

What is especially distinctive about rap music's continuities with West African and African-American musical principles, however, is the rap itself and its prominent foregrounding of an oral mode of expression, the roots of which are more closely associated with the Sahelian cultures of West Africa. These cultures have a long and distinguished lineage of men's societies of court poets and musicians called *jalis*, known as griots in the West, who maintained complex oral traditions of praise, lineage, and celebration. Many of the *jalis'* pieces were extremely long and had to be memorized; others were improvised on the spot for the specific occasion. In either case, a high level of oral skill was required. In these West African cultures, the spoken word was seen as potent and sacred, having the power to evoke that which was being spoken. This supernatural power of the spoken word was called *nommo*. This ancient power is something that hip-hop aficionados are able to recognize in today's raps: "Some people I hear, and it sounds like a long time ago ... These are words of power, like certain words, like positive suggestions of just certain frequencies of sounds" (Gaines, interview, July 20, 1997).

This emphasis on the potency of the spoken word and the oral tradition was to continue after the slave trade brought many of these West Africans to the Americas. During slave times, in the context of plantations especially, the oral tradition manifested itself in more secular forms such as the work song and the plantation tale (e.g. Brer Rabbit or Stagger Lee), as well as in rhyming jokes and singing games. Yet these secular forms preserved elements of the sacred traditions in a way that allowed them to continue in a trans-formed way. The Christian church, as the only officially legitimized context for religious expression allowed to the slaves, was also an important reposi-tory for the oral tradition. This was particularly evident in the preaching style of African American ministers, who relied heavily on rhythm, rhyme, and the skillful use of other rhetorical techniques to raise energy and to give the message greater potency.

The oral tradition continued to evolve in the post-emancipation era, becoming a significant component in both the major forms of African-American secular music—blues and jazz—not so much in the music itself as in the lingo of the subcultures. As African Americans moved from rural southern areas to northern cities, oral expression took the form of urban street talk, which had a more boastful, aggressive quality. Thus practices like sounding, woofing, jiving, signifying, rapping, and telling toasts were raised to high levels of prowess on the city streets in a friendly but competitive atmosphere. Some highwater marks of this oral artistry include the Harlem Renaissance and the poet Langston Hughes, black radio DJs in the 1940s and 1950s, and the game of ritual insult called "the dozens." The Reverend Martin Luther King Jr captivated the nation in the 1960s with the visionary fervor of his preaching style. Malcolm X also had a powerful oral style that strongly affected the African-American community in the 1960s. And the flamboyant and controversial boxing champion Muhammad Ali, widely ido-lized among African Americans, exposed the whole world to his boastful, humorous rhyming.

But perhaps the most important trailblazers for contemporary rap were the poet Gil Scott-Heron and the ensemble the Last Poets. Active during the late 1960s and early 1970s, the Last Poets were a group of black militant storytellers and poets who used the rhythms of conga drums to accompany their spoken political raps. Scott-Heron's brilliant work, including famous pieces like *The Revolution Will Not Be Televised* and *This Is Madness*, was innovative and influential, not only for its marriage of spoken raps with rhythmic grooves, but also for its unabashedly hard-hitting political message. Scott-Heron and the Last Poets were a source of inspiration for many key figures in the first generation of rappers, so much so that some consider them to be "the godfathers of message rap" (Perkins 1991, 42).

There is one more vitally important African-American influence on rap that must be noted, that of the blues, arguably the most quintessential of African-American musics. While there are certainly *musical* continuities among African traditions, the blues, and rap, the continuity of concern here is that of world view or theology, particularly with respect to the oppressive historical circumstances of Africans in the New World. The Christian theol-ogy adopted by many African-American churches sought to escape the hardships of suffering in this world by placing its faith in deliverance in the next. In contrast, the blues refused to look away from the suffering experienced as former slaves in the African diaspora, and sought a measure of whatever this-worldly redemption could be achieved through embodied sexuality and solidarity within the African-American community. As theologian James Cone eloquently writes:

> The blues are a lived experience, an encounter with the contradictions of American society, but a refusal to be conquered by it. They are despair only in the sense that there is no attempt to cover up reality. The blues recognize that black people have been hurt and scarred by the brutalities of white society. But there is also hope in what Richard Wright calls the "endemic capacity to live." This hope provided the strength to survive, and also an openness to the intensity of life's pains without being destroyed by them ... That black people could sing the blues, describing their joys and sorrows, meant that they were able to affirm an authentic hope in the essential worth of black humanity.
>
> (Cone 1992, 96–97)

There is such a strong similarity between this blues theology and that of hip-hop that this quote could well be a description of the world view of recent rappers, a continuity that has been noted by hip-hop scholars:

> Contemporary rappers, like early bluespeople, are responding to the "burden of freedom," in part by relaying portrayals of reality to their audiences through their personal experiences. They also relay positive portrayals of themselves as a means of affirming their personhood (and vicariously the personhood of their people) in a world that is constantly telling them they are nobodies.
>
> (Nelson 1991, 56)

> Rap music can be a profound extension of the prophetic or blues tradition and the legacy of heroism within the African-American experience.
>
> (Craddock-Willis 1989, 37)

In addition to theology, there is a strong continuity in the priestly role of the bluesman and the rapper as well, one which also has important religious implications. Ethnomusicologist Charles Keil writes:

> In spite of the fact that blues singing is ostensibly a secular, even pro-fane, form of expression, the role is intimately related to sacred roles in the Negro community ... As professions, blues singing and preaching seem to be closely linked in both the rural or small-town setting and in the urban ghettos. We have already noted some of the stylistic common denominators that underlie the performance of both roles, and it is clear

that the experiences which prepare one for adequately fulfilling either role overlap extensively.

(Keil 1966)

As I will show in the next section, this priestly function is consciously recognized by rappers and traced back through its African-American articulation to its West African roots. This conscious recognition of the African-American and West African roots of rap and hip-hop is a feature of their considerable religious quality, which demonstrates an extraordinary tenacity and adaptability in not just surviving five centuries of oppressive history, but emerging strong in a vibrant new formulation of these traditions.

Hip-Hop Spirituality

Hip-hop has been represented in mainstream media primarily by the gangsta rap image of dangerous black youth—angry, violent, and destructive. Yet, in my interviews with members of the Oakland Underground, they consistently claimed that hip-hop was exactly the opposite for them—peaceful, loving, inclusive, spiritual, and a force for positive change. This seeming contradiction has been a part of hip-hop culture since its South Bronx origins in the late 1970s, and understanding the dynamics of the dialectical relationship between these two polarities is central to understanding hip-hop's essential nature. To begin with, the situation of young African Americans and Latinos in inner-city ghettos is, as noted at the outset, one of racism, poverty, broken families, substandard housing, unemployment, violence, drugs, gangs, police brutality, arrests, incarceration, and short life expectancy. So, for any form of expression to have credibility, it must address that situation head-on, much as the blues did. In this regard, as Chuck D of Public Enemy has said, rap is black urban youth's CNN, providing information about what's going on in their world. This was a function confirmed in my interviews:

> Hip-hop music is always speaking to me, the lyrics. Especially in the late '80s, there were some real conscious things in hip-hop, and that was what was off-setting high school education, mainstream society, with all the information I was getting from KRS One and Public Enemy and X-Clan, all those groups. So, I just needed it at the time. We all needed it. They were speaking to me and educating me. I know they were. And I felt it. I needed it. It came at the right time.
>
> (Malcolm, interview, July 12, 1997)

In addition to providing information and educating, the raps also serve a crucial function of truth-telling: "It's very important to speak about how you really feel about something ... This is one of the first times in music where you can really say what's going on ... It's very honest. There's a lot of references to whatever's happening right now" (Paris King, interview, July 3, 1997). There is a deeper spiritual aspect of this truth telling beyond simply educating and informing:

> One thing about rapping is always that you've got to come with your heart, who you are. And whatever that be, whether it be L.A. gangster music or New York "righteous" music or anti-government music, whatever. It's all about coming from your heart, saying what you believe in. Whether it was Ice Cube or Chuck D, it was just the spirit there. That's what was attractive, beyond the word itself, because you knew it was coming from the heart, for real.
>
> (Malcolm, interview, July 12, 1997)

In coming from the heart and speaking their truth, rappers are also speaking for their larger community. As one aficionado put it: "There is a culture of people who feel the voices of [rappers] represent them" (Paris King, interview, July 3, 1997). "Represent" is a word widely used by rappers to describe their function. Some take the implications of this even further and explicitly make the connection to the role of the priest and the griot:

> MCs are like the priests or the pastors of the people right now because a lot of children don't listen to their parents anymore. A lot of kids don't go to church anymore. So, MCs have been elevated to this recognizable status that's easily accessible. It's our duty as MCs to try to bring morals to the community, just like the griots in Africa brought morals and they try to pass down things that were basic ... and that's like the role of MCs today.
>
> (Gaines, interview, July 20, 1997)

It is important to remember that the first South Bronx hip-hop crews of innovators like DJ Kool Herc and Afrika Bambaataa arose as an alternative to gang violence and drugs, channeling the destructive impulse into artistic expression. Awareness of this tradition continues today: "Hip-hop—originally, the dancers, the breaking groups—were this alternative similar to the fighting groups. They were just redirecting that energy. That's what they're still doing right now. You know, the energy's there. It's going to happen, it's going to get out one way or another. Hip-hop culture, to me, is one of the best alternatives that I've seen" (Malcolm, interview, July 12, 1997). This, then, is the source of hip-hop culture's seemingly paradoxical valuing of morality and spirituality at the same time it expresses anger and violent impulses—it alleviates the anger by providing a positive alternative direction to channel that energy:

> What it does for me is it calms my soul and all the struggle. I have a lot of anger in me from my ancestors and expressing it through music really

gives me a venue. It's like God gave me a gift and He said, "I know that if I don't give you this gift, you're going to do a lot of crazy stuff." So I accept this gift, and I'm still struggling with it because there's a lot of bad things I want to do still, you know. But the music keeps me centered on what I'm here for.

(Guerrero, interview, August 6, 1997)

And what is it that they are here for? Not anger and violence and destructiveness, but peace and love and spirituality. "One of the basic premises [of hip-hop culture] being based in peace and love for everyone, that also appealed to me. I just got absorbed into it. So, that's one of the messages that you got from hanging out in the scene" (interview with Carlos Mena, San Jose, July 17, 1997).

Hip-hop's always been a spiritual culture. To me, it's just the mainstream doesn't let that show ... I went to something called the B-Boy Summit in San Diego ... and that was just one of the most spiritual things I've ever been to as far as all young people, all different colors, connected by this culture, hip-hop. All peace and love, you know. I mean, the exact opposite of what they'd have you think ... To me, that's what hip-hop is all about. It always has been, that kind of thread, that spiritual thread running through the culture.

(Malcolm, interview, July 12, 1997)

This peace and love spirituality is not simply superficial sloganeering, but something that must be put into practice amid the difficulties of daily life. As one rapper put it: "It's in my day-to-day everyday ... It's not different from my life. It's what I do. It's just what's in life ... It's just onbeat every day" (Guerrero, interview, August 6, 1997). In this regard, another rapper was strongly affected by an experience he had listening to the advice of KRS-One:

He said: "These are the practices we need to do. Act like the god that you know. Whatever god you know, act like him. If your god is loving and merciful, be loving and merciful. The things that you want to happen in your life, visualize them in your mind before you go to sleep." And he said something that was profound to me, because after all that attack, he came back with love, saying, "Here's something you can do for yourself regardless of what I'm saying or what you said." I talked to other people afterwards, and they were saying they do something like that every day of their life, and it works.

(Gaines, interview, July 20, 1997)

This theme of hip-hop as spiritual practice emerged time and again in the interviews: "The people that I know, they're really trying to learn some things about themselves and tap into the rest of the spring that we don't use and these spiritual powers ... I've always taken the spiritual power seriously" (Malcolm, interview, July 12, 1997). "I have to be true to, not just the music and the musics that I'm bringing in, but now there's this religious thing ... I'm trying to reach another level of enlightenment" (Mena, interview, July 17, 1997).

> What it means to me to be a rapper is like, I look around at everything, and everything I absorb is God and I can express that, literally ... So it's really an expression. It's like praying. It's like being with God, literally, like being with God. Hip-hop culture is a spirituality. And it's everything that I can think of. Anything I am that I can do, that happens in this world, it's like that music, it's the culture ... It just gives you a purpose. It shows you why you're here ... It knows that I know God every day ... All those values have become part of the music and now it's in me every day.
>
> (Guerrero, interview, August 6, 1997)

As this last quote shows, one aspect of hip-hop spirituality that allows aficionados to achieve this type of integration into everyday life is the fact that it is part of a larger hip-hop culture. "Hip-hop is not the music; hip-hop is the culture. The music is rap music ... And those fuller aspects of hip-hop are grafitti, break dancing, MC-ing, and DJ-ing" (Paris King, interview, July 3, 1997). "On a spiritual level, I think what now I know as hip-hop culture and respect as such [consists of] the grafitti, the dress, the language, the art, the people, the mindset that's the commonality of thought" (Mena, interview, July 17, 1997). So, immersing oneself in hip-hop culture creates connections and links to many different vital aspects of one's life: "It's just been my link to everything—my own spirituality, my self-knowledge, and music also ... Everywhere I go, everywhere I grow, starts with hip-hop" (Malcolm, interview, July 12, 1997). "It linked me to everything—my future, my past, my family" (Guerrero, interview, August 6, 1997). It also creates links among different races, classes, and ethnicities, as one rapper observed earlier how "people" of "all different colors" are "connected by this culture, hip-hop" (Malcolm, interview, July 12, 1997). This inclusivity of hip-hop culture is expressed beautifully in this description of one rapper's experience at a concert:

> Everybody in the place was going back and forth at the same time. I remember looking back and seeing a whole moving wave of people. And it occurred to me how music brings people together. White people, Asian, Latino, black, different ages. And there wasn't any difference being noticed. Everybody was one. The music was pulling everyone together.
>
> (Gaines, interview, July 20, 1997)

This inclusivity, when combined with hip-hop's power to be a source of political and spiritual awakening in people's lives, leads to a sense that it can be a vehicle for change in the larger world:

> I see it being one of the major forces in the world bringing about change ... Hip-hop culture is worldwide now. It's big in Japan. I know in Germany. And I hear from people all the time in places I would never expect—South Africa. Being one of the major forces bringing about change, new ways, new types of lifestyles, because the old ones, we just can't use them anymore. For young people, that'll be our political party ... it's the closest thing we have to that. It includes politics. It includes spirituality. It includes music. It includes having a good time. It's inclusive of so much ... So, the hope is there in the spirit again, people are putting their hope in spirit, you know, God. Not God as an abstract form, but God in here and in there, you know. That's what we can use to get out of this mess. Hip-hop is just one of the manifestations. That's what we call it in the physical world ... To me, music is the future religion of the world.
>
> (Malcolm, interview, July 12, 1997)

This is an extraordinary statement, not only because it describes a significant new hybrid "manifestation" of nontraditional religiosity emerging within popular culture, but also because its hopeful idealism is firmly grounded in the harsh conditions and contradictions of the real world. In concluding this chapter, I will explore the implications for the larger landscape of religion in America.

Future Religion of the World: High-Tech Universalist Postmodern Bricolage in Popular Culture

The means of musical production has always been central not only to the music itself, but to the symbolism of the musical culture. For example, the drum can be seen as the instrument that symbolizes African music, the saxophone as the symbolic instrument for jazz, and the electric guitar as the symbolic instrument for rock. But, when it comes to rap music, the symbol is not an instrument at all, but the DJ's deck of two turntables and a cross-fade mixer. This simple contrast underlines an important point—that the means of musical production in rap has shifted away from traditional instruments to a new generation of electronic technologies. Moreover, this shift in musical technology has effected a corresponding shift in compositional principles. This innovative transformation in both musical technology and compositional form is a distinctive feature of rap that allows it to retain its African-American orientation at the same time that it points the way toward an emerging high-tech postmodern universalism in contemporary popular culture.

Many critics of rap music argue that the DJ is not actually creating new compositions, but simply taking already existing compositions via samplers and turntables and combining them through the mixer. However, it is precisely this ability to take music and sound from a variety of sources and combine them into an integrated whole that constitutes the craft and the musicality of the DJ, what one aficionado has called "the art of collage" (Paris King, interview, July 3, 1997). According to one DJ, this art "is all about recombinant potential ... Each and every source sample is fragmented and bereft of prior meaning ... [and] given meaning only when re-presented in the assemblage of the mix ... A mix, for me, is a way of providing a rare and intimate glimpse into the process of cultural production in the late 20th Century" (Miller 1996). Thus the DJ mix is a truly postmodern act of creativity, in which the traditional structures have broken down and new forms have been stitched together from the deconstructed bits and pieces in a high-tech bricolage. This postmodern cut-and-paste bricolage illustrates the universalist inclusivity of hip-hop at a musical level: "Every music made in our last millennium ... leads up to hip-hop because it uses every aspect of every music completely ... It's a universal way of connecting all these different styles of music into one thing ... Mixing is like the universal language" (Guerrero, interview, August 6, 1997). The technology used in the creation of the music—drum machines, cross-fade mixers, samplers, sequencers, computers—reflects this postmodern sensibility as well. Originating in the elite, white, corporate world, these technologies were taken by low-income African Americans, used in entirely different ways, and transformed into a new mode of expression.

These new forms of musical technology and composition serve as ana-logical templates for a distinctively African-American approach to life in postmodern America that can be a useful model for mainstream culture as well. In her insightful musicological analysis of rap music, Tricia Rose identifies three crucial elements in its sonic architecture: flow, layering, and rupture. She goes on to spell out how these musical structures reflect a hip-hop worldview, philosophy, and code for living:

> These effects at the level of style and aesthetics suggest affirmative ways in which profound social dislocation and rupture can be managed and perhaps contested in the social arena. Let us imagine these hip-hop principles as a blueprint for social resistance and affirmation: create sustaining narratives, accumulate them, layer, embellish, and transform them. However, be also prepared for rupture, find pleasure in it, in fact, *plan on* social rupture. When these ruptures occur, use them in creative ways that will prepare you for a future in which survival will demand a sudden shift in ground tactics.
>
> (Rose 1994, 39)

As we begin the twenty-first century, "profound social dislocation and rupture" appears to be an accurate description not only of the situation facing African Americans, but the situation facing all of us. Global communication and political economics have put an overwhelming array of diverse cultures, technologies, and information at our fingertips at the same time it is destroying long-standing traditions and paradigms. In this regard, hip-hop culture's ability to combine broken pieces into a new integrated whole can indeed serve as a blueprint for everyone in the new millennium.

Observers of culture and scholars of religion have said many things about the slow decline of institutional religion and the death of God in Western civilization. Yet, for the members of the Oakland Underground I interviewed, and hip-hop culture in general, religion and God are not dead, but very much alive and well and dancing to a hip-hop beat. The religious impulse has simply migrated to another sector of the culture, that of popular music, a sector in which religious sensibilities have flourished and made an enormous impression on a significant number of people. It is clear that hip-hop culture is a powerful religious phenomenon and just one example of many musical subcultures that function as religions in the lives of their adherents. Moreover, as the other chapters in this book show, popular music is just one example of many different arenas of popular culture that also function as religions in the lives of their adherents. From the micro to the macro—the Oakland Underground, rap and hip-hop in general, popular music, and popular culture—these new religious forms have already irrevocably changed the lives of millions of people, not only in terms of the texture of day-to-day living, but also in the way they see the world and the social forms that have sprung from those epistemologies. They signal the emergence of a significant alternative religious choice that bypasses the narrow opposition between traditional religious institutions and secular humanism. These are important changes with large implications that should not be underestimated. Moreover, the dynamic and innovative creativity of these new forms of expression indicates that one can expect them to be a source of religious vitality and evolution for generations into the future. To repeat the words of a DJ: "To me, music is the future religion of the world ... Hip-hop is just one of the manifestations."

References

Cone, James. 1992. "Blues: A Secular Spiritual." *Black Sacred Music: A Journal of Theomusicology* 6, 1 (Spring): 68–97.

Craddock-Willis, Andre. 1989. "Rap Music and the Black Musical Tradition: A Critical Assessment." *Radical America* 23, 4 (October/December): 29–37.

Keil, Charles. 1966. *Urban Blues*. Chicago: University of Chicago Press.

Miller, Paul D. (a.k.a. DJ Spooky). 1996. Brochure notes from *Songs of a Dead Dreamer* (Asphodel 1961). CD.

Nelson, Angela Spence. 1991. "Theology in the Hip-Hop of Public Enemy and Kool Moe Dee." *Black Sacred Music: A Journal of Theomusicology* 5, 1 (spring): 51–59.

Perkins, William Eric. 1991. "Nation of Islam Ideology in the Rap of Public Enemy." *Black Sacred Music: A Journal of Theomusicology* 5, 1 (spring): 41–50.

Rose, Tricia. 1994. *Black Noise: Rap Music and Black Culture in Contemporary America.* Middletown, CT: Wesleyan University Press.

Chapter 16

The Happiest Place on Earth

Disney's America and the Commodification of Religion

Eric Michael Mazur and Tara K. Koda

Our personnel sincerely sell happiness. Hell! That's what we all want, isn't it?
—Walt Disney

It Really *Is* A Small World, After All

In a classic commercial, sports celebrities caught after a contest hear a list of their accomplishments and a question: "Now what are you going to do?" Invariably they respond in what seems to be the only way possible in contemporary, commercial America: "I'm going to Disney World!" (Fjellman 1992, 160).

Indeed, how many millions have neither experienced nor dreamed of participating in "the middle-class hajj, the compulsory visit to the sunbaked holy city," Walt Disney World (Ritzer 1996, 4)? It is just one facet of a global corporation that produces movies and television programs, owns part or all of several other theme parks, television studios and networks, sports teams, housing developments, cruise ships, retail outlets, seminar centers, and training facilities that earned more than $20 billion in 1997 (Miles 1999, 15).[1] One million people visited the California park, Disneyland, in its first seven weeks, and more than four million visited there in 1955–56, its first year of operation (Weinstein 1992, 152). In Florida, 10 million visitors in 1971–72 (its first year) placed Walt Disney World ahead of the United Kingdom, Austria, and the former West Germany as a vacation destination, and more popular than the Great Smoky Mountains National Park (seven million visitors), Gettysburg (five million), and Yellowstone National Park (two million). By the beginning of the 1980s, more people visited Walt Disney World than the Eiffel Tower, the Taj Mahal, the Tower of London, or the Pyramids (Fjellman 1992, 136–39). In 1984 alone, the Florida and California parks drew nearly 20 million customers (Lawrence 1986, 65). "Since the number of visitors to both parks together exceeds the number going to Washington, D.C., the official capital," notes Margaret King, the parks could be considered "the popular culture capitals of America" (King 1981, 117).

Appropriately, the Walt Disney World logo depicts the globe as one of three spheres used to silhouette Mickey Mouse's face; it's a small world, after all, and Disney covers it completely. The American who can avoid contact with Disney must live in a cave; to reject Disney is to defy a major global force, and challenges much that is synonymous with contemporary American culture.

But what has this to do with religion?

In contemporary America, many consider all elements of life, even intangibles, as things that can be bought, and religious leaders now find themselves financially burdened competing for congregants' attention. On television or in the pulpit, they offer salvation along with 12-step programs and childcare. They have developed sophisticated attitudes toward money and fundraising, and some have adopted businesslike attitudes toward their congregants. As George Ritzer notes, "religion has been streamlined through such things as drive-in churches and televised religious programs" (Ritzer 1996, 48). Not surprisingly, many people treat salvation like a product, pursue it for selfish reasons, and often purchase it in seemingly nonreligious forms for seemingly religious reasons. Americans can be found pursuing diverse activities—working out, exploring nature, or watching television— and believing they have obtained the same benefits that they could receive from traditional religious activities. The distinction between religious and commercial activities has blurred, and as one scholar notes, such developments have made "a member of the Jehovah's Witnesses who peddled religion door-to-door on a Sunday afternoon much the same as a vacuum cleaner salesman" (R. L. Moore 1994, 256). In other words, whether it is through eternal bliss or clean carpets, salvation for many Americans is a readily available commodity.

An odd situation to be sure. But even odder when commercial ventures, operating for profit rather than piety, create competition for traditional religion. They are not simply providing paraphernalia for religious devotion— votives, Bibles, or "Pope-on-a-Rope" soap—but are *competing* (if unintentionally) with religious communities by offering similar goods: mythologies, symbols, rituals, and notions of community by which consumers organize their lives. These corporations offer (at a price) salvation from the modern world of twentieth-century American capitalism. And while, as Michael Budde argues, such a situation presents "new and imposing barriers ... to the formation of deep religious convictions," he also recognizes that "[m]ore than any other set of social institutions, these industries collectively influence how people relate to the processes and products of economic activity." They are the "vectors and initiators for ideas regarding the valued, the innovative, the normal, the erotic, and the repulsive" (Budde 1997, 14–15, 32). In other words, these companies create the environment in which even religious ideas are communicated.

The Walt Disney Company is one such business marketing religious symbolism and meaning and providing strong—if indirect—competition to traditional religion in the United States. There are others who are also exploring this market, other purveyors of religious symbols and meaning. However, because of its market penetration, its integrated marketing (also known as "synergy"), and its access to many levels of culture through its corporate network, Disney is uniquely suited for the "religification" of its commodity. And as Margaret King suggests, because a coincidence of factors unique to post-World War II America makes possible, "even obligatory—for Americans, adults as well as children, at least one pilgrimage to Disney Land [*sic*] or World as a popular culture 'mecca' of nearly religious importance" (King 1981, 117), this corporation is able to capitalize on its commodity in a way that is distinctly suited for this time and place.

The Marketplace and Competition in Contemporary American Religion

Once firmly committed to the idea that religion would fade from society as that society became more sophisticated, sociologists have come to use an economic model to explain the continued religiosity of the American citizenry (see Warner 1993). This model argues that religious communities—free of government intrusion or control—benefit from a "free market," and in competition with other religious communities ("producers") *offer* to religious adherents ("consumers") "products" they can compare and select rationally. These "products" (comfort, identity, community, but usually some form of salvation) are like items in a supermarket and compared in terms of their desirability, "market share," and general consumer appeal.

Though this model has its critics, it seems to explain in a more satisfying manner the continued vitality of religion in contemporary America. However, it means nothing if the "consumers" in the model—religious participants—aren't free to pick from religious options; market economies depend on consumers who are free to choose. Thus, over the past decade, scholars have examined the freedom individuals have enjoyed to "go shopping" for religion, and the loss of loyalty to specific religious communities that has resulted. Phillip Hammond argues that restrictions on religious identity have virtually disappeared, and "the social revolution of the 1960s and '70s wrought a major change: a near absolute free choice in the religious marketplace" (Hammond 1992, 168). Similarly, Wade Clark Roof notes that among members of the "baby boom" generation, "religion was whatever one chose as one's own" (Roof 1993, 244, emphasis omitted). The loss of a cultural monopoly by any one religious tradition, matched with the growing role of the individual (rather than the community) as the locus of identity, has made Americans freer to pick from among the various religious options, and to mix and match as they please.

At its logical extreme, this suggests market forces so diverse, and competition between religious "producers" so fierce, that consumers may not only choose more varied and less traditional forms of religious participation (as seems to be the case currently), but might also turn to nonreligious "producers" for the same (or similar) "products." In such a climate, Disney, as much as any other for-profit venture, might be understood as creating, maintaining, and even being depended upon for the images, ideas, and emotions that were once reserved for traditional religious communities. In other words, in a religious marketplace truly free of limits, competition to provide religion-like commodities might include organizations not traditionally understood as religions, and any institution with the wherewithal can compete equally with traditional religions, regardless of its financial or religious goal.

There is a great temptation to equate everything with religion, including Disney. Even a discussion of its founder, Walter Elias Disney, suggests Christ-like comparisons: a man with a vision, lifelong innocence, a message to be shared with the world, and a special affinity for children, envisions a new kingdom of heaven on Earth and leaves his vision with his disciples, who build cathedrals in his honor while he awaits resurrection. The myth of his cryogenic preservation and postmortem corporate participation suggest a continued presence and guidance from beyond (Fjellman 1992, 418, n.33; Ritzer 1996,174–75). One author describes meetings with "the spirit" of Disney in attendance; anticipating his company's future, Walt had himself filmed for screening at meetings after his death, asking questions of participants and commenting on the status of scheduled events (Fjellman 1992, 117).

However, it would be fruitless to suggest that Disney is the same as a traditional religion, or that it is consciously designing its business for religious competition. The first claim would be foolish to make, the second impossible to prove.[2] Instead, Disney's products (tangible and intangible) fill many of the roles often filled by religion. They have entered the market at a time when many people are not only searching for alternatives to traditional religion, but are also flexible with what they find. They have also entered the market at a time when religious institutions are in competition with "global culture industries" (Budde 1997) over the construction and maintenance of meaning at the end of the twentieth century.

Disney as "Religious"? The Religion of Time and Space

Religion scholar Mircea Eliade separates the world into two types of people: nonreligious and religious. While nonreligious people go through life without distinguishing varieties of time or space, religious people observe and maintain sharp distinctions between the sacred and the profane. The sacred (the different, the powerful) is the wholly other that gives meaning and orientation to believers' lives. Writes Eliade, "Something that does not belong to this world has manifested itself apodictically and in so doing has indicated an orientation or determined a course of conduct" (Eliade 1959, 27). This place of manifestation is the center of the universe, the heart of the cosmos and the place where the realms of existence interact. For example, in Judaism, Israel represents the space promised by God to the early Hebrews. Jerusalem remains the center of the Jewish cosmos, and synagogues are built so that worshipers face Jerusalem as they pray. Eliade suggests that "the sacred is equivalent to a power, and, in the last analysis, to reality. The sacred is saturated with being" (*ibid.*, 12; emphasis omitted). For religious people, sacred time and space are bounded by thresholds of power and orientation and provide a sense of the "really real," the order of the cosmos, and the unity of creation. "The threshold is the limit," Eliade writes, "the boundary, the frontier that distinguishes and opposes two worlds—and at the same time the paradoxical place where those worlds communicate, where passage from the profane to the sacred world becomes possible" (*ibid.*, 25). This boundary is well-marked to differentiate space that is common and meaningless from space that is sacred because of the power it represents.

Eliade argues that, for religious people, sacred space exists in a specific relation to sacred time, a return to the time when deities exerted their great-est creative powers, "when the world was young." Eliade notes that sacred time has virtually no relationship to time as experienced by the nonreligious. Instead, the religious person "experiences intervals of time that are 'sacred,' that have no part in the temporal duration that precedes and follows them, that have a wholly different structure and origin, for they are of a primordial time, sanctified by the gods and capable of being made present by the festi-val" (*ibid.*, 71). Eliade notes that "sacred time is reversible in the sense that, properly speaking, it is a primordial mythical time made present" (*ibid.*, 68; emphasis omitted). He suggests that it is "made present" by the re-enactments by believers in sacred space. Contemporary participants in the Jewish holiday of Passover ritually return to the time of their enslavement in Egypt: "It is because of that which the Lord did for me when I came forth from Egypt" (*Exodus* 13:8). "Me," not someone else, but the person at the ritual meal. During the Catholic Mass, the Eucharistic wafer and the wine don't represent Jesus, they actually become him ritually. Eliade's religious people long to return to the sacred time because that is the best way to fully experience sacred space, and therefore be in close contact with the deity. "In short," Eliade writes, "this religious nostalgia expresses the desire to live in a pure and holy cosmos, as it was in the beginning, when it came fresh from the Creator's hands" (*ibid.*, 65; emphasis omitted).

Both sacred time and space are re-created through the use of myth and ritual. According to Eliade, these elements provide religious people with access to sacred space and time by recalibrating life toward the divine. Myths re-insert sacred time into believers' lives. They are, writes Eliade, "the recital of what the gods or the semidivine beings did at the beginning of time. To tell a myth is to proclaim what happened *ab origine*" (*ibid.*, 95). Rituals permit the community to re-enact the myths that reinsert the sacred time into their lives. Myths and rituals permit religious people to demarcate time and space, to orient the world in terms of the deity (or deities), and (according to Eliade) to avoid the meaninglessness of the nonreligious world. He notes that the religious person "lives in two kinds of time, of which the more important, sacred time, appears under the paradoxical aspect of a circular time, reversible and recoverable, a sort of eternal mythical present that is periodically reintegrated by means of rites. This attitude," he continues, "in regard to time suffices to distinguish religious from nonreligious man; the former refuses to live solely in what, in modern terms, is called the historical present; he attempts to regain a sacred time that, from one point of view, can be homologized to eternity" (*ibid.*, 70). Religious people, by operating in sacred space and time, never lose their connection to the deity, and live in a world that is reborn through ritual and myth, constantly young and full of power, wonder, and awe.

"Deep in the Hundred-Acre Wood": Walt Disney World as Sacred Space and Time

As an example of Eliadean sacred space, Walt Disney World (and, to a lesser extent, Disneyland) is bordered, demarcated space in which something out of the ordinary occurs. As part of the agreement over its development, one of Disney's subsidiaries was granted power that, in effect, makes the land surrounding the park an independent governmental entity (Johnson 1981, 158). This entity, which spans 27,000 acres, now produces its own money (the so-called "Disney Dollars," which are legal tender at Disney parks, resorts, and Disney retail outlets), generates its own power, manages its own trash, provides for its own fire and safety needs, and regulates its own local sales taxes on a "semi-autonomous basis approaching a city-state like Vatican City" (King 1981, 121).

As one enters the park, clues reinforce the notion that it is a different, separate space, and therefore significant.[3] Man-made mountains and ordered space carved from the waters remind the "guest" (never "customer") that Walt Disney World, a well-manicured piece of sacred space, is an oasis in the vastness of profane space. The mountains—reminiscent of Eliade's notions of the "center of the universe" and the place "where the realms of existence interact"—are the second and third highest "mountains" in Florida: Space Mountain and the Big Thunder Mountain ride (Fjellman 1992, 75). Disney's empire, like the creation account in *Genesis*, was created by draining swampland and channeling the water into lakes, literally letting "the waters under the heavens be gathered together into one place" (*Genesis* 1: 9). It is fitting that crossing into the park thus re-enacts defiance against the forces of profanity. As Eliade writes, "The threshold has its guardians—gods and spirits who forbid entrance both to human enemies and to demons and the powers of pestilence" (Eliade 1959, 25). Crossing the lake that separates the mundane (parking lot) from the sacred (park) on a boat that is, according to Fjellman, part of the fifth largest "navy" in the world, visitors symbolically move into a world that is spatially and temporally removed from that in which they ordinarily operate.

In the park, the visitor is presented with a choice: to visit the Magic Kingdom, EPCOT, Disney-MGM Studios, the Animal Kingdom, or all four. The decision will determine not only how one spends the day, but also the type of space with which one interacts. The Magic Kingdom, the oldest and mythically richest portion of the park, begins with a journey down Main Street USA and moves to other spaces embodying American mythic time: Frontierland, Adventureland, and so on. EPCOT (Experimental Prototype Community of Tomorrow) is a celebration of American commercialism and technology combined with a multicultural collection of international representatives encircling a man-made lake. Disney-MGM Studios provides a glimpse "behind the scenes" of Disney movies and television, and the Animal Kingdom provides an opportunity to mingle with live and animatronic beasts. Everywhere one goes there are wonderful, colorful, clean, and seemingly educational sights, tempting foods, and picturesque vistas (usually identified for photographing), "a symbolic American Utopia" (King 1981, 123). The park is truly a space unlike anything with which most people are familiar.

Ironically, just like the sacred spaces of any religious community, this space is as powerful for what isn't seen as for what is. Nowhere is there any hint of disorder, nowhere is there any sight of the mundane. Beneath the park (the Disney netherworld?), the veil of sacrality is protected as workers transport products, food, and equipment, and maintain waste removal, all out of sight of the guests. David Johnson notes, "This sequestering makes it easy to forget that work is actually going on, so that the park's operation often seems far more effortless than it really is; visitors can thus enjoy their leisure without being reminded of the everyday world of work" (Johnson 1981, 159). People are free to walk around and forget the crime-, hate-, and poverty-filled world from which they came. As Walt Disney noted, "I don't want the public to see the real world they live in while they're in the park ... I want them to feel they are in another world" (quoted by King 1981, 121).

This total experience of space is a perfect example of what Fredric Jameson calls "hyperspace," which George Ritzer defines as "an area where modern conceptions of space are useless in helping people orient themselves" (Ritzer 1996, 159). Like a shopping mall or a casino, Walt Disney World deprives its visitors of any reference to the outside world by making everything cross-referential. All of the signs, all of the narratives, all of the merchandise relates back to the central theme of the space, the Disney version of

Eliade's "really real." Time itself is expressed spatially throughout the parks. Not surprisingly, there is no significant representation of the present, and while some of the areas purport to represent the future (Tomorrowland, EPCOT), the greatest emphasis is on the past. Much of the space within the park is designed to conjure for the visitor a sense of times gone by—sacred times to the traditional religionist. These times are of two sorts: the romanticized (or actual) youth of the visitor, and a mythic time of national innocence (King 1981, 131). Disney thus successfully exploits its relationship with adults who grew up in the 1950s and 1960s as much as with children who grew up in the past few years. Writes Paul Croce: "Adults, who make up four out of five of the visitors [to the parks], are ushered back to childhood, with playful rides, mouse ears, and buildings designed on a small scale" (Croce 1991, 97). On the other hand, there are signs of a gloried American past everywhere the visitor goes. The Hall of Presidents, the references to the American frontier, the requirement to stroll down an 1890s-style street (Main Street USA is the only way into or out of the Magic Kingdom), all recall an America in its glory, when there was no Watergate, when there were no drugs, when every citizen was strong, and when every leader was honest and wise. In Eliade's words, "when the world was young." Historian Mike Wallace writes of Walt Disney, "he transported visitors back in time" (Wallace 1985, 34).

However, Eliade's vision of the sacred is far too simplistic—religious people live in the real world just like the nonreligious person—and the peaceful image offered in such an analysis is often misleading. It is not surprising, then, that the version of American history provided at Walt Disney World is problematic at best, and fundamentally flawed at worst. The park designers have taken easily recognizable, pivotal images in American history and given them new (and often different) meanings. Notes David Johnson, "the Disney creators have taken the raw material from history, fantasy and other sources and packaged it into units, each with a discrete beginning, middle and end." He suggests that "they have in effect added conventional plots to inherently plotless materials" (Johnson 1981, 162; emphasis deleted). By doing so, Walt Disney World staffers have re-created an American history that is not only sanitized, but also reflective of a particularly Disney version of American history—"Distory"—for millions of Americans and non-Americans who pass through the gates each year (see Francaviglia 1981). This repackaged history changes the perceptions of the visitors, and like all myths, establishes itself as the "really real" over that which is taught in textbooks. "For visitors, and especially the young visitors," continues Johnson, "Disney's version becomes the original version, which is actually more powerful than history since its form is concrete, containing 'real' people and 'lifelike' people with plenty of action and drama by both. By comparison, the history books are static, they require a more studied effort to make the history come alive; the Disney version is more interesting as well as more easily assimilated and remembered for our 'post-literate' generations" (Johnson 1981, 164; emphasis deleted).

Criticizing Disney for such rewriting might be holding it to an unfair standard—does it really purport to teach people American history, or is it a place where people can encounter American history as they want it (consciously or not) to have been? As one Disney "imagineer" notes, "What we create is a 'Disney Realism,' sort of Utopian in nature, where we carefully program out all the negative, unwanted elements and program in the positive elements" (quoted in Wallace 1985, 35). It truly is utopian, almost Edenic. "Cast members" (never "employees") are always "in character"; many of the animals (even at Animal Kingdom) are animatronic and harmless (Danyliw 1998); many of the actors are animatronic and therefore always happy, on cue, and never on strike; the park is always clean; and the visitors are free to live (or relive) their youth (or the youth of the nation) in comfort and leisure from the moment the park opens until the last tram has carried them out. It truly is the happiest place on Earth, even if it seems to represent something real that never actually existed.

"Yo, Ho. Yo, Ho. A Pirate's Life For Me": Disney Co. Encounters Religion, Inc.

Though exploring Walt Disney World through the lens of sacred space and time provides an interesting analysis of the religious experience of that place, it is Disney's ability to market its product beyond the parks' boundaries that makes more powerful the original contention that the Walt Disney Company is marketing religion-like symbolism and competing with traditional American religion. The company encourages people to visit Disney parks when they see Disney films, purchase Disney items when they visit Disney parks or outlets, see Disney movies when they buy Disney products, and so on. By cross-referencing to its other products, Disney creates a consumer world of its own; no matter what you buy, it relates to something else from Disney. "Disney has perfected the art of media synergy" (*The Economist* 2008, 74). Behind the integrated marketing strategy—or accompanying it—are the myths and symbols also found at the parks. Notes Michael Real, "the Disney universe teaches values while it entertains" (Real 1977, 70), and the stories told in the products and the movies reinforce those found at the parks, translating them into a "reality" that, though not always consistent, is pervasive, directive (directing people to the parks and directing their behaviors outside them), and accessible to all who accept it.

Because the animated features are completely constructed Disney products, they are the most powerful conveyors of the symbols and meaning systems outside the parks. They also are a staple of Disney marketing and the centerpiece of its economic revival. Though phased out by the end of the 1960s, animated films are once again being made under the Disney name, and since the beginning of the Michael Eisner era (1984), the company has released 10 full-length animated feature films, as well as mixed- or alternative-media features.[4] These films are the "text" underpinning a world view discernible in Disney stores, theme parks, and other venues. Like the activities at the parks, the movies (which are supported by a diverse pool of popular actors and musicians) take common or familiar stories, sanitize them, and reconfigure them to reflect myths central to the Disney world view; compare Disney's *The Little Mermaid* (1989) with Hans Christian Andersen's original.

On the surface, these films reveal nothing surprising: an optimistic (even moralistic) American vision of the world, in which freedom and independence are appreciated; where difference, though initially distressing, is ultimately affirmed; where outsiders, though initially ridiculed, are ultimately integrated into the group and those who ridiculed them ostracized; where selfless sacrifice is rewarded and selfishness is equated with villainy and destroyed; and where superficial, outward characteristics are overlooked, and all are appreciated. Notes Aladdin in the film that bears his name, "it is not what is outside but what is inside that counts." On the other hand, there is no subtlety about evil; villains are clearly differentiated behaviorally as well as physically, are often drawn or colored differently, and exhibit unmistakable hubris. The animated films also suggest ethical positions to their viewers; good and evil are defined in every Disney movie, and while the villains are offered salvation, many are destroyed—often by fire, hellishly confirming their villainy—because of their continued arrogance and evil. Heroes, though flawed, learn from their mistakes, and are willing to forgive the villains. While some need more help than others on the path toward righteousness, they ultimately do the right thing.

And yet, these seemingly innocent characterizations and ethical positions are not without controversy, and they only hint at larger conflicts over symbols used by Disney and various religious communities. In order to discern the "right thing," characters often seek help from other realms. Scholars and ethnic community representatives have protested some characterizations used by Disney in movies and at their parks as too simplistic, ridiculing a particular group, or misrepresenting them.[5] Some conservative Christians have protested Disney's presentation of morality altogether. During the summer of 1997, the Southern Baptist Convention—the largest Protestant denomination in the United States—announced it was organizing a Disney-wide boycott, an enormous task given the company's diversification. Leaders of the organization complained about Disney policies they considered "anti-family," including health benefits for same-sex partners of Disney employees, toleration toward "Gay Days" (an event at the Florida and California parks organized by gay and lesbian representatives), and acceptance of the open lesbianism of Ellen DeGeneres and her character on Disney-owned ABC. They identified Disney as morally corrupt, implying it was not only unsafe but traitorous. On another front, some members of the American Catholic community decried the release of *Priest* by Miramax (one of Disney's subsidiaries), while others organized a media campaign against *Nothing Sacred*, also broadcast by ABC (Dart 1997a, 1997b). The Miramax film *Priest* and the television show *Ellen* both addressed issues of homosexuality, while *Priest* and *Nothing Sacred* portrayed Catholic clergy as liberal, nonorthodox interpreters of Catholic doctrine.

The use of Disney products in debates over morality and religion is profound not simply for what it says about the Southern Baptist Convention's nostalgia for an American society that no longer exists (if it ever did), but also for what it says about Disney's place in American culture. Disney is not the first corporation targeted by religious organizations for economic boycott. It is a business like any other—"emblematic of capitalism itself," notes Margaret Miles (1999, 15)—and disgruntled members of religious communities may express their displeasure economically, either through boycotts or by establishing competing theme parks (such as Heritage USA). While Southern Baptists are free to own Disney stock, Disney is not a Baptist corporation (Walt was raised as a Congregationalist), and is therefore not betraying anything other than a particular denomination's conception of cultural propriety. Interestingly, while the boycott has elicited little public response from Disney, an objection from the Arab-American community over the depiction of Arab peoples in Disney's *Aladdin* resulted in changes for the video release (Fox 1993). This does not mean that the Arab-American concerns are more significant than those of Southern Baptists. As Michael Budde implies, international corporations like Disney have become "symbolic predators," taking and using familiar religious symbols for commercial purposes. As he writes, "many of the classic narratives of Judaism and Christianity (e.g., exodus, miracles, resurrection) act effectively as deep structures in commercial messages" (Budde 1997, 91, 92). Inevitably, some Christians will be offended (to the point of boycott) at the way Disney portrays important symbols, just as it is inevitable that Disney cannot change such portrayals. Disney uses Christian religious imagery and symbols as the vehicles of the narrative. However, with the portrayal of a particular community type (such as Arabs, Africans, etc.), the image is not woven into the narrative in the same way, and changing images by eliminating cultural stereotypes is possible even when changing the premises of a story is not. Disney refines a virtually religious message, but cannot help but risk offending the religious community that sees its own story woven into the narrative. In so doing, it competes for the attention of largest segment of the consumer market, whomever that might be. And while this is good business sense, the fact that Disney appears to be trading in religious symbols and the categories of space, time, and morality means that the competition may be drawn from the religious as well as the business world.

Real Market Forces at Work

In *The McDonaldization of Society* (1996), George Ritzer uses Max Weber's sociological model of bureaucratization to compare McDonald's assembly-line mentality with all of American culture. He suggests that America has become McDonaldized—operating on the same assumptions that have made the fastfood chain a global phenomenon—because of a slavish devotion to "efficiency, calculability, predictability, and control" (*ibid.*, 9). But like Weber, Ritzer sees the inevitable hazard: the "iron cage," in which activities are robbed of any meaning. "By 'iron cage,'" Ritzer concludes, "I mean that as McDonaldization comes to dominate even more sectors of society, it will become ever less possible to 'escape' from it" (*ibid.*, 143).

Not surprisingly, Disney is one of Ritzer's examples. It is efficient (trash cleanup, people moving, product delivery, etc.), predictable (guests rely on this, since many are return customers), and free of disorder or mess. Like McDonald's, Disney "has succeeded because it offers ... efficiency, calculability, predictability, and control." By cross-referencing its products, it also controls its consumers, robbing them of any ability to "escape" Disney's control once they enter the Disney world. "McDonaldized systems," notes Ritzer, citing Walt Disney World, "generally lack a sense of history. People find themselves in settings that either defy attempts to be pinpointed historically or present a pastiche of many historical epochs" (*ibid.*, 158). By limiting guests' experiences to its own sense of past and future epochs, and by reinforcing those experiences outside the parks through films and other products, Disney has created a world that seems to lack any meaning beyond its own boundaries.

However, Disney *does* provide meaning to its customers, a key to Weber's "iron cage" of meaninglessness that McDonald's and other "McDonaldizers" do not.[6] Disney provides a system of meaning that orients the consumer— albeit mythically, commercially, and with a very American product—to the larger world of consumer capitalism in which they live, whether or not they are Americans. The proof of the reach of Disney's mythology is in how it has been received in different places. Ritzer reports that a French politician noted that Euro-Disney would "bombard France with uprooted creations that are to culture what fast food is to gastronomy" (*ibid.*, 14). In contrast, in its first 10 years, Tokyo Disneyland has entertained the equivalent of Japan's population (Miles 1999, 15), encouraging Disney to explore possibilities for a park in Hong Kong (Reckard and Tempest 1999).[7] This difference in the reception of Disney by two non-American cultures seems best explained by how the French and Japanese cultures integrate different myths. While French and Japanese cultures have experienced periods of xenophobia, the current Japanese attitude toward capitalism makes that culture a much more responsive audience to the idiom in which Disney operates (Yoshimoto 1994).

Ironically, this same idiom has led to seemingly nonreligious controversy in the United States. A Virginia community rejected a Disney proposal to build an American history theme park near a Civil War battlefield, in part out of fear of increased traffic, but also because of the potential misrepresentation that might result from the park's exhibits (Hofmeister 1994). The "Distory" that is so popular in the Florida and California parks, in films, on television, and in stores across the country, and is being exported successfully around the globe, could not overcome a different sacred mythology surrounding an event that, by definition, was not clean, happy, or utopian.

Conclusion

In late-twentieth-century America, the lines between business and religion are often blurry at best, and organizations identified with one may venture into the world of the other—intentionally or not—making for a distinction without a difference. The religion of Disney, if there can be said to be such a thing, is the same as it is for much of late-twentieth-century America— commercialization—and Disney opponents may also be opponents of that aspect of American culture. What makes Disney unique is that its products do not simply feed the commercial needs of its consumers, but—through accessible and pervasive symbols that traditionally have been reserved for faith communities, but now are incorporated into the marketplace—their souls as well. Disney's parks and films exploit the desire to live in a world of peace and beauty, to hope for a better time, and to leave troubles (either personal or societal) behind. Its movies, its television programs, and especially its parks provide a utopian time and space that allows people, if only for a moment, to re-create time and space as they could be, and as they might have been in some mythic (personal or national) past. As Eliade writes, "It is by virtue of the temple that the world is resanctified in every part" (Eliade 1959, 59; emphasis omitted). Disney provides that symbolic and metaphoric temple that resanctifies the world of American consumer capitalism. Through the production and maintenance of meaning and symbol systems, Disney plays the same role of orientation that traditional religion once did exclusively. And because contemporary trends in American religion have created a situation in which nonreligious entities and activities are often used for personal religious (or "spiritual") ends, Americans (and others) can find in Disney many of the elements they once found exclusively in traditional religion. Hey, America—you've conquered the global economy and provided one of the highest standards of living for your citizens. Now what are you going to do? "We're going to Disney World!"

References

Brockway, Robert. 1989. "The Masks of Mickey Mouse: Symbol of a Generation." *Journal of Popular Culture* 22, 4 (spring): 25–34.

Budde, Michael. 1997. *The (Magic) Kingdom of God: Christianity and Global Culture Industries.* Boulder, CO: Westview Press.

Croce, Paul Jerome. 1991. "A Clean and Separate Space: Walt Disney in Person and Production." *Journal of Popular Culture* 25, 3 (winter): 91–103.

Danyliw, Norie Quintos. 1998. "The Kingdom Comes: Fake Animals Outshine the Real Ones in Disney's Newest Park." *U.S. News & World Report,* April 6, 64.

Dart, John. 1997a. "ABC Opts to Extend 'Nothing Sacred.'" *Los Angeles Times,* November 29: B1.

——. 1997b. "Southern Baptist Delegates OK Disney Boycott." *Los Angeles Times,* June 19: A1.

The Economist. 2008. "Magic Restored," 19 April: 73–74.

Eliade, Mircea. 1959. *The Sacred and the Profane: The Nature of Religion.* San Diego: Harcourt Brace Jovanovich.

Fjellman, Stephen M. 1992. *Vinyl Leaves: Walt Disney World and America.* Boulder, CO: Westview Press.

Fox, David J. 1993. "Disney Will Alter Song in *Aladdin.*" *Los Angeles Times,* July 10: F1.

Francaviglia, Richard V. 1981. "Mainstreet USA: A Comparison/Contrast of Streetscapes in Disneyland and Walt Disney World." *Journal of Popular Culture* 15, 1 (summer): 141–56.

Hammond, Phillip E. 1992. *Religion and Personal Autonomy: The Third Disestablishment in America.* Columbia: University of South Carolina Press.

Hofmeister, Sallie. 1994. "Disney Vows to Seek Another Park Site." *The New York Times,* September 30, A12.

Johnson, David M. 1981. "Disney World as Structure and Symbol: Re-Creation of the American Experience." *Journal of Popular Culture* 15, 1 (summer): 157–65.

King, Margaret. 1981. "Disneyland and Walt Disney World: Traditional Values in Futuristic Form." *Journal of Popular Culture* 15, 1 (summer): 116–40.

Knight, Cher Krause. 1999. "Mickey, Minnie, and Mecca: Destination Disney World, Pilgrimage in the Twentieth Century." In *Reclaiming the Spiritual in Art: Contemporary Cross-Cultural Perspectives,* eds Dawn Perlmutter and Debra Koppman. Albany: State University of New York Press.

Lawrence, Elizabeth A. 1986. "In the Mick of Time: Reflections on Disney's Ageless Mouse." *Journal of Popular Culture* 20, 2 (fall): 65–72.

Miles, Margaret R. 1999. "Disney Spirituality: An Oxymoron?" *Christian Spirituality Bulletin* (spring): 13–18.

Moore, Alexander. 1980. "Walt Disney World: Bounded Ritual Space and the Playful Pilgrimage Center." *Anthropological Quarterly* 53, 4 (October): 207–18.

Moore, R. Laurence. 1994. *Selling God: American Religion in the Marketplace of Culture.* New York: Oxford University Press.

Real, Michael R. 1977. "The Disney Universe: Morality Play." In *Mass-Mediated Culture,* 44–89. Englewood Cliffs, NJ: Prentice Hall.

Reckard, E. Scott and Rone Tempest. 1999. "Disney May Expand Its Small World into Hong Kong." *Los Angeles Times,* March 3, C1.

Ritzer, George. 1996. *The McDonaldization of Society,* revised edn. Thousand Oaks, CA: Pine Forge Press.

Roof, Wade Clark. 1993. *A Generation of Seekers: The Spiritual Journeys of the Baby Boom Generation.* San Francisco: HarperCollins.

Wallace, Mike. 1985. "Mickey Mouse History: Portraying the Past at Disney World." *Radical History Review* 32: 33–57.

Warner, R. Stephen. 1993. "Work in Progress toward a New Paradigm for the Sociological Study of Religion in the United States," *American Journal of Sociology* 98, 5 (March): 1044–93.

Weinstein, Raymond M. 1992. "Disneyland and Coney Island: Reflections on the Evolution of the Modern Amusement Park." *Journal of Popular Culture* 26, 1 (summer): 131–64.

Yoshimoto, Mitsuhiro. 1994. "Images of Empire: Tokyo Disneyland and Japanese Cultural Imperialism." In *Disney Discourse: Producing the Magic Kingdom,* ed. Eric Smoodin, 181–99. New York: Routledge.

Notes

1 A commission of the Southern Baptist Convention lists more than 200 subsidiaries connected to Disney. Michael Budde notes that, according to Disney, "on an August weekend in 1990, 30 per cent of all movie theaters in the United States and Canada were screening a feature produced by one of Disney's production companies" (Budde 1997, 30). An *Economist* writer estimates that Disney's 2007 revenues $35.4 billion (*The Economist* 2008, 74).

2 For quasi-religious analyses of Disney, see Brockway (1989); King (1981); Knight (1999); A. Moore (1980). We are thankful to the "Religion and Popular Culture" panel and audience at the Popular Culture Association meeting (Orlando, March 1998) who heard an earlier version of this chapter. We are particularly grateful to one participant who exclaimed that, though she lived near the park and visited often, she did not consider it religious. We are reminded that many residents of Jerusalem—the focus of major religious traditions for centuries—consider it simply another city, but we are grateful for the reminder that sometimes the sacred becomes mundane and needs re-clarification.

3 Likewise at Disneyland, where entering guests are reminded that "Here you leave today and enter the world of yesterday, tomorrow, and fantasy" (Real 1977, 50).

4 In order of release: *The Little Mermaid* (1989), *The Rescuers Down Under* (1990), *Beauty and the Beast* (1991), *Aladdin* (1992), *The Lion King* (1994), *Pocahontas* (1995), *The Hunchback of Notre Dame* (1996), *Hercules* (1997), *Mulan* (1998), and *Tarzan* (1999). Because of the timing of its release, *Tarzan* was not originally included in this analysis. Since the publication of the first edition, Disney has released the following additional animated films: *Fantasia 2000* (1999), *The Emperor's New Groove* (2000), *Atlantis: The Lost Empire* (2001), *Lilo & Stitch* (2002), *Treasure Planet* (2002), *Brother Bear* (2003), *Home on the Range* (2004), *Chicken Little* (2005), *Meet the Robinsons* (2007), and *Bolt* (2008). In 2004, Bob Iger took over for Michael Eisner.

5 Representatives from Native American organizations voiced their displeasure at the depiction of traditional customs in *Pocohantas*, while representatives from African-American organizations have regularly objected to the depiction of African and African-American characters in animated and live action films and at the parks. Margaret Miles notes that African-American employees refer to Walt Disney World as "the plantation" (Miles 1999, 18, n. 2).

6 Even McDonald's mythic world (including Ronald McDonald, Mayor McCheese, etc.) has been overshadowed by characters designed as tie-ins to Disney productions.

7 Margaret Miles reports that Walt Disney World is "presently the #1 honeymoon destination in the country and may soon become the #1 wedding site" (Miles 1999, 13).

Index

Bender, Maurice 46
Benin 295
Bennett, William 254
Benzaiten (goddess) 88
Berger, Peter 5, 240
Berry, Chuck 22, 24
Best, David 163
Beveridge, Albert 23
Bhopal, India 70
Bible 16, 21–23, 52, 53, 54, 121, 142,
    147, 274, 308; *see also* specific books
Biehn, Michael 72
Billboard 20; 21
Bird, S. Elizabeth 192
Black Church, 106, 120, 122, 124, 126,
    127, 128, 130, 131, 132
Black Rock Desert 154, 155, 159, 173
Black Rock Gazette 155
Black Rock City 155, 157, 159, 164,
    166, 167, 168
Black Rock Mountains 159
Blade Runner (1982) 66
"Blessed Assurance" (hymn) 114
blues 24, 27, 125, 127, 297, 298
Blythe, Teresa 187
Bochco, Steven 181–82
Bones 192
brainwashing 189, 190
Branch Davidians 187
Brasher, Brenda 231, 281
break dancing 292, 295, 300, 302
Brer Rabbit 296
British 126
Broderick, Matthew 68
Bronx, New York 291, 292, 299, 300
Brooks, Mel 243
Brown, Mark 272, 274
Bryant, Kobe 121
Budde, Michael 308, 317
Buddha/Buddhas 12, 16, 80–97, 162
Buddhism/Buddhists 17, 18, 80–97; 178,
    220, 224–26, 229–33, 251, 256, 271,
    273; Asian 82, 85, 86, 92, 96; Asian
    American 82, 85; Chan/Zen 87, 92;
    Geluk ("Yellow Hat") School of
    Tibetan 82; Madhyamika 229;
    Mahayana 87, 93, 94, 101n17, 229;
    Pure Land 92; Shingon (Japanese) 94;
    South Asian 93; Tantric 82, 92, 94,
    96; Theravada 92; Vajrayana 82, 92,
    93; Vietnamese-Canadian 96; and
    Westernization 85, 88, 92
Buddhist Churches of America 85

Buddhist News Network/The Buddhist
    Channel 85
Buffett, Jimmy 6, 255, 256, 257, 258–70;
    *Changes in Latitudes Changes in
    Attitudes* 264; "Cheeseburger in
    Paradise" 258; "Cowboy in the
    Jungle" 261; *Fruitcakes* 261;
    "Growing Older but Not Up" 268;
    "Life Is Just a Tire Swing" 261;
    "Margaritaville, [Wasted Away Again
    in]" 258, 264; "Migration" 261; "My
    Head Hurts, My Feet Stink, and I
    Don't Love Jesus" 260; "A Pirate
    Looks at Forty" 261; "Seven Deadly
    Sins" 260
Buffy the Vampire Slayer 51
Burnim, Mellonee 127
Burning Man festival 3, 12, 103, 105,
    106, 154–73
Burkina Faso 295
Bush, George H. W. 238, 254
Bush, George W. 30, 199, 201, 252
Butcher, Sam 140, 147, 151
Butler, Jon 156

Cable News Network (CNN) 299
Calico Mountains 159
Calvin, John 257
Cameron, James 72
Campbell, Joseph 180, 263
Canaan/Canaanites 22, 38
capitalism 2, 44, 141, 142, 145–46, 147,
    149, 150–51
Capoeira 296
Caponi, Gena 122, 130, 131, 134
Carradine, John 43
Carson, Rachel 63
Castaneda, Carlos 191
caste system 222
Catholicism/Catholics 51, 54, 104, 157,
    161, 175, 178, 182, 183, 186, 188,
    189, 190, 191, 232, 243, 260, 271,
    273, 275, 317
Cavaliers (Cleveland) 121
Cavell, Stanley 42
Celtic cultures 112
Celtics (Boston) 130
Central Park (New York) 187
Chang, Michael 84
Charitable Choice Act 199
Chautauqua Sunday School Institutes
    156
Chernobyl, Ukraine 69